'Our leader, as I call him, is proof that you don't have to have played Test match cricket to be able to become an expert on it. If he'd moved his feet a bit more—y'know bent that left knee—he might have played a fair bit at the highest level but, as it is, he has taken his skills into the broadcasting and writing of the game. No one does it better. I know a bit about batting but I could hardly fault his ideas and opinions on the subject. Every chapter is interesting in its own way. I didn't always agree with him but that's not the point. The point is that I wanted to read on.'
GEOFFREY BOYCOTT

'The thing about Mark is his uniquely positive take on cricket. He knows the game inside out and always talks it up. The various television productions with which he is involved, the interviews, the charities he supports, the articles he writes—they all celebrate cricket and its players. He conveys the message that the game may not be easy but it's sure worthwhile. His book is the same, a celebration. *A Beautiful Game* is the perfect title because that is how he sees cricket. More power to him I say.'
ALASTAIR COOK

'Superbly written by someone with intimate knowledge and great affection for the game. Outstanding.'
BARRY RICHARDS

'"Markie boy", as I call him, is a master with words, both written and spoken. He always strives to bring about the good of the game we all love and in doing so he brings a smile to most faces. His positivity is what separates him from others and it's this aspect that shines through in this book. God bless you, Markie boy.'
SUNIL GAVASKAR

A BEAUTIFUL GAME

My love affair with cricket

MARK NICHOLAS

ALLEN&UNWIN

First published in Great Britain in 2016 by Allen & Unwin

Allen & Unwin
c/o Atlantic Books
Ormond House
26–27 Boswell Street
London WC1N 3JZ
Phone: 020 7269 1610
Fax: 020 7430 0916
Email: UK@allenandunwin.com
Web: www.allenandunwin.co.uk

A CIP catalogue record for this book is available from the British Library.

Hardback ISBN 978 1 76029 198 3
Trade paperback ISBN 978 1 76029 275 1
E-Book ISBN 978 1 95253 531 4

Printed in Great Britain

10 9 8 7 6 5 4 3 2 1

To Mum and Dad for making it all possible

*And to Kirsten and Leila for continuing
to make it all so worthwhile*

CONTENTS

PART 1

Playing the game

At home, aged twelve, in the garden where the Test matches were
played. (The door on the right was the entrance to the pavilion!)

CHAPTER 1

In the beginning

The Nicholas family moved house in the spring of 1967. We left a small terrace in Holland Park for the leafy fringes of Roehampton, barely more than a six-hit from the gates to Richmond Park. The new home had a wonderful garden with a lawn and flowerbeds big enough for my mother's interests to sit comfortably alongside mine.

My father and I mowed a narrow strip of grass just beyond the brow of a small tier that hid the white lines we had painted with emulsion as batting and bowling creases. Then I rolled the strip with the barrel of the lawnmower until it appeared flat enough for play. I was nine years old and the game of bat and ball had stolen my heart. The move from street cricket, with stumps chalked on the brick wall outside our old home, to something like the real thing on grass, with a pitch and boundaries, had cast a spell.

My father, Peter, was a decent, if cavalier, club cricketer in the Richie Benaud mould. He struck the ball well and tossed up leg breaks with a splendid lack of concern for their outcome. His interest in cricket came from his own father, who was a wicketkeeper-batsman for the army and Essex and a fine all-round sportsman. With some surprise, I recently found Captain F.W.H. Nicholas, or Freddie Willie Herbie as the lads knew him, in the front row of a huge team photograph in the Lord's museum. Apparently my grandfather was much sought after by philanthropists who took the game far and wide. He was a great mate of the Honourable Lionel Tennyson, who captained Hampshire from 1919 to 1932, and of the entrepreneur Sir Julien Cahn. The picture in the museum is of Sir Julien's XI in Jamaica and I have no idea what it is doing there.

I went with Dad to as many of his games as he would allow, never missing a ball when he was in action and otherwise eagerly playing around the fringes of the boundary with anyone who would have me. He played league cricket for Southgate and wandering cricket for the Free Foresters and the Frogs. Nowhere in the world enjoys wandering cricket like England. It is a throwback to an amateur age of free time and great privilege, and exists to this day. At the top of the tree, clubs such as the I Zingari and the Arabs tell us as much about ourselves as the games we play.

When my father came home from work, he would play in the garden with me each evening. I loved this more than I can describe here. He gave me a coaching book by Sir Donald Bradman, *The Art of Cricket*, and an autobiography by Denis Compton. I was submerged in a world of images, characters, sensations and ideals that were to accompany me throughout my life.

In the late summer of 1968 he took me to Lord's. We sat in the Warner Stand with friends. When Ted Dexter came out to bat for Sussex against Warwickshire in the Gillette Cup Final, I lost the plot, cheering wildly and generally making a goose of myself. Dexter didn't score many but he could do no wrong in my eyes. We had a marvellous day, although Sussex lost. We travelled home together and hurried to the garden, where there was enough light to re-enact the most memorable scenes from the match: a Dexter boundary, John Snow cruising to the wicket and so on. Our shared love of cricket—and music, incidentally, for he was a fine pianist—was an unbreakable bond.

Nine days later my father died. He was 41.

He had moved from Southgate Cricket Club to Wimbledon Cricket Club with a view to playing a little less and more locally. On the Sunday afternoon after the Gillette Cup Final a fellow team member brought him home early from a match. His face was ashen and he went to bed. The immediate diagnosis was that he had picked up a stomach bug from my two-year-old brother, Ben. On Monday, he seemed a little better. That Monday night— or at 2 am on Tuesday, to be precise—he died in bed alongside my mother. Unsurprisingly, the night lives with her to this day.

I was a few weeks short of my eleventh birthday. My sister, Susanna, was twenty months younger. We had no idea why we were whisked off, first thing, to family friends for much of the day.

We returned home around teatime and Mum was waiting for us in the hall. She took us into the sitting room and explained that Dad had died. We were later to hear that a congenital heart condition had betrayed him, and us. These days he would comfortably have survived.

A deep aching sadness overtook our home. It was as if it rained all day and all night. I talked to him in my bed, imagining he would hear, but the deafening silence overcame us all. We slept together in my sister's bedroom for comfort, though little could be found. Our family was always as one and blessed by love, laughter and warmth. Now, the void exposed us as mortal and highly fragile. Honestly, how does a mother cope? We were beyond pain.

Three weeks into the autumn term, my mother took me back to Fernden, the boarding prep school I had started the year before. Neither she, nor my father, had any idea how much I hated it. The saving grace was a headmaster with kindness at his core and cricket set almost as deep in his heart as in mine.

Charles Brownrigg ran an old-fashioned school—not quite Tom Brown's alma mater though along similar lines—but such emotionless authority over young boys did not come naturally to him. Age had taken its toll and so his wife, the matrons and the other masters made the place tick. Mr Charles's true colours were to be found in the summer term, when cricket was played at every opportunity: in the schoolyard during midmorning break; again for half an hour before lunch; throughout the afternoon in organised and disciplined form; and then, for those of us with greater interest or skill, private coaching sessions with him each evening after tea. This was wall-to-wall cricket for three to four hours each day, with matches against other schools twice a week and house matches that were ongoing throughout the summer term. It was heaven.

In the spring and summer holidays at home, I rolled the pitch with even greater vigour and invited friends to play out Test matches. Play began at 11.30 am, lunch was at 1.30 pm and tea at ten past four. Mum never let me down. Even the sausages and mash had to wait until 6.30 when we finished. Invariably, I/England would declare with around 500 on the board and knock over my mate/Australia or West Indies for next to nothing and win by an innings. Friends went by the wayside almost weekly.

I could mimic Geoffrey Boycott's exaggerated defensive positions, Colin Cowdrey's easy manner, Tom Graveney's unusual grip and Ted Dexter's magnificent poise. I copied John Snow's beautiful rhythm and Ken Higgs's angled approach, with his bum stuck out and his snarling response ready for every opponent. I worked right-arm on Derek Underwood's left-arm deliveries and mastered the arm ball with which Fred Titmus trapped Garry Sobers—at least, I thought I did.

The score was recorded each over. At the fall of every wicket, the dismissed batsman had to walk across the garden, into the house, up the stairs and into the small bathroom, where he removed his gloves, put on a different pair and set off back to the middle. Always, the new batsman was applauded to the crease. I think this was more for the sense of theatre than etiquette.

The only times during the summer holidays that these matches were put on hold was during a real Test match, when I sat glued to the television—black and white until the early 1970s—and watched every ball of every game. When we travelled, the car radio crackled with the magic. I could imitate Benaud, John Arlott and Brian Johnston, and did so for anyone who would listen.

At school, I smuggled in a small wireless and hid it under my pillow. During the winter nights of 1970–71, I listened in awe as Boycott and Snow helped Ray Illingworth bring the Ashes back to England. That crackling sound, Alan McGilvray's distant voice, and the news that Snow had nailed Ian Chappell, opened this young mind to a cinematic vision of Australia.

There was an added edge to the second of the two Tests at the Sydney Cricket Ground, when Snow was collared by spectators after his bouncer hit Terry Jenner in the head and Ray Illingworth led his players from the field in a protest for their safety. For me, the SCG assumed almost mythical proportions, and those who played upon it became gladiators in the imagination of a young boy captivated by his heroes. As he ran down the battery and drifted into sleep, his heart beat with the rhythm of the great southern land and from the roar of the crowd whose hard-nosed opinions on the action out in the middle was the stuff of the Colosseum.

I was pleased to move on from prep school. The place represented a deeply troubled time. My nights were filled first with tears and then a challenging nightmare in which I ran downhill from a huge boulder that chased me until the very moment it was to flatten me. I awoke in panic night after night. There was some bullying, of course, as is the way of young boys, and some unsympathetic schoolmastering from men completely unable to deal with such complex emotional trauma.

Cricket was the release. Cricket, cricket and more cricket. I devoured the game in newspapers, magazines, radio and television. I collected those cigarette cards, read the *Playfair Cricket Annual* and even dipped into *The Cricketer* and *Wisden*. Though football and rugby were key components of winter life, cricket still found a place when England toured abroad.

In the spring of 1970, I asked Mum for a new bat. That tested her. She worked her way through the drawers of Dad's desk and found a receipt for cricket kit from a shop in Soho. Soho! She asked me what I knew of Alfred Jameson Sports, a question that confounded me as much as her. She called the number and a man answered who introduced himself as *the* Mr Jameson. He said he had the summer's new range of equipment in stock. And so off we went: me with uncontrollable excitement and Mum with some trepidation. The Soho of 46 years ago was no place for a lady.

We arrived in Greek Street and parked our green Morris Minor outside an old-curiosity-type shop. We descended a small flight of steps and rang a bell. An ageing man with a white moustache greeted us. Peter Nicholas had been a customer for a while now, he said, through a mutual friend at Southgate Cricket Club. Phew. Mum explained that Peter had died. Mr Jameson seemed genuinely sad and promised us the same discount afforded to my father.

I touched the bats, feeling the smooth, cold wood in my fingers. I studied the grains, the bows and the handles. I pulled on gloves, opening and closing my hands inside the soft, fitted leather. I touched pads of all sizes, and admired photographs of Bradman, Hutton, Edrich and Compton.

Mr Jameson pulled out a Gray-Nicolls and began tapping the ball on its face. Then he bounced it, increasingly higher until the odd one hit the ceiling: goodness, he said, what a beautiful piece of willow! This was a long-practised sales pitch and Mum was falling for it. I had other ideas. I picked out a bat with a new logo—a thick black triangle—that I had seen used by Basil D'Oliveira. Mr Jameson disapproved. He said it was heavy and that at my age I needed a lighter bat for greater flexibility. I persevered. On closer inspection the triangle was an image of three stumps and two bails. The bat was called a Duncan Fearnley.

It was an argument I was never going to lose. At the age of thirteen I had my first Fearnley. Better still, Mum decided Dad's visits to Soho had been virtuous. We went back each spring and then, one year, this old curiosity of a sport's shop had gone, replaced by a Chinese restaurant. Alfred Jameson had played his last innings. Hopefully, he was with Peter Nicholas, both bemoaning the fact that the Nicholas son and heir was out in the middle with a bat that weighed more than it should.

Six months later I started at Bradfield College in Berkshire. Initially, the days there were no better than at Fernden prep school but after a year a new housemaster took over and brightened up 'G House'. Chris Saunders had won cricket and football blues at Cambridge and Oxford respectively and quickly understood the individual needs of boys in their early teens, who were often frightened and certainly alone.

Chris had a real gift. He hammered the bad 'uns and stoked the good 'uns. He mixed leaders with losers and let them teach

each other about both sides of the coin. He allowed Johnny Muir—addicted to nicotine by his mid-teens—to smoke in his own house rather than find him out at the bike sheds corrupting others with Embassy Regal or Player's No. 6. He encouraged a lad whose parents lived in Borneo to make the long journey home worthwhile by coming back late after the Christmas holidays. Best of all as far as I was concerned, he encouraged everyone to play sport whatever their limitations.

With a firm but always fair and light-hearted touch, he lifted the general malaise that had overtaken Bradfield—as it had so many of Britain's schools during the early 1970s. Drugs, cigarettes and alcohol were more appealing to many teenagers than Dexter, George Best and David Duckham. Some grew their hair long and then, having rolled it into a bun, held it in place above their collar with pins and clips. When Mike Wright was badly tackled in a 1st XI football match, he hit the frozen ground with enough momentum to somersault forward and into the sideline crowd of masters and schoolboys. Out flew the pins and clips and, to Mike's acute embarrassment, so too the bedraggled locks that hung halfway down his back. As soon as the match was over, our new housemaster frog-marched Mike to the school barber, where the hair was hacked off above the collar and looked ridiculous for the remainder of the term.

In many ways I was lucky at Bradfield. Chris was a brave and enthusiastic wicketkeeper, who knew the game. The head of cricket, Dickie Brooks—another wicketkeeper—had played for Somerset. As one coach, Maurice Hill—formerly of Nottinghamshire, Derbyshire and Somerset—left for other pastures, John Harvey, the recently retired Derbyshire batsman, arrived in his place. I was picked in the 1st XI when I was fifteen and played in the team for four years, the last as captain. I never made enough runs but took wickets with decent outswingers at medium-fast. These three good men guided me on the path to my dream. I was way ahead of anyone as a captain and led an unbeaten team in my final year. Chris appointed me head of house and encouraged me to take charge of everything within my reach.

The runs thing was odd. In my last year at prep school I made four hundreds, a remarkable tally for a thirteen-year-old. Possibly I pressed too hard at Bradfield. Maybe I was promoted too early for my fragile mental state and this had the reverse effect of holding back my performance as I played constant catch-up. Maybe I was too cocky and cricket was already teaching me about myself.

I joined the Bank of England Cricket Club—Mum knew someone, or Dad had, and the ground was next door to home—and played for them in the Surrey League during my mid-teenage summer holidays. The earthiness of the cricket was appealing, more so than the nature of wandering cricket, which was formed around the old-boy network of the British public schools. Some of these clubs—Butterflies, Free Foresters and Stragglers of Asia among them—played against Bradfield during the school term, and my desire to beat them was every bit as great as my desire to beat other schools. With the benefit of hindsight, I now think that I had already latched on to the problem cricket faced with elitism. Bradfield boys had this magnificent ground—still one of my five favourite in England—and the chance to enjoy cricket as a way of life. Youngsters I knew around London had no such luck. There was a smugness about many of the men from the clubs who came to play us. This was not necessarily a conscious thing. It was inherent. The shame to me was that the institution of cricket would not spread its wings.

Once, in a moment of jaw-dropping condescension, an opposing captain won the toss and asked what I wanted to do first. I thought sod him and set out to win the match at any cost. I replied that we would bowl first, to which he warmly agreed. I used our two best bowlers for most of the innings, operating to defensive fields with plenty of cover on the boundaries. We fielded feverishly, denying runs as if our lives depended upon it. By the midpoint of the match, the opposition were not more than 140 for 3 or 4.

These were declaration matches, not limited overs and, on a flat pitch, 140 was nowhere near enough. But no club side of grown men could be seen to bat too long against school-boys. The captain arrived at the wicket looking to push the score along but perished caught on the square-leg fence. He left red-faced. Another half an hour or so passed as increas-ingly exasperated gentlemen came to the crease, only to lose their wicket attempting to catch the clock. Eventually, about 40 minutes before tea, they declared 9 wickets down. We needed about 200 to win. I changed the order round, sending in a couple of hard hitters against the new ball and keeping the opening batsmen for later should the match need saving. It didn't. We got off to a flyer. So much so that after tea we were able to pace ourselves. I got to the wicket with about 90 needed from the obligatory twenty overs in the last hour. We cruised home with time to spare and celebrated long and hard.

In the summer holidays of 1975, I was asked to play for Middlesex Under-19s. I turned up at the Barclays Bank ground in Ealing to find I was playing in a team with Mike Gatting, who was one of the three stand-out young batsmen in England, along with David Gower and the less well-known Matthew Fosh. Though a year younger than Gatt, I hoped to have the chance to compare myself with him but I didn't get in to bat. We won by 9 wickets. Gatt, who finished unbeaten with 70-odd, was in a different class, a completely different class. Within a couple of years, he was with England in Pakistan.

I played a few more games the next summer but lovely old Jack Robertson—briefly an England batsman after the war—who ran the side, thought more of a couple of other lads who had grown up within his radar. Soon enough, I had moved on anyway.

My mother had empowered me to fully embrace cricket. Thus, when the sun shone, I rejoiced. On those summer mornings when it rained, I pined. From the age of fifteen to eighteen, I turned down family holidays on the Isle of Wight, in the New Forest, to France and to Corfu so that I could catch bus and train, cricket bag in hand, to turn up everywhere and anywhere for a game.

Dad may have gone but his memory lived on through this shared passion for cricket. A beautiful game was the friend to whom I had turned in September 1968 and the friend who remains firmly by my side to this day.

CHAPTER 2

Hampshire, 1977

There were Jim the Fizz, Pops, Pokers and PT; Hillers, Murt, Elvis and Pissy Pete; Lew the Shag, Jungle Rock, Herbie, Trooper, Dougal and Dicey Rice. Most of us, and a few more, were based in a small room in the bowels of a pavilion building so dilapidated it was noteworthy that the council passed it fit for business. Assuming it did.

Hampshire County Cricket Club was run by Desmond Eagar and had been since the 1950s. His second-in-command was the club captain, Richard Gilliat. My first year—as a wet-behind-the-ears triallist set on a life in cricket—was 1977, Desmond's last. We freshers saw little of Eagar and not much more of Gilliat but there was no mistaking that they were in charge.

We were the County 2nd XI, the Brat Pack, uncapped staff players who bowled in the nets in pretty much all weather. We ran the scoreboard at 1st XI home matches and helped the ground staff with the covers and such. We took turns to act as 12th man for the gods who lived in the little cottage upstairs: the capped 1st XI players. This was a mystical chamber into which we were rarely allowed. Entry to the first-team dressing room came via knocking and then permission, even as 12th man. This was a coveted role, simply to rub shoulders with some of the best players around—Barry Richards and Gordon Greenidge, for example, Andy Roberts, Trevor Jesty and Gilliat himself. But after a few days at it, you understood that the public-school fagging system was far from dead.

First up, before play, you served the lads tea, coffee and a couple of digestive biscuits. At lunch you turned waiter for the bowlers or unbeaten batsmen—ham rolls usually, or the tasteless fare from the dining room, plus lashings of Heinz salad cream. At tea, you ran for cover if things were going badly out on the field but not before ensuring the sandwiches had been delivered by the kitchen and the teabags had drawn. If Hampshire was in the field, you made your way to the scorer's hut to collect the bowling figures and deliver them to the captain. Weirdly, he tended to look in the maidens column first, as if maiden overs were the route to a pot of gold. Yes, wickets were okay, 'but maidens, lad, maidens: give 'em fuck all'.

Towards the close of play you filled the huge communal bath into which the naked gods descended as one, having supplied their order for drinks—beer, lager, Coke, orange juice or milk, mainly—and ran various other errands. That bath was an unhealthy thing all right, unless you got there first and were gone before the bowlers' feet began their long and weary soak.

I was first taken upstairs to this holy place by Mike Hill (Hillers), the 2nd XI wicketkeeper, when the first team were playing away from home and we were doing six-hour days in the nets. He showed me an enormously heavy bat, made from dark wood, that he said Barry Richards used in Sunday League games. He claimed it weighed 4 pounds, which I had no reason to doubt. It was enough for me to just to hold a bat used by Richards, the cricketer who could do no wrong in my eyes. Swooning, I made to drive, cut and pull, shadowing the great man's stance and technique, with an exaggerated position of the left elbow and a flourish in the follow-though. But the bat weighed me down. The strokes seemed near impossible. This was a club, not a bat. What was I to believe? That Richards was immortally strong? That the journey I so badly wanted as the bookmark to my life was already beyond me because I could not lift the great warrior's sword?

Hill had now been joined by Nigel Cowley (Dougal, after the dog in *The Magic Roundabout*) and Tim Tremlett (Trooper, for his military gait and Roman nose). They began to laugh among themselves. This was no bat used in matches by Richards but a demo, made from oak, which he used to warm up immediately before going out to bat. It made his actual bat feel like a wand, allowing his muscles to adapt quickly to the challenge of the new ball. I disappeared to the bowels below, tail between my legs and their laughter in my ears.

Hampshire was an old-school club: institutionalised in that shabby English way, financially poor but mainly happy. The place chugged along, just about breaking even in an age when no one talked about money, only manners. Eagar was as much headmaster as former captain and secretary. Much loved and respected, he was to die suddenly late that September, aged 59.

Once, he offered the young leg-spinner Alan Castell a drink in celebration of his first five-wicket haul. 'I'll have a pint of bitter, please, Mr Eagar,' said Cass. 'Castell, a word in your ear,' Eagar replied. 'When a senior member of the club offers you a drink, ask for a half, Castell, a half. Now then, Castell, let me buy you a drink to celebrate your bowling today.' 'Thank you, Mr Secretary,' said Cass, 'I'll have two halves of bitter, please . . .'

Occasionally, something—or someone—arrived to break the ever-so-slightly-grey rhythm of life. To a degree, Castell was one of those but his cricket never kicked on and soon enough he too was one of the game's lost souls. Long before my time was the first and very best of them, Colin Ingleby-Mackenzie, the Old Etonian who led the county to the championship in 1961 with outrageous flair and abandon. The stories of that summer have become the stuff of legend. Wild optimism; dashing parties in London decorated by beautiful 'It' girls; wads of cash laid down, won and lost track-side at Ascot; crazy declarations on the cricket field and miraculous victories from nowhere all came together to beat Yorkshire—far and away the best team in the land—to the championship title. When not gallivanting around London, Colin lodged at the Eagar family home in Southampton, frequently getting in as Desmond was getting up.

Hampshire's approach was well summed up by Ingleby's response to the interviewer's first question at the BBC Sports Personality of the Year night in London. 'Well, Colin, this was quite a performance by your chaps. What was the secret?' asked Peter Dymock. 'Oh, I don't know really. A bit of luck, I suppose,' replied Colin, 'and a simple enough rule that I wanted the chaps in bed by half past ten, to be sure that they got an hour's sleep before the start of play.' Boom, boom. 'Gosh,' or some such thing, said Dymock. 'So it's true, Colin, that you did it with wine, women and song?' 'Well, I don't remember much singing, Peter,' replied Ingleby, before howling with laughter.

It was a long time before I came to know Colin personally but when I did there was no going back. He was the best of men—joyous, charming, generous of heart, spirit and pocket, and very funny. My greatest privilege was to be asked to speak at his memorial service at St Paul's Cathedral, an occasion attended by almost two thousand people whose lives he had touched.

Afterwards, the family gave a reception at the Merchant Taylor's Livery Hall in the City. I was talking to Colin's wife, Storms (née Susan Stormont-Darling), when a hard slap at my right shoulder caught us all by surprise. I spun round and there, tall and elegant and wearing a black velvet Fedora with a cream silk scarf draped around his shoulders, was Peter O'Toole. Can you imagine! 'Bloody good, dear boy, bloody good. I did Lean there. It's a fucking awful place!' And then he smiled, the most majestic smile in all the world, and disappeared from view. I never saw him again.

The last time I had seen him was on stage as the lead in Keith Waterhouse's mischievous play *Jeffrey Bernard is Unwell*, a role to which he was ideally suited. Years earlier, in the winter of 1979–80, we shared the same net in the indoor school at Lord's. He was a mate of the coach and former England left-arm spinner, Don Wilson, and liked to hang out with the young wannabes of the professional game. On occasion, he would buy us Chinese dinner up the road after the nets were done. He was just about the most alluring man I have met. How anybody avoided falling in love with him, I do not know.

'Lean' was David Lean, who directed *Lawrence of Arabia*, and O'Toole was right about St Paul's from a speaker's point of view. Because you perform from the other side of the dome from the audience, you feel isolated and the sound of your voice feeds back at you—'It's a fucking awful place.' Having said that, it is beautiful place too, and as I began to talk about Colin, the sun came out, flooding the circle beneath the dome with a golden morning light. It was as if his spirit had dropped in to reassure us that all was well upstairs and though today was very nice, we should dry up the tears and crack on without him from here on in. Truly, we could feel this spirit, and who was to argue with the most optimistic man any of us had known?

After Ingleby, the white Barbadian Roy Marshall became the club captain. Marshall could really bat, the first of three truly great cutters of the ball that came from overseas to thrill Hampshire fans: Marshall; then Gordon Greenidge, also from Barbados; and finally Robin Smith, from Durban. But Marshall was a dreary captain or, if that is unfair, he was not a patch on Ingleby, who was the hardest act to follow. These were fallow years.

The club trod water until the arrival of Richards in 1968. After Ingleby-Mackenzie, Richards was probably Eagar's best signing, though it brought controversy because the South African was on a higher percentage of 'talent money' than the other players. (Effectively, talent money was a performance-based bonus. Salaries were negligible but talent money could make a summer's work properly worthwhile.)

Richards announced he would make 2000 runs in his first season and was scoffed at by the embittered old pros who played alongside him, especially when he failed on a green pitch in his first match. Though no one knew it then, Richards was among the finest batsmen on the planet. He made 2000 runs all right, and earned more talent money than the rest of them put together. Jealousy bounced all around the dressing-room walls. I was soon to discover that jealousy bounced all around the professional game.

That first year, I lived with Nigel Popplewell—Pops—in a flat halfway up Bassett Avenue, the main drag heading north out of Southampton. We lived off cornflakes, and roast chickens that were half-eaten one night, left to fester for the best part of 24 hours in the bowels of the oven in which they had been cooked, and then finished off the next day. Pops had a red Mini that took us to and from matches and to the pub. Rather too often, it brought us back from the pub, too. If there was no chicken in the oven, it was a pie and chips from the joint around the corner that the health inspector eventually closed down.

Pops's father, Oliver, was a barrister before he became a judge—he chaired the inquiry into the Bradford City stadium fire—and was later knighted. He and my father completed national service in the navy together, which is how we all knew each other. One morning, we rolled out of bed for a game against the Middlesex 2nd XI in Winchester, gave the corn-flakes a miss because the milk was rancid and hurried out to the avenue to find the Mini had been nicked. This was a blessing in disguise. Upon our hasty return to the flat to call both the coach, Peter Sainsbury, to tell him we would be late—not funny—and the police to report the theft—quite funny—we found the bathroom flooded and the floorboards giving way—very funny. The landlady, who lived in the flat underneath us, was banging at our door.

Pops, or maybe me (who cared, except her?) had run a bath and forgotten about it. By the time the cops turned up, the landlady had lost the plot. Our bathwater was a steady flow into her living room. The cops found the car two days later, abandoned in a derelict part of town. The landlady charged us proper money for the fix-up. We were on £21.50 a week so, with a few caveats, Judge Popplewell and Mrs Nicholas agreed to pick up the tab.

Stressed, we arrived by taxi at the St Cross ground in Winchester just before the lunch interval. The coach lost the plot too. He said it was our last chance, which seemed a little extreme, but it wasn't the moment to point out that we had not been alerted to a first chance. The fact was, we were two public schoolboys, and the reasonable perception was that we had lived a life fed by the silver spoon.

Actually, Sainsbury—or Sains (what imagination we had for nicknames!)—was a fabulous man. He had played for the county from 1954 to 1976 as an accurate left-arm spinner, brilliant close fielder and gutsy middle-order batsman. Then, in a jobs-for-the-boys appointment, he became coach. He had no qualification other than a long and worthy playing career but county second elevens were run by former professionals who simply passed on their stock in trade. Frankly, Sains was not very good at it but he was a top bloke and we all adored him.

Popplewell didn't make the end-of-term cut, sadly, but Somerset snapped him up, so somebody else lived off dried old chicken and stale cornflakes too. I was offered a two-year contract, starting 1 April 1978.

These contract announcements were made early each September and filled most of the playing staff with dread. Young players dreamt of glory in the game they loved. Fellows in their mid- to late twenties needed the job. Those in their early 30s, many of whom had long fallen out of love—with the game and often their wives, too—prayed for the chance of a benefit year and a tax-free windfall in recognition of their long service.

That autumn of 1976 had spelt the end for two splendid characters, Richard Lewis (Lew the Shag—though Lew went on to marry the daughter of the chairman of the club's cricket committee and to become cricket coach at Charterhouse School, so not bad) and Pete Barrett (Pissy Pete, who loved a drink). Famously, when hit in the nuts by Michael Holding in Hampshire's match against West Indies the previous summer, Pete lay writhing on the ground and looked up to see Clive Lloyd asking if everything was intact. 'Think so, captain, but 'ere,' said Pete, 'would you mind asking yer fast bowler t'slow down a bit?' Both were playing Minor Counties cricket in 1977 but hung around with us the rest of the time. Pete was a ripper bloke who tragically died in a motorcycle accident a year or two later. It took us a while to smile again.

Hillers and Andy Murtagh (Murt) stayed on to become 2nd XI senior pros, an oxymoron if ever there was one. John Rice (Dicey Ricey) was playing more first-team cricket, which was better than living on the fringe, so he got a two-year deal too. Same for Nigel Cowley. Rice played another five years and Cowley twelve. Both were destined to leave Hampshire unhappily—there is no easy way to release a professional sportsman—though they, thankfully, found fulfilment in the game elsewhere. Rice got the bullet in 1982 but was soon appointed coach at Eton College, a job he held for 30 years. His wife, Sue, ran the school shop, and together they became a popular and integral part of Eton life. Cowley played in our team that won the Benson & Hedges (one-day) Cup in 1988 before a brief spell at Glamorgan led to the end of his playing career. He turned his mind and spinning-finger to umpiring, and is still at it now. Increasingly, cricket takes care of its own.

The County Ground in Northlands Road, Southampton, was a quaint place. The pitch was good and the boundaries were shortish. I had first been there on a school trip to watch the 1975 Australians. Richards made runs in both innings, though Australia won the match with a convincing run chase in which Ian Chappell made a hundred. Absorbed and star-struck, I resolved to return one day and bloody well play out there myself.

Now here I was, on a month's trial for which I was paid expenses but would have come for nothing. I was beyond nervous on arrival at those Northlands Road gates. Most of the guys had come through the Hampshire youth system but, having grown up in London, I played for Middlesex Young Cricketers where one or two others were ahead of me in the pecking order of Under-19s county cricket. The trial at Hampshire was courtesy of Gilliat, who had been contacted by my housemaster at Bradfield, Chris Saunders, who knew Gilliat from Oxford University playing days. Sainsbury then called the school coach, John Harvey, once of Derbyshire, and heard Saunders' view endorsed.

I was shown to a small, cold, unglamorous changing room with pale-blue walls and a stark concrete floor in the basement of the pavilion, and told to change then report to the nets pronto. The first team were practising and I was sent to bowl in net 3. I looked up to see Richards on strike. Jeeesus. I ran in and bowled a gentle long hop, which, with a distracted air, the great man smashed off the back foot over my head. I ran to get the ball from the fence some 70 yards away. On return, I peeled off the long-sleeved Bradfield College jumper and tried again. Same ball, same result. Shit.

Nine months earlier, I had opened the bowling for the Public Schools XI against the English Schools Cricket Association (ESCA). That event had nothing to do with bowling at Barry Richards. I tried again, this time fuller and quite straight. Richards blocked it. At this stage of my life, it was the single most exciting thing I had ever done: bowled a ball that one of the two or three best batsmen in the world had blocked. I walked back to my mark, turned to face my hero and take him on again, only to see him walking into the next-door net. Please no. But yes, Richards had gone. That was it. Three balls in paradise. Over.

We bowled for a couple of hours in damp and chilly conditions before breaking for lunch, which, to my surprise, was at the pub down the road. I had chicken pie and chips. One or two of the lads introduced themselves properly. Tim Tremlett (Trooper) was kind and asked some questions about where I had come from and what cricket I had played previously. I think we drank pints of lager and lime or blackcurrant and lemonade. There were a lot of in-jokes to which I was not privy but I learnt that the 1st XI were done for the day and off to an away match at Lord's. There was a whisper we would all have a bat later. Not so. I just kept bowling. Fun but not great for my lower back, which was iffy at best. Jim Ratchford (Jim the Fizz—physio, though not really, more a masseur with a good line in sweet talk) noticed me clutching the area of the sacroiliac joint. He offered Deep Heat and a rub. Christ, I thought,

I can't be seen on the physio's bench on day one. 'No thanks, Jim,' which others told me was a wise move. Fancy that, some of the best players in the world and no qualified medical man in sight. Just Jim, who barely knew a calf muscle from a fetlock but gave a damn good rub when the aching soldiers presented themselves. Them were the days.

I stayed in a bed and breakfast next to the pub, slept well after the day's excitement and woke to find rain chucking it down. My worst nightmare. I wanted to play cricket every day—yes, that's every damn day. In general, old pros loved the rain and young pros hated it.

Thankfully, it relented by midmorning and we were back in those nets. I bowled better but was outplayed by David Rock (Jungle Rock, after the song), a young talent out of Portsmouth just a few months older than me. He had an easy upright stance and drove the ball through mid-on with authority. A few weeks later he was playing for the 1st XI at Portsmouth against Essex.

I had a chat with him at lunch—more pie and chips, pint of lager and lime, I kid you not—about his bat, which had a black triangular motif over the splice. Rock had used Fearnley equipment from the start of his career and explained that Duncan Fearnley was a former Yorkshire and Worcestershire batsman who now made his own bats at a factory in Worcester. This was a revelation to me. I had no idea there actually was a man called Duncan Fearnley. A year later, Rock took me to the factory to meet him. Duncan made me a bat, for goodness' sake, and gave it to me, along with pads and gloves—all free. Mum liked that. (From that point on, every spring, I would spend a day with Duncan at the factory in Worcester. We got along famously and after mornings at the work-bench would break for long and alcoholic lunches before returning to sign off on bats and then load the car with gear. We are close mates to this day and often reminisce about Basil D'Oliveira and Alfred Jameson's quirky little sports shop in Soho. In seventeen years as a professional cricketer, I never used any other make of bat.)

After lunch we went back to the nets and I was told to pad up. With a beating heart, I took guard at Hampshire County Cricket Club for the first time. The net pitches were grassy and soft. 'Herbie' (Richard Elms, a left-arm quick who had just been signed from Kent) made a fool of me. In fact, in general, I made a fool of myself.

Nerves have never served me well. I completely disagree with the theory that you need at least a sign of nervousness to perform at your best. This has not applied to me in any walk of life. Not at the wicket; not on the tee; not in front of the camera, on the stage or at the lectern; never at a party, nor in a meeting; and definitely not with women. Nerves are my enemy and surely were this day at Northlands Road. The surface was difficult. The ball moved around off the seam and refused to come onto the bat. I missed it, nicked it, slapped it in the air, shut the face on outswingers to lose my off stump and got bowled through the gate by inswingers. It might be the most excruciatingly embarrassing twenty minutes of my life.

I could sense the disapproval. After the net session we were to drive to Dover and then play the Kent 2nd XI in a three-day match the next day: the biggest game of my life. Mike Hill told Sainsbury they couldn't possibly leave a staff player behind and take me. Others whispered in corners with a similar sentiment. Andy Murtagh sensed the general unease, told everyone to pack their gear and that he would have the travel arrangements for the journey to Kent fixed in half an hour. Then he took me aside and told me to forget about the net session. Tomorrow was another day, he said. Murtagh's brother, Paul, taught at Bradfield. Perhaps he had heard I was all right. Sainsbury came into the dressing room and confirmed I was playing. I suspect he was under orders from the Eagar–Gilliat corridor of power.

In those days, we travelled to matches by car. Quite how any of us afforded a car, I don't know. Popplewell wasn't with us at this stage; he was still up at Cambridge bowling those medium pacers for top county players to batter around Fenner's, the university ground. Murt drove Jungle Rock and me, in the back seat, to Dover.

That week, the back of the passenger seat in Hillers' car broke, so Freddie Ireland, the scorer, who always travelled with Hill, lay down all the way to Dover and back. Freddie couldn't pronounce his Rs and, for that matter, wasn't much good with Fs either. So he called himself 'Pweddie', which we all did, and it was bloody funny. We used to tick-tack en route, stopping at a pub or fish and chip place for supper. All these old bangers, bought on the cheap, in a peloton to far-flung parts of the land for cricket games that no one watched and of which few took notice. Pweddie liked fish and chips and told Hillers to stop near Canterbwe at a chippy he had known since god was a boy for pish, chips and mushy peas. Certainly, said Hillers, so that is what we all did, in town after town, month after month, during the summer of 1977.

The following year, I shared a house with Hillers. He ironed his socks and underpants, and made sure his trousers had a perfect crease. He left his bathroom gear—toothbrush, paste, shaving kit and so on—in symmetrical lines. If you knocked something out of place, it would be realigned when you returned. He was always bathing or showering. Super bloke, ordinary cricketer. And he never got the seat fixed. Pweddie had to travel thousands of miles lying flat on his back.

In August, Elvis Presley died. When Hillers came to pick up Pops and me to go to a game in Bournemouth (quite how we fitted in with Pweddie spread-eagled in the passenger seat

I don't know) I was on the staircase inside the front door doing 'Blue Suede Shoes'—voice, knees, air guitar, the lot—and given my long dark hair and the pound or two of excess weight I was carrying, it was an easy call. I was Elvis for the rest of the summer.

Elvis made a hundred at Dover. Kent were strong, as were we. The cricket was a good standard, much the best I had played. And I made a hundred, which was orgasmic. Chris Cowdrey got one for Kent, too. It was the first time we had met and we had a terrific night out, whizzing into town in his black Ford Capri. The girls loved him. Everybody loved Cow. There was a magic about him.

My hundred shook the boys up. Nick Pocock (Pokers—as I say, we cricketers could sure cook up a storm with nicknames) was another of the public schoolboys flirting with cricket as a living. He was a good front-foot driver of the ball and a brilliant catcher anywhere close to the bat. He made a hundred too. We were out soon after one another, and as the others took us past 350, he walked me around the ground.

'It's pretty obvious you can play a bit. You'll probably get offered a retainer for the rest of the summer,' said Pocock. So far so good. 'But be careful, the long-time pros think you're cocky. Turning up and making runs doesn't make life comfortable for any of them. Keep your head down and for god's sake don't sound like you know it all, even if you do. Though you don't.' Right. Blimey. Not how I had imagined life as a pro at all.

Pocock was spot on. They sure thought I was cocky and they were right, though it wasn't a conscious thing. I was enthusiastic and had spent most of my life in love with the game. I read every book and watched every televised ball. By the standards of most nineteen-year-olds, I knew a lot about cricket. The challenge was to not let anyone know. I was offered a retainer—£21.50 a week—for the rest of the summer.

And that was pretty much how we rolled. Hours in the nets. Not enough fielding practice. Unhealthy food. Lots of beer. Long car journeys, often at night after matches. Stops in provincial English towns and villages. (Pokers refused to stop at motorway services for any reason except fuel. He said Ingleby wouldn't dream of it—'Ghastly places.') Fines for just about any indiscretion that included dropped catches and not wearing the club tie after play, along with daft ones such as the failure to drink anything and everything with your opposite hand on a Friday.

(After the offer of a retainer, I couldn't afford the bed and breakfast full time, so Sains and his lovely wife, Joyce, put me up at their home. Every morning, he would bring me in a cuppa, with a 'Wakey, wakey, rise and shine'. On Friday mornings, as I yawned and knocked back the tea, with the cup in my usual right hand, he would exclaim 'Got ya, 50p!' One day, Dougal threw his toys out of the cot when he was battling away to save us the game and at the tea-break slugged back a pint of orange squash only to be told it had cost him fifty pence. Believe me, enough little mistakes and £21.50 a week didn't go far, especially if you couldn't catch.)

We won a few games and lost a few. It felt special to represent Hampshire, and a place in the 1st XI remained the Holy Grail. When Rock was picked to play at Portsmouth, we all went along to watch him. There were a few thousand spectators at the United Services ground and our boy briefly looked the goods. The sun shone that day and all was well with the world.

The biggest thrill of the summer came in mid-June at Northlands Road, where Hampshire had a home semifinal tie against Gloucestershire in the Benson & Hedges Cup. A few of us watched the game from inside the scorebox, urging on those of our number—Ricey and Dougal most notably—who were playing.

If Barry Richards was the cricketer on whom I most doted, Mike Procter was not far behind. His buccaneering style, both on and off the field, mesmerised opponent and spectator alike. He and Richards had grown up in Natal at the same time, and both played for the Gloucestershire 2nd XI after impressing on a South African schools tour to England in 1963. Procter is one of only three men—Sir Donald Bradman and C.B. Fry are the others—to have made six consecutive first-class hundreds. But it was as a fast bowler that he most caught the eye, sprinting in from near the sightscreen to bowl with an unusual, almost wrong-footed action and swinging the ball prodigiously in to the right-handed batsmen.

Procter won that semifinal almost before it had started. He took four wickets in five balls, including a hat-trick. And not any old four, if you don't mind. He trapped Richards and Jesty lbw, and bowled Greenidge and Rice. He had Cowley stone dead lbw for five in six but dear old Tommy Spencer's heart was pounding too much to get his right forefinger out of the holster for a third time in one over. As Cowley says to this day, he was the most out of the three of them. Watch it on YouTube: it is as captivating now as it was then. Imagine seeing and hearing this drama from the scorebox. We couldn't change the tally fast enough. The chants of 'Proctershire, Proctershire' live with me to this day.

Inspired, I took to bowling in the nets like Procter and batting with my chin tucked into my left shoulder like Richards. I imitated their voices too, having edged close enough to Procter in the bar that June night to hear every word. Neither playing method much worked as I recall but mimicry was to become a common theme over the months and years that followed, especially of John Arlott and Richie Benaud.

Pops and I won Sains over, and Hillers began to enjoy our happy-go-lucky look at life. Paul Terry (PT—I know!) teamed up with us for the second half of the summer after finishing at Millfield and playing a lot of representative cricket for England at Under-19 level.

It was an awful feeling when summer turned to autumn and we were sent on our way. In those days, and until fairly recently, county contracts applied to the period from April through to September. We said goodbye to friends and went out into the big wide world to find a job. I headed back to London, lived with Mum, and ended up in the City doing analyst work with the stockbroking firm Hoare Govett. As the days became shorter and the nights longer, I was overcome with the desire to return to the little downstairs dressing room at Northlands Road and the banter that had quickly become a soundtrack to my life. I missed bat and ball and I missed the people. I missed the way cricket had wrapped its arms around me. I knew there was no going back, no chance of a life in the City or anywhere else except Northlands Road. I had been offered a two-year contract and I was damned if I wouldn't make it work.

CHAPTER 3

Australia

In the late English summer of 1978, Mike Taylor, the experienced Hampshire all-rounder, asked me if I fancied a season in Australia. Kerry O'Keeffe, who had spent a period at Somerset with Mike's brother, Derek, had been on to him about a young pro playing for a club he knew that needed shoring up. I could barely contain myself.

Come season's end, I packed a couple of bags and set off on the second real adventure of my life. Two winters earlier, I had captained an English Schools team, under the name the Dragons, to Rhodesia and South Africa. We had some success and after the tour I took the overnight train to Durban to play three months of club cricket for Berea Rovers. I was eighteen, hung out at the youth hostel in town, and lived the life of a young man besotted by cricket and the avenues down which it led.

But the dream was different. I had a cinematic vision of Australia, in which the blue horizons cut a sharp line between sea and sky and where the terracotta desert stretched so far from view that no man could ever occupy its space. My father had told me about Richie Benaud, my mother about Keith Miller. I had seen Dennis Lillee at Lord's and Jeff Thomson at

Southampton. The Chappells had spent many a summer's day in the garden at home in London, and on many a winter night their deeds had been transmitted via radio to a little boy who could repeat their figures more easily than his times tables.

The Australian captain's wicket had been the greatest prize, both at home and on the telly. It was a love–hate relationship. I could mimic Ian Chappell's stance, and his back-and-across move to play the hook. I could chew his gum, reposition his box and tug on the brow of his baggy green cap. The buttons of my shirt were undone to the breastbone, the sleeves were turned up at the cuff, the collar pointed to the sky. I could run in like Lillee, leaning well forward, pumping my arms and reaching the crease with a raucous surge of momentum. I could scream his appeals on my haunches, a finger raised to the heavens and a look of disgust at the umpire's decision. And I could wipe the sweat from my brow with a single swipe of my right index finger. Only Chappell and Lillee could stop Dexter, Boycott, Higgs and Snow in the backyard of 106 Priory Lane, London, SW18.

During Ashes tours Down Under, I would listen to the wireless until the small hours claimed me. In 1970–71, I heard Alan McGilvray and John Arlott talk of Ray Illingworth and Bill Lawry; of Snow and Terry Jenner; of Boycott and Johnny Gleeson; and of the Sydney Hill and the old scoreboard. Once, a mean teacher at boarding school left me bereft when he confiscated that wireless. It was returned when the rawness of the loss became apparent to the headmaster, Charles Brownrigg. He reasoned that a little boy's tired mornings were a fair trade for enthusiasm and the knowledge of a game that he suspected would play a huge part in that boy's life.

Through the northern winter of 1974–75, we watched highlight reels of Lillee and Thomson doing terrible things to English batsmen. One ball from Thommo hit Keith Fletcher on the badge of his cap and flew 25 yards to cover, where Ross

Edwards took the 'catch'. Another hit David Lloyd in the nuts, where a small, pink Litesome box (protector) inverted and shattered. Colin Cowdrey arrived from England aged almost 42 and rotund. He walked out to bat at Perth and diverted to the non-striker's end to introduce himself to Thomson, who was pawing at his mark. Thomson told him to piss off and bat. Within an over Cowdrey had been hit twice. Legend has it that county batsmen hid behind the sofa when the BBC played the news footage of these frightening moments.

Australia had, in no particular order, the Harbour Bridge, the Opera House, the Sydney Cricket Ground, the Melbourne Cricket Ground, the Adelaide Oval, the WACA and the Gabba. It had sheilas, beaches, barbecues and cold beer; Rod Laver, Ken Rosewall and John Newcombe; Malcolm Fraser, fourteen million people, Norman Gunston, Paul Hogan; sharks and crocs, the bush, the outback; AC/DC, Clive James and cricket. And I wanted to see it all.

I was at the very back of the plane, coincidentally sitting next to Wayne Larkins, the Northamptonshire opening batsman. I didn't know him personally but had admired his sparkling strokeplay from afar. We were soon friends and instead of sleep, we smoked a million cigarettes and drank a lot of beer. It was a long, hard flight and I emerged for the first time into the bright, early morning Australian light with a weary step. I was met by the club captain, Robert Holland.

———

William Holland and Emily Dickson married on 20 May 1909 in Northern Ireland. They produced seven children, five boys and two girls, the second of whom was Bill. In 1927, just before the Great Depression started to bite, they took the monumental decision to leave their home and start a new life in Australia. Bill was fifteen years old.

They sold the family shop for £400 and used most of the money to pay the fares. This was long before the assisted-migration scheme that spawned the phrase 'ten-pound Poms' and encouraged many families to search for a brighter future in the great southern land. The tickets were bought in Pomeroy, County Tyrone, and with bags packed, the family caught the ferry from Northern Ireland to Liverpool on 17 December 1927. They carried all they possessed for almost a mile along the docks to find their ship, the *Demosthenes*. It is about as brave a thing as you could imagine: no money and no idea of what lay ahead. The journey at sea took eight weeks.

On arrival into Sydney, they were told to head up the hill to the employment agency. Bill was asked if he could ride a horse, to which he replied yes—a mighty lie but he figured he would learn pretty quick if needs must. He was sent to Warren, 333 miles north-west of Sydney, where two Irish brothers took him in and taught him the ways of the jackaroo. By day he ran the cattle; by evening he worked the farm, washed the clothes, cooked and cleaned. He was well liked and never grumbled about his lot. He wrote regularly to William and Emily, who had stayed around Sydney.

After two years of this uncompromising life, and having saved every penny he earned, Bill told the brothers he was returning to the city. They paid him out and wished him well. He knew how damn lucky he had been to find kindred spirits deep in the heart of country Australia. He was not so lucky in Sydney, where there was no work and so, after a brief period in New Zealand where he learnt the finer details of farm life from his uncle, he joined the army in 1933. Corporal Bill Holland was stationed in Darwin, where he helped build the military base and married Marjorie. With a stroke of good fortune, and with Marjorie pregnant, he was transferred back to Sydney around the time the Second World War broke out. Their first child, William junior, was safely born in a Sydney hospital. The next day, the Japanese attacked Sydney Harbour in mini-subs— two-man submarines—forcing a total blackout of the city. Marjorie was pleased to find she still had her boy a week later.

Bill left the army in 1946, receiving an 11-acre parcel of land at Kanwal, near Wyong, for his efforts. With his own hand, he turned next to nothing into a home: the home in which his second son, Robert, lived for the first three years of his life. Then the family moved to Morisset, where Bill built a chicken farm. But it wasn't the chickens that Robert first recalled.

'Dad made me a cricket bat when I was eight years old. He made it from an old piece of hardwood timber, like a fence paling. I can recall him cutting the timber and shaping the handle to a round shape, using a rasp. I thought the bat was great and it was well used in cricket matches at the Pipers' house and also at the Dewhursts' place. Though the bat was suitable for use with a tennis ball, it could not be used with hard cricket balls because they jarred your hands badly.

'We played cricket on the long and wide concrete footpath that led from the Pipers' front gate to the high front steps that were also made of concrete. The location was ideal, as we didn't need a backstop [wicketkeeper] because any deliveries the batsman missed would be stopped by the steps. Cricket was also played in the sloping paddock at the rear of the Dewhurst house across the road from our place. The batsman would bat at the higher end of the paddock and hit the ball down- hill. Charlie Dewhurst, the father of Danny, Sally and Laurie, used to play with us from time to time. He used to bat and hit the ball a long way down the sloping paddock. I remember thinking, "How can anyone hit the ball so high and so far?"

'Charlie used to arrange a number of cricket matches each summer, for kids up to, say, twelve years of age, because there was not any junior cricket played in the Morisset area. The only opponents that I can remember were Dora Creek and the patients of Morisset Psychiatric Hospital. My brother was one of the best players for Morisset, while Noel Thompson was the star player for Dora Creek. I played in a couple of these matches and would have been about nine years old.'

Having enjoyed holidays at Coal Point, on the fringe of Lake Macquarie, the family decided to move there and Bill built them a family home. In fact, Bill took to building as a profession, and single-handedly developed and sold ten properties that gave his family a comfortable life. Days by the lake and in the local town of Toronto were a joy and Robert played more and more cricket, especially in the yard at Coal Point Primary School.

'Conditions were horrendous. We played on badly laid concrete or any piece of grass we could find. I was very competitive. By the age of thirteen I had begun spinning a ball out of the front of my fingers off the laundry-room wall. I learnt about side spin and over spin. My wrists and fingers became very strong. Soon, albeit under-arm, I could flight the ball too.'

He played fourth grade at the local club, Southern Lakes, at thirteen. He was picked in third grade because he held two catches. Gaining confidence, he had a crack at leg spin and took 50 wickets at 10 apiece. The next year, aged fourteen, he played first grade.

He remembers jumping off the bus from Booragul High School each afternoon at five minutes to four and running home to catch the start of the last session of live play in the televised Sheffield Shield matches. Richie Benaud, Peter Philpott, Gamini Goonesena and Johnny Martin were the glamorous wrist spinners of the time, and young Holland could not get enough of them.

'Everybody bowled leggies in those days. Television allowed me to see stuff I'd never seen, to see the standard that I needed to achieve. I worked on landing the orthodox leg break ball after ball. Then I worked on the square leg break, the 45-degree leg break, the topspinner, the little wrong 'un, the big wrong 'un and the slider. I never truly mastered the wrong 'un and never got close to the flipper.'

Bob played representative cricket for Newcastle at all age groups but there was never a sniff from the New South Wales selectors. In the late 1960s, he worked in Sydney as a draughtsman at the Department of Lands and commuted back home to play for Southern Lakes at the weekends. In the summer of 1970–71, while working on his Civil Engineering diploma, he was talked into a season for Bankstown with Jeff Thomson and Lenny Pascoe. It was a memorable experience.

'We only had four bowlers—Thommo; Lenny; Barry Thebridge, an off spinner; and me. Often enough one of Lenny or Thommo wouldn't turn up so I'd take the new ball. Lenny fought with everyone—umpires, captains, fielders— and would frequently take it out on the opposition by bowling six bumpers in an eight-ball over. Thommo was quick but bowled mainly half-volleys and yorkers, with the occasional short one. He definitely wasn't so bloodthirsty back then. Though having said that, we did have some fun saying to blokes who came out to bat after a night on the lash, 'Hey, mate, Thommo put two in hospital last week. How you feeling?!'

After that and a successful degree, it was back to Toronto and seasons in the sun with Southern Lakes. Invariably, the team would finish bottom of the log and Dutchy, as the cricket bubble now knew him, was among the leading wicket-takers in the league. Matches for Northern New South Wales against touring sides were the highlight, and he vividly remembers bowling to Boycott at Newcastle Oval in 1978–79.

'I got 4 in the first innings but don't remember bowling to him. In the second innings, I bowled eighteen wicketless overs, most of them to Geoff, whose bat was as wide as the lake. He made a second-innings hundred to ensure England won a match in which they had not played especially well. Each morning and evening of that game, he lined up voluntary net bowlers from the local clubs and they wheeled away from dawn until dark. On one occasion, only a fellow called Gordon Geise was left standing, and even he gave in when his boots split at the seam of the sole and the upper. Boycott asked what size he was and upon learning they were both size 9, lent him his spare pair so that Geise could bowl on and on, through the fading evening light. "Do they fit well, lad," said Boycs at nightfall. "They do, mate," replied the exhausted Geise. "Then they're yours for 20 bucks," said Boycs!'

Dutchy finally made his debut for New South Wales that summer, against Queensland at the Sydney Cricket Ground. He took 1 for 113 in nineteen overs, while Trevor Hohns, the Queensland leggie, took 11 in the match. At last, though, the selectors had identified the talent and Dutchy was to become a regular feature at New South Wales practices. The following summer, Kerry Packer's 'rebels' returned to the dressing room. The tension was obvious, he says. There was jealousy and mistrust.

'We all arrived for pre-season training and the WSC guys sat on one side of the room, the rest of us on the other. So, Rick McCosker, Trevor Chappell, Doug Walters, Len Pascoe, Kerry O'Keeffe over there; Peter Toohey, Steve Rixon, John Dyson, David Hourn, me and others over here. I remember a meeting when the team was announced with Chappell opening and Dyson left out. Dyson was beside himself, Trevor was by no means a natural opening batsman. You could have cut the air with a knife.

'I played the fifth Shield match of the summer instead of David Hourn but mainly scurried around with the drinks and bowled in the nets. Anyway, I got picked more regularly in the early 1980s and began to take wickets. In the 1983–84 season I was one of the leading wicket-takers in the Shield and started the next season just as well.

'In late November 1984, it happened. Carolyn and the kids had been in Sydney watching the Shield game and we loaded up the Cortina station wagon to drive back to Toronto. We were just past Hornsby and Carolyn turned on the six o'clock news. Almost immediately, the Test team was announced. I was in it. Well, we drove onto the shoulder of the highway and just sat there in shock. Then, impromptu, we all started cheering: the three kids, Carolyn and me, cheering away. Then we drove home. When we got there, our neighbour Joy had a huge white sheet over the front of the house and had written in big, black marker "Dutchy in Test team. Congratulations, Dutchy Holland!" All around the town people seemed pleased.

'It was quite a debut. [Holland is still the third-oldest cricketer to make his Test match debut for Australia and remains the oldest to do so since 1928.] They could play a bit, those West Indians. We were smashed through but I got a couple of wickets. It was the match when Kim Hughes resigned and cried in front of the television cameras. I've always got on well with Kim and felt badly for him. I went to the manager, Bob Merriman, and suggested we look after him, take him away from the spotlight and certainly not let him be left alone in his room. Bob said they had it covered. I suppose he thought "What would this new boy know?" But I was 38; I knew enough.

'Allan Border took over in Adelaide but we lost again. Kim played but was mentally shot. I should have bowled around the wicket at Viv Richards and certainly the left-handers, Larry Gomes and Clive Lloyd, but I didn't. Don't know why, really. Was nervous about it, I think, and there wasn't much communication between the senior guys in the team and us new boys. Funny that. There's this long journey to play for Australia, and when you get there you feel like you're starting out again, even at 38. I was left out of the Boxing Day Test (22–24 and 26–27 December in those days), when Craig McDermott and Murray Bennett made their debuts and Viv got 208, so that was a lucky miss! It was a time of great change after Greg Chappell, Dennis Lillee and Rodney Marsh had retired. We weren't to know it then but Kim Hughes was on the brink of leading a rebel tour to South Africa too.

'Anyway, I was back in the side for the Sydney Test, as promised by Rick McCosker, who was one of the selectors. We played four bowlers—shades of Bankstown days—Geoff Lawson and McDermott, Murray Bennett the left-arm spinner, and me. We won the toss on a damp pitch and chose to bat. Kepler Wessels played a fine, brave innings of 173 and I took 6 for 54, including Viv, having had him dropped by Greg Ritchie at mid-off in the previous over. Then I got 4 for 90 in the second innings and was given the man-of-the-match award. Can you believe it? Man of the match against West Indies! So it's not difficult to answer the question when I'm asked about the highlight of my career.'

Holland toured England later that year but felt he bowled too much in the early part of the tour—taking wickets, mind you—and was therefore jaded by the time the tests reached the pointy end. He found the margins of error against David Gower close to negligible and, in response, began almost exclusively to bowl flatter leg breaks simply to retain some control. He kept reminding himself of a brief meeting with Bill O'Reilly, who told him much as Benaud told Shane Warne: 'Master the leg break, ball after ball. Don't let the bastards off!' Warne always says that the wrist spinner's first challenge is to stay on. After that he needs a lot of love. In all, Dutchy claimed

34 wickets in eleven Tests. He played a season in New Zealand in 1987–88 and finished second on the list of wicket-takers in the Shell Trophy. In 1988 he hung up his first-class boots, aged 42. Any regrets?

'I'd like to have played more!'

His story is typical of country cricketers around Australia, whose ambition often outweighs the opportunities before them. Some wither on the vine, others make sacrifices to save themselves from doing so. Glenn McGrath is famous for taking his boots from Narromine, near Dubbo, to the city. His mum saved some money to buy him a caravan, which they towed from home to Hurstville in the Sydney suburbs. McGrath lived there on his own for thirteen months, while working at the bank and spending hours in the nets at Sutherland Cricket Club. Holland preferred to stay with Southern Lakes and commute when necessary. But then Newcastle is not Narromine.

Let's hand over to Dutchy's wife, Carolyn, to bookend the stories of Bill and Robert.

'The first thing I wish to say is how very proud Bill— Grandad, as we all knew him—was of his youngest son, Robert. Robert achieved academically and also in the sporting arena, and this was of great delight to his parents.

'Robert's father became a fierce supporter of the soccer he played but he also became a huge cricket fan, and when his son was first chosen to play for New South Wales as a leg spinner there was no one with a bigger grin than Grandad. However, when Robert was chosen to play for his country, that grin became the biggest smile you would ever see.

'Robert, Bob, Dutchy was selected to be Australia's 326th Test cricketer, making his debut against the West Indies in the second match of the 1984–85 series. Grandad and Grandma would always enjoy packing the thermos and muffins and turn out at the cricket in Newcastle. They would stay all day and enjoy every moment. Of course, Craig, Rohan and Naomi (our three children) were always at the cricket, so it was pretty much a double-delight day for them to watch the cricket and see their grandchildren.

'They would hang off every word whenever Robert's achievements were mentioned in the newspaper and added their own interpretation if the newspapers were not positive. Robert played district cricket from when he was fourteen years of age and first-class cricket for over ten years. He still plays golden-oldies cricket today at age 69. Robert now places all his knowledge into coaching and administration. So as you can imagine he provided much delight for his parents. Bill was so proud of Robert, his brother Bill junior and all his grand-children.'

The man who left Northern Ireland in 1927 aged fifteen, died peacefully in Toronto 62 years later. He led his life the hard way, getting his hands dirty and beating the odds. Billy's story is very typical of the generations who have made a great land the place it is. If you wonder why Australians are competitive, imagine arriving after eight weeks at sea to a country that has fires in one state and floods in another during the same week. You have next to no possessions or money and are immediately told to report to an employment agency that sends you 333 miles inland to a town you have never heard of to do a job for which you have no skills. You say goodbye to your parents and six siblings and have not the faintest idea when, or if, you will see them again. The sun burns your pale skin and the dust chokes your young throat. You are thirsty, hungry and just fifteen years old.

Bill and Marjorie's second son, Robert, made the journey from enthusiastic schoolboy cricketer to the Australian Test team. His particular talent, the leg break, is the most difficult to foster and every bit as difficult to perform under the spot-light. He played in a New South Wales side that won three Sheffield Shields. He twice took 10 wickets in a Test match—both at Sydney—against the West Indies in 1984 and New Zealand eleven months later. He also spun his name onto the honours board in the away dressing room at Lord's with his 5-wicket haul in 1985. In all, he managed 316 wickets in 95 first-class matches at 31.19 each. Good job, Dutchy.

It was Dutchy who met me at Sydney airport. I was to play in the Newcastle grade competition for Southern Lakes. He greeted me warmly and introduced Bob McLeod, an academic who ran a building firm and opened the batting for the club: slowly, I was to discover. On the drive north, they told me about the club its ambitions, limitations and charms. On arrival in Toronto, they hung a left and took me to Awaba Oval. I loved it. Then down the main street of this one-horse town, past the workers' club and the fish and chip shop to the small marina at the water's edge. From there we turned right and headed out of town, a mile or so, to Coal Point. They had found me digs in a small apartment on the edge of Lake Macquarie but to allow me to find my feet after the journey from England, the Holland family were putting me up for a week or so. I stayed for three.

That night there was a reception in my honour in town. The chairman, Les Edwards, said some generous words of welcome and the players gathered enthusiastically around me. They gave us chicken drumsticks, sausages, party pies and beer—either Tooheys New, a pale lager, or Tooheys Old, a dark stout that kept the mining community happy. I was knackered and suddenly terrified. These good folk clearly expected a decent return from the new pro. I was twenty years old, embarrassingly overweight and not quite as good as they, or I, thought I was.

We practised the next afternoon. The net pitches were concrete and Dutchy made the ball bounce steeply. The faster bowlers made the ball bounce too, past my nose. I returned the compliment when I bowled. There was a fielding session of sorts but it was a shambles. We practised at Ron Hill Oval in town, where the second grade played. At least 40 people came every Tuesday and Thursday, and most expected a real go.

There were two separate associations in which Southern Lakes had teams: four of them played in the District Competition and two in the City and Suburban, which was more knockabout. There were junior teams too, and I had a couple of games for the Under-21s. Although the two associations have since merged, the structure remains similar today.

Dutchy was player, captain and president—had been so since 1975 and stayed president until 2005. That is some clubman. He played first grade from 1961 until 1998, which hardly seems believable. In that time he took 799 wickets for the club to go with the 316 for state and country. This is not to mention other rep games and activities. Then he played lower grades until 2011. After that, he became coach and mentor. Now he is the curator of two fields and many pitches. Can there have ever have been a cricket club more indebted to one man? To this day, he spins them as hard as the old fingers will allow and last March toured South Africa for the first time where, he said, big men slogged him into trees. He is close to 70 years of age, still slim, fit and in love with the sport that has given him a way of life.

If the spirit of cricket is best illustrated by respect for the game and a determination to leave it in a better place than the one in which you found it, Dutchy is a fine example. To this day he plays with a fiercely competitive edge but with the lightest touch. He is a gentleman in the truest sense of the word.

Our first game of the season was against Wallsend and we were hammered. Annoyingly, their opening batsman, John

Gardner, who had left Southern Lakes for Wallsend at the finish of the previous summer, made runs. He then sat at the bar in the workers' club drinking middies of Tooheys New and telling us where we went wrong. 'Tosser,' I thought. I'd buy him a beer now.

The Toronto Workers Club was a feature of life that season. Cold beer was served in cold glasses of all sizes—5 ounce, 7 ounce, schooners and more—and cricket was spoken day upon day, night upon night. We ate burgers, pies or fish and chips. Occasionally, I splashed out on a steak but the pennies were tight. We played the pokie machines, more as recreation than anything, and watched the little money we had fall down the blackhole of hope and despair.

I moved into the apartment by the lake and missed Carolyn's cooking. A rumour went around that there were sharks in the lake, thus I missed the Holland family swimming pool too. I was homesick but hid this with endless hours in the nets facing Dutchy's brilliant leg spin. I ran club practices with enthusiasm and the rest of the time was back at the pad by the water to watch hour upon hour of cricket on television.

The flat was a well-appointed studio on the ground floor of a double-brick house—very typical of Australian residential development of the time and the lake was but a cricket pitch from the glass-fronted sliding doors. It was owned by Peter and Sue Merilees, whose constant encouragement and support was appreciated by a young boy ever so slightly lost. I couldn't make a damn run for the club and moped at home most evenings, wondering why the gods were so cruel. Peter's happy disposition and Sue's jolly approach to all things homely were invaluable allies. They are still there. Dutchy and I went over to see them early in 2016. It was as if the world had stood still.

The cricket, though not better than anticipated, was every bit as tough as a young Englishman might have expected.

Batsmen hit the ball hard, bowlers hit the bat hard and fielders threw in hard. No one played for laughs, only to win. Sometimes selfishness overrode common sense but in the main the greater good was at the heart of the players in that league. This was in contrast to the professional county game, where self-interest dominated so much of the cricket at second-eleven level.

I had played three first-class games for Hampshire the previous summer, none of them with any specific triumphs, but I had not disgraced myself. I was surprised by the gulf in the standard of county players. Gloucestershire, for example, had Mike Procter, Zaheer Abbas, Sadiq Mohammad, Brian Brain, Andy Stovold, John Childs and David Graveney to shore up Alastair Hignell, Jim Foat, Jack Davey, Julian Shackleton and Andy Brassington. This is in no way meant to be disrespectful to the latter group of five, only to point out that this was a pretty typical team sheet around the shires: made up of world-class cricketers, county cricketers and good club cricketers. Frankly, in 1979 and 1980 Hampshire were worse—barely a decent Minor Counties side until Malcolm Marshall and Gordon Greenidge returned to play in the latter part of the summer after the West Indies tour of England. First-class cricket in England has always been spread too thinly but the counties can't see it, stuttering along as they do, utterly dependent for survival on income from the English Cricket Board's (ECB's) sale of international television rights.

I was a decent young talent, signed by a first-class county, but that summer I was unable to take a trick in Newcastle grade cricket where, incidentally, the standard of club cricket was below that in Sydney. I took some wickets but struggled badly with the bat, going from bad to worse the more I practised and the harder I tried. By the end of that season, each of my innings had become a self-fulfilling prophecy of doom.

There were many differences between amateur cricket in England and Australia, not least the standard and attitudes. A key one for me was the lack of opportunity to play during the week, or on Sundays, in Australia. In England, you can pick up a game anywhere, pretty much any day, but not in Australia, where there is no culture for a recreational game and no history of wandering cricket. I was sure that a few innings away from the pressure of performing in grade cricket could revive my game but I couldn't find a match in which to play them.

I was invited to play one midweek representative game in Gosford for a Newcastle team against a Sydney rep team in the Tooheys Cup. Bob Simpson, Allan Border, Steve Rixon, John Dyson and others played. It was a valuable exercise and I did fine, taking 3 wickets and guiding us over the line with a calm, unbeaten 12 from number six in the order. Dutchy played and took 3 wickets too, so I guess Southern Lakes knocked over the Sydneysiders and won the laurels.

After a couple of games—and before the run drought had truly set in—Dutchy suggested I take over as captain. He had done it for years and felt that a new hand on the tiller might benefit everyone. It was fun and the guys responded well. Wayne Hackett, a great lad and a big, strong new ball bowler, ran in all day, as did the former captain. The ball swung out at Awaba and so I bowled a heap of overs too. Between the three of us we kept most opponents under control. We just didn't get enough runs. In hindsight, I should have dropped myself down the order but was nervous of appearing weak.

God, it was hot there. An airless heat that sucked the oxygen from the lungs of willing men. In general, I like the heat but after just six or seven overs on a Saturday morning, you sure knew you had been in a fight. In the first match I played, Dutchy came over and said, 'Good stuff mate, have a spell,' and in a moment of splendidly confused interpretation I replied, 'A spell?

Christ, I've just bowled six off the reel and it's 38 degrees!'
A spell in Oz is a rest. A spell in England is a period of bowling.

Awaba Oval was surrounded by a white picket fence. Beyond
it was the bush. Huge gum trees towered above thick scrub
and undergrowth that swallowed well-struck cricket balls.
We could take an age in there looking for balls, for this was snake
country—red-bellied black snakes and the more dangerous
brown. We saw one on the footpath from the dressing shed
to the oval one afternoon, before it hurried away to the very
hiding place that gobbled up the hits for four and six.

I loved that cricket ground. It had a character of its own,
and demanded character of those who played upon it. The pitch
didn't have much pace and therefore results were hard to force.
You could play good cricket and finish a match with next to
nothing. You could lose the toss on beautiful Saturday morning
and spend hours in the field, only to arrive the following
Saturday to see it pissing down with rain. What's more, I was
paid a few bucks to work at the oval—paint the sightscreens,
fix up the pickets, roll the pitch and mow the outer—which
made wet weather doubly depressing.

Not much has changed. They use it for the lower grades
these days, having smartened up Ron Hill Oval in Toronto for
the first team. The pickets had gone, replaced by wire, which
is cheaper but looks pretty unattractive. The dressing sheds are
a monument to another age, with splintering floorboards and
peeling paint. The view of the play is good, though, and there
is plenty of space. The path where the brown snake lay has
been concreted over but, on the Saturday before my visit, the
fourth-grade team had seen a brown snake in exactly the same
spot, basking in the afternoon sun.

Awaba Oval wasn't the only place I worked that season of
1978–79. Bob McLeod hired me to tile and grout for his building
firm. What a hoot that was. My immediate boss was a ripper

bloke called Bruce—oh yes, he was. Bruce was a dead ringer for Frank Zappa—same hair and moustache—and smoked as much dope. He would pick me up at 7.30 am in his ute, we'd stop for a sausage roll somewhere, and start on the bathrooms and kitchens at about eight. Then we had a smoko around 10.30—a roll-up cigarette and a cup of tea or a can of Coke. Come lunch-time, I was up for a sandwich. Bruce, who was a skinny bugger, had a joint. Next day, same pattern. On the third day, I tried the joint too and fell poleaxed to the floor. It was a first and not to be repeated, for there was serious weed in Bruce's blend. On the fourth day, he drove us out to a creek where the water was clear and clean. We swam and then Bruce smoked his joint and me a roll-up, after which we crashed out to sleep. As the summer days wore on, his brickwork lost its shape and my grouting missed its mark. We howled with laughter and figured we'd better crank it up pre-lunch because post-lunch was hopeless. Sometimes in the evening, Bruce asked me out to his tin shack in the middle of nowhere but I couldn't do the dope and, anyway, he soon faded into oblivion. I wonder where Bruce is now.

One night I took a sheila to the drive-in cinema to see *Grease*. When Danny put his arm across the back of the seat of his Chariot and made a pass at Sandy, I tried the same. That faded into oblivion too.

One afternoon a week I practised with Phil Slocombe of Somerset and Richard Williams of Northamptonshire, who were playing for other Newcastle clubs. A couple of gifted local lads mucked in some days, one of whom could really play. His name was Greg Geise, the son of the Geise who had bowled at Boycott and was offered the shoes for twenty bucks. He was on another level from the players I had grown up with, both tech-nically and in the power of his shot-making. Just eighteen years old—tall, strong and confident of his ability—he would have walked into the Hampshire team of the moment. To attract the attention of the New South Wales selectors, he knew he had to play grade cricket in Sydney and it was another five years before he got his chance. In all, Geise played eight Sheffield Shield games. Dutchy says his 84 at Adelaide played a major part in an important win against South Australia but that the acquisition of Imran Khan for the summer blocked his further progress: either that or Greg didn't quite have the mind for Shield cricket. A cricketer can have all the talent in the world but his temperament counts for as much, otherwise no deal.

I spent Christmas with Slocombe and a mate of his on Bondi Beach. It rained for much of the day and we retreated to a drab apartment, ate takeaway chook and drank beer. Bondi in 1978 was not Bondi in 2016. Not close, not recognisable, not even very safe back then. Older folk say the streets were lined with needles and the storm drains dumped the worst of stuff into the shallowest water. I live a part of the year there now in a wonderful apartment on the rocks at North Bondi that the owners bought in 1981, much to the horror of many of their mates. 'You wait,' said Edmund Graham, the landlord, 'Bondi will be summer gold one day.' The place is worth a small fortune now. Back then you could not have paid me to return.

I made two other trips to Sydney in my plodding dark-grey 1963 Holden, with its column-shift gears and padded leather bench seat. I met up with Paul Terry, my Hampshire contemporary, to go to the first floodlit match at the Sydney Cricket Ground—coloured clothes, white balls, black sightscreens and all under the banner of WSC. Unable to control the crowds outside the ground, Kerry Packer opened the gates and let everyone in. It was a thrilling experience. Australia played in canary yellow and the West Indies in shocking pink. It was the night Packer knew it had all been worthwhile, the night that changed cricket forever.

Since arriving at Coal Point in late September, my voracious appetite for the game had been satisfied by television.

The ABC showed the six-Test Ashes series against England and Sheffield Shield matches. Channel Nine showed WSC. I couldn't get enough of it. I was a cricket junkie.

England won the Ashes 5–1 against Graham Yallop's understrength Australians, effectively a second eleven that was lambasted in the media. Though Boycott had a poor tour after the death of his mother and the loss of the Yorkshire captaincy—he told the selectors he wasn't up to going but they persuaded him otherwise—David Gower, Derek Randall, Bob Willis, Ian Botham, Mike Hendrick and Geoff Miller were simply too good in a team ruthlessly led by Mike Brearley. Most of the best Australian players were playing alternative matches around the rest of the country for Packer. I went to watch England play Northern New South Wales at No. 1 Sportsground Newcastle but didn't stay long. The truth is that I had begun to doubt myself.

The season had been a real eye-opener. I did a make a fifty and a few good thirties but never kicked on. I spent hours beating myself up, wondering if I was any damn good at the game at all. Dutchy reckons I carried too much of the club on my shoulders—captain, coach, number three batsman, front-line bowler, sightscreen painter. I had just turned twenty so maybe he is right. He adds that had I wanted to come back for the next summer they would have been delighted to have me, which cheers me up no end.

I wish I had known that then. Perhaps I would have gone back to repay their faith. As it was, I decided that Newcastle was not for me. We often say we wish we knew then what we know now. Well, it truly applies to my time with Southern Lakes. I felt I let the club down and thought that if I ever had another crack at Australia, I would commit to making a better job of it.

———

In the early part of the summer of 1977, the story broke that an Australian television and publishing mogul was hijacking the game. On 13 May that year, Tony Greig, the England captain, was sacked. Greig had signed for Kerry Packer to play in a series of privately arranged and funded matches in Australia that would feature the best players in the world and be televised live on Packer's network, Channel Nine.

Television was the root and branch of the WSC adventure. Packer had inherited a media empire from his father, Sir Frank, but specifically his heart was in television. He loved sport and sportspeople. It became fundamental to him that the Nine Network should be the home of the world's greatest sporting events. A couple of things were on his side. In March 1975 colour television came to Australia and the transition from black and white had a huge effect on viewing numbers and advertising revenue. Nine was already strong in news but drama was expensive. Relatively speaking, sport was cheap and, best of all, it was inherent in the Australian lifestyle.

In March 1976, Packer made a play to the Australian Cricket Board (ACB, later Cricket Australia) for the exclusive rights to all Australian cricket but was snubbed. Incandescent, he famously said to the ACB chairman, Bob Parish: 'There is a little bit of the whore in all of us. What's your price?' 'There isn't one,' replied Parish, who stuck with the ABC. Packer then proposed a joint agreement to promote a series of matches over a five-year period, played in January and February each year, that would not clash with existing international schedules. He offered to underwrite the costs. That received a slap in the face too.

Meanwhile, there was growing discontent among the high-profile Australian players, who were unofficial world champions with filmstar status. They played in front of huge houses but were paid peanuts. As Richie Benaud was to say later: 'We wanted a fair day's pay for a fair day's work.' Dennis Lillee advocated a series of matches to raise funds for retired players who had nothing to fall back on. Lillee had Austin Robertson, his manager, and John Cornell, a television man well known to Packer, in his camp. The ACB's attitude was best explained by the secretary Alan Barnes, who said: 'If you don't like the pay and conditions, there are plenty of others who will take your place.' It was much the same in England, where the Test players received £50 a day. Cornell approached Packer to back Lillee's scheme. Packer told them to hold tight for something on a much bigger scale.

Packer's first masterstroke was convincing Richie Benaud to guide the development of the product, advise on strategy and work on the telecast. Benaud was authority and Benaud was street cred. Other than Sir Donald Bradman, no man was more powerful or better able to transcend the great divide between Melbourne and London. Better still, he was one of only a very few men to tell it to Kerry as it was. In the weeks leading up to the start of the first season of WSC, Packer made a final plea in London to the International Cricket Conference (later the International Cricket Council, or ICC) for mediation in the rights dispute with the ACB. The ICC refused and he stormed out in disgust, saying to the media, 'It's every man for himself, may the devil take the hindmost.' Benaud was not impressed and fired off a memo to Packer's henchmen: 'Please, when you get back to Australia, can we start making love not war. The press since you made the devil comment has been dreadful.' Benaud's velvet glove and Packer's iron fist were a perfect fit.

Then Packer seduced Greig, who was ripe for the plucking. Greig was a good-looking and ambitious 30 year old but, in his own view, just a few failures from being axed as captain of England like so many before him. He wanted good money, a job for life and a low-interest home loan. He got the lot and, in return, Packer told him to hunt down the best cricketers in the world and sign them up.

Greig left for the Caribbean almost immediately, where Clive Lloyd took some persuading. 'Can we really commit to an untried project,' wondered Lloyd, 'and was the risk worth the possible end of our international careers?' The answer was yes, especially when he was reassured by the news that Benaud was onside. After Lloyd came Gordon Greenidge, Viv Richards, Michael Holding and Andy Roberts, among many others. Holding has talked about his sense of disbelief when he was offered US$25,000 to play a season of cricket. 'I went to the bank with my savings book and in those days it used to be put into a machine that updated the account. When the teller handed it back to me, I stared at it in shock. For the first time in my life there was a comma after the first number!'

Greig then targeted the Pakistanis: Imran Khan, Majid Khan, Zaheer Abbas, Javed Miandad and Asif Iqbal. No problem. Nor with most of the Poms, many of whom were friends and hung on their captain's every word. Mind you, not all of them agreed for fear of their future in the English professional game. Easier still were the South Africans, who were starved of international cricket and ravenous at the opportunity. Ten minutes over a Castle Lager was good enough for Barry Richards, Graeme Pollock, Mike Procter, Eddie Barlow and Clive Rice.

There was a late threat to South African involvement when a key clause in the Commonwealth Gleneagles Agreement that discouraged sporting contact with South Africa was invoked by Michael Manley, the prime minister of Jamaica. Malcolm Fraser, the Australian prime minister, was obliged to ban the South Africans from entering Australia until Packer found a loophole that allowed freedom of movement to any South African player with a UK county cricket contract. Fraser, more wary of Packer than Manley, relented. This meant that only Pollock, who had not played county cricket, missed out. In general, Fraser went out of his way to accommodate Packer, once allowing Greig—back from a recruitment foray—into the country without his lost passport. That's power.

Lillee, Cornell and Robertson had the Australians they needed and then some. The only hiccup was with Jeff Thomson, who was contracted to a Queensland radio station that would not, even under Packer's relentless pursuit, release him.

It was an astonishing raid on the game as most of the world's best players deserted the established corridors and signed to play in the closest thing cricket has ever seen to a rock'n'roll circus. For a cricket-crazed teenager in London at the time it was a seminal moment, and as much fun as the album that changed the look and feel of the 1970s, David Bowie's *Ziggy Stardust*. We watched open-mouthed as the footage from 12,000 miles away had Lillee and Lenny Pascoe, Procter, Rice, Imran, Holding and Roberts bowling a white ball at the speed of light, under lights, dressed in tight, coloured clothes with bell bottoms and butterfly collars. These guys were Kerry's band and, boy, could they play guitar. Depending on your take, Packer was either the Man Who Sold the World or Starman. Either way, he would have his way and cricket's commercial transformation had begun.

Having said that, the first year was far from a smash hit. Crowds were desperately disappointing, and some of the logistics hit a wall. Because the major Test-match grounds refused to give Packer any access, the first Supertest was at VFL Park, an Australian Rules Football ground in a relatively inaccessible part of Melbourne's eastern suburbs. West Indies won in three days but only 13,885 people turned up. The next Supertest was played at the Sydney Showground, slap bang next door to the SCG. Again, West Indies won in three days and this time 23,762 people turned up. Another disappointment.

There was, however, a Machiavellian upside to the downsides. David Hookes had his jaw broken by Andy Roberts, a moment that convinced the public WSC was for real.

Though crowds and publicity warmed to some degree, Packer needed the Australians to win more matches. Soon after the end of the first season, Barry Richards was summoned to the Packer stronghold in Park Street and told that he would play the second season for the Australians. Packer knew that Barry was living with a Sydney girl and had talked of moving to Australia full time. To soften the blow, he offered the South African permanent residency in Australia and a ten-year $30,000 interest-free loan on a house in Crows Nest he knew Barry wanted. Tony Greig and Ian Chappell were in the room and neither liked the idea, partly because it compromised both teams and mainly because it compromised the credibility of the cricket. Packer was not for moving.

The following morning, Barry was summoned again. 'Change of plan,' said Packer, 'you're back with Greigy's mob.' Surprised, relieved but also a tad disappointed, Richards made to get up and go. Packer said, 'Hang on, son,' and handed over the residency papers he had promised, plus a cheque for AU$30,000. *That* is why the World Series cricketers revered Packer. Ten years later to the day, Barry received a call from Packer's accounts department calling in the loan. Barry smiled and sent off the cheque.

Very quickly, the players began to realise they had done the right thing. The press, however, continued to hound them, and the various boards of control to threaten them. While the WSC executive team liked the high quality of the cricket, the intensity of the competition and the positive television ratings, they were deeply concerned by the spiralling costs and the PR.

Then something simple but game-changing happened: a television commercial blew everyone's socks off. It showed close-ups of the leading Australian players in their canary-yellow trim and was set to a catchy tune with an easy partisan lyric. 'C'mon, Aussie, c'mon' was brilliant, still is. It launched the second season and was every bit as big a boost as winning the battle against the New South Wales Cricket Association to have matches played at the Sydney Cricket Ground. When I arrived for my season in Toronto the ad became the soundtrack of the summer. We all sang it and knew every word. The next thing I wanted to do was get to the SCG and see these guys in action.

The ACB team was being flattened by England; in Toronto, WSC was the talk of the town. I watched in the workers' club; I watched at Dutchy's place and I watched even more, day and night, in my own joint by the lake. I knew the past and present of every player, and I was soon pretty good at predicting their future. In his mid 30s, Barry cut it with the big boys, confirming the suspicion that, along with his namesake Viv, the absent Pollock and Greg Chappell, no one on the planet could bat better.

So, to be at the SCG, sitting on the Hill with Paul on the night of the full house—the night Packer threw the gates open—was electrifying. Official figures record that 44,377 people were there. It felt like double that. By the now the players had moved from coloured trim into full colour—canary yellow for the Aussies and coral pink for the West Indies—and the night-time spectacle drew gasps of admiration from us all. The stage the players had been given was beyond our imagination. WSC formed the aspirations of a new generation of cricket lovers. I was hooked, and all of us were awash with the originality and sense of optimism provided by Packer's largesse.

Tony Greig could see this and started to realise the enormous impact they were all having on the game. His courage had been extraordinary, his honour intact. Greigy's one great regret is that he never squared it with the important old-school figures who had backed him throughout the journey from his native South Africa to the England captaincy. Packer had insisted that he sign a confidentiality clause, and then he went underground to recruit the players. By the time the story broke in the early summer of 1977, many of the best were known to be on board and Greig was sacked at the start of that Ashes summer in England.

At the time, England was paying him £200 per Test match, less than the cost of the tickets he had to buy for his family to attend the 1976–77 Centenary Test. He had no doubt he was down the right road but was shocked by the way some turned on him. Writing in *The Times*, John Woodcock said that Greig was an Englishman 'not by birth or upbringing but only by adoption', implying that his disloyalty was no surprise. Greigy hated that: after all, his father, Sandy, was a proud Scot who had been sent to South Africa to train aircrews during the war. Greig fiercely believed that he had sacrificed the most coveted job in English cricket for a cause that would improve the lot of all cricketers.

WSC was a fusion of five-day Test cricket, 50-over hoe-downs, country fairs, day time and night time, red balls and white balls, piped clothing, pink, blue and yellow clothing, bouncers, helmets, drop-in pitches, and two Richards from previously untouchable boundaries batting together in the same team. It was played up-country and in the metropolis, in showgrounds, in parks and even, occasionally, on cricket grounds. Pakistanis, West Indians, South Africans, a Kiwi, the Poms and the Aussies all bust a gut on behalf of the same man. Camera, lights, action.

It is often overlooked that Packer loved cricket deeply and that beneath the bluster was an unseen pastoral care for the game's roots and its people. He took the successful history of cricket and revamped it for the future. The major matches were played with a gladiatorial intensity and at an immensely high standard. The only disappointment was that the circus never came to London town. After two memorable, seismic summers in Australia—and brief flings in New Zealand and the Caribbean—it was all over, gone as suddenly as Ziggy. The rights were secured and Packer, via a High Court restraint-of-trade challenge in London, was in the winners' enclosure. He had got what he wanted and so drew down the curtain.

Benaud and Greig, both sadly gone now, departed this world very sure of their influence in the most important period the game has seen. Without immediately becoming rich, the players at last earned a decent whack for their ability to fill a stadium. Having said that, it was a long time before their income truly reflected their worth to cricket's global expansion.

To those of us lucky to have been in Australia for any small part of this show, the memories will never fade. The players reached remarkable heights and each glimpse of them provided a moment when the world stood still. Swathes of women hung around the hotels and Australia's youth was at one with the chorus of that brilliant jingle that rang out across the second year of this great adventure. It was cricket porn.

Tall, slim and charismatic, with a shock of blond hair that set him apart, Greig somehow led the World XI to victory in the defining Supertest shootout at the Sydney Cricket Ground—a place of redemption at the end of the road. Incredibly, I was there, nervously watching from the ground floor of the Members Pavilion as Barry made a gritty hundred to guide Greig's team home. I hung around afterwards hoping to see him and was not disappointed. He asked me into the dressing room and introduced me first to Greigy and then to Alan Knott, who chatted away as if he had known me all his life. I met Procter, Le Roux and Asif Iqbal too. I mean, please, can you imagine? When I drove away from Sydney that night I was floating on a cloud.

I didn't know it then but 25 years later I was to work for Packer at Channel Nine. Perhaps it was meant to be. Perhaps the experiences of 1978–79 were the catalyst for a life-changing story. Certainly, my time spent in Australia helped me understand a passionate, driven people and allowed me to see how, in just a couple of hundred years, they had built a formidable culture of their own.

The storm that hit world cricket soon calmed. Packer negotiated pretty much everything he needed—a list that included ten years of exclusive television rights, a 50 per cent share of the gate and of sponsorship and merchandise revenue, both of which came under the remit of his firm, PBL Marketing. He also designed the pattern of summers to come, with five home tests and the fifteen-match triangular one-day tournament that was to be called World Series Cricket. Lastly, he said every major ground should have floodlights. All that, 37 years ago.

In return, the ACB was relieved to have its game back.

While WSC cost PBL $34 million, the Nine Network was pulling in record revenue and could bear the cost—within two years it was breaking even. All the players were paid out in full, and most of the international players were signed to Mark McCormack's US-based sports management group, IMG.

WSC changed the game irrevocably and for the good. It is wrong that there is no mention of it in the record books for the cricket was played at the highest standard. The administrators, who at last began to understand the value of their product, should have put that right. It is not too late to do so now. Television coverage improved out of all recognition. Night cricket pulled in new audiences and generated more income. In the greatest form of flattery, other sports imitated much of cricket's new journey.

Packer's influence on the game is unparalleled. In fact, some days I wonder if the game as we know it would even be here were it not for him. The vast wealth provided by television rights has made modern sport but Packer's impact goes beyond that. He understood the Esperanto of the moment and used his own network to drive a rethink in cricket's global aspirations. It is quite some legacy.

CHAPTER 4

The Hampshire captaincy

Richie Benaud said captaincy is 90 per cent luck and 10 per cent skill; but don't try it without the 10 per cent. I agree with most things Richie said but not this. My guess is he was tongue-in-cheek or, if not, then certainly self-deprecating. The balance might be 50–50. You need luck with your players for sure, specifically the quality of your attack, and with the toss. You need magic from people who can turn a game on a dime. But that is not luck. When teammates used to wish Geoffrey Boycott luck, he would mutter about its irrelevance and the requirement of skill.

Is it luck to place a fielder in a new position and see a catch go there next ball? Yes and no. In the 1988 Benson & Hedges Cup Final at Lord's, I put Derbyshire in to bat. After four overs the score was 27 for no wicket. Stephen Jefferies panicked and insisted we spread the field. Instead, I called for a helmet, placed myself at forward short-leg and brought in another slip. At the end of the over the score was 28 for 2 and a slip catch had been dropped. The 2 wickets had fallen to easy catches at forward short leg. Was I lucky that Jefferies bowled two beautiful inswingers? Was I lucky that the batsmen, Peter Bowler and

Bruce Roberts, played forward and edged from bat and pad into my hands? No, I had considered it possible. Was it a fluke that John Morris edged to third slip? I don't think so. But I was lucky to win an important toss and lucky that Jefferies got it right at that moment, though I would argue that my aggressive tactic focused his mind. Was I lucky that the ball looped into my hands at short leg? Of course, but I was standing in the right place. On the BBC, Benaud called it brilliant captaincy. Jefferies took 5 for 13 and we bowled Derbyshire out for 117 before going on to win comfortably. My reckoning is that you make your own luck and much of it comes from self-belief.

Ian Botham and Shane Warne were luckier than most, but they would argue they made their own luck. Warne told me the real reason he retired was that he had 'run out of arse'. I felt the same towards the end of my captaincy career. Some senior Hampshire players did not agree. Paul Terry thought I became more defensive as I grew older. My view is that the players were less gifted, which limited my options. In that Benson & Hedges Cup Final (when I was young and fearless) I wanted to shock the players out of their nervous and sloppy start with a bold statement. I also thought the long delay to fetch the helmet from the dressing room and the animated, almost theatrical, changing of the field might niggle the Derbyshire batsmen and ever so slightly change their approach. I hoped they would think, 'I'm not getting out to this bullshit,' and, thus, change down a gear. Am I lucky that it worked? Maybe, maybe not.

In mid-July 1984, Nick Pocock walked me around the United Services ground at Portsmouth and told me he was going to stand down from the captaincy of Hampshire forthwith. He said he wanted me to take over and the cricket committee did not need much persuading. Neither did I. With Pocock in the wings, I led the side for the rest of the season and was appointed formally that autumn, after ratification by the main committee. I had secured a place in the Hampshire team in 1980, blown it in 1981 but come back convincingly enough in 1982 and 1983, when I was the first English-born batsman to 1000 runs. By 1984 I was settled at number 3 and, although infuriatingly inconsistent, played enough substantial innings to justify the club's faith.

Pocock was a strong character and a tremendous supporter of mine. We are good friends to this day. He warned me of the likely dissenters, first among whom was the richly gifted Trevor Jesty, a man whose numbers never quite reflected his ability. If my theory about luck is right, and Botham personified it, we could use Jesty as an example of the opposite of Botham, for the extent of their talents was not so far apart as the result of their efforts. Jesty's brilliant stroke-making, late outswingers and safe hands were almost apologetic in comparison to the compelling certainty in Botham's similar skills and the confident manner in which he applied them. Botham won many a moment through the power of his personality. Jesty was more reticent and fortune was not as kind to him. He served the game with distinction, retiring from life as a first-class umpire at the end of the 2013 season.

Trevor had been with the club a decade longer than me and felt he deserved a crack at the job. He told the press that you could only be appointed Hampshire captain if you had three initials—M.C.J. Nicholas, N.E.J. Pocock, R.M.C. Gilliat, E.D.R. Eagar—and that plain old T.E. Jesty had no chance, so he was leaving and moving to Surrey. I could hardly blame him, though I did point out that Hampshire's longest-serving captain was L.H. Tennyson—albeit, the Honourable L.H. Tennyson. It was sad when Trevor and his wife, Jacqui, moved on. They had been at the heart of the club for a long time, and Trevor had played a good hand during the summer of 1973 when the County Championship was won under Gilliat's savvy leadership. Now it was my turn. There was a job to do.

Cricket captaincy involves many variables, requires clear lines of thought and attitude, and assumes responsibility for group interaction that is initially driven by individual ambition. The key is to trust the players, not to nanny them. It is a challenging and stimulating job. The captain must have a modus operandi that the players understand and into which they buy. Mine was to keep the game alive at all costs and to risk losing in order to try to win. Most of the players were up for this. Those with doubts kept them to themselves.

There is a lot of talk in sport about team spirit. We had long been known as 'Happy Hants', which implied we were good blokes but a bit of a pushover. I was sick of seeing sides arrive to play against us looking as if they expected to beat the nice guys. I preferred us to play a bit tougher and with an air of self-confidence. This was often perceived as arrogance but even our more understated characters approved. Chris Smith was the most committed supporter of this approach, and Malcolm Marshall too: after all, the West Indies personified it. If it meant losing a few friends, then so be it.

Team spirit is natural when you are winning but often forced if you are not. At these times, players begin to talk behind each other's backs, retreat into cliques and undermine the greater good. There are two options here. The first is to sit everyone down together and thrash it out, something I tried in my early years as captain but abandoned. The problem was that one or two players dominated these gatherings and others kept their powder dry for dark corners. Complaints became personal—batsmen versus bowlers was common—and too subjective for a solution.

The second option is to meet the players one on one, understand their view and ensure they understand yours and what you expect from them. This is the moment to encourage individuals to think for themselves within the role you have mutually agreed upon; it is also the moment to set targets, both personal and for the team. It allows for a shared point of view and therefore provides a platform for support. It also allows for a shared burden, as the explanation of someone else's anxiety relieves tension and encourages more generous consideration for others outside the self-contained bubble in which most professional sportsmen live.

In general, we had a very good collective spirit. Understandably enough, it could go missing when we were losing. Very little can be done about this, except to encourage talent and self-belief, and hope to start winning again quickly. In hindsight, the Hampshire dressing room might have benefited from being more confrontational, so that personal misgivings came to the surface rather than festered. This was probably my fault. For one thing, a dictator doesn't much like being dictated to; for another, I learnt it was safer to keep everyone calm because it's a long old county season if you are at each other's throats.

Mike Brearley encouraged plain speaking at team meetings, both with England and Middlesex. The very strong characters around him frequently laid into one another but then crossed the white line as a unit. I felt such democracy was a risk. Yes, you want the players to have ideas, not only about the cricket but also about the running of the club. But the risk of too much discussion is a loss of decisiveness and, frankly, I procrastinated enough as it was. Most people react well to authority if it is thoughtfully and consistently applied. Consultation can lead to better leadership, especially when a captain has much to learn about himself. The fact is, I had some players I trusted and others I did not. So I tended to listen to a few but not to them all.

Traditionally, cricketers are sceptical about team meetings and tactics. So much happens so quickly that plans conceived over breakfast are worthless by lunch, or sooner. Ranjitsinhji said he had seen 'men go grey in the service of the game' without considering tactics or other people's roles or problems. In proof of this point, I captained Derek Underwood in a match at Lord's between MCC (Marylebone Cricket Club) and Australia in 1985, and was astonished by his indifference to the placing of the field. 'Up to you, matey,' he said with a smile. 'You're the captain, I'll go with whatever you think.' Blimey, I was in short pants and long socks when this bloke was first knocking over Australians. Underwood was a special cricketer and the loveliest man, who never understood why cricketers were so eager to be captain.

Of course, a captain needs to balance the input of his colleagues against the final say. He must, above all, rely on his own instinct. If the gut says it, then do it, for if you wait a split second the moment will be gone. This further suggests that prolonged analysis of a situation is unnecessary—in other words, think about it too much and the horse has bolted.

The longer I did the job, the better I was at man management but the less adventurous I became tactically. I think you know too much after a while and a kind of fear takes over. Instead of thinking, 'If we try something we could win,' you think, 'If I do that we might lose.' Initially, I could trust the team to deal with losing but not as the years went on. I guess we all grew up. Or I did, which, after the best part of twelve years in the job, was understandable. Some of the team of the 1980s had moved on and therefore the social make-up and dynamic of the team shifted. I have said that during my last two seasons as captain, 1994 and 1995, the players were not as talented as the world-class cricketers we had previously. Neither were the majority as experienced. By definition, then, we were less likely to win and therefore the collective ambition was tempered by self-doubt, which exaggerates self-interest. This completely threw me in the 1994 season but, after a dreadful start to 1995, I began to work it out and came to enjoy that summer very much. Heath Streak, the Zimbabwean, was the overseas player and John Stephenson had arrived from Essex to assume the captaincy the following year. You could not wish to meet two men with bigger hearts.

Of course, the most important thing was for the players to trust me. Simply wearing the stripes cannot guarantee respect. Brearley said, 'The name on the box is often not the same as the contents inside it.' Respect comes from performance—an occasional problem for me; from decision-making, both on and off the field—generally okay; and from the qualities you display as a human being—the good was pretty good, I'd say (!), and the bad either a) unintentionally demeaned others or b) was too driven by emotional highs and lows. On one occasion, three of the senior players took me aside to discuss a) and b) and point out the problems they created. This was difficult for me and for them but it served a valuable purpose for us all. It was to my advantage that our team began as friends. Most of us had been together since the days in the underground dressing room, and we had come to accept idiosyncrasies and flaws in one another. My knowledge of the game was sound and I loved bringing people together. On balance, I was thought to be the right choice. Equally, I was able to see their honesty as crucial to the bigger picture of Hampshire cricket.

As soon as I became captain, I asked for Paul Terry as my vice-captain. He was tactically sound, popular with young and old, and had a lovely way with the bowlers, who trusted his counsel. I was hugely fond of Paul and, having rejoiced in his selection for England the summer before, was now able to work alongside him as we planned our path for success in the years to follow. At least that was how we saw things then. In our mid-twenties we were idealists and none the worse for it.

We were a very happy team, or teams. Over the twelve years that I steered the ship, there were few periods of truly rough water. Of all the possible angles one could take on playing the game professionally, the most important seemed to be to enjoy it, and we certainly did that. There was the odd hiccup but only in the cause of the greater good. I don't suppose any group of people live together for twelve years in perfect harmony. Most of the key players back then are still friends now. I wish we saw each other more but the global spread of residency makes that impossible. We speak well of each other and respect both our past and present. I am sure we are respected by those against whom we played.

The more I have thought about cricket captaincy, the more I have come to realise that the key is to harness the collective input and expertise of the group. Each of the players has strengths, and therefore captains should play to them rather than spending too much time attempting to shore up weaknesses.

Like most captains, I was could be guilty of reacting negatively to a mistake. This makes players fearful and less free to express themselves. I love the way the modern captain tells his players to let go of inhibition. I suggested this to a number of our players and some responded better than others. The fear of failure is both inherent and applied: letting go is simultaneously an opportunity and a risk. Go figure. I became less reactive and more patient over time. Eventually, just about anything could wash over me. It is a complex balance to show that you care, without caring too much.

THE INTERREGNUM

I took over the captaincy of the team in the late summer of 1984, and Hampshire cricket was formally mine to make something of by the start of the summer of 1985. I had watched the club disintegrate as a school of learning for the young through the summers of 1978 and 1979. A chippy attitude had developed, especially around the performances of

Barry Richards and Andy Roberts, who were not pulling their weight. For close on a decade, Richards had been a magnificent cricketer for Hampshire, the biggest drawcard around the counties post Garry Sobers and pre Viv Richards. Roberts had an outstanding first year in 1974 but never found the long-term commitment later displayed by Malcolm Marshall. Fast bowling is hard enough but the grind of the county circuit sent many a speedster to the knacker's yard. Two-thirds of the way through the 1978 season, both walked out on their contracts.

The feeling from senior players was that the captain, Richard Gilliat, was losing his grip. This whisper was hardly a surprise; county pros liked to blame those around them and the captain was first in line, followed by the blokes earning more than they were.

I played a couple of first-class games in both 1978 and 1979 but was no more than a good club player and neither physically fit nor mentally strong enough. Most of the old pros were jealous of any youngster who got a game, and their reluctance to embrace us left a very bad taste. Mike Taylor was an exception but his influence was limited by the demands on his own performance as the years took their toll. Frankly, we were happier in the 2nd XI. Imagine that, a professional environment in which young players had no desire to move up the ladder!

Peter Sainsbury, our coach, did all he could to inject discipline and set standards but he was more follower than leader. The only man who had been a part of Ingleby-Mackenzie's triumph in 1961, Sains was a tough all-round cricketer. Good-humoured, diligent and enthusiastic, he had no illusions about his limited but well-applied abilities: 'When I started in 1955, I took wickets with balls that went straight on as batsmen played for the turn and I am still doing so now,' he said when he was chosen as one of *Wisden*'s five cricketers of the year for the 1974 edition. Modesty was his byword and, though he never said so himself, many a lesser cricketer has earned the colours of his country. When he hung up his boots at the conclusion of the 1976 season, he had 1316 first-class wickets, 20,176 runs and 617 catches. Not half bad.

The single breath of fresh air during this two-year hiatus was the arrival of Malcolm Marshall from Barbados. Maco was a slip of a thing with a fast arm and natural way of bowling, batting and catching. Not much, however, suggested he would become the best fast bowler in the game. During one of his first matches for Hampshire it snowed. He wore jeans, T-shirt, a cheap leather jacket and sandals without socks. Seeing him curled up beside the dressing-room radiator, we doubted he would return the next day, never mind sign for another year with the club. We could not have been more wrong. After an entertaining team shopping spree for thick woollen jumpers, thicker socks, an overcoat and mittens, he bowled like the wind, took 7 in the match and stayed at our side until the end of the summer of 1993, when his appetite for county cricket finally ran out.

At most counties, the cricket was run by a 'cricket chairman' as distinct from the elected chairman, who directly represented the members. I suppose this non-executive position was a forerunner to the directors of cricket, football and rugby that are so prevalent now. Our boss was Charlie Knott, a former off spinner for Hampshire, and very obviously the man around whom the club revolved. He signed the players, negotiated the wages, defined the small print in the contracts, appointed the 'cricket subcommittee', ran the meetings and chose the captain—albeit with approval from the main committee.

He conducted most of his meetings with players in his car, breaking news—both good and bad—with the same face of foreboding. He was a shrew-like man who wore a pinstripe suit, county tie and trilby. He watched the cricket closely but rarely passed comment on the team's performances, preferring to let the captain run the show and be accountable. He protected the players in the face of the general committee, a body that rarely, if ever, argued the toss with him. I rather admired Charlie, for this was no easy job. He did it for nothing more than a genuine love of the club and, I imagine, the pleasure of something meaningful late in life.

In 1980, Knott gave the captaincy to Nick Pocock, a decision that raised blood pressure around the place but a brilliant one all the same. Nick was very public school—a disciple of Ingleby-Mackenzie but in a less forgiving age—and therefore a constant butt of the old pros' humour. He had never quite commanded a regular spot in the team, which meant there was a mighty fuss over his elevation. The more the old pros whispered in corners, the more the rest of us loved it. We now had a captain who cared about the young talent available to him and this reawakened our enthusiasm. We were not world-beaters but we awoke each morning eager to play and learn, which was not necessarily the case in a county system that all too often drained the exuberance of youth.

Nick gave Hampshire cricket a brighter face. He was an attacking captain with a splendid innocence that led to some unforgettable moments and matches. Marshall loved him and Gordon Greenidge could see the upsides. He gave faith and love to the more gifted players and rotated the others in the hope of striking it lucky.

When we finished bottom of the County Championship in his first year, winning only the penultimate match of the season—and that because Marshall returned to the Hampshire ranks after the West Indies tour of England—he gave a memorable team talk telling us not to forget the pain of such humiliation. With conviction, he said that the sweetness of victory in the future would be every bit as striking as the bitterness of defeat right then. It was really quite Churchillian.

We were better the next year and really very good in 1982, when we finished third in the championship. This was one of only a couple of summers during his thirteen-year Hampshire career that Marshall had a genuinely strong new ball partner. Sadly, Kevin Emery disappeared almost as quickly as he arrived. A tall man and ideally built to bowl fast, he took 78 championship wickets alongside Malcolm's 134—yup, 134, of which, incidentally, only 14 were numbers nine, ten or eleven in the order. Emery came close to selection for England's tour of Australia that winter but a suspect action persuaded the selectors, who feared the result of television exposure and the reaction of Australian crowds, to leave him behind. Emery was never called for throwing and remedial work began behind closed doors that led to a purer release of the ball but without any of the venom that had previously been his trademark. He was not the same bowler again. Unsurprisingly, these events led to a difficult and sad period in Emery's life.

I must tell you about a couple of 'Pocock moments'. There was Chris Old at Bournemouth nicking Marshall to slip, where Nick took a good low catch on the bounce. We gathered to celebrate and I said, 'Skip, that didn't carry,' to which he replied, 'Hmmm, true, but look where "Chilly" is now,' and we all turned to see that Old had scarpered and was already up the steps, past the members and just yards from the dressing room. The catch carried then, we all agreed.

On the flip side, there was Eastbourne, when John Barclay didn't walk for a catch at the wicket off Marshall. The situation was tense because both teams were going well in the championship. The decision was tricky, because Barclay spun his body hard left in trying to ride the bounce of a short ball. The umpire, David Evans, was obstructed by the way in which Barclay's back had now turned 180 degrees to face him. Uncertain of any deflection and deaf to any noise, he ruled it not out.

At the end of the over, two charming men from the hotbed of the old school network came together. Pokers (Shrewsbury) asked Barkers (Eton) if he had hit it. 'Yes, I'm afraid so, captain. I'm awfully sorry, has it caused a problem?' Damn right. Marshall was losing the plot.

At the start of his next over Marshall ran out Barclay, backing up at the non-striker's end: a Mankad. This is a form of dismissal named after Vinoo Mankad, who twice in the same series ran out Australia's Bill Brown in this fashion. Seeing the batsman out of his ground, the bowler whips off the bails in his delivery stride. Usually, the bowler would give a warning but not this time, just revenge for the previous over. Evans asked Marshall if he wanted the appeal to stand, to which Marshall said yes. Barclay said fine, and left. The crowd went hostile.

'What do you think?' Nick asked. 'Call him back,' I replied, which he did. Maco went into orbit. Barclay turned down the offer, saying he was comfortable with the decision and that since he had started the whole sorry affair in the first place he should pay for it now. The hostility from the boundary edge ramped up, an embarrassment Barclay later blamed upon himself.

Maco was incandescent: 'I get he out twice in two balls, skipper, and he still fuckin' here? I no fuckin' bowl.' And off the great man went to long leg. He had a point but not an argument.

Nick left him alone during the next over and then called to him at long leg to bowl again. No luck. Ouch. Then he told him to grow up or bugger off to the dressing room. Brave, given Marshall was the stardust in his bowling attack. For a moment the impasse stopped the game. I thought they should kiss and make up. Nick disagreed and called Nigel Cowley to bowl. Brilliant move. Marshall arrived from the boundary edge saying that Cowley couldn't bowl a hoop up a hill and he'd better bowl himself or we'd never win the effing game.

He tore in, as his heart told him to, but we didn't win the effing game. Chasing 171, Sussex were 122 for 8 at stumps. We finished third in the championship and joint fifth in the Sunday League: one bowler took 134 wickets and another 78 yet we finished third. How badly we needed a top-drawer spinner! It was a similar story in 1983. We finished third again, though this time without Greenidge and Marshall for a month or so. They were helping take West Indies to the World Cup Final, a match they inexplicably lost to India. It was a win for the romantics, crazy and joyous, but our two Bajans found it hard to appreciate the way simple Indian faith had overcome a seemingly invincible superpower.

In late July of 1984, Nick dropped the bomb. He had done all he could, he said, and was standing down. It was my time. He left me with a good team, though still short of a quality slow bowler, just as the county had been since Sainsbury retired.

THE CAPTAINCY

I was immediately aware of the wider responsibilities. Players, committee and supporters alike wanted success and looked to the captain to drive it. I felt we were blessed with batting talent, adequate catching and a great fast bowler. I urged the committee to strengthen the bowling. I had always been struck by the speed at which other, perhaps more ambitious, counties moved to sign available players from elsewhere.

During my first few years we tried to sign Neal Radford, Graham Dilley and Greg Thomas, each of whom would have been a perfect foil for Marshall. The committee could not be convinced about Radford, was pipped by Worcestershire's newfound riches over Dilley, and let Thomas slip through its fingers to end up at Northamptonshire for the matter of a few quid. Money was tight. Hampshire operated to break even at best but this risk-averse approach was in contrast to my tendency for acting now and asking questions of the accountants later. To me, investing in quality had no downside. Incidentally, I thought Thomas got it wrong when he chose Northants. Time spent with Maco would have improved him beyond measure.

Hampshire cricket had a poor record of raising its own talent. Not a single member of the 1985 team was born in the county. The club had a far better policy with overseas players. The best were sought and, mainly, signed. Thus, we had Greenidge and Marshall, who did not disappoint.

Gordon, like Trevor Jesty, was sceptical of my appointment, doubtless thinking he was a candidate for the job himself. Malcolm worked quietly on him and we developed a day-to-day relationship that allowed us, at the very least, to bat together, if not paint the town red at night. A mistake perhaps was to not involve him in strategic discussions or team management. I had the best sidekick one could imagine in Paul and leant on Maco, Tim and Chris Smith as an unofficial management group. Gordon's moods led me to doubt his counsel because I suspected he had a different agenda. Having said that, he was terrific with the young players and never stinted in his efforts for the team. In fact, on big occasions, I felt he tried almost too hard, as if it were Gordon against the world. But that is not a criticism, more a reflection.

Ted Dexter thinks Greenidge the most complete right-handed batsman he has seen. In full flight, he was a glorious sight. I was at the non-striker's end when he hit a nicely flighted ball from Ravi Shastri back over his head and onto the road at the Mumbles in Swansea—the ground where Sobers hit six sixes in an over off Malcolm Nash. As Ravi let go of the ball, he saw Gordon coming at him and exclaimed, 'No!' We watched it disappear from view and Ravi said

'There is no bowler, I don't care who he is, safe from a Greenidge assault.' Technically sound, physically strong and driven by an almost irrational intensity, he became one of the outstanding batsmen of his own or any other age. For many years, we Hampshire cricketers have talked about the weekend when he made three hundreds against Lancashire— two at Liverpool in the championship match and one at Old Trafford in the Sunday League. He went to each of them with a six. The blow at Old Trafford landed on the railway line, as it was then.

Thankfully, during my first summer as captain, I played a couple of key innings that he rated and were to help us win matches from tricky positions. They kept the wolf from the door, so to speak.

The other old sweat left from the early 1970s was David Turner, a gutsy and powerful left-handed batsman who had no designs on the captaincy at all. He was a straightforward Wiltshire lad, a cobbler by trade in the off-season, who gave 100 per cent of himself every time he walked onto the park. An hour or so before the first game I captained in 1984, Turner took me aside, said I was the right bloke for the job, wished me well and said he would 'keep an eye out' for any backstabbing. Some senior pro.

I was soon pretty wrapped up in the job. Once, after a defeat that followed a long run of cricket around the country, I announced a practice session for the next morning—our first day off in a fortnight. Paul Terry told me to go and find a wife and kids. I agree that I became one-dimensional during the cricket season but I cared, I really cared. A wife and kids were the last thing I wanted to think about. I thought about Hampshire County Cricket Club, the game and the players. These were a set of responsibilities that I enjoyed and believe are important to this day.

THE SUMMER OF 1985

We had the most marvellous season and won nothing. The County Championship was ours for the taking but we blew two huge chances and were scuppered by rain on a couple of other occasions.

In one-day cricket we finished third in the John Player (Sunday) League, lost by four runs in the quarterfinal of the Benson & Hedges Cup to Leicestershire and, after finishing with the scores level, lost again in the semifinal of the NatWest Bank Trophy having lost more wickets than Essex. That was the most painful defeat I had suffered in cricket.

Having said that, in most ways it was the happiest and best year of my cricketing life. The high standard of first-class cricket in England was assured by the quality of overseas players all over the land and the presence of the England players for much of the season. We were properly tested and, in the main, did ourselves justice. Should we have won some silverware? Yes, but then Bradman averaged 99.94. Nothing in cricket is either certain or perfect. It took us three years to learn to win.

The County Championship
22 May
This was one of the great county matches, an advertisement for the game in every way. Ian Botham made 149 in the first innings and Viv Richards made 186 in the second—with ten sixes and nineteen fours, if you don't mind—but Somerset were beaten. Tim Tremlett and Kevan James made maiden first-class hundreds, rescuing the side from 107 for 7 in the first innings. Chris Smith crafted a match-winning hundred in the second innings. I didn't play. I was at Lord's where, captaining MCC, I made 115 not out against Australia. Allan Lamb and I put on 239 in just over three hours, before I declared. Then the rain came to ruin any chance of a result.

Though my head was in London, my heart was at Taunton, where the sun shone. I followed Teletext much as we follow Cricinfo or Twitter now. Botham set Hampshire 323 in 77 overs, and Smith and Paul Terry put on 180 in thrilling style before the chase faltered. Twelve runs were needed from the final over, to be bowled by Joel Garner. Nobody slogs Joel Garner. Oh, yes they do. It took Marshall three balls to finish it—2, 4, 6. Pity he hadn't played in the first championship match of the season, against Kent, when having lost only 3 wickets in the run chase we finished 2 short of Cowdrey's feisty target, with me and Jon Hardy at the crease flailing away in vain. What a waste of a chance.

Tim Tremlett's father, Maurice, was once a fine all-rounder for Somerset and England. His son took 5 wickets in that match against Somerset, including Richards for nought in the first innings, and made a hundred in a famous win on the old man's patch. We all thought we would win the championship after that. Even conservative Tim.

8 June

Oh shit, maybe not. Rain denied us a certain win at Edgbaston— like we bowled Warwickshire out for 127, made 400 plus, declared and had them 198 for 7 with more than four hours left—and a very likely one at Middlesbrough the following week.

Then . . .

To Bournemouth and a key match against Middlesex, who were second in the table behind us, but were without Mike Gatting, Paul Downton and John Emburey—all away with England. We declared our second innings leaving them 265 in 67 overs and knocked 8 of them over for 82. The tea break was a party.

But we never took another wicket. Jamie Sykes, remember him? Exactly, but we bloody well do. Sykes and Simon

Hughes—I still hate you for this, Yozzer—batted for 29 overs to save the match. The pitch was dead. We dropped two catches and I bowled Maco into the ground. I switched the bowlers around ten times in the last twenty overs. Nothing. Maco took 8 in the match but the rest of us couldn't help, not even accurate Tim.

24 August

This was the start of Bournemouth week, a festival of cricket that included two championship games and one in the Sunday League. Good holiday crowds attended and the boundary was lined by marquees that sparkled in the summer sunshine. In those very different days the club took cricket around the county, playing four matches at Bournemouth, two at Portsmouth and one at Basingstoke. We enjoyed them all and invariably got results on pitches that offered more to bowlers than Southampton.

The day before the start of the first match of the week against Gloucestershire, I drove to Bournemouth and met with the head groundsman. My view was that the pitches needed more life if we were to regenerate our championship ambition. I asked him to leave more grass on the surface and water it, which he did on the promise that I should answer to the committee if it backfired. Then it hammered down all night and continued raining for most of the morning. When the covers came off around lunchtime, the pitch was emerald green and sweaty damp. A start was agreed for three o'clock. I won the toss and put Gloucester in. We bowled them out for 140—the gifted young quick bowler from Lymington, Stephen Andrew, took 6 wickets. We made 197 ourselves and then bowled them out again for 157. Rajesh Maru, the little left-arm spinner we had signed from Middlesex the previous winter, took 5 for 16, which I cannot claim was in my master plan but then Marshall was hustling in with some venom at the other end, which sure forced some shots against Maru.

We needed 101 to win the game against Courtney Walsh, David Lawrence, Kevin Curran and David Graveney. Walsh trapped Greenidge lbw and had Chris Smith caught at slip. It was 19 for 2 when I walked to the wicket, very conscious of both the pre-match gamble and the fading championship dream. An hour and twenty minutes later, the game was over. We won it by 7 wickets. I made an unbeaten 71 in 68 balls. It was the best I ever batted.

In a later chapter, I refer to what Sachin Tendulkar calls his 'floating technique', a dream-like state where he responded intuitively to conditions and tactics. By this, I think he means a Zen mind. Barry Richards describes it as the magical place where you feel as if you have control over the bowler's thoughts and come close to an accurate premeditation of each ball you receive. I swear I felt exactly this that day. I can only think of three times in my professional career that I found this magical place. There were other days when I had a clear mind, moved well, had the requisite desire for a performance and was technically sound enough to produce it. But to float? No. The floating technique truly is magic.

Long after the crowds had left Dean Park and the Gloucester players had departed for home, I went out to the middle to see the groundsman again. He was preparing the pitch for the next day's championship match against Leicestershire. 'More of the same, skipper?' he asked. 'Sure thing,' I replied, with the same caveat. This one looked really green, more naturally so than the Gloucestershire pitch, which had been coloured by the sweating under the covers. Again I won the toss. We bowled them out for 100 on a pitch tailored to Tremlett's medium-paced seam and cut. He took 5 for 42 and Marshall 3 for 12, in 15.2 overs!

We made 371 for 5. This time I went in at 15 for 2 and made 146. I can't say I remember floating but I played pretty well. At my side, in a partnership I shall not forget, was Robin Smith, who made an unbeaten 134. We put on 259, demanding concentration from one another between the bursts of laughter that were part of the beauty of time at the wicket with the Judge. He could spot a pretty girl from a distance: 'Skipper,' he said, 'do you see the gentleman just left of the sightscreen in the third row, the chap in the blue towelling sunhat?' 'Indeed I do, Judgey.' 'Well, I'm going to ask the girl next to him out for a drink tonight!' We declared 271 ahead, knocked over Chris Balderstone by the tea break, and the Judge, instead of following us back to the dressing room, headed for the bleachers and his date. We won at a canter the next morning. Judge said his night out was a modest success. Our championship dream was alive.

11 September

I have said that it was usual practice to set up games of cricket on the third afternoon of championship matches because, if not, so many of them drifted into nothing. In the original structure of county cricket, the pitches were left uncovered and this made for more interesting surfaces in general and more results. There has never been much pace in English pitches and once they were covered it became harder and harder for bowlers to take twenty wickets. In the mid-1980s I was a young buck on the Test and County Cricket Board's (TCCB's) cricket subcommittee and strongly supported Bob Willis's argument for four-day county cricket. As the position stood, however, I was damned if three-day games would be left to die. At the denouement of the 1985 season, I was more desperate than ever to keep one alive.

On the last afternoon of the penultimate match, I set Northamptonshire 241 in 60 overs on a flat deck and with a very short boundary on the far side of the Northlands Road ground. Most of the team thought this target too easy, and their fear was substantiated when Wayne Larkins hit the first ball he received from Marshall over extra cover for six. Larkins made 48 quickly and then I had him caught at slip by Maru, soon after nailing Geoff Cook lbw. Generally, my bowling was a thing of little interest, though I could always swing the ball. A career-best haul of 6 for 37 against Somerset beggars belief but on this day, the Northamptonshire wickets of Cook and Larkins were much celebrated.

Allan Lamb took us on, accelerating the chase in his inimitable style while we dropped him twice. Then Maco came back to have him well caught by Chris Smith. Now came the crunch. Roger Harper, the West Indies all-rounder, was at the wicket and hitting sixes. I turned to Maru because I felt we had to take pace off the ball and get it to spin while Northants were chasing so hard for victory. Neil Mallender promptly holed out. I wish I could recall the exact details of the final over but I know that, come the final ball of the match, Northants were 9 wickets down needing 6 runs to win.

I went to talk to Maru, who looked terrified. I said he must look to rip it, not worry too much about where it pitched, but pitch it and spin it, not roll it. I had most fielders around the boundary but three up—backward point, extra cover and straightish mid wicket—all for top edges. I told Raj that in less than a minute from now he would be a hero and that we would go on to win the championship. 'Spin it,' I said, 'just spin it.' He nodded and turned pale.

I got to my position at mid wicket and turned to see Raj already moving in to bowl. He is rushing it, I thought. Slow down. Too late. He fired the ball at the pitch, landing it back off a length where it stood up and, said our wicketkeeper, Bob Parks, turned just a little from leg to off. Harper took the stumping out of the mix by stepping back and then opening up the left side of his body in the modern way. He waited, as if he had his finger on the trigger, and then he fired. I can see the ball now, in its long, slow arc high over the sightscreen, over the wall and into the road. It was never found, neither was the championship won.

We were devastated. In the dressing room there was only silence. Laces were undone, boots pulled off, drinks taken. Maru sat slumped as most of the guys commiserated by patting his shoulder or ruffling his hair. Eventually the silence was broken by Greenidge, who said: 'Which idiot told you to bowl it there?' 'Me,' I said. 'No one is to blame. It just didn't work out.' And that was that.

The NatWest Trophy quarterfinal

A funny thing happened at Taunton. Fifteen minutes before the start, Mike Taylor—former player, friend and, in 2005, the club's marketing manager—came into our dressing room. He said the pitch hadn't been rolled. We had lost the toss and been put in by Ian Botham on a humid morning. Mike was convinced we were entitled to seven minutes of a roller of our choice. I asked the umpires, who agreed but said it was now too late to be rolling the pitch. I took issue with the second judgement, saying the start should be delayed while the playing conditions were honoured. Truculent as this may sound, Garner and Botham with the new ball on a hard and greenish pitch was a potential game-breaker so I stuck to my request.

The umpires sent for Botham, who was immediately incensed. He argued that thousands were out there who had paid good money for a game of cricket not a roller. I said fine, you bat then. There was no love lost between us back then. He stormed off, telling the umpires it would be on their head.

Botham was the biggest figure in the game; the umpires were petrified. I pushed harder and said they surely should call the TCCB offices at Lord's and speak with the cricket secretary, which they did. He confirmed that we were entitled to have the pitch rolled and that though it was not usual practice to delay the start, they had the power to do so. This was especially challenging at Taunton, where the groundsman's shed was behind the covers, which were behind the sightscreen, which was behind the boundary advertising boards, which were behind the ropes. It took ten minutes to get the heavy roller out there and seven more to roll the pitch. We started about half an hour late and Botham stormed in, bowling fast and short. To this day, Paul Terry says it is the quickest bowling he ever faced. Unusually, Garner pitched short as well and though the ball flew through, the stumps weren't threatened. Terry and Greenidge dodged the bullets until a mix-up, a run-out and 2 cheap wickets brought Robin Smith to the wicket at 51 for 3. He loved the pace in the pitch and, first with Paul—who batted with a serenity given to few county cricketers against such a high-quality new-ball attack—then later with the left-handed David Turner, smashed all comers to the shortish boundaries while running the rest of the Somerset fielders ragged. We made 299 for 5, a big score in those days, of which Robin made a swashbuckling hundred.

The whole match was played at fever pitch. We knocked over Peter Roebuck and Viv Richards quickly, and took 3 more quick wickets before the second unusual occurrence of the day. The score was 43 for 5 and only the mighty Botham, who had just arrived at the crease, could deny us. Given the storyline of the day, I thought I'd bowl against him myself, on the basis that he would almost certainly look to hit me most of the way back to Winchester and just might hit one straight up in the air. I started with a decent outswinger that he missed and then a straight ball that he blocked. Then another that he blocked. I wasn't that good. He walked down the pitch and told the umpire that the low evening sun was blinding him. I said the scoreboard was his problem, not the sun but he said no, really, he couldn't pick the ball up. He then asked the umpires to come and stand in his crease and see for themselves. The crowd was restless. Somerset's terrific team of the late 1970s and early 1980s had reached its zenith and was falling back down the mountain. We were, potentially, the heir apparent. The people suspected it and had now seen it with their own eyes. Incredibly, the umpires upheld Botham's appeal for light—good light—and we all left the field. The crowd went nuts, though this time not at me, at him.

Back in the dressing room, and I suppose it was close on seven o'clock by now, we were resigned to coming back the next morning. To our surprise, Botham put his head in the door and asked for a private word with me. I met him back in the umpires' room, where we'd had our face-off eight hours earlier. He said the crowd was getting out of control, demanding their money back and blaming him. He asked if I would appear on the balcony and explain the problem with the sun in the hope of defusing the increasingly emotive situation. This was like Caesar requesting that Marcus Brutus come to his aid in the Forum.

But I did as he asked. I stood on the dressing-room balcony, microphone in hand, looking out over thousands of angry cricket fans, and said that the sun had suddenly dropped to a point just a fraction above the sightscreen that made seeing the bowling from the River End pretty much impossible. I added that it wasn't of Ian's doing: blame the fellow who laid the pitches all those years ago, I said.

Well, it worked a treat. Even the police came to say thanks. Botham was hugely grateful, and how about this? We have been mates since that day. So much so that his family asked me to MC his son's wedding; that Ian asked me to take that son, Liam, in at Hampshire—Liam was a very good all-round cricketer by the way; and that I have hosted many of Beefy's charity foundation events over the years and do so to this day. (His knighthood came on the back of unflinching commitment to Queen and country on the field and to people in need off it, particularly children suffering from leukaemia.) We play golf together and share a love of food and wine. Staying at the Botham home in North Yorkshire is a delight, the only trick being to disappear to bed before he disappears into the cellar for the night. When they built Ian Botham, they broke the mould.

The NatWest Trophy semifinal

Hampshire had never made it to Lord's for a cup final. All those fabulous players—from Roy Marshall to Malcolm of the same name, from 'Butch' White and Bob Cottam to Andy Roberts, from Derek Shackleton and Peter Sainsbury to Trevor Jesty and David Turner, from the start of Barry Richards to the completion of Gordon Greenidge as the world's greatest opening batsmen—none of them had managed to negotiate the dreaded sea of a semifinal.

In 1985, neither did we, though we got so close we could touch, feel and smell that Lord's turf. Essex beat us by virtue of having lost fewer wickets in a match so tense that nerves and tempers were stretched to breaking point.

We batted first in damp conditions and did not make enough runs. I got to 39, our top score, before playing all around a straightish ball from Stuart Turner. I was incandescent when given out lbw. On the BBC, Richie Benaud said, 'I don't know that Mark Nicholas is very pleased with that . . . it looked pretty straight to me.' He was right.

We had to defend 224 on a pitch that was drying out. We got rid of every Essex batsman who mattered except Gooch. In the final over before tea, he called for a tight single to mid wicket, where Robin Smith swooped to hit the stumps direct with Gooch clearly short of his ground. The umpire, Barry Meyer, gave him not out. Fuck, fuck and FUUUUCK again.

At tea the BBC kept replaying it. Gooch was a foot short. There were toys everywhere and we were throwing them. Then I thought, 'We'd better get this thing back on track. The game is by no means done yet.' (Later, bad light stopped play and the match went into a second day with Essex needing another 94 off 21.2 overs with 6 wickets in hand.) We fought, by heaven we did, but there just weren't enough runs to play with. It was like trying to squeeze toothpaste from an empty tube—there was nothing there. Essex inched closer, Gooch in control—one of the best players anywhere, going nowhere except Lord's. I took some gambles, specifically using Marshall for all his allotted overs in an attempt to collar Gooch. But bloody hell, that Gooch had some game. I told Cowley to lob it up and buy his wicket; I even bowled a few at him myself, some proper poo, but he resisted everything, including temptation. We were left with Greenidge bowling the last over—the 60th. Gordon never bowled, ever. Gooch was at the non-striker's end when Stuart Turner safely blocked the final ball of the match. The scores were level. Essex had lost 7 wickets to our 8. Stupid rule. We batted when the ball was nipping around all over the place, for goodness' sake. Essex should have won easily but we pushed them as a decent side should. I was proud of that. Mr Meyer, a lovely man, cost us the Lord's dream.

WHAT I THINK NOW

If I had my time as captain again, I would give more attention to fielding—my own and that of the team. Had we caught better, we would have won the championship, despite our relatively thin bowling. That summer of 1985 was the closest we came and the most fun we had. We were third on a couple of other occasions and certainly had enough players of a standard above the line to carry those beneath it. I have already said that we needed one other top-class seam or swing bowler— something Cardigan Connor later became, though was not quite while Malcolm was in his pomp. I suspect he revered Malcolm too much for his own game to flourish. Above all, we needed a big spinner of the ball. Shaun Udal arrived not a moment too late but his greatest gift was accuracy and deception in the one-day game, not revs on the ball to win championship matches. The more he played, the craftier and more reliable he became. So much so that England took him to India in 2006, where he captured Tendulkar's wicket, among others, to help England win in Mumbai. Game-changing spinners are a rare breed in the county game. It was, and is, a lonely job, espe-cially on English pitches that are prepared with an increasingly uniform soil that binds them together like cement.

At the end of the 1987 season, we were left with a dilemma. The TCCB changed the regulations on overseas players to one per team and just two per county staff. There was no point in either Greenidge or Marshall kicking his heels in the 2nd XI so, reluctantly, we did not offer another contract to Greenidge. I was a part of that decision, explaining to the cricket committee that cover for Marshall was crucial, given our ongoing struggle to take 20 wickets. Expecting him to play every match was unfair and likely to shorten his career. We signed the South African left-arm quick, Stephen Jefferies, who was grateful for the deal, good with the youngsters in the 2nd XI and, when the stars were aligned, a brilliant matchwinner.

Greenidge was deeply hurt by the decision. He had come to England from Barbados as a ten-year-old boy, living first in Reading. Hampshire picked him up and he more than returned the county's faith over the eighteen-year period he was with the club. The general view was that his surprising insecurity, which could manifest itself in an apparent bitterness, came from two things. First, the cross-pollination of his life—was he English or Bajan, and how did others perceive the answer to that question? Second, the fact that a couple of Richards stole much of his thunder.

As I have said, Gordon was an exceptional cricketer. In West Indies colours, he laid much of the groundwork upon which the others, notably Viv, paraded their talent. At Hampshire, he stood at the non-striker's end while Barry was consistently feted as the best opening batsman on the planet. He was overlooked for the captaincy of the county three times—first when Gilliat retired, then when Stephenson moved on and later when Pocock stood down. Now, he surmised that I had fired him. He had a fair bit to grumble about.

He did not make life easy for his captain. Indeed, we all trod on eggshells around him. He infuriated me when he refused to play in a county game the day after the 1987 bicentenary match at Lord's between MCC and Rest of the World. He made a superb hundred in the second innings, hobbling between the wickets for much of it. This melodrama was a Greenidge speciality. Indeed, many an opposing bowler was glad to see him arrive fully fit because, when limping, he invariably made runs. Anyway, I got through to the dressing-room phone at Lord's and he told me he wasn't up for it the next day. I said if he could limp through a hundred against the World XI he could surely limp through one against a county attack. He said he couldn't and would not be there in the morning. Marshall, the stand-out bowler in the match at Lord's, turned up on time and played with his usual commitment.

I cannot pretend that my relationship with Gordon was always as it should have been. I have long thought it would be interesting to hear him talk about his sense of identity as a cricketer. Much water has flowed under that bridge, however.

Probably too much. It remains one of only a very few things I regret about my time as captain.

We see each other once a year at a charity match for Well-being of Women. It is wonderful that he plays. He has softened, as have I. His life after cricket has not always been easy and I care as much for him as for the other Hampshire players of my time. His friendship with Marshall grew stronger as Malcolm became terminally ill with cancer. He nursed him until the end, which is a kindness and spirit given to few men.

On the international stage, Gordon played some of the greatest innings in history. For Hampshire, he did the same but under the radar. I'll pick just one, at Northampton on a wet pitch. With Paul, he put on 250 for the first wicket. When Paul raised his bat for 50, an innings he considered among the most technically accomplished of his career, Gordon was 202 not out. We declared at 338 for 2 on a terrible pitch and won by 169 runs. That is how good Gordon was.

Decisions on players' careers were much the most difficult part of the job. I well remember walking Bob Parks around the United Services ground at Portsmouth to tell him that we were going to play Adrian Aymes ahead of him. That was a most unpleasant experience. I also told my dear friend Peter Sainsbury, the man who had backed me on every step of my journey, that his number was up as a coach. In discussing the Sainsbury decision, the chairman of the cricket committee, Charlie Knott, had said 'and tell me when I should go too, please'. So one day I did, in his own house.

What else? I had to wrestle with dropping myself on a couple of occasions but both Knott, and the man who replaced him, Jimmy Gray, insisted I should not do so. They thought such a decision the thin end of the wedge and, anyway, they preferred their captain out there, in charge. Paul could see the argument but it was sure tricky explaining to Robin Smith that he was heading for a 2nd XI match while we were off to try to win the championship. Paul was no fan of Gray, a former player in Ingleby-Mackenzie's golden team, primarily because of his misinterpretation of a letter Paul handed to him when he resigned the vice-captaincy. I, however, was fond of Gray. He had helped my batting, read the game well and, like Knott, was an effective buffer between the dressing room and the general committee.

I was upset when Paul stood down. A few niggling issues had come his way, not least my interference in matches that he captained when I was ill or injured. He was also disapproving of my approach to certain complicated issues that arise over a long period of governance. He regrets the decision now, much as I regret interfering with his brief spells at the helm. While working on this chapter I called him to talk these things through. The next day he wrote me a kind note, clearly explaining his thoughts back then and apologising for not resolving them with me face to face. We were so damn subjective about everything, we agreed. Oh, for the time and space to have stood back and taken stock. Malcolm took up the cudgels of vice-captaincy and loved the day-to-day involvement.

Malcolm's offsider, Cardigan Connor, was a lion-hearted cricketer and an utterly charming and self-deprecating man. He had been plucked from Minor Counties cricket and, over a long career, proved to be one of the club's finest signings. The Smith brothers, Robin and Chris, were outstanding batsmen, whose professional approach to the game sat comfortably with their innate sense of fun. I knew Udal from a young age and ushered him though the early days of his long and fruitful time in the game. A touch more maturity would have made him a regular international player: as it was, he served Hampshire with unconditional love and enthusiasm before finishing up at Middlesex, where he took over from Ed Smith as captain.

There were two wicketkeepers during my time, Parks and Aymes. Parks had a lovely, natural way with the game and a fine brain for it. Aymes was tough as teak and the sort of soldier any general would want by his side. There were two vastly different all-rounders, Kevan James and Jon Ayling, the first an import from Middlesex, the second a Portsmouth Grammar School boy. Jon could really play the game but never quite recovered from two freak injuries that badly affected his confidence. Kevan simply gave all he had, in the most honest way. He made hundreds from most positions in the order and took 6 for 22 with his left-arm inswing against Australia in 1985. Raj Maru toiled away, too tiny to bounce the ball much, but spinning it just enough to ask questions. He was a fine close-catcher and brave lower-order batsman, who had not found a regular place at Middlesex but instead found a home at Hampshire. There were two promising fast bowlers— Stephen Andrew and Kevin Shine—both of whose ability was overshadowed by self-imposed anxiety. There was a damn good, if ageing, Dutch medium pacer called P.-J. Bakker— nickname Nip, get it?—who brought a little sophistication and perspective to the workplace. These fellows, along with Paul, Tim and the superstars, were the nucleus of Hampshire cricket for more than a decade. My admiration for them and the wonderful memories of our time together live to this day. We were all lucky.

IT ISN'T OVER UNTIL IT'S OVER

We played Gloucestershire on a lively pitch at Cheltenham in late July 1992. We were largely on the wrong end of the game and, with an inexperienced batting line-up, fought coura- geously through the last afternoon against Courtney Walsh, among others, to save the game. In those days, if the captains and umpires agreed there was no chance of a result, the plug could be pulled on first-class matches with half an hour's play remaining. Well, with half an hour left in this match our score was 274 for 8, 102 ahead of Gloucestershire. The umpires saw me waving my arms around, beckoning the players off the field. The Gloucestershire captain, Tony Wright, agreed the game was up and the umpires pulled the stumps from the ground. I went to the middle and explained that far from calling a halt to proceedings I was, in fact, declaring our innings. A sense of confusion was immediately evident, which I admit I enjoyed. The umpires put the stumps back into the ground, at which point Wright said there were only nine available overs left in the match. I agreed and pointed out that he required 103 runs from them to secure a famous victory. He studied me like I should be consigned. The younger players in the Hampshire team were excited. The older ones less so.

Richard Scott, a former Hampshire player and everyone's friend, thought the whole thing hysterically funny and came out to open the Gloucestershire innings with exactly the right approach. He could see nothing to lose; Wright could see the loss of everything. Scott immediately picked up Marshall for a couple of sixes over square leg. I switched to spin and he hit a couple more. At the other end, wickets were tumbling. Bill Athey was stumped and Walsh, promoted up the order for a slog, holed out on the boundary off Udal. Then Scotty nicked one to me at slip. Gloucestershire were 70 for 5. Wright himself, with Jack Russell, steadied the ship—as far as they could in a couple of overs—but Wright fell to the excellent Udal and Justin Vaughan followed as the game returned to its previous breathless state. Russell invented shots that are commonplace today until we all surrendered to the ticking of the clock with the home team 95 for 7, just 8 short!

The friendly Cheltenham spectators were on their feet. Wright warmly shook my hand and said, 'You're mad,' by which I suppose he meant, 'Good declaration, you clown.' To me, that 45 minutes, or whatever it turned out to be, well illustrated the spirit of cricket. It was also a useful reminder not to take the game too seriously.

A CONVERSATION WITH MICKY STEWART

We were playing Surrey at Guildford in mid-July 1988. I came off the field at tea and Micky Stewart, who was the first full time England manager–coach, asked to see me privately. Odd, I thought. We sat in a small room in the old pavilion.

'I wanted you to know that this morning you lost a three–two vote to captain England in the next test.'

That got my attention.

England were being thumped by the West Indies. Gatting had been sacked after the First Test on the premise of some-thing embarrassing with a barmaid in a Nottingham hotel but really it was a retrospective punishment for his on-field spat with Shakoor Rana in Pakistan the previous winter. Then, after two Tests in charge, John Emburey was sacked too. The Headingley Test was next, a difficult place to play but where competent English seam bowling could, conceivably, match the West Indian attack. When I heard Emburey had been removed, I assumed Graham Gooch would get the job. At least, I thought he should.

'Oh, right, that's a pity,' I said to Micky. 'Very good of you to come and tell me, though. What cost me?'

'I voted against you,' he replied.

'Whoa, that's full-on. Why?'

'I just don't think you can play your first Test against this side as captain. It's too hard. To bat against them is a job in itself but to captain as well, with all that goes with it and for the first time, the press would be all over you. It's not the right time.'

'Yes, I see that.'

'We want you to know that you're in the forefront of our minds for the tour to India this winter. You play spin well, it's a tough tour to lead. You're a real candidate. The chairman [Peter May] is a supporter. Keep making runs, and having Hampshire in contention for trophies helps too.'

'Great, thanks, much appreciate the line of communication.'

I was a fan of Micky: there was no bullshit with him. Hampshire had won the Benson & Hedges Cup a week or two earlier and we were rolling around mid-table in the championship, which Kent were leading. I was hugely encouraged by his honesty and realism. I remember thinking the England team were in good hands and that it would be interesting to work with him. I also remember thinking that besides Mr and Mrs Gooch, Micky was Gooch's greatest fan.

Before heading back to the dressing room, I said: 'Presumably, if Goochie goes well, he'll get the job in India.'

'It's not Goochie,' he said.

'What! Not Gooch?'

'Chris Cowdrey.'

Chris was Peter May's godson. The press made a lot of that. I didn't. The selectors decided they wanted a specialist captain—the Brearley theory—to lift the team in the face of an all-conquering opponent. Chris and I were the candidates, neither of us quite justifiable selections on playing ability alone but add in captaincy skills and a case could be made. They chose Chris who, as Micky pointed out, had played a few Tests in India under David Gower on the successful 1984–85 tour. Fair enough.

And that was the last I heard of it. Chris captained the Headingley Test and tells a very funny story of the toss with Viv. As was the tradition back then, each captain recited his team to his opposite number. The home captain went first and halfway through Chris reciting the English team Viv interrupted and said: 'Don't worry, man, you play who you want. Now, we got Greenidge, Haynes, Richards . . .' To which Chris said: 'That's fine, you play who you want as well!' And he could feel himself turning white. It was the first and, sadly, last time for Chris, who had a toe broken by Walsh and could not play at the Oval, where Gooch did captain the side. The tour to India was cancelled. 'My father and I,' says Chris, 'captained England 28 times between us.'

Gower was brought back to the job in the summer of 1989 against the Australians and then immediately fired after the 4–0 humiliation. Ted Dexter had taken over from May as chairman of selectors. Gooch finally got the England captaincy he deserved for the tour to the West Indies in early 1990. I was appointed captain of the England A tour to Zimbabwe. Michael Atherton was my vice-captain. Such are the lines of succession.

We had an excellent trip to Zimbabwe, beating a good side led by the formidable David Houghton—one of the finest batsmen against whom I played. Atherton made plenty of runs and displayed an uncompromising approach to the game, allied with a notable level of self-confidence. At a team meeting before the first one-day international, he remarked that we needed to start fielding better and, 'Captain,' he said, 'we better start putting key fielders in the key positions.' 'Expand on that, if you will,' I said. 'Well, backward point is imperative against these guys who love to cut the quicker bowlers, so we need our best catcher there.' Yup, I agreed, but before I could complete the sentence he added: 'And that's me.' In the first over of the match, he took off high to his right and held on to a blinder. When he came up with the ball, he looked at me and said, 'Told you.'

That tour, and the England B tour I led to Sri Lanka in 1986, was the closest I came to international cricket as a player. The new generation included Atherton, of course, and another who was with us in Zimbabwe, Graham Thorpe. Both showed all the signs of high-class batsmen, which included poise and an encouraging ruthlessness. I thought it a pity Atherton was made captain of England so young and a greater pity that some of the wrong people were in management alongside him. Through the 1990s, England's team became increasingly guilty of a siege mentality that distracted from the job at hand. Had Atherton been left to observe a while longer, I suspect he would have unravelled many of the problems that were to halt the progress of his side.

DAVID GOWER

I could not persuade the Hampshire committee to invest in bowlers but the most beautiful batsman of this or pretty much any era was an easy sell. David was out of favour with the England selectors and kicking his heels at Leicestershire, the club at which he had forged his career. He chose Hampshire ahead of Kent, primarily because of his admiration for Marshall.

There was much excitement about his arrival, not least from the players, who saw him as a proper star. He made a hundred at Southampton against Sussex in his first home game, putting on 256 with Robin Smith. Their partnership gave us a near-perfect canvas of batting—David with his neat elegance and exquisite timing, Robin with his intimidating presence and rugged power. We made 600 for 8 declared and romped home.

David was so gifted it was a joke. Some days it was as if he didn't know what to do with all the time he had to play and the myriad options at his disposal. When in the mood, he made even the very best bowlers look pedestrian. To see him up close was both a joy and a revelation. He saw the ball early, played it late and hit it surprisingly hard. He also manoeuvred it beautifully, creating angles that accelerated the game what-ever the obstacles set before him.

As long as net practices didn't happen too often, he took them more seriously than generally perceived and appeared to enjoy catching and fielding drills. We all marvelled at the way he could turn his back to the coach hitting the ball at him and then spin on command to pluck just about everything out of thin air at the last possible moment.

As with many of those who are so outrageously gifted, there are risks and occasional complications. After a couple of weeks of preseason training, he asked for a quiet word. There was a car in the bottom of the lake at St Moritz, he said, which he had left there. The problem was the Swiss police and the insurance company, he said, half amused, who wanted the car out of the lake pronto. He was looking to schedule a couple of meetings in London. Would it be all right to miss practice for a day and get the thing sorted?

The nuts and bolts of the story were these: Gower and Lamb had been with a bunch of mates in St Moritz for the Cresta Run, a joyride on a bloody dangerous British-built toboggan track. After a night on the piss, a couple of them—one of whom was David—had driven their hire car across the lake for a bet, only to hear the alarming sound of ice breaking beneath them at the halfway stage of their journey. It was well past midnight and, unable to see much, they abandoned the car and made it to safety themselves. On their return the next morning, broad and chilling daylight revealed no sign of the offending vehicle. It, and they, were sunk. Now, a month on, the ice had melted and the authorities and environmentalists were on his case.

How splendid, I thought, and immediately my mind went back to Colin Ingleby-Mackenzie in the late 1960s. Ingleby-Mackenzie and Denis Compton had a hard winter's afternoon on the gin at the Cricketers Club in London until, in some panic, Compo suddenly said: 'Christ, it's 6.30 and I'm due to introduce the guest speaker at the Denham Golf Club dinner at half past seven. I'll never make it to the station for the next train.' To which Colin said: 'Borrow my car, old boy, it's parked outside. I'll get a cab home.' 'Marvellous,' said Compo, who left in a flurry of coats and hats and tie-straightening. As he shot out of the door, Ingleby shouted: 'It's rather a wreck, master. Write it off for me, will you, and I'll talk the Admiral into something a bit more fancy for you next time!'

The following morning, Colin came down to breakfast, where his father, the Admiral, was at the head of the table reading *The Times*. 'Rum old business with your chum Compton last night, dear boy,' said the Admiral. 'He was speeding up the A40, swerved off the road and drove his car into a tree. Wrote it off, apparently.' 'Marvellous!' exclaimed Ingleby-Mackenzie. 'Followed my instructions to the letter.' And the Admiral's scrambled eggs shot across the table.

I'm no Ingleby-Mackenzie but I did think Gower's story rather entertaining. I said he could have as long as needed. Unfortunately, this little sojourn coincided with a friendly against Sussex. One or two of the boys, less than impressed, asked why he wasn't there. I said he was attending to important business in London. 'One rule for one, one for the others,' said somebody. 'Absolutely,' I replied. David got the car out. It cost a small fortune.

Later in the summer, Ted Dexter rang me to ask about him. I said he was in tremendous nick and that no one in England could touch him. David was picked against India at the Oval and made a beautiful, unbeaten 157. Then he toured Australia, where he infuriated Gooch, the captain, and the management by slipping away during the England innings with John Morris for a ride in a Tiger Moth—a journey that included flying low over the match England were playing against Queensland. Was that a laugh or was he a liability? Gooch and Gower were different animals. I greatly admired them both and could see how the contrasting soundtrack of their lives made for an awkward relationship.

David often slept before he batted, literally. At the fall of the wicket we would shake him awake, upon which he would splash his face, pick up his gloves, bat and helmet and head off. He figured that watching every ball made him tense and his best batting came when he was relaxed, so he might just as well switch off. I figured if it worked for him, it might work for me and, by heck, it did. Sleeping offered the advantage of a clear mind with no preconception of what lay ahead. It meant you watched and played the ball, not the expectation of it.

On balance, David was a terrific signing. We had the odd row over the fact that I insisted he turn out in the Sunday League, which he hated, but in general he was a good influence in the dressing room, using a lifetime of experience at the highest level to encourage, delight, defuse, calm and simplify. Very occasionally, his own explosive temper would clear the dressing room but he was hardly the Lone Ranger there. It is why dressing rooms must be private places, because only those inside can fully appreciate the highly charged and emotional nature of what happens outside.

MALARIA

At the end of the 1990 England A tour to Zimbabwe, I flew back to London, stayed the night with my girlfriend and was up early to head back to Heathrow, where I was meeting the Hampshire team for our preseason tour to Barbados. I told her I felt achy, like I was about to come down with flu. She whacked a couple of Panadol into me and suggested drinking less wine. On the plane, Chris Smith suggested vodka, so I gave that a go too. By the midpoint of the flight a doctor was called. Fifteen minutes later I was on oxygen. I was wheel-chaired off the aircraft and transferred to hospital. In casualty, I told them

I had malaria. There is no history of malaria in Barbados so they thought I was delirious and simply did all they could to keep my temperature down.

I was in a large ward, too weak to take any initiative of my own and, frankly, frightened. The England team had just arrived in Barbados from Trinidad. The first people to come and see me were Gooch and Lamb, along with the parents of the Smith brothers, Joy and John. Lamby wanted me moved to a private ward and made a lot of noise about it. He sensed I was worse than just running a high fever and he was right.

The next morning a consultant arrived who had studied all the tests and told me I had falciparum, or cerebral malaria. Later, we traced this back to the England A visit to the Victoria Falls. He said that effective drugs had been ordered from the tropical diseases hospital in London but in the meantime they would treat me with quinine, and a lot of it.

My mother, stepfather, sister and brother were on holiday in France and read about it on page three of the London *Daily Telegraph* while having breakfast in Paris. Mum, in understandable panic, eventually got through to me but I wasn't for talking. I stayed in hospital for a week, bloody ill and living through the four-part cycle of a potentially fatal strain of malaria. Goochie, who had his thumb broken by Ezra Moseley in Trinidad and was therefore unable to play in Barbados, visited most days, as did Lamby, who was leading the side in Graham's place. The Smith parents and Ted Dexter were regular visitors too. David turned up and said, 'I signed up to play with you, not visit you in hospital!' The Hampshire guys visited once or twice but were otherwise busy playing and partying without having to worry about me bossing them around.

I then spent another week being nursed by the wonderfully generous Tyrwhitt-Drake family, who had a house on the polo field at St James. I am forever in their debt. The England team welcomed me into the dressing room for the Test, which I watched for a few hours each day from the balcony. I recall Alec Stewart being especially supportive. A fine family, those Stewarts. I was hopelessly weak when I flew home, having lost a stone and a half, and therefore missed the first couple of games of the season. Paul captained typically well and I should have left him to it more than I did. My first game back was the one in which David and the Judge added 256 together. They said they would turn it on for me, and how!

It took more than a year to get the malaria out of my system. The 1990 season was extremely difficult and, truth be told, I should not have played. I crawled out of bed each morning, barely practised, got through the day and crawled back into bed at night. I would not do the same again. In fact, I would have ignored the committee's urging and left the bulk of the season to Paul—with David, Chris Smith and Maco at his side. The summer of 1990 was not one during which I felt cricket to be a beautiful game.

TRIUMPHS

We had a few. Four trophies in the six years from 1986 to 1992. Over the period September 1991 to July 1992, we held both the knockout cups—the 60-over NatWest Trophy and the Benson & Hedges 55-over tournament. We didn't believe anyone could beat us at home and doubted they could when we played away. It was a great feeling.

The John Player League (aka the Sunday League), 1986
I recall very little of the season other than we played an enterprising brand of the 40-over format. Marshall was so bloody good around this time that I convinced him to bowl with at least one slip in almost all situations, which gave us the mindset of attack in what was an essentially defensive game.

He did so reluctantly at the death but I reckoned your average county batsman was as likely to nick him as hit him back over his head, so I won that argument more often than not. (I was still pursuing this belief six years later and, against his will, brought in a slip for Mark Ealham in the 1992 Benson & Hedges Final against Kent. Ealham hit the next ball onto the top tier of the Compton Stand—a huge blow. Maco gave me the most withering look.)

Gordon batted brilliantly for most of the summer and the rest of us pretty darned well. The bowlers fed from Maco's confidence and developed both a pattern and rhythm. The fielding was mainly good and athletic, though some needed hiding more than others. The trick was to get the right fielders in the right places at the right time. (I didn't go so far as to use Paul as a stalker in the way Johnny Barclay used Paul Parker at Sussex. Parker always fielded at cover point in his Sussex cap, or at least we thought he did. Cleverly, Barclay, who wore a white towelling hat, and others, would swap headgear with Parker and then swap position too. Thus, if you were stealing a single to the slowcoach in the floppy at mid-on, watch out, it might not be Blogs, it might be Parker.)

We won the John Player League on a fine day at the Oval, which should have led to the jolliest of parties but a Surrey member had a heart attack on the balcony above us. Apparently, the tension in the match had got to him and while we were receiving the trophy our physio, David Newman, was up there trying to save his life. We drove home subdued that night and later the next day heard that he had died in hospital. That sure took the gloss off our first trophy together.

The Benson & Hedges Cup, 1988
In the quarterfinal, Robin Smith played one of his finest innings on an uneven New Road pitch that suited the strong

Worcestershire attack. Without him we would have fallen but with him, and with the magnificently positive Stephen Jefferies alongside him, we rose to the task of an improbable run chase.

In the semifinal, Paul made a most impressive hundred. This was the innings that no Hampshire batsman had managed since one-day cricket first appeared as a 65-over competition in 1963. Back then, amateurs and professionals changed in different dressing rooms and talent money further split the rooms. Paul had long believed that if one of the top order batted through the innings, a vast majority of games would be won. At times, he attempted this to the detriment of the run rate, putting such pressure on the middle order that collapses became inevitable. My support for him was unconditional but unrest among his peers demanded we throw the debate open to the floor. The problem was not his theory but its practicalities, and they needed ironing out. Everyone had their say and then, on the day that it really mattered, he conjured up something close to perfect. Always an elegant batsman, Paul got down and dirty while Essex scrapped in their never-say-die way. Then, having wrestled control, he paraded his talent to take us over the line. Like Robin Smith in the quarterfinal, Paul had shown just how much Hampshire cricket meant to him. He spoke for all of us with the innings that finally took Hampshire to Lord's.

Everyone was so pleased. Demand for tickets reached a provincial version of fever pitch, which was exciting. As Nigel Cowley said, 'I've got family I didn't know existed.' There are aspects of the day that will live with me forever. I had a good match personally with two catches when I moved in to short leg and some runs that ensured we chased a low target without a drama. Best of all, I remember the cracking dressing-room party. As cheers rang out from thousands of Hampshire folk on the outfield, those of us lucky enough to have played were awash in the sensations of achievement and joy.

The NatWest Trophy, 1991

A few days before the final against Surrey, Waqar Younis smashed up my hand in the Championship match at the Oval. Oddly, he was late out of the home dressing room on the second morning and jogged past me and Kevan James as we were walking out to continue from where we had left off the night before. He was very jokey and said how much he was looking forward to the final on Saturday. I agreed and, tongue-in-cheek, told him to keep a bit in reserve for the big day. The simplest way to describe how fast he bowled on an uneven pitch is to relate that the Judge, who had only ever batted in a helmet with side pieces, called for a visor. Fitting it took an age. When we settled down to play again, Waqar's wrath could not be contained. He bowled every bit as fast as Thomson and Imran had bowled to me when I was starting out, only on this pitch the ball flew from shortish—but not bouncer—length to be close to unplayable. To this day, I can see and feel the one that got me. It trapped my left hand, which was in front of my face, against the bat handle and immediately I knew he had landed a knockout blow. I was soon in casualty, and then touring Harley Street in search of an answer. The best offer was a pain-killing injection from a needle the size of my middle finger. The consultant said it was unlikely to help much anyway. Waqar had crushed the left knuckle of my left hand and broken the little finger in two places. No cup final for Mark Knuckleless.

This helped selection in one way and challenged it in another. We had been wrestling with which bowler to leave out and favoured the use of the two spinners, which had worked so well in the journey to the final—one, incidentally, during which we had not lost more than three wickets in any round. The Lord's pitch had no great history of helping spin, however, and with a 10.30 am start we thought we would need another seamer if we bowled first.

Just as in 1988, there was no Marshall. In both those summers he toured England with the West Indies, causing havoc. In 1988, Jefferies had been a magnificent replacement, more than justifying the difficult decision about Greenidge, and winning the man-of-the-match award in the most clear-cut choice there can ever have been—he took 5 for 13! Now we had Aqib Javed, the young Pakistani outswing bowler, whose wholehearted approach was typical of his countrymen.

Neither was there Chris Smith. His sudden retirement in the middle of the summer of 1991 was a surprise and a disappointment. We were more than fortunate that Tony Middleton stepped into his shoes with such conviction.

The team had changed since 1985—no Smith C or Greenidge with the bat; no Parks with the gloves; no Marshall, Tremlett, Andrew or Cowley with the ball. In their place were Middleton and Gower, Adrian Aymes, Aqib, Jon Ayling, Kevan James and Shaun Udal. Making up the 1991 NatWest Trophy champions were Terry, Smith R, Connor and Maru.

Someone had to lead them on the day but should it be Terry or Gower? Over the year or so that it took me to recover from malaria, Paul and I had drifted apart. Almost everything at the club revolved around me, too much so in his view. He argued that this affected my own play and therefore the make-up of the team. He had a point, though it was more the illness than the workload. He went quiet on me but I knew what he thought. In turn, I felt that our long friendship warranted greater support. Time is a remarkable healer. We catch up in Perth these days and things are much as they once were when we were starting out.

As for David, he had led England to the Ashes, for goodness' sake. His calm authority was easy to follow and we asked him to do the job. The truth is, we were lucky with such riches. Hampshire would have won the match with either of them in charge. Each of our carefully considered ideas worked a treat, not least using the two spinners for their full quota of overs. David handled the day as if he had done it all his life, which, of course, he pretty much had. When he received the trophy he called me forward to share the moment, a kind and thoughtful gesture.

I had sat on the home dressing-room balcony with my arm in a sling and smoked cigarettes provided by one of the rival one-day cricket sponsors, Benson & Hedges. You think you are nervous playing but watching was unbearable. We chased a decent Surrey score, sticking closely to a rate that did not leave too much to do against Waqar's reverse-swinging yorkers at the death. The two highlights of this chase were the Judge's cover drive off Waqar that all but burnt the turf on its way to the Warner Stand boundary—a statement shot that put the chirpy Waqar back in his box—and Ayling's uppercut for six into the Tavern off Tony Murphy as the night closed in. Those 60-over games were a long haul, especially in September. Photographs from the presentation and the resulting celebrations were taken by flashlight.

We had a lively celebration dinner on a boat on the Thames with Gary Lineker and Tim Rice making guest appearances. The chairman of NatWest was Bob Alexander, one of the brilliant legal men employed by Kerry Packer for his battle against the TCCB thirteen years earlier. He came in with a couple of magnums of serious champagne for me and I made the mistake of taking them with me to the boat. I should not have been surprised when the Gower–Lineker–Rice axis cracked them open. It was a memorable night, though waking the next morning to a violent hangover, fully dressed and with your broken hand stuck awkwardly under your hip is a most unpleasant experience.

The Benson & Hedges Cup, 1992

Maco finally had his day in the sun—or two days as it happened. He scored some runs, took some wickets and lifted the cup. No county cricketer can have more deserved his triumph. I hit a huge six over square leg off Martin McCague and held on to a good catch at mid-off. The video footage of my celebration is embarrassing. We were better than Kent and rode the loss of the toss on a misty, damp morning—conditions that hung around all day—with a minimum of fuss. The weather had delayed the start and most of the Kent innings carried over to Sunday, which takes a little of the sting out of the after-party. We were the happiest team and perhaps the best in the land. We should have won the County Championship too but so badly lost focus after winning at Lord's that we missed our slot. Bloody silly, but I can't remember enough of how this manifested itself to explain it here. It was probably as simple as taking our eye off the ball, losing a couple of games and, with them, our rhythm and momentum. There is no doubt that in the weeks that followed the winning of the 1992 Benson & Hedges Cup we failed to justify the talent in a good team.

ANYTHING BUT A BEAUTIFUL DAY

Our three-day match against Pakistan in 1992 was a grim affair. Javed Miandad's team arrived to do a number on Robin Smith, whom they saw as a threat in the Test series. He was in the nets bright and early, as ever, when the Pakistan team bus pulled in. Waqar came over, stood behind him and made the sign of the cross on his forehead. An hour later, just before the toss, Aqib approached Julian Wood—with whom he had played the previous summer, for goodness' sake—and said, 'There will be blood on the pitch today, you ****, and it will be yours.' The match played out in this vile atmosphere and I became involved in an incident that did neither me nor the game any service.

I had about 25 when I played forward to Mushtaq Ahmed and failed, not for the first or last time, to read the wrong 'un. The ball looped from the inside edge of my bat to the top of my pad before bouncing an inch or so short of the diving hand of the substitute fielder at short leg, Rashid Latif, who came up claiming the catch. Collectively, the Pakistanis appealed with venom. I was nervously given out by Ray Tolchard, who was new to the umpires list.

Furious with the appeal, the decision and the general spirit of the match, I turned in the direction of the pavilion but stopped after 15 yards or so to speak to the vastly experienced square-leg umpire, Kenny Palmer.

'I'm not going, Kenny,' I said. 'He caught that on the bounce and I'm sick of this game and their attitude and I'm not fucking well going.'

'But you gotta go,' said Kenny. 'You've been given out, captain, you've got to go.'

'Well, I'm not, Kenny, I'm sorry, I'm not. You go and speak with your mate over there and tell him the catch didn't carry.'

'I can't to do that, captain, I couldn't see whether it carried or not but he could and he gave you out.'

'I'm not going, Kenny, so go speak to him.'

Can you imagine! The Pakistanis were incensed. Javed Miandad came over and gave me a mouthful. I told him to piss off and mind his own business. He said it was very much his business.

David was the non-striker. He came over. 'Skip, I know your frustration. We've all felt it this game but you should accept the decision and go. Believe me, no good will come of you staying here.'

'I know,' I said, 'but I'm too far down the road now. I'm sorry, I'm not going. They've abused us from first to last and we have no idea why. Now they're trying to cheat me out. I'm staying.'

Palmer went to talk to Tolchard. Incredibly, Tolchard reversed the decision and reinstated me.

The place went off.

Waqar and Wasim Akram came back to bowl immediately. Every ball was at my head. Even when I ducked or swayed, they appealed. If I played the ball down at my feet, a fielder would pick it up and make as if to run me out. They followed through almost to my face and told me what they thought of me. Unaware of the facts in the middle, the crowd began to cheer my every run and catcall the Pakistanis. The match descended into chaos. Writing this, I am in disbelief at what I did. Indeed, I have been so ever since.

Eventually, Wasim and Waqar were taken off. Mushy returned and again they appealed or exclaimed against every ball I played—even a well-struck boundary. Then I played forward to another googly, misread it again and watched as it looped off my pad to Latif. Now, they really went up, en masse, like a pack of wild dogs. Tolchard gave me out, or did he give me not out? It's a blur. I hadn't hit it, nowhere near. Either way, I walked off, deeply distressed.

I bought *The Times* the next morning to read John Woodcock, the writer whose opinion I most respected. He had given me a mighty roasting. During the lunch break, I went to seek him out in the press tent. I explained the atmosphere of the match and the facts out in the middle. He had no sympathy. In fact, he fired everything back, saying the greater the provocation, the greater my responsibility to the game. John reminded me of more innocent days when the manners that were once an integral part of cricket's charm were taken for granted. He said it was the chippy English pros and the sly remarks they passed off as banter that were to blame for the attitudes so prevalent on the modern-day field of play. Banter all too soon turned into sledging, he insisted, and the arrogance of the English game was inexcusable. He said that if I honestly thought that cricketers from the subcontinent were the root cause of such crass and aggressive behaviour, I was deluding myself. In summary, he said that anything that came out of the mouths of Pakistan players today could be traced back to the haughty English and the hostility of the Australians. Anyway, he said, you should know better.

I left with my tail between my legs.

It took a while to get over. I apologised to the umpires at the end of the match but the damage was done, especially to Tolchard. The part of it I most regret is making it so difficult for him. I think it is why I now strongly support the principle of the spirit of cricket.

I have often spoken about this with Wasim Akram, who is a dear friend. He puts it down to white-line fever. He does not doubt that the catch may have been claimed on the bounce but neither he, nor any other member of the team, could have seen for certain. None of which, we agree, is the point. I should have walked off when given out, end of story. He laughs about the bouncer barrage, as does Waqar. Neither of them, nor Javed, nor Mushtaq, hold a grudge. Indeed, quite the opposite. In Lahore and Karachi I have been a guest in their homes, and I remain in close and regular contact with Wasim to this day.

But I learnt a lesson. Don't mess with a beautiful game.

HAMPSHIRE'S NEW GROUND

At a restaurant in Leeds in 1987, the Hampshire president Wilfred Weld, the vice-chairman Bill Hughes and I made plans that would change Hampshire cricket forever. The old ground at Northlands Road was small and dilapidated. There was no space to expand and no sense in patching the place up. Let's build a new one, I said. Early the next morning, after our long and enthusiastic dinner conversation about the potential of such a project, Bill, who was a surveyor, rang my room to say he had drawn up some plans.

Initially, it was as straightforward as finding a new site and getting a good price from developers for Northlands Road, which was in a prime residential location. This all went well enough until the developers ripped us off and the club ran out of money. Rod Bransgrove, a true fan of the team and a successful businessman, saved Hampshire County Cricket Club from ruin with his own money. He was neither fuelling his ego nor searching for reward, as bitterly suggested by a prominent figure at the ECB. He did so for love. Rod took over the club in 1999 and remains chairman to this day. The 'new' ground at West End, a few miles outside Southampton, is finally complete a mere 27 years after its conception. It is magnificent.

The only sadness is that Wilfrid died early in 2016. His great heart, his humour and his unwavering devotion to the club will be greatly missed. Bill smiles on, the embodiment of Hampshire cricket at all levels and for all ages.

I was very involved in the early stages of the project, hosting lunches and dinners, pitching to investors and sponsors, and driving a series of crucial meetings with Lord MacLaurin, then chairman of the ECB, to ensure the new ground received international status. I made a short three-dimensional graphic film that we used for promotional events and even wrote a marketing paper that included a new constitution for the club based around the model of a Southampton city franchise. Such ideas are all the rage now.

More generally, I 'sold the dream'. I relate this to illustrate just how embedded in Hampshire cricket I had become. In 1995, alongside the Judge and Shaun Udal, I dug the first sod of earth at the site on which the ground sits so impressively today. I retired from first-class cricket four months later. At that dinner in Leeds in 1987, we had discussed the size of the boundaries because I envisaged setting fields for Udal that brought him wickets with catches in the deep rather than the dispiriting mis-hits for six that were so prevalent at Northlands Road. As it happened, I was six years out of the game by the time Hampshire played first-class cricket there.

Rod moved the business model from a members' club to a limited company. I was on the board for a couple of years but stood down once I began to spend almost half the year in Australia. Our dream was truly realised one balmy summer's evening in 2005 when England thumped Australia in a T20 match before a full house of 18,000 people at the Rose Bowl. It wasn't the first international match on the ground but it was surely the most memorable. Since then, England has beaten India in a Test match at the Ageas Bowl—rechristened courtesy of a loyal and important sponsor—T20 finals day has drawn fans of the game from far and wide and Hampshire has won many a nailbiter in front of the television cameras. Members have space to stroll around the outer and appreciate the cricket from many different angles, while the facilities offer all that is expected of a modern sporting venue.

When we set out on the journey we wanted a contemporary cricket ground, not a modern sports 'stadium'. The great legacy of Hampshire cricket can live comfortably in this new arena, nestled as it is in the green hillside that looks directly back over the Hampshire Downs. Even the access for spectators has improved. Long queues and some crowd rage have haunted the club's executive from the moment the Eastleigh Borough Council withdrew its plan for an ancillary junction of the motorway that would service the ground and the local community. Nowadays, the council is a shareholder in the business, so perhaps we can persuade its officers to reconsider.

My part in the story of the Ageas Bowl was substantial enough and I am proud of it. It has become a popular place, especially with the players who visit from around the country and from all over the world. There are stands named after Colin Ingleby-Mackenzie, the club's most irresistible personality, and Shane Warne, one of the two greatest cricketers to have represented the county. Malcolm Marshall is the other. As for Rod? Well, the pavilion honours his name, which is a fair reflection of the many miles he has travelled for the benefit of the club.

I had eighteen years within the heart of Hampshire cricket, almost twelve of them as captain. Come rain or shine, I gave it all I had. I look back with fondness and pride on the cricket we played, the people we produced, the manner in which we conducted ourselves (with the odd exception) and the prizes that were won. I think I can safely call it a love affair.

CHAPTER 5

The Smiths

This is the story of a beautiful family that lived vicariously through the achievements of its two sons, Christopher and Robin. For better or worse, cricket has written the storyboard of their life from 1980 to the present day.

We first met Robin Smith at the county ground in Southampton in 1981. He was seventeen years old and already something of a prodigy. At the age of twelve, he had featured as the model in Barry Richards' coaching book and then went on to beat Richards' record for runs in a season of Durban club cricket. They called him the Judge because of his hairstyle— sort of crinkled and cut tight to his scalp, like a judge's wig. His shyness disguised a wonderful sense of fun and an entertaining ability to mimic other cricketers and famous folk, most especially Archbishop Desmond Tutu. His modesty could not disguise his talents.

The Smith family lived comfortably in La Lucia, an attractive suburb fifteen minutes from the centre of Durban. The father, John, ran a thriving leather business. The mother, Joy, taught dance. Robin's elder brother, Chris, was a good cricketer already forging a career with both Natal in the Currie

Cup and Hampshire in the County Championship. Chris—or Kippy as we knew him because when a toddler he couldn't pronounce Chris and used his own interpretation—and I were close friends. Robin hung out with us a bit but had his own circle and, boy, could they party.

John Smith doted on Robin—we all did, really—and was determined that the gift of batsmanship given to his youngest son should not go to waste. Each morning at 5.30, John would wake the Judge with a cup of tea and then drive him to the nets, where a family friend and former Natal batsmen, Grayson Heath, taught him the finer points of batting and rehearsed them in forensic detail.

Frequently, Robin would have a night on the tiles and sneak in through the garden doors to leap into bed fully clothed, pulling the sheets to his chin just seconds before John appeared with the tea. 'Good morning, my boy!' And Robin would act out a yawn, rub his tired eyes and grunt, 'Morning, Dad,' before curling back under the sheets. Once John had disappeared Robin would slug back the tea, jump into the shower, switch from nightclub finery into training gear and emerge into the morning sunlight with John none the wiser. John never did work out why his boy invariably needed a siesta. Then again, perhaps he knew full well.

South African cricket was immensely strong in the 1970s and 1980s. At all levels, the game was enthusiastically played in a tough and fair-minded way. Provincial cricket was blessed with talent and commitment. The Natal team was led by Mike Procter and included a collection of players who fed off Procter's charismatic performances. Both on and off the field, they went hard. At the end of the first day of the first match in which the sixteen-year-old Robin Smith was made 12th man, he changed out of his whites and into best bib and tucker—blazer, slacks, white shirt and Natal tie. The team was strewn around the dressing room, soaked in sweat after a long and humid day in the field. Smith made to leave, eager not to over-stay his welcome or, indeed, to keep his mother waiting in the car park to take him home.

'Where do you think you're going, youngster?' said Procter.

'Er, to meet my mum, Mr Procter.'

'Not yet, you're not. Get that jacket and tie off, go down to the bar and order 60 cane and Cokes.' (Cane is a favourite South African spirit.)

'Sixty?!' exclaimed the sixteen-year-old.

'Yup, there's eleven of us and you and we're having five each.'

From that moment on, the Judge was one of the lads. Procter, the best of men and most outrageously brilliant of all-round cricketers, took to Smith. Soon he had him in the team and, unsurprisingly, the boy ate from his master's hand.

South Africa's ban from the global game—which had come in 1970 because of the government's apartheid policy and was to last until 1991—meant that the Currie Cup was the only stage for these richly talented cricketers. Provincial matches were as much about the need for self-expression as a simple and youthful desire to play the game they loved. Some—most notably Richards, Procter, Eddie Barlow and Clive Rice—had a career with counties in England. A few others—Garth Le Roux included—had also been a part of Kerry Packer's WSC.

Matches against Transvaal were war. Rice, Ray Jennings and Alan Kourie let the younger Smith have it with every weapon at their disposal. The games against Western Province were hardly less intense. Le Roux bowled fast and aggressively, Stephen Jefferies swung the ball at pace and Denys Hobson ripped his leg spinners. The quality and approach of these opponents gave Robin a foundation for the challenges he was later to face against the West Indies, India and Australia.

Joy's parents were Scottish. John's family was out of Walsall, near Birmingham. Therefore, the boys qualified to play for

England. Tony Greig had gone down this road successfully; Allan Lamb was in the process of doing the same. Chris was keen to make a living from the game, and county cricket was the place to do just that. As luck would have it, he made a hundred for the Glamorgan 2nd XI, with whom he was having a trial match or two, against the Hampshire 2nd XI at Bournemouth in 1979. I bowled some of my Procter impersonations at him but, given he had the real thing to contend with in the nets back home, he didn't appear much bothered. The Hampshire coach liked the look of him and nipped in with the offer of a contract, which Chris quickly signed.

This was a profound moment for Hampshire cricket and a masterstroke by Peter Sainsbury (not that he knew it at the time), because Robin followed suit a year later. Hampshire was perfect for the Smith brothers, who had grown up with almost daily reports and pictures of Barry Richards in the club's colours on the back pages of the South African papers.

The boys were a terrific addition to our number: engaging and enjoyable, if jaw-droppingly naive about life outside the walls of South Africa's residential palaces. Chris asked us what sort of trees spaghetti grew from and left the plug in both basin and bath. Robin panicked when he travelled to Cardiff for the first time in Chris's car. A mile before the Severn Bridge, Chris produced his passport and told his brother to do the same. The Judge went pale. Chris hid him in the boot and let him out at Newport. They were a breath of the freshest air and this natural, positive energy gave us all hope at a time when the club was languishing near the bottom of the county cricket heap.

Chris made an instant impact, with a work ethic previously unseen among lazy young English pros. He spent hours in the nets, perfecting a defensive technique that was the basis of the many hours he spent at the wicket. There was something of

Geoffrey Boycott about his single-minded pursuit of runs, if precious little about Geoffrey after hours.

In the off-season, they returned home to play in the Currie Cup. The scene in South Africa was changing. Rebel tours, brilliantly conceived and executed by Ali Bacher—who had captained the last South African side before the ban took hold and then became chief executive of the South African Cricket Board—were the centre of everyone's attention because they brought overseas teams to the Republic for the first time since 1970. (Notwithstanding an International Wanderers side that had toured in 1976, with Dennis Lillee making a marked impression upon the South African audiences starved of international cricket.)

First, in 1981–82, Graham Gooch captained an England side that broke ranks with the TCCB to earn some decent money and mercenary status. Then came a substandard Sri Lankan team before two West Indian teams in consecutive years, both led by Lawrence Rowe. After that, Kim Hughes took a group of Australians, all of them taken aback by the strength of South African cricket through the 1985–86 and 1986–87 seasons. In 1990, Mike Gatting led another English side, the last unofficial group to tour a country that was on the brink of political revolution. The tours had helped to maintain high standards in South African cricket and offered players the chance to wear Springbok colours but they barely compensated such magnificent cricketers as Rice and Le Roux, Jimmy Cook, Peter Kirsten, Kevin McKenzie, Kenny McEwan and Vintcent van der Bijl for the loss of a Test career.

Procter had played seven Tests in two home series against Australia before the ICC voted to outlaw South Africa. Barry Richards had played four against the Australians in 1970 and Graeme Pollock, arguably the greatest player of the three, had thrilled audiences in 23 Tests against England, Australia and New Zealand. A team that included these three cricketers and any number of the above from the talented pool in the Currie Cup would have given the full West Indian side a run for its money.

All of which meant that the Smith brothers had a choice to make, one that changed the course of the family's life in a way they could never have imagined: stay home and be limited to provincial cricket and the hope of the odd rebel touring team to set the juices running, or change allegiance and relocate to England. They went for the second option, as many of their teammates would have done had they too possessed British passports.

Even with a British passport, players who were not born in England had to complete a four-year qualification period. Allan Lamb had done just that and, after four dynamic seasons with Northamptonshire, was picked to play for England at home to India in 1982. Meanwhile, Chris was making mountains of runs for Hampshire in an exhibition of what could be achieved if the mind was properly tuned to the matter. He was a lesson to us all. If only we had taken more notice.

Meanwhile, Robin was having an outrageously good time in county second-eleven cricket where he slaughtered feeble attacks and burnt the candle at both ends with great relish. I have often wondered if this period of relative cricket inertia tempered the natural development of his game. The brothers continued to play for Natal in the English winter, a rhythm that was disturbed in late 1983 by Chris's selection to tour New Zealand with England.

This was a remarkable achievement. The plan had been for Robin to play for England, not Chris. But with the straightest bat and a weight of runs, the elder brother had prised open the door at a time when few had barely turned the handle. Gooch was banned by the TCCB for his adventure in South Africa and turned instead to a contract with Western Province in the Currie Cup. Boycott was winding down. The other candidates could not match the senior Smith's consistency.

Back in Durban during that English winter, in the garden at La Lucia, Robin was beating balls. John had installed a bowling machine and, hour upon hour, the garden boy was required to load up, fire balls at the Judge, see them scorched across the Durban turf, pick them up and start over. At midday, Robin would change into training gear, run for 40 minutes or so around the suburban streets ('Run in the heat of the day, my boy,' John would say, 'to prepare for long innings in hot climates'), return home to jump in the pool, swim lengths, tuck into one of Joy's splendid salads, have a kip and then head for organised practice with Greyville-Northlands or Natal in the late afternoon.

Frequently, Paul Terry and I would join him in this routine. Paul and I arrived at Hampshire at pretty much the same time and our careers had followed similar paths. The clear differences were his greater ball sense and athleticism, and my greater confidence and natural timing. Paul had a fine cricket brain but little inclination to force it upon people. He could bat all right, but didn't always appear to believe it himself. Paul was as introverted as I was outgoing.

In a wonderful triumph for the Brat Pack of 1977, Paul was to open the batting for England against West Indies in the summer of 1984. His selection came on the back of a good county season but, specifically, an innings of 102 at the Oval against Sylvester Clarke. His linear approach and fine back-foot play impressed the chairman of selectors, Peter May, and his predecessor, Alec Bedser, who had watched it together.

In 1984, a Test against the West Indies was the toughest ask in sport. Paul survived the first one at Headingley with modest returns and, depressingly for us all, had his arm broken by

Winston Davis in the second at Old Trafford. His international career was over almost before it had begun. The pictures of him in a plaster cast, batting one-handed to see Lamb to a hundred and eke out a few more runs towards England's total, are all that remain of so much early promise.

My own career was stuttering along: good periods and bad, the gulfs between them quite ridiculous. Heath, a marvellous man, generously spent time with us visitors too. He pushed me to establish a more consistent method based on sharper footwork, a skill I found difficult. Later in my career, I learnt to stay still for longer and to base my batting on the position of my head.

Joy and John were immensely kind to us and to the other English cricketers who migrated to Durban during those winters long ago. Their unflinching loyalty and friendship are one of the sweetest memories of my time in the game. John cleared our path in the pursuit of runs, wickets and catches. Joy soothed our fragile egos. Their boys had charm and a common touch that made them widely popular and often emulated.

While Chris was away, we spent more time with Robin, both practising and partying. This was not for the faint-hearted. As the sun went down, the beer flowed. Come the witching hour, we found ourselves at the Beverly Hills Hotel, Father's Moustache or Raffles, admiring the beauties that were drawn to him. Eventually, we would disappear—self-esteem crushed and pockets empty—leaving the Judge to his girls, his mates and to the small hours before that dash home to beat John's early morning call.

Which brings us to an interesting aspect of the brothers' development. These dawn-patrol coaching sessions fashioned a style of play and, from it, came an almost robotic mindset. Though Heath was a fine coach and a delightful man, he was driven by surprisingly inflexible thinking. An example of this was the requirement at every opportunity for batsmen to get forward. Thus, Robin honed a big stride towards even the fastest bowlers. In the main, this served him well but on occasion it led to bombardments that more nimble footwork might have avoided. He was famously brave against the quicks and, in general, highly effective but had he been able to resist the temptation to come forward as a matter of course, he might have developed a wider range of response and a more delicate touch. In turn, this would have improved his play against spin, which was compromised by that big front-foot move and the hard hands that were its result. This may seem picky about a man who averaged 43 at Test-match level, but hear me out.

Heath had a formula: $A + H = C$ which meant Arrogance plus Humility equals Confidence. Robin did not have the arrogance, nor did he need the humility. Paul was the same. Chris had it and, I was often reminded, so did I. Yet Chris and I were the least talented of the four of us. Chris filtered the methods offered by Heath and applied much of his own thinking to a career that surpassed expectation.

It is what you do with talent that counts. Robin was led to believe that practice and training—the 10,000-hours theory— led to success. Heath's drills and disciplines were valuable during development but less essential in the long term, as the requirements of batting evolved on different pitches and in different circumstances around the world. Heath provided grounding and consistency but, by definition, he imposed limits. The more Robin analysed and was analysed, the more he retreated. The more he knew, the more he feared. As he grew from boy to man, the key to teaching Robin was to encourage him to let go.

I was at the crease in the 1988 Benson & Hedges Cup Final when Chris got out and Robin replaced him. We were chasing Derbyshire's low total and he asked how best to go about it against Michael Holding, Devon Malcolm, Ole Mortensen and Alan 'Jack' Warner. I said, 'Show off.' He made 38 from 27 balls, sparkling with a series of back-foot drives and cuts before a freak catch on the boundary by Steven Goldsmith ended the fun. On commentary, Benaud said, 'The game needed an innings like that.' Within a fortnight, Robin was picked to play for England against the West Indies.

Lamb was at the non-striker's end when his South African mate took guard for England at Headingley against Malcolm Marshall. The Judge went through the calisthenics and then the sprints on the spot that became a signature of each of his innings. Obviously tense, he was about to settle into his stance when Lamb called for him. 'Hey, Judgey, Judgey, come here, my china. Can you see Kath [his wife]? Look, Judgey, she's there in the wives' area in the middle of the stand next to the pavilion. See her? . . . Jeeesus, she's twitching with excitement and completely flushed in the face. See how you do it for her, Judgey . . . Fuck knows what she'll do next!' Judge roared with laughter, relaxed his shoulders and arms and worked Marshall off the stumps for a couple of runs through mid wicket. He was away. Good job, Lamby.

I have long thought that the flaw in Robin is that he listens willingly but does not always hear. By the time his Test career ended prematurely in 1996, he was a marginally less good version of exactly the same batsman Lamb met in the middle at Headingley in 1988. Most cricketers change. The nature of the hurdles they face, the opponents who study them and the march of time demand that technique, method and approach become subject to rethinks. Robin had stayed pretty much the same, if understandably scarred by the years of battle. At his best, he was exceptional, but he had fewer gears than others less gifted. This was the reason the England selectors, who could not possibly have understood his complex character and the upbringing that came with it, were to mess him about in the latter half of his career.

Let's go back to 1981. Robin was immensely strong. The Hampshire coach, Peter Sainsbury, banned him from hitting sixes in practice because we were running out of balls. He rained these hits into back gardens almost a hundred yards away, where increasingly furious residents refused to return the Dukes and Readers they found in their flowerbeds.

This was a kid whose life had been bathed in sport. He was a rugby centre with pace and power, a record-breaking schoolboy sprinter and a batsman with the world at his feet. He was loyal, self-effacing and bloody good value. He hung on the words of his elders and especially loved his old man's eccentricities.

Once, with moments remaining in a school rugby match, Robin received the ball on the halfway line and began a memorable surge, riding tackles and handing off all comers along the way. When he reached the final 25 he was close to the touchline and somewhat surprised to see John sprinting alongside him. 'Go, my boy, go!' screamed John Smith as startled parents hurriedly cleared a path. When Robin threw himself over the line to secure the brilliant winning try for his team, John went with him, flying through the air in his trademark white shorts, white short-sleeved shirt and tweed cap, landing on top of his son in a moment of unparalleled madness.

And so it was, in the privileged environment of African servants, bowling machines loaded by gardeners, private coaches, myriad friends, gorgeous girls and great swathes of love and attention from his delightful parents, that Robin Arnold Smith grew up.

He made his first-class debut on New Year's Day, 1981, in the B section of the Currie Cup, and first played for Natal in 1982 alongside the incomparable Procter, who had made his own first-class debut in 1965. Robin's career finished in 2003 alongside James Tomlinson and James Adams, who are still playing for Hampshire today. That is one hell of a wingspan. During this time, he played some innings that were out of this world. His hundred against West Indies at Lord's is a popular video on YouTube. Another against Australia in Manchester was considered near perfect by Richie Benaud. For all his trials against spin, he made 128 in Colombo against Sri Lanka in 1993 and averaged 63.37 in six Tests against India.

The steel with which Robin applied himself to the game occasionally manifested itself in surprisingly opinionated responses for one so apologetically polite and courteous. Over a weekend before a Test against Sri Lanka, Hampshire played the tourists in a three-day match at Southampton. Unnecessarily, I told him to field at silly point on the off side to Ranjan Madugalle, who was thrashing Raj Maru's gentle left-arm spinners around Northlands Road. Robin said he'd rather not, given he had a slightly more important event to come for England on Thursday at Lord's. I said, 'Hampshire pay your wages, pal, you'll field where you're damn well told.' To which he replied, 'Who's your fucking pal, pal?' Game, set, match to the Judge.

His Test average of 43.67 includes nine hundreds in 62 matches. Robin was a stellar attraction, playing the game in a way that appealed to audiences worldwide. He was a brilliant one-day cricketer too. In the summer of 1993, he scored a breathtaking unbeaten 167 against the Australians in a one-day international at Edgbaston, a match England duly lost. He was used to that. He once made 155 not out for Hampshire against Glamorgan in the Benson & Hedges Cup and lost that game too. There were some muppets alongside him in those days.

Many of his innings for Hampshire stand out, but the two I would pick if pushed were both played in one-day cricket.

Against a good attack on a poor pitch at Worcester, in the quarterfinal of the 1988 Benson & Hedges Cup, his unbeaten 87 saw us home by 3 wickets. In the final of the 1991 NatWest Trophy at Lord's, his 78—run out, if you don't mind—did much the same. One off drive from Waqar Younis who, as the light was fading, cranked it up in an attempt to win Surrey the game, was truly the stuff of a champion.

In the opening home championship match of the 1990 season against Sussex, Robin put on 256 with David Gower, who was playing his first game for the club. They dovetailed perfectly, finding a synergy that delighted the healthy crowd. It was as if the clock had been wound back to the days of Richards and Greenidge—one elegant and easy, the other at first flexing muscle and stretching sinew before finding an unlikely lightness of being. Freed by the hints of bonhomie that characterised Gower's play, Robin made 181 alongside David's 145. For an all too brief period, these two wonderful cricketers floated on the same cloud.

From that first day we saw Robin, it was clear that he intimidated bowlers. He drove the ball supremely well either side of the wicket and cut the thing as if he were a boxer delivering a knockout punch. He could pull and glance and sometimes sweep. His unerring and imposing ability to punish the bad ball was pre-eminent in the English game. He rarely gave his wicket away and, while he was at the crease, any team for which he played had a better than even chance of success. I am certain he won more of the big points for Hampshire than anyone else, including Richards and Greenidge.

As a young man, he thrashed the fast bowlers into the bleachers and frequently launched all but the best spinners into space. Age and inevitable disappointment led to the retreat into self-doubt that affects sportsmen who know too much about failure. Having said as much, the opposition celebrated his wicket with transparent relief and joy to the very end. Hugely popular and much admired, there was not a man you would rather have on your side, in the trenches or at the bar. He had time for everyone—to his cost, actually—and everyone had time for him. I believe him to be Hampshire's greatest ever cricketer and strongly believe that a Robin Smith Stand should honour his name.

At this point of the Robin Smith story, you would not think much could go wrong. But it did.

Wind the clock forward to January 2011 and the living room of a barely furnished apartment in Perth. It was there that the same Robin Smith was found on the floor, curled up and contemplating suicide. This gentle and beautiful man had been dragged into an abyss of alcohol and antidepressants. His life, once secure and bright, was suddenly dark and uncertain.

This story is not as unusual as we might hope. Professional cricket provides a mainly secure life, 24/7. The modern-day professional has his path cleared by numerous support staff, but it was pretty cushy back in the 1980s too. Expenses covered the daily cost of life. Salaries provided enough to pay the bills. There was no financial incentive to a career in cricket, only the burn of ambition and the joy in fulfilment. The family of sport ensured friendship and a common theme. Together you ate every meal, practised, travelled and played before waking up to the morning's alarm and doing it all again. Back then, you shared a hotel room with a teammate too.

It is a career that takes the best years of your life, often for little reward. At some point in your 30s, 40 if you are lucky, you are all washed up. Alone and frightened, you face a world about which you know next to nothing. You bat, bowl or keep wickets—and for this you are paid a livable wage and often applauded—but god knows, the game offers you little comfort for the next phase in your life.

It is a worryingly well-trodden path: alone, often lonely, frightened. Such trauma leads to a diminished self-worth. There may be a wife to cherish and kids to feed but the pub provides respite. No job. Too soon, no money. Then comes the self-absorption and the retreat. The family notices your moods. So it's back to the pub. Then the embarrassment, the hiding, depression, sometimes the drugs. Often the alcohol. Sometimes divorce. Alone, frightened. To the bookie, or the tables. Then debt.

It is upon exactly this that the professional cricketers' associations and the benevolent funds spend most of their time. Call it after-care, because ex-pros need help. Not all of them, not by any means. But it is no coincidence that approximately 140 cricketers of first-class standing have committed suicide.

Back to Chris for a moment. He played eight Tests for England, four of them against Richard Hadlee, between midsummer 1983 and spring 1984. He did all right but not well enough to merit a crack at the West Indies in 1984, about which he was mighty relieved. Kippy loved most bowlers, though not the really fast ones, who tested his nerve and reaction more than he had planned when he came into the job. Hadlee was just about manageable. Holding, Marshall, Garner and Walsh, en masse, were not. He wasn't scared, just practical about his chances. Chris Broad, Tim Robinson and Graeme Fowler went past him in the affections of the selectors. Gooch was soon to return from the ban. Though neither knew it at the time, Chris Smith and Paul Terry had said goodbye to test cricket by their mid-twenties.

For the remaining five years of his county career, Chris went about his work with typical attention to detail and equally typical outcomes: runs, runs and more runs. He settled in England, married a lovely girl from Gloucestershire and flirted with business projects in the off-season. The sight each summer morning of Kippy and the Judge at the Northlands Road nets, facing up to the bowling machine lovingly loaded by their father was a staple of Hampshire cricket life. John would read out the notes he had taken during the Grayson Heath sessions in the late 1970s and early 1980s, and Robin—more than Chris, whose independence remained a virtue—would cross-check his game. Their bats would be pockmarked in black, a strange residue from the heavy yellow dimpled balls that were the brothers' fodder.

If Robin had a daily spring in his step, Chris had a weary, if rather amusing, plod. He played down his own gifts, giving the impression that he would really rather not be there. He once admitted to me that in all those runs was only a reflected glory, and that the physical and mental effort that went into producing them would lead to an early retirement.

He could be very funny. Briefly, having talked him into fielding at slip, we christened him the Claw, because he held on to eleven consecutive catches. Then he dropped an easy one and was so disgusted that he walked out of slip down to third man, where he stayed for the rest of his career. It was the oddest thing, given he had the strongest mind of us all: a mind smart enough to win cricket matches and numerous man-of-the-match medals. It was a mind that was already plotting the future.

In the latter part of the summer of 1991, he dropped the bomb. He was, he told us, retiring with immediate effect from professional cricket and emigrating to Perth, Australia, where he had been appointed commercial director at the Western Australia Cricket Association (WACA). Wow! We urged him to stay until the end of the season but he buggered off all the same, leaving us an opening batsman short for the NatWest Trophy Final at Lord's. No worries in the end: Tony Middleton stepped up from the 2nd XI, made 78 and we beat Surrey in a thriller— the game where Robin won the bout against Waqar Younis.

With Chris kicking on Down Under, his brother began to visit Perth more often. He had spent a couple of winters playing for the Claremont-Nedlands and South Perth clubs in the mid-1980s after parting company with Natal. Needless to say, he broke the record for the number of runs scored in a season for South Perth in 1987–88, just as he had broken Richards' record in Durban all those years ago. Nice habit.

By the late 1990s, Chris had become chief executive at the WACA. It is some story: a South African who played for England running a leading Australian state association without a jot of previous experience. Then, when he moved on from the WACA, he set up his own embroidery business, working around the clock to make a handsome return. It is impossible not to admire the sheer resilience and ambition of this savvy and driven man.

After Paul retired from professional cricket in 1996, he too followed the exodus, playing and coaching at Melville Cricket Club, where he was popular and respected. Paul's family have settled well in Perth and the kids, both in their twenties, have Australian accents. I marvel at the sheer guts of such a move. For a while, he ran a cricket academy for aspiring English county cricketers, but the well ran dry and, in search for work, he took on coaching positions at Hampshire and, more recently, in Bangladesh.

I hardly need tell you that Robin took his family to Perth too, though not without a dip at an afterlife in England, where he was happy in a little village to the west of Southampton as you head for the New Forest. Friends invested in Chase, his cricket bat and equipment company, and Masuri, the cricket helmet brand for which he held the franchise. The raw truth, however, is that Chris was the businessman. Robin left England in a hurry in 2008, taking Kathy and two children, Margaux and Harrison, with him. Rumour had it there were unpaid bills. They are paid now.

Throughout these upheavals, Joy and John were thrown from pillar to post. They owned a flat in Southampton and spent increasing amounts of time away from Durban. John cashed in the leather business, only to see the South African rand weaken against both the sterling and the Australian dollar. They eventually sold up in both Durban and Southampton before setting sail for Perth, where they are content to be alongside the boys and the grandchildren. Having said that, they must look back wistfully. Their journey from La Lucia, with a couple of acres, a pool, a jacuzzi, a dance studio, a fine garden, a cricket net and all the trappings of a white man's life in Southern Africa, to a one-bedder in South Perth—via a two-bedder in Southampton—almost beggars belief.

By the time Robin hit rock bottom, I was in Sydney for part of the year, working for Channel Nine. Two decades on, the four boys whose lives had collided at Hampshire County Cricket Club in 1981 found themselves entrenched in the Australian way of life.

Three of us were fine. We didn't know that one was not. Robin was on the booze. He had always loved a drink and at the close of each day's play, the social hub of friend and foe gathered around him. It was in him to take this to a dangerous limit but, overall, he handled his taste for a beer pretty well. His marriage was a different thing. It was in trouble.

His brother did what he could to help but Robin was beyond help. He hid, ashamed. He pined for the Hampshire dressing room. He ached for the crossing of that white line. For the raising of the bat. For the applause. He hurt for the loss of friendships and a lifestyle that had sustained him over 22 happy and celebrated years. There was more booze and there were more issues at home. Then there were problems with the Masuri business that he had brought with him to Australia.

The antidepressants controlled his life. He was free-wheeling to oblivion. Former teammates and colleagues tired of his excesses and feared for his sanity. Phone calls bounced around the ether. The news was that the Judge was struggling for air. Just occasionally, that wonderful and precious smile could be activated but mainly by alcohol. The fact was that a beautiful and much-loved man had become a shadow.

Barry Richards, who had been looking for an investment property in Perth and heard Robin was in need of accommodation, bought a place into which Robin moved. But Robin couldn't do this alone. So he sank further into the darkness. Which is why, one day, he was found curled up in a corner, shivering and thinking the worst. It is a lesson to us all and to the game, which owes pastoral care to those who have graced it. Thankfully the game has come to understand this. Depression of any sort is no longer taboo.

It was Chris, and his commendably patient and delightful wife Julie, who stuck with it and saved Robin. They cleared out the guest cottage at the back of their own property and moved him into the sanctuary of a home. They found common ground on the issue of drink. Robin was not allowed any. Chris gave his younger brother a full-time position at the embroidery factory and took on the Masuri franchise. Indeed, there were olive branches for Robin at every turn. Chris was worried but Chris was kind. On occasion, tough love replaced brotherly love, but blood was proving thicker than water. The plan began to work.

I remember a dinner there one night, only a few years ago. Just the four of us—the Smiths, Paul and me—at Kippy's Australian home, where the Judge lodged. We bounced off each other much as we used to do—old jokes, in-jokes and bad jokes. Kips told the Cardiff passport story again—imagine how many times!—and we doubled up as one brother took unmerciful piss out of the other. We recalled good and not-so-good innings and matches, and rejoiced in our luck to have had such a life.

Robin drank Coca-Cola and we knocked back the wine. He did some of those old impressions and we laughed some more. We slagged off the players of our era we didn't rate and drifted into misty-eyed memory of the great Malcolm Marshall, and of Cardigan Connor and Tim Tremlett. Over a decade, give or take, we were the very core of Hampshire cricket. Chris said there were more than 100,000 runs for Hampshire between us (101,746 to be precise), so the club should be bloody grateful!

Marshall was greatly fond of the Smith boys. He liked their appetite for both life and runs and found fun in their dry humour, occasional madness and strange idiosyncrasies. One night in Leicester before a Sunday League game at Grace Road, Robin and Malcolm were sharing a drink at the hotel bar. Three fellows interrupted them, ostensibly for an autograph, but were soon taunting Maco for the colour of his skin. In search of peace, Robin and Malcolm left the hotel for some food, only to find these same blokes following them to the restaurant. Same story: racial taunting. Robin threatened to put an end to this nonsense with a blow to the snout but they sneered at his bravado. Maco urged Robin to leave it and for them to head back to their hotel rooms. The lads followed them back, goading and abusing, and by the time they returned to the hotel lobby, Robin had had enough. He warned the main culprit one more time, but to no avail, before letting fly with his right fist. The man hit the deck like a sack of shit. The other two recoiled in shock and pulled their mate from the fray before hurrying from the hotel.

The rest of us knew nothing of this. Even Maco wasn't fully aware of the collateral damage. During fielding practice,

I noticed Robin drop a couple of skiers. Most unusual. Kippy said I should talk to him away from the others. Robin showed me his right thumb, which was badly swollen and bruised—I could see immediately that it was broken. He told me the story of the night before and we agreed he could not play in the match. By a strange twist of fate, Kips was 12th man after a poor run of form. He replaced his brother in the side and made a crucial unbeaten 54. We won the match by 5 runs.

There was a price to pay on two counts. Robin was out of cricket for a month and the Hampshire committee wanted to know why. Upon hearing the story, they urged disciplinary action, which I forcefully resisted. Of course, we didn't want punch-ups in hotels. Equally, I admired Robin for the way he stuck close to his mate and took action on his behalf. His nature was gentle and not remotely confrontational, therefore I was sure such a reaction had been severely provoked. Maco, the sole witness, agreed with me. I backed his judgement unconditionally and told the committee that if action were taken against Robin it would be without my support. Thankfully, we heard nothing more of it.

Judge remembered the night well and, in particular, his excruciating sense of embarrassment. Over dinner, he told us that he knew he should have a) woken me up with the news and b) gone to hospital for an X-ray. But he'd had the stomach for neither. He thought the rest of us would be angry with him but I was more taken aback than anything. I'd have been more pissed off if he had woken me up. On the morning of the game I felt I had to be careful not to lose my own focus, so I made a quick decision about selection and moved on. Privately, I was proud of him.

In many more ways than were obviously apparent, the four of us, and Maco, set the tone and standard of a good club that fulfilled some, though certainly not all, of the promise that was evident from the day we met. Now we sat over dinner, 30 years and some 12,000 miles away from Southampton, crystallising our past in a happy few hours together.

After almost a year, Robin moved out of his brother's place and in with his folks. He sleeps there on a sofa bed to this day. He looks after his mum and has become closer than ever to his dad. He has fallen in love with Karen, a gorgeous and spiritual girl who lives in the flat above. She has three children in a small two-bed space. They live a simple life and are devoted to one another.

There was a hiccup in September 2015, when Robin drifted back towards an uglier self, but he has ridden out the storm. Chris was furious and cut back his brother's responsibility at work. Karen said simply, 'I can live with a drunk but not a drunk and three kids. The choice is yours.' For him, there was no choice. For a year now he has looked well and fit, if a tad too thin and greyer on top than most men his age. He is off the turps and the old smile still sparkles. My affection for him burns as brightly now as it did 30 years ago.

He called recently to say he had some coaching work and was planning to become less dependent on Kippy. He called again to say the coaching work had doubled in the last few months and that his old club, Claremont-Nedlands, had hired him to work with the juniors. Lucky them. He added that he had bought an apartment for the children in the same block as him and the folks. I could have cried.

He sounds alive. A good mind is ticking over in a way it may never have done previously. No one gave him much credit for his mind, just for his cricket and sense of fun. Maybe there is another man in there that we missed. He even did some television analyst work in Pakistan and it went down well.

I think Robin Arnold Smith has turned the corner. For the moment, we can say that a tragedy has been avoided. But there is something Shakespearean in the narrative. I both admire and love this family. I shall never desert Robin, whatever the provocation. He is a good man and I care for him in a way that is hard to explain adequately. I care for them all. Perhaps, it is simply how a captain cares for those who follow him over many long summers. Cricket both shaped and determined the first part of Robin's life, during which he was at once fearless and fragile. Now he faces the challenge of the second part. Cricket changed the life of all of his family. I wonder if they still see it as a beautiful game. I think so.

PART 2

Thinking about the game

In the dressing room at Hampshire—on the verge
of retirement and looking to the future.

CHAPTER 6

The art of batting

Batting is frequently difficult and frustrating but even the most prosaic of batsmen can give pleasure with a moment of brilliance. It is mainly an instinctive skill and yet relies on method for its excellence.

Nothing, not even ballet, could be more graceful than a cover drive by David Gower or an on drive by V.V.S. Laxman. Batting pleases the eye because it is a thing of straight lines that are subject to angles and dimensions. Each innings is an interpretation.

Above all, batting is fragile. One minute you have it, the next it is gone. A single ball will undo hours, days, weeks of preparation. For sure, batting—cricket, indeed—is not to be trusted. It is played out on the edge of nerves. It examines character, explores personality and exposes vulnerabilities. A batsman scores a hundred one day and nought the next. This is wicked, it is unkind, but it is tempting and it is exhilarating. Raise your bat once and you will ache to do so again.

The art of batting is a beautiful journey with a beautiful result. This beauty holds its place in our heart even at a time when all roads point to change. It is why there is an immense responsibility as we search to modernise a game that has its roots in the past. After all, it is those roots that define cricket.

TECHNIQUE

I once asked Barry Richards how it was that he unfailingly played forward when the ball was pitched up and back when it was short. Most of us see a blur a couple of yards away and do our best. He looked at me almost sympathetically. 'It's all about watching the ball in the hand and then from the hand. If it's released here [marginally behind the bowler's head, he demonstrated], it will be pitched up, so you can start thinking of transferring your weight forward. If it's released here [marginally in front of the bowler's head], you can reckon on playing back. Somewhere in the middle is a good length.' Blimey.

Finding this hard to comprehend, I approached Sir Garry Sobers at a cocktail party in Barbados. I told him of the conversation but did not mention with whom. 'Yes, exactly right,' said Sobers. 'How else do you pick up length?' How else indeed. Then he asked who it was I had spoken to. When I answered Barry, his face lit up. 'That man could really bat,' he said. The great journalist and broadcaster Tony Cozier was with us and we whiled away the evening with rum and talk of great players and teams. It was hard to imagine anyone beating the best of Barbados: Greenidge, Desmond Haynes or Conrad Hunte, the three Ws—Clyde Walcott, Everton Weekes and Frank Worrell—Sobers, Seymour Nurse perhaps, Marshall, Joel Garner, Wes Hall and one of Charlie Griffith, Wayne Daniel or Sylvester Clarke. The Transvaal side of the early 1980s would have given them a good game, along with a New South Wales team or two. Sir Garry wanted a punt on his own blokes.

When Gower came to Hampshire, I told him about my question to Richards and Sobers. He said that after a rough time against Dennis Lillee, he approached Greg Chappell for some advice. Chappell told him he was playing the wrong half of the ball. 'Dennis is running it across you, so you have to play the outside half of the ball. You're committed to the inside half.' Good grief. Gower said he understood it and responded with some better returns.

Justin Langer told Ian Chappell he was sick of getting hit by the short ball. Chappell told him to focus on the hand that had the ball in it and nothing else—in other words, not a general area but specifically the ball in the hand. 'You pretty much can't get hit if you do that: your eye and brain will work faster than the ball.' Langer was staggered at the improvement. I wish I'd asked Chappell the same question 40 years ago.

Most average batsmen watch an area and predict an outcome. Few actually follow the ball from hand to bat. It is such a common fault in batting that I am surprised it is a not a feature of coaching and subject to intense training of eye and mind.

The usual instruction is to move your feet but to do this you must pick up the length of the ball quickly. After a difficult season against fast bowling in 1987, I sought the advice of Jimmy Gray, who had played in Ingleby-Mackenzie's 1961 championship-winning side and had been recommended to me by Mike Gatting. He suggested I worry less about my feet than my head. To exaggerate this point, he tied my feet together and attached the rope to the side netting in the indoor school at Southampton. Two things happened: a) I stayed still— obviously—and timed the ball consistently well; and b) my head and eyes stayed level, which made it easier to hit the ball back from whence it came. It occurred to me that I was watching the ball more closely because I was less concerned about where my feet should go and more concerned about the ball. I backed eye and instinct and reacted accordingly. Gray noticed improved footwork, which I imagine came from my head being in the right place. The only difficult shot in this practice routine was the cover drive, so I ignored it for a while and soon found that I was leaving the ball alone outside off stump with more confidence. I spent the back end of a winter with Gray, working on these two aspects of batting, and played pretty well the following summer. I noticed that bowlers were forced to bowl straighter and that I could pick them off more easily. The law, I suppose, of unintended consequences.

Batting is a subjective skill and has changed considerably in the time I have been involved with the game. On uncovered pitches and before the introduction of helmets, the tendency was to play back. This allowed more time to judge the speed of the ball's arrival, especially if the pitch was wet, and more space to cope with uneven bounce. The clarion call on uncovered pitches was for 'soft hands', meaning a loose grip and a gentle method of letting the ball come to you before dropping it safely at your feet. If you study footage of Denis Compton against Keith Miller, for example, or of the Australians being bowled out by Jim Laker at Old Trafford in 1956, you will see back play almost exclusively. Just occasionally, a player emerged to buck the trend. Foremost among them was Tom Graveney, who was best known for his cover drive and much admired for his ability to hook and pull off the front foot.

We were taught a sideways-on game, both in stance and execution of strokes, but it always struck me as odd not to line up the ball with both eyes. Thus, I believe the ideal stance has the right eye (for right-handers and vice versa for left-handers) less closed off than in some coaching manuals and level with the left. This means that the head and shoulders will be a little more open than in a perceived classical stance. The hips should be on the same plane as the shoulders, approximately pointing at the non-striker. Then the knees should be flexed and the weight of the body on the balls of the feet. In the modern era, no one has proved the value of this set-up better than Sachin Tendulkar, though it looks as though Virat Kohli has taken a lot from him.

Tendulkar's longevity is testament to such detail in batting. Rarely, for example, did he fall over to the off side and play around his front pad. Occasionally, he was lbw playing across the line of the ball but that error came from judgement not technique. The set-up that allows the right eye to help pick up the ball clearly also gives the batsman a better feel for his off stump and the option to leave deliveries that target Geoffrey Boycott's famed 'corridor of uncertainty'. Importantly, this stance creates freedom for the straight drive, which is the best of all strokes because there is no fielder behind the stumps at the bowler's end.

Bradman set up this way and nobody picked length quicker than Bradman. Alec Bedser told me that he consciously over-pitched to The Don, because the speed of his footwork turned good-length balls into short balls that he pulled through mid wicket. This was the hardest stroke to defend against, added Bedser, because Bradman never seemed to miss his spot.

Greg Chappell, Viv Richards, Gordon Greenidge and Martin Crowe are further examples of such a set-up. Ian Chappell and Javed Miandad were a touch more open; Ted Dexter and Barry Richards a touch more closed. Sobers made sure his eyes were level and wasn't bothered about being opened up on the back foot. In fact, he came to advocate it but, then, Garry was a one-off. Sobers simplified the issue of footwork by going back to fast bowling and forward to spin. There is a fabulous picture of him facing Dennis Lillee during his brilliant 254 for the World XI at the Melbourne Cricket Ground in 1971–72. Lillee has let go of the ball and not a muscle in Sobers' body has moved. I guess you don't need a trigger movement if you already know where you are heading.

In his book *The Art of Cricket*, Bradman advocates a small movement back and across to trigger the muscles and mind.

This was the accepted norm among players in the era before the covering of pitches because it bought time to watch for and counter awkward bounce and allowed for more options against the short ball. Loading up on the back foot allows a natural move forward to drive, but the player must be careful not to have his weight stuck only on the back foot. The key is keep the body weight evenly spread, as it would be in the stance.

Many a fine batsman has used the forward press as his trigger, Greenidge among them. He preferred loading up on the front foot and then springing back to cut, pull and hook. He was also flexible enough to adapt his technique for pitches and opponents. Once, on a dangerously uneven surface at the Oval, he took on Sylvester Clarke almost exclusively from his back foot. This was the innings during which he swapped his helmet for a sun hat. 'To sharpen up,' he said.

Generally, batting requires a few non-negotiables and offers plenty of variables. Among the non-negotiables are a still head; high left elbow (we are still using a right-hander as the model); gun-barrel straight bat; body shape maintained throughout the hitting area; dominant left side of the body; and the left hand— the top hand—as the guiding force in both defence and attack.

The backlift is definitely a variable. Bradman, Boycott and Viv Richards all picked it up towards second slip and looped in back down the line. A surprising majority pick it up straight and swing it back down the same line. Ted Dexter and Barry Richards led the call for an open face with the wrist-cock opening the blade of the bat during pick-up. Others prefer the face closed.

Tony Greig stood with his bat aloft at about stump height. Graham Gooch and Clive Rice, too. Greig, being so tall, did so purely for comfort. Gooch wanted to ensure his eyes were level and found that holding the bat low and tapping it in the crease led to his head falling over to the off side, which, in turn, led to a tendency to play around his front pad. Rice didn't feel any great need for the trigger, choosing instead to be in position as early as possible and drop the bat on his drives rather than hit through them.

Experimentally, I tried most of these and found the greatest comfort with the bat held up—like Gooch, for whom I had the greatest admiration. I was looking to counter fast bowling by being as ready as possible as early as possible. This, though, became a trade-off against getting properly forward to pitched-up deliveries and I found myself constantly tinkering and modifying this part of my set-up, much to the amusement and sometimes frustration of my teammates. Boycott says I played with my feet 'in a piss pot', so I wouldn't say I found the answer. In the little cricket I played after retiring from the first-class game, I went back to a more orthodox stance and found it easier. We do tend to over-complicate.

Martin Crowe preferred to tap the bat near his right foot as the initial trigger before making a small move back and across. He felt this sparked a reaction to the delivery of the ball and then, with the bat remaining low to the ground, his shape held firm and level through the execution of the shot. Martin paid close attention to technique but worried about its boundaries and inhibition. He was at his best, he said, without 'traffic'— either emotional or technical. He wanted his movements and bat-swing to be in sync with the arrival of the ball. When they were, he had rhythm . . . and rhythm is the holy grail.

Jacques Kallis and A.B. de Villiers pre-set themselves with the bat held slightly aloft but not high. These things trend and change as the game moves through its ages. Right now, many of the best players hold the bat up and a number of them pre-set in the way of Kallis/de Villiers—Kane Williamson among them. Increasingly, and particularly in T20 cricket, batsmen are setting themselves like baseballers, ready to strike. The left hip is cleared and from this comes a free swing and a near 360-degree field of opportunity. This technique is unlikely to sustain defence against the moving ball and, like it or not, Test cricket will always provide passages of play in which the batsman must protect his wicket. Thus the question, how many batsmen can be as successful as David Warner in making the transition from the shortest form to the longest form of the game? And, on a slightly different issue going forward, how many will want to?

Dexter points out that young English cricketers were brought up to think defence before attack, which may have been a legacy of uncovered pitches and, if not, then of senior county pros who saw the glass half empty. That was not the case in other parts of the world and is not the case today. Dexter points out that if you are ready to attack, you will be in the best position to defend. He does not advocate the baseball approach but he does support a full and open backlift. Boycott would argue that you have to stay in to score runs. He believes in big strides, especially forward, because the soft and grassy pitches on which he was raised demanded that you be as near to the pitch of the ball as possible. Batsmen schooled on hard pitches tend to transfer their weight with smaller strides and, thus, create a wider hitting arc.

Dexter thinks Boycott's 142 not out in the second innings at Sydney in 1970–71 was the best innings on a difficult pitch that he has seen. John Snow then took 7 for 40 to see England home. Boycott feels that his upbringing on uncovered pitches served him well in that innings. He rode the uncertain bounce against the quick bowlers, restricting himself to the cut and to straight and on drives. He finally worked out John Gleeson, mainly defending, but also using his feet to get to the pitch of the ball on enough occasions to change Gleeson's length. He says that, in general, he tried to maintain a flow in his batting, even in defence.

It is important for the body to remain fluent, not static, through all the strokes since each one is the extension of another. A straight drive is best played by hands and shoulders that are working with the forward momentum of the body. Sobers could drive the fastest bowlers off the back foot past the stumps at the non-striker's end in one fluid motion and, for good measure, with the most magnificent flourish. Tendulkar played the same shot but with more of a forearm punch. Were they boxers, Sobers would be looking to finish the fight with this stroke, Tendulkar to do so with accurate jab after jab.

Given the bowler is generally aiming to hit the top of off stump, either of the triggers—back and across, forward press— must be the first part of the move to cover that line or, at the very least, to understand it. There are batsmen who choose to stay leg-side of the ball but this is fraught with danger, as the hands are bound to be separated from the body in the danger area just outside off stump.

Essentially, a batsman is trying to make the bowler bowl *at him*. In return, bowlers are looking to move a batsman away from his secure space and out of his mental comfort zone. These vignettes, or sidebars, to cricket make the game appealing on many different levels.

Ideally the ball should be played late, beneath the eyes, but swing bowlers look to draw the batsman into playing early, which is fatal; seam bowlers look to close down foot-work by working a batsman away from his chosen position; fast bowlers can traumatise the mind. Spin bowlers work on patience, and hope to use flight and cunning to outwit and outlast their opponent.

Most of the basic principles of technique apply to batting against all types of bowling. Having said that, it is impera-tive to use the feet to get to the pitch of spin. Michael Clarke has been superb at this, as were the two Sri Lankans Mahela

Jayawardene and Kumar Sangakkara. Before them, any number of Indians and, foremost of all, Javed Miandad, were masters of the art. A couple of small skips, back foot crossing front foot along the way, make for the smoothest move at the ball. It should not be forgotten that the use of the feet is as valuable in defence as it is in attack.

The softest hands are imperative, as the spin and extra bounce of the ball must be cushioned. Woe betide he who goes hard at spin bowling. In essence, batsmen should not let spinners settle. Look first to read the spin, either from the hand or off the pitch, and then find a way to work with it. It is no surprise that Shane Warne says leg spinners need a lot of love. The fact is, batsmen love to smack spinners out of the park. The trick is for them to do so with a clear plan. Warne would goad batsmen into departing from their plan—into playing the man not the ball—but he needed his captain to understand the thinking.

In England's second innings at the Gabba in 1994–95, I remember walking around the Gabba with Barry Richards and Greg Chappell as Warne bowled around the wicket and into the well-worn footmarks outside the right-hander's leg stump against a bemused England. Graeme Hick, who had managed well in the second innings, was out shouldering arms to a ball that spat from the rough and ran up his arm to his glove before ricocheting to Ian Healy. Richards said the only hope was to take guard outside leg stump—in other words, to set up on the line of the ball's release, and open up the off side. Chappell said he would prefer to stay off side and either come down the pitch to drive straight or through mid-on or to slog-sweep. Both added they would have to force him to drop short by taking some risks themselves, otherwise scoring opportunities were too limited. We suspected that no spin bowler had previously asked such complex questions of batsmen. Muttiah Muralitharan and his various challenges were to come a little later.

My father—able seaman in the Navy, 1947.

Mum and Dad at their wedding, June 1954.

Middlesex vs Southgate CC, 26 August 1951. Dad is second from the left. For a few years in the mid-1960s I would go every weekend to watch him in action and spend hour upon hour batting and bowling on the sidelines myself.

We spent most of our summer holidays at Seaview on the Isle of Wight playing beach cricket . . .

and most of the rest of the time playing cricket in the garden at home. Here, I am mowing and rolling the pitch for my homespun version of England vs Australia, 1968.

The real thing: 1968 at the Oval, a famous and favourite photograph. After volunteers from the crowd helped to dry the square, Derek Underwood did the rest. Every England fielder is around the bat as John Inverarity is given out lbw by umpire Charlie Elliott with six minutes left in the match.

Batting at my school, Bradfield. Not the best view of a beautiful ground.

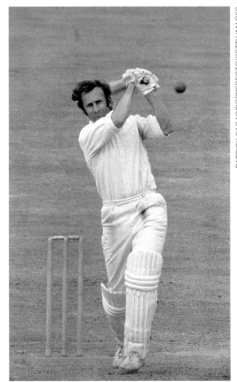

Colin Ingleby-Mackenzie and Ted Dexter—two free spirits who captured the very essence of cricket and of life.

John Snow traps Ian Chappell lbw in the semifinal of the 1975 World Cup, a low-scoring match won by Australia after Gary Gilmour took 6 for 14 with his left-arm swing. Battles between the Chappells and Snow captivated me.

Peter Sainsbury leads out Hampshire against the Australians in 1975 at Southampton. I was there that day, on a school trip, and saw Barry Richards bat for the first time. The little cottage in the middle of the buildings behind the players is the dressing room in which I was to spend many happy summers.

September 1978—arriving in Australia for the first time, tired and embarrassingly overweight. Goodness knows what Dutchy thought when I entered the arrivals hall at Sydney Airport.

Tony Greig and Kerry Packer, two men who pushed cricket—kicking and screaming— into the commercial age. Twenty-six years later I was to work alongside Greig—and to discover there was more to Packer than this smile.

I was in the crowd at the WSC Supertest Final at the SCG, February 1979. Barry Richards made an unbeaten hundred to see the World XI home, and asked me into the dressing room for a drink afterwards. Imagine the thrill of that. It was when I first met Greigy.

Dennis Lillee—a primal force and magnificent sight. Basil D'Oliveira looks remarkably calm, but then he was.

Barry Richards, master.

Mark Nicholas, pupil.

Greg Chappell, elegant even in the pouring rain, at the Oval in 1977. Chappell finished unbeaten on 125 and Australia won in a thrilling finish at 8.15 in the evening.

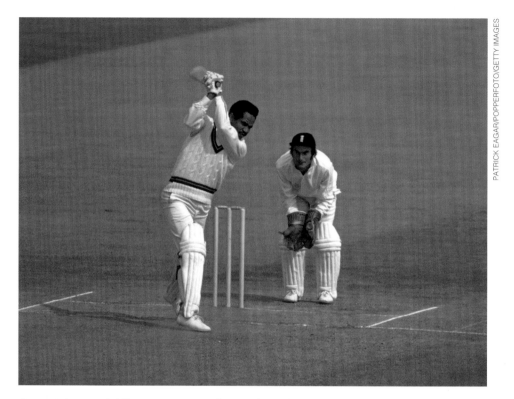

Garry Sobers and Allan Knott—a perfect study in the art of the game.

Mike Procter taking 4 wickets in five balls during his raid on the 1977 Benson & Hedges quarterfinal at Southampton. We watched from inside the scoreboard, spellbound.

Graeme Pollock—disbelieving bowlers were left stranded by drives and pulls that destroyed their spirit.

A characteristic image of Gordon Greenidge: left knee up, hooking. How about Brian Close at short leg—no helmet and eye following the ball into the bleachers. What a man!

An amazing shot of Thommo about to fire the catapult. Rodney Marsh is a long, long way back and not a muscle has moved in David Gower's body.

BOB THOMAS/GETTY IMAGES

Ian Botham finishes the match at Edgbaston in 1981. 'Hampshire were playing Kent at Canterbury and during tea we all watched the TV in the Kent dressing room. Things didn't look good for England but Alan Knott said, "Don't worry, the gorilla will take 5 for none and we'll win by 20." Botham took 5 for 1 and England won by 29.' The wicketkeeper is Bob Taylor; he seems pleased!

PATRICK EAGAR/POPPERFOTO/GETTY IMAGES

The deck chairs create a false sense of peace. There was no peace against Imran Khan at Hove. This superb athlete and hugely charismatic man was a frightening opponent for a wannabe young cricketer.

A few fast bowlers might be thought of as the best ever. In the modern age of the game, Malcolm Marshall and Dennis Lillee are the two who tend to receive most votes. This dramatic picture of Maco gives a sense of energy, athleticism, strength and speed.

We were all delighted when Paul Terry was picked for England but, in his second Test at Old Trafford, Winston Davis broke his arm. Bravely, he came out to help Allan Lamb get to a hundred, which Lamby did. Paul kept out the first one from Joel Garner but not the second!

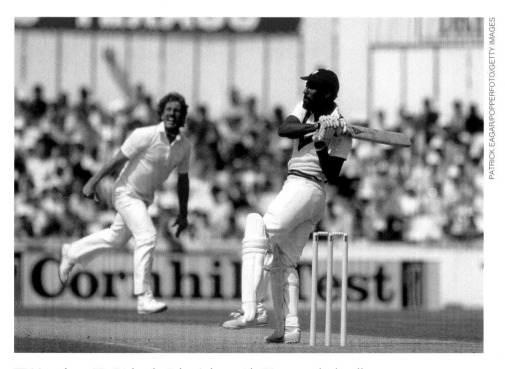

Writing about Viv Richards, John Arlott said, 'He exerted a headlong mastery even more considerable than Bradman at the same age.'

PATRICK EAGAR/POPPERFOTO/GETTY IMAGES

The Smith brothers, Robin and Chris—it was a profound moment for Hampshire cricket when they were signed, a breath of the freshest air.

GRAHAM MORRIS

Batting in the Parks at Oxford with David Gower, soon after he came to Hampshire. It was fun, an almost surreal experience.

Benson & Hedges Cup winners, 1988. Hampshire had never made it to a Lord's final. This was one of our proudest days.

With Maco and the Benson & Hedges Cup in 1992. He was a dear friend and unflinching supporter, whose death from colon cancer at the age of 41 broke a lot of strong hearts.

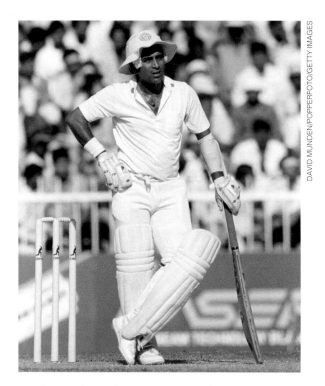

Sunil Gavaskar—the expectations of a billion people were about to be passed on to a rising star . . .

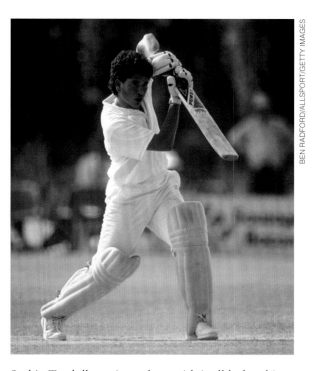

Sachin Tendulkar—just a boy, with it all before him. 'Have faith in your talents and trust your instincts,' he said.

A CONVERSATION WITH SIR DONALD BRADMAN

Bradman rated the Sobers tour de force for the World XI at Melbourne the best he ever saw, marginally ahead of Stan McCabe's epic 232 at Trent Bridge in 1938—an innings he said he wished he could have played himself. I know this because he told me. During the Adelaide Test, on the same England tour of 1994–95, Doug Insole fixed it for me to meet Bradman. We sat in the back left-hand corner of the committee's outdoor seating area for about 40 minutes. Bradman and Nicholas, chewing the fat. Dad would never have believed it.

We began talking about Shane Warne, who was bowling at that moment. He said Warne was the best young spinner he had seen. He was impressed by his accuracy and competitive spirit and likened these attributes to Bill O'Reilly, who was the best bowler he had seen—full stop. Best of all, he liked the way Warne entertained us all: an attribute, he said, not to be underestimated. He admired much about modern cricket and wished he had played the one-day game. It would have suited him, he thought, and he liked the idea of playing under lights.

I asked him if there was a secret to batting. Concentration was first on his list, after which the words I recall are courage, character, footwork and speed of movement—both around the crease and with his strong hands. He said he spent hours chopping wood as a child, which had strengthened his wrists to allow the slightly unorthodox grip that gave him such surprising power.

He said his aim was to score runs quickly—a reason, claims Roland Perry, the author of the book *Bradman's Best*, he selected Barry Richards in his all-time team ahead of Sir Leonard Hutton and Sunil Gavaskar. The object was to win the game, said Bradman, so you better crack on with it. He alluded to the fact that he didn't have especially good eyesight, which amazed me, but he moved quickly on to talk about Tendulkar and, annoyingly, I forgot to come back to it. He said that much of Tendulkar's play was similar to his own—he suspected that an average eyesight was included in this—and pointed out that he (Bradman) didn't have to keep a billion people happy every day of his life. He said that Sachin was a superb cricketer, whose modest example was an inspiration at a time when the world was losing much of its modesty.

I picked him up on Barry Richards and brought Graeme Pollock into the conversation. He was convinced that had the two of them been allowed a full Test-match career, they would have been the greatest right- and left-handed batsmen of all time. He admired Pollock for his error-free commitment to an innings, without in any way compromising a natural leaning towards attacking the bowlers. He particularly loved the imagination in Richards' game and the desire to dominate.

Perry quotes Neville Cardus, who knew Bradman well, describing one of Bradman's innings: 'He was never uninteresting, he merely abstained from vanity or rhetoric.' That might have been the pattern of our conversation, though he didn't completely shy away from talking about himself. He was adamant that all batsmen should be looking to score, even if defending, and felt that his ability to keep the scoreboard ticking was paramount to his success.

I pressed him on other matters. He was less keen to discuss Bodyline—bored by it, probably—but he did say that the real problem was scoring runs against the tactic, as was the case in the 1980s against the West Indies. He was impressed by the way Tony Greig and Allan Knott had tried to score against Lillee and Thomson by making room to upper-cut. He wouldn't be drawn on whether Thommo was the fastest ever, though he did bring Larwood, Tyson and Holding into the conversation.

He preferred an eye for the future and predicted an increasingly commercial game and huge income for the best cricketers.

This, he thought, might bring issues with player behaviour that the ICC would have to confront more quickly and firmly than administrators of recent years (pre-1994–95) had done. Having said that, he was generous in his praise of the modern cricketer. He even spoke well of Kerry Packer, realising I'm sure that Packer had been good for the professional game. Bradman was an amateur, of course, a stockbroker by profession. He was glad of the feeling that, whatever else, he had something other than cricket to fall back on. It seemed an odd thing for a man whose whole life had been dedicated to the game to say. Perhaps the overriding emotional difference between amateur and professional is that one needs it so much more than the other.

When Insole reappeared it was clear our conversation was over. I thanked Sir Donald and left, having barely scratched the surface. As I walked back to the press box, I wondered if he might be the greatest sportsman of all time. Figures support the idea. Effectively, he was twice as valuable as any other batsman ever. On reflection, Muhammad Ali; Jack Nicklaus and Tiger Woods; Rod Laver and Roger Federer; and Pelé and Lionel Messi, to name a few, each have impressive credentials of a different type.

I heard a mischievous story about Bradman from Henry Blofeld. He had twice been dismissed for low scores against New South Wales, which had adopted a tactic of putting on a bad off spinner to bowl well wide of off stump. Twice, the frustrated Bradman threw his bat at the ball and got out. In 1937, Queensland went to Adelaide and his old mate Bill Brown used the same approach. Bradman studied the bowler a while and then called Brown over. 'Here, Bill,' he squeaked, 'I was going to get a quick hundred today and then give it away, but now I'm going to get 250.' He fell four short.

It is well worth making a visit to the Bradman Museum in Bowral, New South Wales. Many of today's cricketers are cynical about those of yesteryear, particularly when they watch the old newsreels. But go to Bowral, see him on the big screens and you will marvel at this genius of run-making. Such power and precision. Such authority. He would smash anyone today, too.

Thommo on The Don

In late January 2016, Jeff Thomson was inducted into the Australian Hall of Fame. He made a very funny speech, reminding us all of a more relaxed and less politically correct age. The next day, Kerry O'Keeffe interviewed him on radio. Here is a transcript of the last part of their conversation.

Kerry O'Keeffe: Mate, there's not many of us from our era that can claim to have bowled to Don Bradman. But you can, can't you?

Jeff Thomson: Yeah, yeah, yeah.

KO: When did that happen?

JT: On a rest day in a Test match in '77. We were playing India.

KO: Can you talk us through that experience, the Bradman experience?

JT: Yeah. Yeah, sure. Well, I was—a rest day. Just got married. You know, so instead of the usual rest day where I wrecked myself, you know, getting drunk or going fishing, what we used to do—I mean on a rest day, you just cut loose. Only two days to go. We can do that easy.

KO: Yeah.

JT: So, anyway, I've got my wife with me now, so all the fun's gone out the window. I've got to toe the line, so I've gone to a lunch party. Can you believe, Jeff Thomson from Bankstown going to lunch at a doctor's place drinking wine? And it was hot as buggery. It was about 40-odd degrees. Anyway, I'm there. And who's there? On the table is Bradman and his wife, my wife and myself, Doc Beard, who was the host, and his wife, his two boys, who were seventeen and nineteen, and Bishan Bedi and a couple of Indian officials on the other side. Right, we're playing against them.

KO: Mm.

JT: And I'm sitting there drinking. I remembered distinctly drinking a XXXX there. That's what I used to have. And it was hot. And Bradman had a full suit on—the whole deal— tie and all that. And I just had casual, neat casual. And the next minute we're going out in the backyard at Doc's place. And I reckon he's asked us along there because his kids want to play cricket against Don Bradman and Jeff Thomson in the backyard. And this is fair dinkum. I hadn't seen them before this, except down on the ground. And Doc was a tragic cricketer. He would have loved to have played cricket, but he wasn't good enough, as you know. So he was hoping his boys were going to be good enough. So he figured he would give them a lesson with Bradman and myself. As we were walking out to the net, and it was a full turf wicket, Bradman said to me, he said, 'Gee, Jeff,' he said, 'I don't know what I'm doing this for. I haven't done this for 30 years.' In 1948 he finished. This is in 1978, right.

KO: Mm.

JT: So it was '78. And I'm thinking to myself, 'I don't need to do this either. I'm bowling tomorrow. I don't need to waste my energy on this. I'd rather enjoy my beer. But it's Don Bradman, and when Ian Chappell and Greg Chappell find out I've been mates with Don Bradman, they're going to be spewing. And when people find out I've bowled to Don Bradman, how cool is that?'

KO: Mm, yeah.

JT: You know? So I had a double-edged—double-blade sword, if you know what I mean?

KO: Yes, indeed.

JT: Anyway. We go out there. I thought, 'Wow, I'd better bowl some leg spinners to this old bloke. It's not going to look too good if I kill him in backyard cricket, you know, in Adelaide.' This is what an idiot I am. Anyway, so I bowl a couple of leggies. And I used to be able to bowl good leggies. And I'm sort of lobbing them, and Bradman's got nothing but a bat, right. He's taken his coat off. Still got his tie on and his full, you know, dress gear. And he's just batting them back. And I looked for where these kids are, and they're off their long run, right. I thought, 'Oh, no, they're going to kill him.' And before I could stop them, this kid's running in. And the kids are bigger than me, right. They're seventeen and nineteen, but they're tall. And I thought, 'Oh, mate.' I'm looking at Bradman, and he's going from sort of trying to smile at me—because you know what he's like; he didn't smile that much.

KO: No.

JT: And he's got this serious face on. And I thought, 'Good luck, old man. You're going to be hurting in a minute.' And he goes smack and hits this kid—like, hits the ball. Like the best shot you ever want to see. Like the ones you see on TV, you know. And I just thought, you know, when you watch those old film clips, it's like when people watch us, you know. They probably say, 'They cut out all his bad balls and all this sort of thing. You'd never think Bradman played a bad shot.' Anyway, he belts this kid. And I thought, 'Well, that was lucky.' The next kid comes in and he belts him some-where else. And I thought to myself, 'Oh, beginner's luck.' So I stopped playing, and for 20 minutes he has absolutely destroyed these two. Like, if it was Viv Richards or Greg Chappell or Ian Chappell out there at the same day, you know, in their prime, they wouldn't have done it. They would have backed off and said, 'Look, I've got no pads, protectors,' and all that and got out. He just launched at these kids. Like, he just said to himself—I could see him saying he is not going to miss a ball. And he didn't. He just destroyed them. And he walked out and just sort of winked at me with a bat under his arm as if to say, 'They thought they were getting me out. I've got news for them.' Oh, mate, you know, Skull, it was up there as one of the highlights of my career.

AN INNINGS (OR TWO) BY VIV RICHARDS

Viv Richards played the greatest innings I ever saw at first hand. He was with Glamorgan for a couple of years at the end of his career and occasionally wound back the clock to the days when he carried all before him. We set them 364 on the final day, a target well within reach on the flat pitch at the small Northlands Road ground. They were about 140 for 5 at tea but Viv was still there and, for some reason, he was blocking. He seemed to be in a filthy mood, exaggerated by the fact that the Glamorgan captain, Alan Butcher, had come out on the dressing-room balcony waving his arms around as if to say get the hell on with it. It was like Viv had decided the others were pretty useless and, in protest, was going to block out the draw. We definitely thought we would win. No way could the last five Glamorgan wickets survive a whole session.

Tim Tremlett bowled the first ball after tea and Viv made as if to block but then, almost imperceptibly, followed through on his forward defensive shot. The ball disappeared over the sightscreen, out of the ground and across the road. We all looked at each other and thought, 'Ah, here we go!' And there we went. Glamorgan needed more than 200 in the session and he just murdered us. It was fantastic to watch, up to a point.

Fast forward. With one over of the match left, Viv was 150 not out. They needed 14 to win and the greatest fast bowler in the world was bowling to the greatest batsman in the world.

The Welsh were 7 down now and Colin Metson was in. So I said to Malcolm, 'With all of us on the fence, Viv gets a single and you have five balls at Metson and the rest, who can't bat. We might even win.' So Maco ran in and bowled a good length ball on off stump. Viv blistered it through cover for four. Our two quickest fielders were at deep point and deep extra cover. Neither moved. I'm thinking, 'That should have been a single, Maco.' 'Maco,' I screamed from long off, 'give Viv a friggin' single!' Next ball, Maco bowled a quick bouncer and Viv hit it over the flats. We never saw the ball again, ever.

So I moved in from the boundary and said, 'Give him a fucking single, bowl him a yorker and you've got three balls at Metson!' So the very great Malcolm Marshall ran in and bowled a good full ball—not quite a yorker, though—and Viv dug it out and drilled it wide of mid-on towards the boundary, scorching the turf in the process. Before it crossed the line, he took his gloves off and ran towards me to shake my hand and say, 'That was one helluva declaration, skipper, let's go drink some beers.' He was 164 not out. It was one hell of an innings, Viv.

'As if he'd have taken the single anyway,' said Maco in the bar at ten o'clock that night.

And another thing . . .

Swansea, three years later. Marshall to Richards. It was *still* Marshall to Richards. Malcolm runs in and Viv pulls away at the very last moment. There's a hush. On the field we're all looking at each other. No one dares say anything. 'Hey!' screams Viv, now marching down the pitch, past Marshall and on, past the umpire. 'YOU!' Nothing, bar a horrified look on a few nearby spectators. 'That's YOU!' Now Viv's pointing to a spot just above the sightscreen, pointing to a man who is sitting on his own, flicking through the pages of his newspaper. 'That's right, YOU!' The man looks up from his broadsheet, startled, and points to himself like, 'What, me?' 'Yes, YOU!!!

You've got David Gower and Robin Smith at slip,' screams Viv, 'and you've got Malcolm Marshall, the greatest fast bowler in the world, bowling to Vivian Richards . . . And you're reading the fucking newspaper?!' Priceless.

I asked him the same question I asked Bradman: is there a secret? 'Keep it simple, head still, watch the ball,' he said. 'These fellas these days want to over-complicate this thing which is batting. Come forward, come at the face of the man who challenges you, show him who's boss, then spring back if you must. Be the boss, because if you don't think you are, no one else will.'

WHO IS SECOND BEST?

This chapter on batting has not turned out quite as planned. Talk of the distance between Bradman and others such as Richards makes me wonder who the best is after Bradman. The first thing to say is that I have no more idea than the next man, but it makes a good yarn and something that mates and I have debated over many years. Had Bradman not averaged 99.94— say it was 59.94—we would judge him alongside everyone else. There would be arguments for substance and for style and, again, they would be entirely subjective. There is no wrong or right, just opinion. Unless it is Bradman, of course, then the bets are off.

Figures have to feature in the criteria because they are the one constant but these alter with time, laws, equipment, opponents and conditions. Comparing W.G. Grace, Victor Trumper or Ranjitsinhji with Kevin Pietersen, A.B. de Villiers or Virat Kohli is nonsense—other than to say they all liked, or like, a dash. Grace could impose, Trumper could invent and Ranji could improvise. Today's batsmen have such attributes as their starting point. Certainly, our man must bat in a fashion that wins matches for his team. Runs themselves are a necessity.

Runs made when specifically needed, or in difficult circumstances, assume much greater value. How do we measure this? We can't, not through the ages anyway. Some form of *Moneyball* algorithm might soon separate the modern players, but, thankfully, the many misty years that have seen cricket evolve from a game of top hats, curved bats and underarm bowling to the kaleidoscope it has become today prevent us from too much forensic exploration. Anyway, there is a romance to cricket that should be preserved. We can compare and contrast but we should not judge. The sensational achievements of W.G. in his time have to sit alongside anything A.B. achieves in his.

The *Wisden Almanack* provides us with the records—a good starting point. At the time of writing both Steve Smith and Adam Voges average more than 60 but of those whose careers are past only George Headley, Graeme Pollock and Herbert Sutcliffe, other than Bradman, finished beyond that mark. Headley played 22 test matches and Pollock 23; are these enough to prove a man's place in the pantheon? How do we judge Kenny Barrington's 6806 runs at 58.67 against Jacques Kallis's 13,289 at 55.37 in twice as many matches? Or the celebrated techniques of Sir Jack Hobbs, Walter Hammond and Sir Len Hutton against the gifts given to Stan McCabe, Sid Barnes and Neil Harvey? And so on.

Of all Bradman's figures, one that requires a second look is the 56.57 he averaged during the Bodyline series in 1932–33 with a strike rate of 74 runs per 100 balls. He wore the traditional green cap of Australia and was thus exposed to physical danger, while at the same time being unable to score in various areas of the ground because the law permitted any number of fielders anywhere. Those who played against West Indies from 1976 were confronted by multiples of this physical danger. Helmets came to build confidence but, by then, laws were long in place to restrict negative field setting. How would Bradman have played Larwood had he worn a helmet and been able to attack the leg-side field behind square? We have no idea, of course, which is why achievement can only be judged within the parameters of the moment. We can, however, be certain that helmets have changed technique and expanded options. As Kerry Packer famously said to Justin Langer, 'Son, if we hadn't invented helmets, you'd be dead.'

On a general level, the best batting I ever watched came from Sachin Tendulkar during the 1998 series against Australia in India, the series when he plotted for Shane Warne and then mauled him. In the build-up to the tour, Tendulkar set up shop for a week with Laxman Sivaramakrishnan, the former Indian leg spinner who brought a bunch of young leggies with him. Three pitches were prepared—one new but very dry, one totally underprepared and dusting, and one torn apart by spikes and rakes. Each day, they moved from pitch to pitch as Tendulkar defended, attacked and slogged his way into a method to combat anything Warne put before him. That series confirmed Bradman's idea, first conceived a few years earlier by his wife, Jessie, that there were definite similarities between the two of them: the man with the highest average and the man with the most runs and most hundreds.

During the Channel 4 television days I did a masterclass with him and asked, as I had done with Viv, if there was a secret. 'Not really a secret,' he said. 'For a batsman, each day is different. The mental set-up, the way the feet move, the bat swing, all of it. You have to adjust to mood and moment. Have faith in your talent, keep coaching to a minimum and trust your instincts.' Good advice. He had previously talked to me about his floating technique—or the Zen mind—and agreed with Barry that it is a magical feeling. The masterclass was broadcast live from the Rose Bowl in Southampton and even Richie Benaud came out to watch and listen.

The best single Test-match innings I have seen was Brian Lara's epic unbeaten 153-run match-winner in Barbados in 1999, again against the Australians. Lara loved the Aussies. He first announced himself with a classic at the Sydney Cricket Ground in 1992. They eventually ran him out for 277 and, as Warne often says, they weren't going to get him out any other way. Lara named his daughter Sydney after that day, and likes to tell people that it is lucky he didn't play the innings in Lahore.

Wisden recalls the performance in Barbados as 'transcendent' and played by 'the hand of a genius'. There is more: 'Exhibiting the new awareness and maturity he discovered in Jamaica, he brilliantly orchestrated the conclusion of an unforgettable match. He guided his men to victory as though leading the infirm through a maze.' It was one of the greatest Test matches, won by a single wicket and signed off by one of the greatest innings. Lara is flattered by the judgement and rates his double-hundred a week earlier in Jamaica even higher, though I think that is as much for the emotional circumstances in which it was played as the quality with which it was played. During this series, Lara matched anything Richards or Sobers had managed before him.

Twice, of course, Lara held the world record Test match score. First with 375 against England at the old St Johns Recreation Ground in Antigua in 1994. Then with 400 not out in 2004: same opponent, same ground. It is one thing to hold the world record, and quite another to go and get it back a decade later. Angus Fraser, who played in the first of those matches, says it is the only time he bowled at someone who, he thought, could hit every ball for four. (Peter Sainsbury said that of Peter May.) For good measure, Lara has the world-record first-class score too, 501 not out for Warwickshire against Durham. Chris Scott, the Durham wicketkeeper dropped a sitter when Lara had 18. He turned to Wayne Larkins at first slip and said, 'Shit, I suppose he'll get a hundred now.' Sure did Chris, and some.

When I asked Lara the same question, he quite understood what Barry Richards and Sobers had said about reacting to the point of the ball's release. He had not consciously done so himself but he thought it probably happened subconsciously. 'What else would I watch?' Quite so. He had no other insight to his own mastery except to say that he gave the first 40 minutes of any innings in the long form of the game to the bowler. After that, good luck.

As previously established, my cricket addiction took hold in the mid-1960s, when I was starstruck by Ted Dexter and John Snow. Watching, reading, listening and impersonating until lights out, I came to see the 1970s as a golden age. The finest batsmen I set eyes upon were—in a batting order, for the sake of it—Sunil Gavaskar, Barry Richards, Viv Richards, Graeme Pollock, Greg Chappell and Sobers. Others could do marvellous things, but these six men captured the essence of my dream whether as underdog or bully and, occasionally, there were moments of both for all of them. Only Tendulkar and Lara have stepped in their footprints since.

Ricky Ponting, Jacques Kallis and Kumar Sangakkara were very close. A.B. de Villiers and Virat Kohli are on track. In fact, having watched the two of them bat in all three formats over the past two years, I would say that greatness is theirs for the taking. Both have appeared routinely capable of the obvious, the oblique and the outrageous—but we must not be lost in the deeds of T20 cricket. Rather, we should reference their performances in Test-match cricket where they have set new standards for the aspiration of others.

To illustrate this, I would pick de Villiers' 91 against Australia at Centurion in 2014, when he resisted Mitchell Johnson and Ryan Harris at their most punishing. While gifted colleagues such as Hashim Amla and Faf du Plessis were laid to waste, de Villiers moved smoothly forward and back as if he were batting on a magic carpet. Unhurried and unshackled, he transcended the pattern of the Test match. Perhaps he, too, has discovered a way to float while batting.

Of late, much has been made of Kohli's high level of fitness and feverish desire. This has come from an astonishing series of performances in one-day and T20 cricket. But these attributes were first made unarguably apparent to the world in the two superb hundreds he made against Australia at Adelaide in 2014—the first match after the death of Phillip Hughes. In reference to the second of them, Sidharth Monga, writing on Cricinfo, said that Kohli attained 'batting nirvana' during an unlikely run chase that he threatened to complete almost single-handedly: 'This was the "zone" batsmen talk of, when conditions, match state, batting partners, bowlers don't matter. You just watch the ball, and react to it. No premeditation, no eye on the future.' The thing I most remember was the exasperation of the bowlers at the moment when they seemed to have beaten him, only for instinct and the fastest hands in the game to react and recover.

These two have held my attention and frequently led me to gasp at the wonder of it all. The more I see of Joe Root, the more I think he can be included in this elite. The three of them are pioneering a total form of batting that can be applied to all three formats of the game. Their reference to the demands of footwork and bat control is close to flawless and yet, at the same time, they are redefining movement, range and risk. Best of all, there appears to be no limit to their ambition. Indeed, when Root went to 200 against Pakistan at Old Trafford in 2016, he did so with a full-blooded reverse sweep. He certainly appears to play in an untroubled manner. Crowe would be envious of this, while being full of admiration for the rhythm that Root brings to batting in all situations and all formats. These three men remind us of the beauty of progress.

But, as I say, it is the first six from the golden age who got me at hello. It is with their completed careers that we can advance discussion. Because all were either at their best, or somewhere near it, in the ten-year period between 1968 and 1978, it is more straightforward to compare and calibrate them. Batting for the World XI against the Australians in a WSC match at Gloucester Park in Perth, the two Richards went through the gears together and it is hard to imagine a better dovetail. (Kohli and de Villiers achieved something similar while at the crease for the Royal Challengers Bangalore in the IPL.)

We have already established that Viv's ability to overwhelm an opponent cannot be matched. He began each innings as if it were a crusade, emerging from the pavilion with the innate conviction of right and the promise of dominance. Has any sportsman made such an entrance? Sir Leonard once noted that Richards 'goes on about being descended from slaves and cotton pickers, but he walks to the wicket as if he owns the plantation'.

The best Viv Richards innings were the most spectacular cricket shows on earth: inflammatory, irresistible, inspirational. After the English heatwave summer of 1976, John Arlott wrote that Viv 'exerted a headlong mastery even more considerable than Don Bradman at the same age'. The bats were balsawood compared to those used today and the boundaries bigger. His leg-side play fuelled the legend but it was the power of the riposte—the sense of vengeance for a suppressed people—that rang out the loudest. No wonder Bob Marley's 'Redemption Song' is top of his hit list.

The other Richards, Barry, had everything: the purist might argue more even than Viv if technical accomplishment is the benchmark. The South African government's apartheid policy denied Barry the one thing he most deserved, a relevant place in the game's history, but he should travel happy in the knowledge of the pleasure he gave in the parts of the world his passport allowed.

At his best, he was pretty much flawless but the unpredictability of his mood meant he flirted with audiences, sucking them in to his unique gifts but too often spitting them out in a careless departure from the business at hand. Batting for Hampshire in a 40-over match at Southampton in 1976, he went from 95 to 101 deliberately playing John Lever with the edge of his bat. Then he hit a long hop up in the air and walked off. That arrogance rankled with even his most devoted followers.

There is an apocryphal tale about Barry batting for his club, Durban High School Old Boys, in an important league match. So hard was it to motivate him for such a trivial affair that Dennis Gamsy, a Test player himself, challenged him to hit ball after ball to predetermined areas of the ground. Suitably amused, Barry made 70-odd in less than an hour and never once missed a chosen target.

There are any number of such stories. Clearly, his gifts were as extraordinary as the politics that denied their fulfilment. Sadly, as Barry tired of the limitations of first-class, epics were replaced by cameos and the game that had once been his inspiration became a chore.

Few players have had such time to play the ball. He stood side-on to the bowler, chin tucked in tight to his left shoulder, and held the bat with an orthodox grip and an exaggerated high left elbow. This made him immensely strong through the off side from either foot and, until Root, I had not seen anyone—not even Tendulkar—drive the ball off the back foot through the covers in such sublime fashion. The brilliance in the placement of these strokes seemed to mock the opponent.

Like Tendulkar, he applied straight lines to the art of batting, which leads to a geometric effect. If the great stylists among left-handers—Frank Woolley and David Gower; Sobers and Lara—had the more vivid brushstrokes, the right-handers, such as Richards, Tendulkar, Greg Chappell and a couple of others not yet mentioned here—Mahela Jayawardena and Mark Waugh—brought linear brilliance to their contrasting artistic impression. One man's Picasso has always been another man's Rembrandt.

At Perth in 1970, Barry made 325 in a day for South Australia against Western Australia. Ian Chappell says that in the hurry to get to 300 before the close, their new recruit from Natal farmed the strike to ensure he was hitting downwind. Chappell adds that the final ball of the day, bowled by Dennis Lillee, was driven back over Lillee's head with such ease that it appeared to be the sort of thing Richards did every day.

The originality in his stroke-play came from an inquisitive and unrestricted sporting mind. He hated the mundane, still does, and was the first to back away from the line of the ball and either late-cut straight balls or smash them over extra cover. He sees batting as something beautiful and believes that with his talent for it came the duty to entertain.

Frustratingly, there is little video evidence: snippets from South Africa's 4–0 win over the Australians in 1969–70; some clips from WSC; a hundred for Hampshire in the Gillette Cup against Lancashire, though the grainy footage and sloppy editing show us little of the magic. A worthwhile piece of film to study is the charity match at the Sydney Cricket Ground in 1994, when, aged almost 50, he opened with Sunil Gavaskar against Lillee and Thomson for a World XI against a Bradman XI. Look at the economy and the precision of the strokes. It is an innings of just 24 runs but, other than the first and last balls, it is a lovely 24.

No batsman I have seen brought such grace and style to the nitty-gritty of the workplace. It was perfection, touched by something almost risqué, and satisfied all the requirements of a young boy in love with the game and its aesthetics.

As Bradman indicated, Pollock was really something—an executioner, albeit a graceful one with an insatiable appetite for runs. South Africans flocked to watch him in action and then, as the Castle lager took over, became almost tribalistic in their appreciation. As Graeme grew older, his stance became wider and his bat heavier, but the no-frills Pollock game stayed the same. Keep it simple, stupid, he seemed to say: rock back and forward and thump it for four. Disbelieving bowlers were left stranded in their follow-through by cover drives and pulls that destroyed their spirit.

In order to see him and Barry in the flesh against some of the bowlers we confronted daily in county cricket, Paul Terry and I went by ship (it was a cheap ticket) from Durban, where we were playing club cricket, to Port Elizabeth for a one-day match between South Africa and the rebel West Indians. Barry made a hundred but Graeme stole the show with an astonishing assault after being hit on the forehead by Sylvester Clarke. Having been stitched up in hospital, he returned to the ground in time to see Clarke knock over Garth le Roux with the first ball of a new spell. The crowd murmured both approval and concern when they saw the great man walking back to the wicket in a helmet. The first ball from the powerful Barbadian was quick, short and aimed at the stitches. It disappeared into the band of Cape Coloured musicians at square leg. So did the next one. All five balls went for four or six. He finished unbeaten on 66.

The England cricketers of the hour talk in awe of the 125 he made at Trent Bridge in 1965; Australians the same of the 274 at Durban in 1969–70. Like Richards, Pollock was cut down by apartheid but at least had 23 Test matches to make a case in the history books. It is hard to look beyond Graeme Pollock.

Unless you look to Sir Garfield. He was a shadow of himself when I caught him at Lord's in 1973 but imagine the thrill of even the shadow of Garry Sobers in the flesh. Each step he took was an event, every stroke an imitation of art. He made 150 that day. Thanks, Garry. Rohan Kanhai made a tasty hundred too. We went home and suddenly West Indies were beating England in the back garden. We pushed up our collars, rolled our shoulders and thrashed back-foot drives without a care in the world. That was the thing about Sobers: it was as if he had not a care in the world. He had an amazing eye for the ball, fast hands and feet that danced—cricket's Muhammad Ali, without the mouth. He could thread a gap where there seemed none and he could clear the ropes like few batsmen of the era. An hour of Sobers invariably changed a whole match. Geoffrey Boycott insists that of the players he saw, only Sobers, Richards and Lara had genius—no one else. I defer to Geoffrey occasionally. Anyway, if Bradman says Sobers' 254 at the MCG was best innings he watched, so be it.

There was something of the Roman emperors in Greg Chappell. His walk to the wicket was brisk, shoulders back, head held high as he appeared to survey the enemy in pity. The strokes were from the classics, upright and surprisingly powerful. There was an on drive to die for, and uncanny placement through point and the covers. Everything about him was precise and serene; the only surprise came when he was out, as it seemed so unlikely.

We played against him once at Southampton, when the Australians were over for the Centenary Test in 1980. He had an aura, and some game. At tea he was 86 not out and we heard that he was going to retire on the basis that the Hampshire attack did not merit a first-class hundred. It was a fair call: we were rubbish. In the end he decided against it and, instead, ran past a straight one from the left-arm spinner John Southern. My memory is of the utter certainty in his batting, and of its elegance. I can hear the cleanest sound of bat on ball and still see a cruel beauty in the way he picked us off.

People talk of his bad run against West Indies in the early 1980s, but it was brief. Across seventeen tests against the most formidable fast-bowling attack in the history of the game, he averaged 56, a performance that brooks no argument.

Finally, then, to Sunil Gavaskar, whose batsmanship carried the hopes of a billion people long before Tendulkar was around to assume the responsibility. Gavaskar was the man who tucked in behind the ball to apply a perfect technique and the soundest judgement in the making of 34 Test-match hundreds. His defiance spoke for new India before it was fashionable to do so: 'We will not be bullied, we will fight them on the fields of Mumbai, Georgetown, and Melbourne [where he once attempted a coup, so angry was he at being adjudged lbw to Lillee] and we will never surrender.'

We saw Sunny up close and personal at Southampton. An Indian journalist had written him off before the 1979 tour of England, so he took it out on Hampshire. Sunny explains: 'I was furious with this irresponsible man who knew nothing of the illness I had been through and the conversations I had had with the selectors prior to the tour. So I dug in for a hundred come what may against Hampshire and then, once I got there, decided to have some fun and entertain the crowd who had put up with me blocking for most of the day!' He made an unbeaten 166.

His thirteen hundreds against West Indies at an average of 65.45 are the stuff of a true champion, though it should be acknowledged that a fair whack of his career against them came before the best of the four-pronged pace attack came together.

Having said that, his unbeaten Test best of 236 in Chennai against Marshall, Roberts, Holding and Davis was a reminder that all things are possible if you have a mind for them. He batted at four that day but came in at 0 for 2! Only a handful of batsmen have used the strength of their mind so effectively.

In the second part of his career Sunny wore a skullcap, mainly beneath his sunhat, but the foundation of his many hours in the middle was a rock steady head, set bare to the bowler. He benefited from a sharp eye, trained on the badminton court, and a compact and orthodox stance that allowed him to pick length quickly and respond efficiently.

So who is it to be, this mythical best after Bradman in the modern age of the game? It is tempting to say that Sir Donald might have been right about the two South Africans but there simply is not enough history to go on. Barry has been my own favourite batsman; only Sachin nudged him for me. Tendulkar might well be the perfect answer, linked as he was to Bradman himself. Think of the many miles he covered without compromise and the way he inspired a nation, much as Bradman had done before him. Bradman, of course, never played outside Australia or England. Tendulkar was a global phenomenon who defied Imran Khan in the late 1980s, Shane Warne in the late 1990s and Dale Steyn in 2011. Bradman and Tendulkar were both able to isolate the challenge and apply themselves whatever the expectation. Sachin could be my man but for the helmet.

I am taking Tendulkar and Lara out of this argument; Kohli and de Villiers too. Helmets have changed batting. There is no question that the merits of the modern greats sit alongside those of the past but this mission has altered the longer I have thought about it. I have concluded that our champion must have played within the same parameters as Bradman, in other words in the days before helmets.

I go for the majesty of Sir Garfield Sobers, for his ability to make cricket a thing of beauty and joy; for breaking the world record score as a young man and playing with the same instincts as an old man; and for scoring more than 8000 runs at an average of nearly 58. Remember, he had all those late nights to recover from, never mind that he bowled quick, quicker and slow—both left-arm orthodox and over the wrist. Oh, and he caught flies wherever he fielded. Yup, it's Garry.

BACK TO THE BEGINNING

Batting is a craft that has evolved over a couple of centuries. Film of W.G. Grace in the nets does not tell us much, other than how different the game was back then. The same can be said about grainy footage of Jack Hobbs, although 199 first-class hundreds must count for something. Photographs at the MCG of Walter Hammond and Bill Ponsford remind us that many of the pitches of the day were barely identifiable from the outfields, and therefore the balance between bat and ball was far less weighted in favour of batsmen than it is today. In 1937, the lbw law changed so that bowlers could trap a batsman in front by pitching the ball outside off stump and bringing it back into his pads. Previously the ball had to pitch on the stumps and be going on to hit them, which takes some bowling. Imagine the hurried changes to technique upon the introduction of that new law.

For what it is worth, John Arlott told me that Hobbs was as good or better a technician than Barry Richards, and E.W. Swanton said the same of Walter Hammond. Bradman had Hammond as 12th man in his team that included Tendulkar in the middle order.

The evolution of batting has been slow and precise. Batsmen have responded to the equipment, conditions, formats and public demand with rhythms of their own. Only of late has the evolution become revolution. In T20 cricket, sixes are like confetti. In Test matches, hundreds are sometimes scored at better than a run a ball. At Newlands, Ben Stokes and Jonny Bairstow put on 399 at nearly 7 an over. A few days later, a fifteen-year-old Indian, Pranav Dhanawade, made 1009 in one innings over two afternoons. Not even Tendulkar did that.

The bats are bigger and better, the men using them are stronger, the pitches are flatter, the balls do precious little, the boundaries are shorter and the coaches and captains grant a licence as never before. It is a wonderful time to bat.

For as long as Test cricket maintains its place at the top table, we can be reasonably assured of an ongoing reference to the techniques that have made batting an art form. Its talent can be defined in various ways, among them resilience and application. Of late, no one has better illustrated this than Alastair Cook, whose ten thousand Test match runs are the work of a clear mind and strong body. A good, relatively orthodox method is adaptable to all forms of the game and is one reason cricket remains aesthetically appealing, even as we have moved from touch and timing into this era of brutality. Kohli, de Villiers and Root have crossed this divide with élan.

Batting is moving so fast it is hard to predict what will come next. The nature of cricket has always led to one inherent fear: failure. T20 all but eliminates this for batsmen. It is virtually impossible to be bowled out in 20 overs and therefore the currency of wickets has lost value.

A couple of years back, Kevin Pietersen and I were talking about risk. Well, I was. He just laughed. He said I was missing the point and that he didn't care about getting out, only that he had given himself the chance to do something different. He added, 'As long as I prepare well and play to my ability, everything will take care of itself. Either way, the sun will come up in the morning.' Such an attitude is incomprehensible to players brought up in an age when the preservation of your wicket was a lifelong pursuit.

The best batsmen of the day weigh up myriad different options compared to those of the past. When Viv first hit balls from outside off stump through mid wicket and Barry backed away to leg and drove over cover, the sheer bravado drew gasps of admiration. Nowadays, if you bat at eight and can't hit over cover, you're not good enough. The zeitgeist of shot-making is a straight half-volley ramped over third man or a wide one reversed over long leg.

Can the ball survive this heady advance of the bat? If it is to do so, the size of the bat must be limited. While that piece of legislation is being drawn up, the ball needs a more prominent seam again. The challenge for cricket is to keep all the skills of the game moving forward together, reflecting, as far as possible, the times in which we live. If batting is to remain artistic, it cannot become easy and neither should it be reduced to the lowest common denominator. Artists make their achievements look easy but it is the ten thousand hours of exploration, experimentation, practice and rehearsal that make perfect. Not even in batting is there pleasure without pain.

CHAPTER 7

The week we wished that wasn't and the spirit of cricket

Sydney, 25 November 2014

In the middle of the afternoon, a newsflash came on the car radio. Phillip Hughes, the South Australian batsman, had been hit by a short ball in a Sheffield Shield match at the Sydney Cricket Ground. The match was between New South Wales, the state in which Hughes grew up and had played most of his cricket, and South Australia, where he was now playing. He had been rushed to St Vincent's Hospital in a critical condition.

I was en route to the New South Wales Golf Club in La Perouse and immediately pulled the car into a lay by. I knew Hughes quite well and liked him immensely. I recalled the various blows I had taken. Gladstone Small broke my cheekbone; Waqar Younis some of my hand. Courtney Walsh, Sylvester Clarke and Graham Dilley had all damaged me at one stage or another during an eighteen-year first-class career in which I bore the brunt of many a fast bowler's aggression. (Something to do with a public-schoolboy swagger, apparently.)

Though the physical threat was relevant, I don't ever recall being frightened of the ball—only of humiliation and failure.

Helmets were just coming into the game when I started in first-class cricket. Few players wore them and virtually no one wore the visor too, only the side pieces. In 1980, I went out to bat against Sussex wearing a sunhat. From long leg, Imran Khan shouted to Le Roux, 'Look Garth, no helmet!' and they bombed me for the brief period I was at the crease. After a couple of overs I was caught at the wicket: a brute of a ball from Imran that brushed my glove at throat height. Though I stopped short of shouting 'Catch it!' I was relieved to be out of the line of fire. It was typical of the time that the fast bowlers thought nothing of such threatening intimidation, and it was stupid of me not to have practised in a helmet and to not have had one to hand at the match. Like plenty of others around the country—our team included—the pros at Sussex revelled in the machismo given them by the overseas stars. They fed off this frenzy of short-pitched bowling and I was unable to cope.

In the dressing room, I cried.

Until you bat against the fastest and the best, you can have little idea what is involved. The experience is far removed from anything else in a young cricketer's life. You see the ball but not in a conscious, responsive way. It appears first as a small, dark missile screaming towards you—the size of a squash ball perhaps, before nearness brings reality of size and colour—and then, when it hits bat or body, the immediate impact feels heavy, dense and hard. Ideally, as discussed in the previous chapter, you have pre-set movements to cope: back and across; forward press; an early move to off stump, then repo with your head still, are the most commonly used triggers that help find the right place from which to react. After that, you trust hours of practice and your instinct. The best batsmen see the ball earlier than the rest of us and therefore have more options. The

Richards and Sobers ability to pick up length from the point of the ball's release from the hand seems almost impossible to those of us not blessed by such speed of eye and reaction.

I was lost in these thoughts when the phone rang, making me jump. Did I know about Phil Hughes? Yes, I did and yes it is terrible. I have no recollection of who called. I started the engine and headed on to La Perouse in a daze. On arrival at the golf club, desperate to know more, I telephoned Michael Clarke but it went to voicemail.

After thirteen holes in the evening sunshine, all of them punctuated by worried conversations about Hughes, helmets and bouncers, a text from Clarke appeared on my phone. It said, 'I'm at the hospital, mate. Fuck me, I'm scared.' Clarke had long been both buddy and mentor to Hughes—an older brother in all but blood.

An operation to release the pressure on Hughes's brain had already taken place. He had been hit on the neck, just beneath the left side of his skull, behind his earlobe. Footage on the news showed him to be through the attempted hook shot a fraction early. The Australian doctor Peter Bruckner explained the procedure and added that Hughes remained critical. He did not say the operation was a success or that Hughes was stable. He did say that Hughes was in an induced coma. Clearly, he was fighting for his life.

Channel Nine's *Today Show* called. They wanted to interview me live in the studio at seven the next morning. I hate that early morning thing but said yes. Going to bed, I felt much the same way as Clarke: scared.

26 November

A terrible night's sleep. Tossing, turning. At 1.45 am I took half a sleeping pill. When the alarm went at 5.45 am, the duvet was on the floor and my body had contorted in such a way that

I was lying almost upside down. All the news bulletins said Hughes was a little battler and would pull though. 'How do you pull through if in a coma?' I wondered.

Karl Stefanovic, co-host of the *Today Show*, asked me some good questions. He had a helmet there and he asked me to explain how the ball had missed it as Hughes turned his head. After doing so, I suggested that a modification was required, as much to the shape of the design as to the membrane. I had shown how he was through the shot too early, which is as dangerous as too late. I talked about the 25-year-old Hughes I knew and went on to say that the bowler, Sean Abbott, had a difficult time ahead and would need support. As Mark Taylor put it on Nine News: 'I only hope Sean can forgive himself, which will be doubly difficult because there isn't actually anything to forgive himself for.'

I was home at 7.45 am, knackered. I tried to go back to sleep but it was hopeless. By 11 am, I was at the Australian Golf Club for the pro-am event on the eve of the The Australian Open. Rory McIlroy was back to defend the title he had won the year before from Adam Scott in a thrilling finish at Royal Sydney. But everyone was talking about Phillip Hughes.

On the way there I had got to talk to Clarke at last. He was keeping a long vigil at the hospital and was doing all he could to support Hughes's family. He sounded nervous and tired. There was no change to Hughes's condition. I didn't say as much to Clarke, but I was worried that the surgeon had said nothing encouraging. One might expect 'Phillip is stable' or, better still, 'Surgery was successful', but there was nothing positive. In fact, there was nothing.

Throughout the afternoon, 30 people must have asked me about him and I had no idea what to say. 'He'll be right,' they said. 'Yes, I hope so,' I replied. My golf was off-the-chart bad. The pro in our group was Richard Green, who liked his cricket. Hughes remained the topic of conversation.

27 November

Up early again. It was a cool, grey morning. I was on the tee at 7 am to see McIlroy hit off with Geoff Ogilvy. Rory looked as tired as I felt. He had won the Race to Dubai on Sunday, flown to Australia on Monday, played the course for the first time on Tuesday, spoken at the dinner, headlined the pro-am on Wednesday and all the while barely slept because of the time change.

At the turn, the drizzle began and I was cold. I ducked into the coffee shop and stayed there until eleven o'clock before venturing out again to see him play the last three holes for a two-under-par score of 69. Not much to report, really. The weather took the occasion out of the golf. His ball-striking was magnificent but his putter was as cold as the rest of us. The spectators were mute, the course difficult; 69 was a good effort, if not the effort we came to see.

At 2 pm I switched on the telly, hit the sofa and nodded off. The last thing I remember is Scott missing a putt to go to four over par.

Sometimes you have no idea why you have woken up. A noise probably or a niggling concern. Channel 7 had interrupted its coverage of the golf with a newsflash . . . The life support had been turned off.

Phillip Hughes was dead.

———

This what I wrote for Cricinfo in the moments that followed.

Cap 408 has moved on. There was no chance to say goodbye. Phillip Hughes won his Baggy Green in 2009 at the age of twenty. The cap is a symbol for Australia, made famous by Trumper and Bradman, but worn with equal pride by all who have followed them. Not least among those is Hughes.

These past 48 hours, the game had gathered around him at St Vincent's Hospital in Sydney. They had flown from across the vast southern land, sensing danger. Their loss has no explanation. Their grief has no boundary. Their mortality is set before them.

Cricket is proven to be brutal. Men have wilted before men. The strength of one is the weakness of another. There are bullies, there are heroes. The game sorts them all out. And it takes care of its own. The cricket family was suspended in fear. The cricketers who came to Phillip's bedside wanted to take care of their own. When the dreadful news came, the opportunity had been taken from their hands.

The photographs of him tell his story. Gifted, cheeky, kind, honest and humble are words that reflect the images. Others might be 'generous of spirit', 'self-effacing in reflection', 'unconventional in play'. His batting was an adventure. From it, came 26 first-class hundreds and the certainty of many more. Maybe he was to return to Australian colours next week at the Gabba, maybe not. But he would have done so soon, for he had a quite unique talent. It was a matter of time. But he ran out of time.

The blow to his head might happen to any cricketer, any day. A regulation ball—not too slow, not too fast—that he went at too early, by just a fraction. That fraction meant the end of his life. It really is that thin a line. The brutal game.

Helmets became a regular part of cricket in the late 1970s. So fast and aggressive was the bowling in WSC that Kerry Packer wanted his batsmen protected. Tony Greig, who had previously borne the brunt of Dennis Lillee and Jeff Thomson in a cloth cap, was among the first to wear the white, motorbike-style crash helmet. Lillee hit him on it as if to make a point. Greig mimicked the buckling of his legs. Phillip Hughes was not mimicking. The ball missed his helmet by enough to strike what we now know to be a weak area. So weak there was no way back.

Australia is devastated. That is not an exaggeration. Cricketers are an important part of the country's history and of its culture. Cricket is more than the national sport or the summer game. It is a way of life. The game is the soundtrack of summer, its players the orchestra. Around the land, as families rejoice in sunshine, warmth, light and space, cricket continues to resonate. Children play and imitate. Adults do the same or collect around barbecues, drink beer and select teams.

Many thought Hughes should be back in the team. Others disagreed. Everyone had a view. Whatever that view may have been, people liked Hughes. There was something infectious there, something quite thrilling in the expectation of him. The loss of that expectation has shaken the country to its core.

What people saw was a hunger for cricket and a respect for life. This is not a combination that every player has found, though the lesson is clear. From it has come unilateral support and national distress. He was, as Andrew Flintoff said in a tweet, 'a cracking lad'. Flintoff roughed him up in Test matches, and the way one man reacts to another in such a situation reveals a great deal.

Just before Flintoff got to him in the English summer of 2009, he played two innings in Durban that were extraordinary. The South African pace attack was the best going around and the splendid little fella flayed them. In the first he made 115, hitting 19 fours and two sixes. In the second, he made 160, with a further 15 fours and three sixes.

It is difficult to paint the picture of these performances, because that is what they were. Unusual and uncomplicated, compelling and irresistible, Hughes left a brushstroke on the canvas of the game. It was a different, almost brave new world that he created in that match with his prize fighter's approach set before an artist's flourish. The sadness was that it was brief. Soon, Flintoff exposed a flaw and the selectors responded with a lack of faith. The will-he, won't-he story had begun.

Now it is over. The death of the man, Phillip Joel Hughes, is a tragedy that will live with us forever. He was not yet 26, for goodness' sake. Not yet in his prime. We pray he had some idea of the joy he brought to so many.

I wrote this while the various television networks devoted every minute to the tragedy. Mainly, I shivered a little.

The game I have loved all through my life had killed a man.

19 November

Clarke made an official comment to the media. He spoke about his friend and the loss that he, along with the whole team, was feeling. He appeared beyond pain, frequently breaking down or stopping to suck in huge gulps of air. He had been at the side of the family, so had suffered their grief as well as his own. He spoke for all Australian cricketers about the many merits of their friend. It was agony to watch. I imagined he would give a tribute at the funeral on Wednesday, so he had more of this to come. His most recent text to me said, 'Mate, I only wish I could have done more to save my little bro. So sad, bud. I have to do media again tomorrow as captain. Going to be so tough. Not sure I have it in me.' Well, he did have. Clarke's stock was rising. His leadership qualities had never been more relevant.

THE HUGHES LEGACY

3 December 2014

'Is this what we call the spirit of cricket?' asked Michael Clarke. And indisputably the answer was yes. In a concise, brave and hugely pertinent tribute to Phillip Hughes, the Australian captain opened the eyes of the game. The spirit of cricket is in its people, in their respect for one another and in their respect for the game. Clarke recognised this and found the words to say so.

Since the appalling news that Hughes's fight had been lost, a beautiful thing had emerged. Cricket had united through a cascade of love and compassion. The town of Macksville led the way with its dignity and strength. From Macksville to Mumbai and on to Manchester, people had grieved for the passing of one so gifted and for the scar left upon the game. Now the players could heal that scar and, again, Clarke said as much: 'Phillip's spirit, which is now a part of our game forever, will act as a custodian of the sport we love.' Clarke paused, drew breath, held his nerve and added, 'We must listen to it, we must cherish it, we must learn from it, we must dig in and get through to tea. And we must play on.'

With those words, Clarke threw down the gauntlet. Stop the rancour, stop the sledging, play the game and ignite the friendships that make it so special. Sledging is not 'a part of the game', as is so loosely proposed. Playing 'tough' cricket does mean playing ugly cricket. Witness Hutton, Benaud, the Nawab of Pataudi and Sobers, and the standards they set that have long since become extinct.

Instead, applaud your opponent for his skill and his courage, for without these there is no game. Do not be ashamed of kindness because the energy that comes from it is the energy of life. Cricket deserves more than had come its way of late. Now it was a game at the crossroads, and where we took it from there would define its future forever. None of these ideals can bring Phillip back, but they can begin the path of his legacy.

A remarkable service was held in Macksville that day. Through excruciating pain, messages of love, faith, family and belief were driven home to the thousands present and the tens of thousands more who watched on television and listened on radio. The Youth Group cover of 'Forever Young', a gloriously simple hymn of popular music by the band Alphaville, opened the occasion, and Elton John's 'Don't Let the Sun Go Down on Me' closed it. Phillip's father, Greg, carried the coffin front left, and etched upon his face was the terrible truth: he was saying goodbye.

As the funeral cortege made its way through the streets of a typically loyal and united Australian country town, people lined the pavements with bats and hats and stumps and balls, and signs emblazoned with the words that best described one of their own. A young one and a good one had been ripped from their grasp, and their ashen faces told you they knew not why. Even the people of the church struggle with that one. No one knows why. But some can find a reason and can see hope.

Lessons must be learnt. This shocking accident was not such a one-off. David Richardson, chief executive of the ICC, told me how South African businessman Michael Meeser and his wife lost their eleven-year-old son, Daniel, in an eerily similar incident in 2009. Daniel was practising at the Daryll Cullinan Cricket Academy in South Africa and, though wearing a helmet, was struck just behind his left ear attempting a sweep shot. He remained standing for a while before collapsing, much as Hughes did at the Sydney Cricket Ground. The neurosurgeon operated to remove some of the skull in order to relieve pressure on the brain from the bleeding, but Daniel never regained consciousness. Three days later, he died.

Many years ago, the father of a close friend of mine died from almost exactly the same blow in an English club game. Nick Kemp was playing for Kent against Middlesex in a Sunday League match when told that his father, John, had been rushed to hospital and was undergoing brain surgery. John Kemp spent three months in a coma and did not recover.

This was before helmets, of course, but the point is that this area of the neck and skull is weak, and an urgent modification of the helmet was now required to provide protection.

The reactionary call for a limit on short-pitched bowling made little sense. The same argument might recommend that tackles be taken out of rugby; obstacles removed from the British jump racing season; and tight and potentially dangerous surges ruled off limits for Formula One drivers. The very nature of sport demands courage and instinct. From this comes much of its appeal. The hook and pull strokes that made batsmen such as Viv Richards and Ricky Ponting so admired came from bowling that was pitched short. Many of cricket's most thrilling moments have come from brilliant and dramatic exploitation of the short ball. What is needed is strong, intelligent umpiring and a sensible understanding of a late-order batsman's ability.

Around the time of the funeral, Shane Warne showed me a picture of New Zealand players in Sharjah he had seen on Twitter. The words and stats on it read: 'NZ bowled 1135 balls in the 3rd Test match, not even a single bouncer. Took all 20 wickets, didn't even celebrate a single wicket. Williamson didn't celebrate his 50, 100 and 150. McCullum didn't celebrate his 100, 150, 200. McCullum dedicated his double ton to Hughes, played with jersey written "PH" on it. This team has won a million hearts as well as the Test match.' Now that is the spirit of the game. Of course, it is not the only way to do it—and the absence of bouncers sure works best on the pitches in the Middle East—but it is an attitude and an option worthy of review.

There is a banter to cricket that should never be disregarded, and an effervescence in personality that can be encouraged in myriad guises. We don't want soft cricket. Or a game without emotion or reaction. Even anger has its place, especially when funnelled into performance. Cricket is a game for all people, of all temperaments, in all moods. It has long run parallel to life—and we live in an impatient and contrary age—but it need not reflect the lowest common denominators of that life. As Martin Crowe wisely wrote in the pages of Cricinfo, we need to move 'Towards a kinder, gentler game'.

Before leaving Macksville I came face to face with Greg, Phillip's father, whom I had not previously met. I told him how much I admired his son. He replied that he was immensely proud of both Phil and his siblings, Jason and Megan, who had spoken so well. And then he gave me a great big, teary hug.

Many of the very best to have played the game were in town to honour and celebrate a young life that had been cut down after just 26 years. Yes, he had more, much more to give. But if Clarke was right, if the spirit and the energy that were Phillip Hughes can live on, the game and its future will be safer, richer, brighter.

THE SPIRIT OF CRICKET

In addition to being responsible for the laws of the game, the MCC has long believed that cricket should be played in accordance with its traditional 'spirit'. In the late 1990s, I was asked on to a small subcommittee, originated by Lord Cowdrey and chaired by Ted Dexter, with the brief to enshrine the 'spirit of cricket' in the game's laws. At first I hesitated because of the risk of it sounding pompous, imperial. In the end, I accepted because I felt the need for a reference to the spirit of the game that was clear and direct and hoped to help find it. Anyway, Dexter, who had taken on the role after Colin Cowdrey died, is anything but pompous.

The task was not as easy as it may sound. Everywhere, and everybody it seemed, had a different interpretation of the spirit of the game. We therefore ended up with something vague, not by intention but of necessity. In England, for example, young cricketers have been expected to 'walk'. But at the first Cowdrey Lecture in 2000, Richie Benaud said that as a boy he was taught to wait for the umpire's decision and then to accept it without rancour.

Tony Greig was astonished to find that English county cricketers walked, but then came to understand the value of such self-policing in a game where every player and umpire knew each other well and soon rooted out the good from the bad. Greig told his England players that he respected their right to walk in county cricket but that he wanted them to stand their ground in Test cricket, given the obvious advantage it gave to the opposition if they didn't.

Wasim Akram says that no one told him of similar rules and tradition as he grew up. He says he just sort of learnt along the way. Clearly, the child brought up in the streets and markets of Lahore or Karachi will see the world very differently from one educated at an English private school. In Pakistan, every fielder appeals for lbw, and they may ask why not? In other parts of the world, it is frowned upon to appeal unless you are the bowler, wicketkeeper or first slip.

Such issues are open to wide interpretation, which is why we have laws. Adam Gilchrist and Brian Lara were walkers but the modern game has not seen many others. Television has proved that catches claimed have not carried. Equally, television has proved imperfect and ruled that many others have not carried when they almost surely have. This humiliates a fielder and exposes technology as flawed and therefore misleading.

The preamble to the laws that we came up with says, 'Cricket is a game that owes much of its unique appeal to the fact that it should be played not only within its laws but also within the Spirit of the Game. Any action which abuses this spirit causes injury to the game itself.' We went on to outline the various areas of concern and interest—responsibility of the captains, players' conduct, fair and unfair play, authorisation of umpires to intervene—and then to list a few examples of actions that we considered, without argument, to be against the spirit of the game, such as disputing an umpire's decision or abusing an opponent or umpire with foul language or violence.

We also included the word that seemed most relevant to me—'respect'—and applied it in such contexts as respect for your opponent, for your captain, for the umpires and for the game's traditional values. As I related earlier, I myself had been wildly guilty of abusing the spirit of the game when Hampshire played Pakistan in 1992. I hope I was able to apply some of what I learnt that day to my brief time on this committee.

I know that many current and former first-class players doubt the value of the preamble, thinking it idealistic and unworkable. I don't agree. I believe a guideline is necessary and I hope it will be an inspiration to schoolchildren who presently too often see unpleasant behaviour when watching cricket on television and consider it the norm. I don't say we got the guideline absolutely right and should add that I completely understand the need for different interpretations. The fact is that the Spirit of Cricket is not a law and therefore does not dictate what is permitted or otherwise. It is an appeal to keep certain values in mind and, as such, offers a broader context than the laws themselves.

———

I include these thoughts here because I see Phillip Hughes as the best of the spirit of cricket. Think of that delightful, innocent smile; think of the flair with which he batted; the country upbringing that sat so well on grander stages; the absence of histrionics when poorly treated by selectors; his lack of cynicism; his generosity to fellow man; his myriad outside interests; and the sense of a life that sparkled, all too briefly.

Perhaps most remarkable was the global outpouring of grief at the news of his death. From one side of the world to the other, in places far flung and little known, candles were lit, wreaths and bats were laid down, vigils were held, prayers were read, songs were sung, concerts were interrupted and schools stopped in silence. Think of it: almost everyone who had been touched by cricket, and many who had not, reflected upon the life of a human being they did not even know. Each one of us had been confronted by our own mortality and left devastated that a young man so innocent and free had been taken.

We needed no inquest. Cricket was responsible. And that is why the spirit of cricket matters so much.

CHAPTER 8

Fast bowling

I did not pick up the ball from Gladstone Small that broke my cheekbone. The one from Jeff Thomson that hit me in the nuts was a full toss—imagine. Sylvester Clarke broke my right index finger with a good-length delivery that spat at my hand like fat from a frying pan. Allan Donald hit my shoulder so full on and with such force that my body gave way and I collapsed to my knees. I tried taking a ball from Courtney Walsh on the chest, very Brian Close, but it took the wind and guts out of me. Javagal Srinath hit my helmet and the ball ricocheted, one bounce, all the way to the long-leg fielder who assumed I had hit it and threw himself forward for the catch. Waqar Younis smashed up my left hand with a ball so fast I barely knew he had let it go. Wasim Akram broke my toe with a spearing yorker that went on to shatter the stumps. I hit the deck after that one too and people thought it was very funny. Having had a laugh and then shown some sympathy, Wasim told me I was out. These are the ones I clearly remember. There were more. Cricket is a dangerous game.

I think it is right to say that my own standard of batting swung above and below the median line. This inconsistency was hugely frustrating. I put it down to the demands of captaincy, a lack of application and too much cricket. In good times I was talked about by media and selectors as a possible Test cricketer, though I came closest to being chosen to play for England as captain. Simon Barnes writing in *The Times* once said: 'Mark Nicholas' main role in life seems to be to decorate the argument about the England captaincy without ever being very likely to receive it.' Ouch.

In bad times, I should have dropped myself from the Hampshire team but the culture was different then. The club wanted the fellow appointed captain to be on the park. Now, with the influence of managers and coaches, that would not be the case.

Fast bowling could be a problem—not always, but often enough to become an Achilles heel that troubled me during two or three different periods of my career. My reactions and footwork were slow, so I relied on native instinct and timing. I was at my best when I took on the quicks because it got the feet moving and improved my mindset. Occasionally I had my day and especially remember a warm handshake from Curtly Ambrose upon reaching a decent hundred against Northamptonshire, along with a rare back-slap from Courtney Walsh after an unbeaten 70-odd that carried us over the line in a tight match with Gloucestershire. If I had a message about batting against fast bowling it would be to look to score, otherwise the crease can become a dark place. To defend well against real pace, you need a damn good method. In attack, you can get away with a bit of luck.

I made an unbeaten 115 for MCC against the 1985 Australians and was within a hair's-breadth of being caught in the gully off Thomson first ball. I had gone in after Gooch was dismissed by Thommo twice in two balls—bowled off a no ball, then bowled next ball. Nervous, I fended at a bouncer and watched it loop a centimetre or so over Kepler Wessels' outstretched fingers. I played some shots after that. The other bowlers were Geoff Lawson, Simon O'Donnell and the slow left-armer Murray Bennett. I got stuck into Bennett.

I am often asked who was the fastest bowler I faced. Thomson is the answer and by the time I had sniff of him, he was five years past his most frightening. He took 7 for 22 for Middlesex against Hampshire in a Benson & Hedges Cup match at Lord's in 1981 and didn't win the man-of-the-match award. (Incredibly, Alec Bedser, the chairman of selectors, was adjudicating and gave it to David Turner, Hampshire's Wiltshire-born battler, who made 69 in a low run chase.)

It is said that Thomson's action delivered the ball as if it came from a catapult, which is about right. It was as difficult to pick up as it was thrilling to face, like one of those insane rides in an amusement park where people scream out their mixed emotions. That same summer he came down the hill in the championship match at Basingstoke and hit me in the groin with a full toss. Strewth, he was quick. I lay writhing just 20 yards from the very spot where Wasim Akram was to shatter my toe some years later. Mike Brearley looked down at me and said, 'It's very apparent your mother was an actress. Now, if you're okay, would you mind if we got on with the game.' Bastard. A month later, Brearley was back as captain of England and winning the Ashes. Genius.

In short spells, others I have faced briefly matched Thomson— notably Imran Khan and Garth Le Roux, Akram and Younis, Andy Roberts, Ian Bishop, Rodney Hogg and Donald. Joel Garner could get a wriggle on too, by the way. Marshall took three balls to bounce me out in an exhibition game in New York—that was fast. You can't count three balls, though. It was the only time I ever appeared on an 'England' team sheet and my contribution was instantly forgettable. Marshall might have been the best fast bowler of them all. I faced Dennis Lillee and he wasn't too dusty, either. They have to be the top two, with Roberts and Akram nibbling at their heels.

Richie Benaud maintained that the fastest bowler he ever saw was Frank Tyson, marginally ahead of Thomson. Tyson hardly ever bowled short, said Benaud, just zeroed in on the stumps and your toes. The Typhoon only played in seventeen Test matches, taking 76 wickets at 18.56 each. When asked the same question, pretty much everyone else says Thommo. Others in this rarefied speed space are Harold Larwood, Roy Gilchrist, Michael Holding, Shoaib Akhtar and Brett Lee.

Shoaib Akhtar bowled cricket's first recorded 100-mile-per-hour ball in Cape Town in 2003. Thommo reckons 100 miles per hour was his stock ball. Nick Knight played the Shoaib delivery to square leg as if he were facing a county trundler in a Sunday League game. Paul Terry maintains that the fastest bowling he faced was from a seething Ian Botham in a cup match at Taunton, and Paul played a couple of Tests against the West Indies in 1984. The cricketers of Lancashire and Worcestershire say that a match on a lightning-quick pitch at Old Trafford in the early 1990s made the county bowlers feel like Lillee and Thomson in Perth. Mind you, one of them was Patrick Patterson. Michael Slater will never forget Devon Malcolm in Perth on the England tour of 1994–95, just as the South Africans still shiver at the thought of Malcolm at the Oval a few months earlier.

In the mid-1980s, Robert Maxwell launched *Sportsweek* magazine. The mag's advertising campaigns on television were brilliant. The best of them was cricket-specific and opened with the back view of Joel Garner returning to his mark. The picture was 'soft'—maybe a touch defocused—and relayed in slow motion from a locked-off camera just above the bats-man's stumps. The soundtrack was a beating heart and over it a man's voice, speaking slowly and deliberately, said: 'You've got two-fifths of a second. He can bowl full, he can bowl a good length, he can bowl short; you can play forward or you can play back.' At which the audio is turned up: boom-boom, boom-boom, boom-boom.

Now in the distance, Garner turns to face the camera and begin his approach to the wicket, head bent forward, knees high like sprinter, long powerful arms working hard at his side. 'He can swing the ball, he can seam the ball, he has got the yorker and the bouncer. What have you got?' Audio up: boom-boom, boom-boom, boom-boom.

By now Garner is close to the stumps and bringing himself to his full height. He is six feet and ten inches tall, immensely strong and menacing. The heartbeat soundtrack has sped up: boom-boomboomboomboomboom . . .

'You can block or drive or cut or pull, or hook, if you dare.' Boomboomboomboom . . .

'The close fielders can smell fear. Is it yours?' Boomboom-boomboomboomboom . . .

At which point Garner releases the ball from his hand and the action cuts to normal speed. The ball comes at the camera like a bullet from a gun.

'You can play for . . .'

Whereupon, in full frame, sheet glass—previously undetected by the camera but encased around the stumps—violently shatters at full impact and volume. It is as if a grenade has exploded.

'Too late.' Pause. 'Get inside sport, get inside *Sportsweek.*'

Which is pretty much it. Against fast bowling there are a number of options but no time. The things that matter are preparation and instinct. There is physical danger, so you are either up for that or not; there are a lot of balls from which you cannot score, forget them; from those you can, make sure of your timing, for if you try to hit the ball too hard you will miss out. You don't actually think about these options as the ball is travelling, you just react, trusting practice and eye. Eye is the key. Don't even think about taking your eye off the ball. If you do, the glass shatters.

When I heard the news about the blow to Phillip Hughes, I was reminded of Imran and Le Roux at Hove in 1980. I was wearing a sunhat and my Bradfield College thigh pad. I had never been much interested in thigh pads, backing myself to make contact with most balls bowled on that line and to score from them. The sunhat became a target for bloodthirsty opponents. Here I was, a naive public schoolboy, swaggering out in a floppy sunhat. Thinking back I cringe.

Imran bowled up the hill at alarming pace. He was loose, having just made an unbeaten hundred, and motivated by the sunhat. He moved with a feline grace that disguised the devil; Garth came down the hill like a battering ram. Garth bowled the heavier ball, the one that hurt most. Imran bowled the one more likely to get you out: the fast inswinger from wide on the crease that, if pitched up, homed in on the stumps and, if short, homed in on you. The Hove pitch was quick and bouncy back then and Imran and Garth loved playing this bully-boy game with county batsmen who were woefully short on experience, technique and, in many cases, courage too.

Imagine standing by the side of the motorway and watching the cars in the fast lane flying past you at 90 miles per hour and more. There is a drama and excitement in both that sight and sound, and there is shock in its potential. The cricket ball weighs 5 and a half ounces and is hard as a rock when new. The seam is strung tight and feels rough, like sisal. The new cricket ball is a potential weapon of destruction. You are standing 20 yards away and you are the target. You are the 'too late' in the ad.

Try standing directly behind and close to the net when the professionals are practising. If a batsman plays and misses, you will instinctively recoil your head and maybe your body too. You will be surprised by how fast the ball comes and the threat it poses. Multiply this by double the effort, double the adrenaline, often a faster pitch, the presence of an opponent at the crease to awaken the senses of the bowler, and add in the urgings of colleagues and crowd. There is no way to replicate fast bowling, only to imagine what it might be like. Honestly, a high percentage of recreational cricketers would be shocked by how fast Shane Warne bowled his leg-break and certainly by the sound of the revs he imparted to the ball fizzing through the air. So imagine Imran and Le Roux or Lillee and Thomson.

What to do? I think the first thing is to stay very still. Allan Border flexed his knees and dipped his head a little, just before the bowler released the ball. Then his head was still when the ball began its journey. Of course, you need courage and you need to stay smart. You will get out—everyone does eventually— so worrying about the loss of your wicket is wasted energy. As Ian Chappell advises, watch the bloody ball from the hand in the bowler's approach and follow it like a hawk until it reaches you. By all means have trigger movements but be as near to off stump as suits your game when the ball is delivered. In other words, leave yourself as little to do as possible. There is no time, so improve the odds by being secure and ready.

In this two-fifths of a second, you are not processing ideas and coming to conclusions. You are simply reacting. Your brain already has preconceptions and responses. Let your instinct work with those. Limit your options and reduce the likelihood of error. Decide, for example, if you'd prefer to duck or sway from the short ball; to stand and defend or to ride the bounce; to hook or to uppercut. Have the answers as your default position. Keep your grip on the bat soft and defend very straight, back down the pitch, but allow the pace of the ball to create angles and deflections off the blade. You will get ones and twos, even occasional boundaries, simply by timing these defensive actions. Be on the balls of your feet so you can move late and quick, to respond when the bowler is off target.

If you get it wrong, you hear the sound and feel the sting of ball on flesh. Or you will recoil from the impact of ball on helmet. Or you will need to manage the pain of your compressed thumb against the handle. Or sense the break of bone. Or see your middle stump fly out of the ground.

In 1980, I could not cope with Imran and Le Roux. Certainly not on that pitch anyway. We also faced Lillee that year as the Australians warmed up for the Centenary Test. I couldn't cope with him either. Not even close: caught Yallop, bowled Lillee for 0. In the second innings it was caught Marsh bowled Thomson for 7. A legion of better players than I went to their cricketing grave with Lillee and Thomson as the executioners on their headstone.

Ashley Mallett told me a story of being at the pub after the first day's play in that match at Southampton, when a young bloke came up to him and asked how it had gone. 'Not bad,' he said, 'not that I did much myself.' He paid for his drinks and turned back to the lad who had asked the question: 'Good workout for the fast bowlers, albeit against a pretty ordinary Hampshire team. The top-order batting was weak as piss,' he added, 'the number three a shocker for a first-class team.' I was the young lad. I was also Hampshire's number three.

One major issue that hounded me was the playing of the man not the ball. I was in awe of these guys. I tried to isolate the ball, god knows I did, but my mind beat me. And then beat me up. I tried visualisation. I saw a shrink—recommended by Bob Willis and Viv Richards—who used hypnosis. His name was Arthur 'Two Sheds' Jackson and he saw people at his home in North Sydney. Some nickname. But even Arthur couldn't help. I sat in Viv's chair but the magic stayed put. I had to face the fact that I was stuck with my perception of the game's past, which insisted these guys were too good for me.

I searched for something present, something real. Reality is neither a memory of what has gone before, nor is it the future. Reality is the ball bowled there and then, but I couldn't damn well grab reality.

I wish I could have had another crack a few years later, by which time I was helping out young cricketers with this sort of stuff. My ecstatic celebration upon reaching a hundred against Ambrose in 1994 was tempered by the realisation that Ambrose, who was busy taking 7 for 44, was another young kid's nightmare. My conclusion is that you can train a mind but not change it.

To explain further: I thought that every ball Lillee bowled to me had my number on it, even when he came back with creaking joints to play for Northamptonshire. Roberts played against Hampshire for Leicestershire one season and I thought much the same about him. They weren't all like that, probably they were the only two with such a hold on me. The rest became manageable—no doubt you become better equipped and less starstruck as you grow older.

Having said that, in 1991 Donald bowled me two balls so fast I must relate them. Chris Smith's wife, Julie, was due with their first child so he refused to play in a championship match at Portsmouth—refused! I opened the batting in his place and on the way to the middle asked Paul Terry which of us would take the first ball. He said he usually did but we could go left and right. I said fine and went left. Donald marked out his run to the right. I took guard and looked at the field. Very funny lads. Keith Piper, the Warwickshire keeper, and the slips were miles back. Like miles. I laughed. But there was no joke. The United Services ground at Portsmouth had a quick pitch and this one had a green tinge upon its granite-hard surface. There were four slips and a gully, a short leg, a leg gully and behind him a long leg. Andy Lloyd, the captain and a mate of mine, was at short point. I looked at him as if to say, 'Hoho, me old mucker.' He just winked, a pretty mean wink I should add, and then turned to give A.D. a final push before battle.

Well, the first ball came at my head with a ferocity I had not seen since Imran and Le Roux. It was like a guided missile and I was the target. I threw back my head and, by a whisker, avoided destruction. Piper leapt to gather the ball above his head and then jumped around as a man jumps on hot coals, before wringing his hands as a man who has burnt his fingers upon a hot plate. The slips loved it. Lloyd urged for more from this monster. Christ.

I thought, 'I need time here.' I walked towards Paul, who was not eager to talk but I insisted. I said I would leave the next ball alone, assuming it wasn't straight, and we should run the bye because no way could Piper get it to the stumps in time to run us out. I added we might have more byes than runs by lunch. Paul neither liked the idea nor found the follow-up funny. He said we shouldn't take the piss. I said, well, maybe not, but we should do all we could to piss them off.

After some choice lines from Lloyd based around 'Get the fuck on with it', I settled back into my stance. Jeeesus. The next ball was quicker and marginally better directed, this time at my throat.

As I began to throw back my head I sensed it was too late and my hands instinctively rose to protect my life. The ball brushed my right glove. 'Too late' . . . Piper flew high to his right but the ball arced a fraction in its flight, touching only his fingertips, and as he hit the ground so too did the ball—a few yards behind him. We ran. The umpire signalled bye. Shit. Paul played out the over. Now I was to face my old nemesis, Gladstone Small. It didn't take him long. Stranded on the crease as he nipped one back off the seam, I was plumb in front. Given out for 0, although I actually made 1, sort of. The Warwickshire players began ahoopin' and ahollerin'. Paul went on to make a hundred and never once ran a bye.

Next morning I paced out the distance between me and Piper, 30 yards. Try it some time. It looks so ridiculous you won't believe me. Paul reckoned we were that far back a couple of times ourselves: once when Maco bowled to Glamorgan in a Sunday League game (I do recall that we didn't have a fielder in front of square that day, a 40-over match); and another time when he mowed down Derbyshire in a championship match.

In the second innings I made 5 and see from *Wisden* that I was caught Piper, bowled Donald. I have a hazier memory of this. I remember that the Warwickshire players were all over me, hyenas every one. Donald pounded in and delivered a ball that kicked from short of a length around off stump, of that much I am sure. I either nicked it or gloved it. Donald sprinted past me, right arm aloft in salute of the moment. I was flattered that my wicket mattered to him so much.

MY BUSTED FACE

Gladstone Small wasn't fast but he was extremely nippy. Gladstone was nippy enough to hurry Test-match batsmen and nippy enough to make me wish I had worn a helmet. I was on about 60 when Bob Willis returned to the attack. I remember David Turner calling for a helmet and asking if I wanted mine. 'Don't think so. Pretty flat out here. I'm seeing it fine.' Big mistake, huge.

Willis bowled an over at Turner. Not much happened. The first ball of the next over was from Small to me. I'm pretty sure I saw it pitch but saw nothing else. It was shortish and reared from the easy-paced pitch like it was angry. I hardly moved. At the very last moment, fear of the unknown made me jerk my neck. Too late. It hit me flush in the left cheekbone and ricocheted straight back down the pitch. I collapsed like a sack of shit. Everyone came running but I felt nothing and knew only the shock. There was blood. They called the medics, who called the ambulance. I was taken off on a stretcher. I remember the ambulance journey specifically because of my fear of the extent of the damage and the likely surgery. I hate all that hospital stuff. They had to operate pretty quickly. My mum turned up from London not long before the anaesthetist started to count me out: five, four, three, two, one. Goodnight and good luck.

God, it was like I had been hit by a bus. Everywhere around my head felt heavy and tight. My mouth was dry. My eyes stung. I was straining to breathe through my nose. Oh god. I drifted back to sleep.

Mum was there when I woke up. The nurse came in and then the consultant surgeon. He said the operation was complicated but a success. They had decided not to cut into my face but, instead, to make an incision by the side of the back of my ear, raise the flesh on the side of my face and lift the compressed cheekbone back into place. I could play again in six to eight weeks but would be well advised to wear a helmet. Thanks for that.

The areas around my left eye socket, the left side of my nose and the upper left teeth are still numb to this day. The hair round my left ear grows funny. That's it, no more collateral damage. I went back to the ground the following evening after play, all bruised and bandaged up. The boys were in the communal plunge bath and in a spirited mood after a good day. They briefly went quiet when I appeared around the corner with my mummified head. Then they cracked on.

It wasn't Small's fault. I should have worn a helmet or watched the ball more closely. Bloody stupid. Gladstone is a great bloke, salt of the game. We laugh about it now, or I do;

he gets a bit sheepish. It happened near the end of the English season and I played in South Africa about six weeks later. I hated the compulsory helmet thing. It took the winter to get used to it and I was okay by the next county season. In fact, I don't think I thought about it again at the crease.

I have often thought how lucky I was not to have been hit in the face by Imran or Le Roux at Hove. I reckon the ball would have come out the back of my skull.

———

I remember Wes Hall's long run-up and gold chain. I remember listening to the wireless when John Snow hit Terry Jenner in the head at Sydney. I loved Snow—what a bowler, what a dude. And I came to be a friend of Jenner's. I remember Thommo terrifying England in 1974–75 when, watching the news clips from 12,000 miles away, English county batsmen hid behind their sofas.

We all remember Lillee, perhaps the most dazzling sight of them all. I remember David Steele lunging bravely forward to West Indians and Australians alike. Steele was chosen for England by Tony Greig, who took a survey among county umpires: 'Who do the fast bowlers around the circuit find most difficult to get out?' asked Greigy. After Boycott, who was unavailable, the reply was close to unanimous: 'David Steele.' So Greig told the other selectors he wanted the grey-haired chap with specs in his team and Greigy was a hard man to argue against. It is true that Steele went down a flight of stairs too many for his first Test innings at Lord's in 1975. Nerves will do that to you. Instead of entering the Long Room and making his way to the pitch, he found himself in the gents while 28,000 folk waited for him outside. Luckily he had a sense of humour. He shook a few well-wishing hands, climbed back up a flight of stairs and made a brave fifty against Lillee and Thomson, who at first thought him a joke—'Who the hell is this guy, Groucho Marx?' Soon enough they came to respect him. Steele became a national celebrity. Littlewoods sent him cheques and butchers sent him steaks. He was voted BBC Sportsman of Year in 1975, the unlikeliest winner they ever did have.

I remember Michael Holding at the Oval in 1976, the driest English summer of them all, and his 14 wickets. I don't recall England being much good—with the notable exception of Dennis Amiss, who was a seriously fine player. Holding bowled so fast it was funny to watch England try to bat. The ground was bone-dry, Viv made 291, and Mikey bowled at the speed of light to blokes without helmets. He ran in smoothly and so light of foot that they christened him Whispering Death. He bowled mainly full, to hit the stumps and the pads.

I went to the 1973 Cup Final at Lord's and when the public announcer said, 'From the Nursery end, Mike Procter,' I rushed to my seat. I shall never, ever forget Proccy steam-rolling Hampshire at Southampton in the Benson & Hedges Cup semifinal in 1977. He took a hat-trick and 4 in 5. What a cricketer. He sprinted in and bowled fast inswing with an unusual and thrilling action. Yes, Proc was a proper hero. In the age of the four great Test-match all-rounders—Botham, Hadlee, Imran and Kapil Dev—he had them all covered. But, of course, like Barry Richards and Graeme Pollock from the same era of South African cricket, he was denied a Test career by the government's policy of apartheid.

After that, I was playing against (and with) some of these guys.

A BEER WITH TIGER WOODS

The Emirates lounge at Melbourne airport was much like any other in 2009, just before it was tarted up. I cruised in, chuffed with my week's work for Channel Nine on the Australian

Masters. The tournament was won by Tiger Woods who, in just four sunlit days, had taken Australian golf back to the days of Greg Norman, when huge crowds followed the Shark's every step and rejoiced in his ability to transform the golf course into a theatre of dreams.

I had just interviewed Woods on the 18th green in front of 10,000 people. There was not a cloud in the sky nor an inkling of the fact that within a fortnight Woods's world was to be turned upside down by a fire hydrant, among other things. He had slipped on the gold jacket (a tournament tradition knocked off from the better known US Masters green jacket that is won each year at Augusta) lifted the trophy, thanked us for the cheque—'which Mom can buy some more koalas with'—and answered a series of Nicholas questions with charm and humour. I didn't know it at the time but he then made a dash for the international terminal at Melbourne airport. As did I.

Upon entering the lounge, I saw Geoff Ogilvy, who is such a good bloke. 'Hi Geoff, decent week, mate. Looked like the putter let you down.'

'No kidding,' he replied. 'Fancy a beer with us?'

'Sure.' And with that Tiger appeared with a couple of Crown lagers.

'You guys know each other,' said Geoff. 'You just had a chat on the 18th green.'

'Sure do. Hi, buddy,' said Tiger. Surreal.

'Thought you had your own plane?' I said.

'Gave it to Mom. She needs the space for all those fluffy kangaroos and koalas and stuff she's been buying.' Of course. Lucky Mom.

Geoff said, 'Mark is the face of cricket on Australian TV.' Good intro.

'Okay. Cool. Helluva game that,' said Tiger. Honest, he did.

'You watch cricket?'

'Yup, hours in hotel rooms, often through the night. Wish I understood it better. I mean, damn, those pitchers, they run at full speed, sprinting speed, right?'

I nodded. 'Bowlers,' I said.

'Right, bowlers. Then they jump, turn their body pretty much sideways during the jump, land in an unnatural position and pitch with a straight arm at around 90 miles per hour. That looks hard, buddy.'

'It's hard, Tiger.'

See, it was worth waiting for. Tiger Woods is into cricket. He said the biomechanics interested him, alongside the many parallels with baseball. He said Roger Federer really liked it, which had fired his own interest.

'What about their ankles, knees, hips? From the point of landing that front foot to the point of releasing the ball, the stress on the three crucial mid- and lower-body joints is extreme. The injuries must be long-term damaging. How many years do they play for?'

'Well, it's a . . .'

'And don't they move the ball in the air, like a baseball pitcher?'

'The best of them do, but . . .'

'And why do they land the ball in the field, not pitch it direct on the full to the batter?'

'Good luck,' said Geoff. 'Another beer, guys?'

Sure.

So I sat in an airport lounge explaining to Tiger Woods the detailed skills of fast bowling and the courage required to do it effectively and over a long career. That job done, he asked about Adam Gilchrist (he knew the name) hitting home runs. I told him Gilchrist was a freak, the ultimate game-changer. Then he asked about Warnie.

'I'd like to meet Warnie,' he said.

'And he'd like to meet you,' I replied.

'The Nike guys tell me he's a cool guy. I reckon we'd get on.'

'Yes, Warnie is a cool guy and you would.' We called him. No luck.

After 40 minutes of this, during which time I got in one question about golf, his people came to take him to the plane. He said Geoff and I should go with him. Riveting, a VIP route, hidden from the crowds. It was fun. I had been upgraded from business and guess where I was sitting? Across the aisle from Tiger. I tried Warnie on the phone again. No luck. (When we landed in Dubai there was message after message from Warne—'Give him my number, mate' overrode most of the others. So I did.) Tiger had a glass of champagne and then wine with his dinner. We chatted a bit more about spin bowling (I know, how bizarre is all this?). After that he put on headphones, pulled shut the doors of his Emirates first-class suite and the next I saw of him was thirteen hours later when we said our goodbyes.

I interviewed him exactly a year later, at the gala dinner on the eve of the 2010 Australian Masters. His manager told me not to touch upon 'you know what'. I thought, bugger that. He was on stage with Warne, two of the greatest sportsmen the world has ever seen. I began by asking if they had met before. 'Just now, upstairs, we had a beer together,' said Warnie.

'Do you have anything in common?'

———

No fast bowler performs without pain. Day in, day out, pain is a given. Tiger nailed that. Most have surgery at some point or another—back, knees, ankles mainly. Pace is the greatest gift but it comes at a price. Every decade or so different theories arrive to guard against injury. These tend to revolve around the physical action of bowling, which is subject to trends and change, and the workload. Footwear has evolved from a heavy boot made with leather soles and uppers, which was designed for strength and support, to a shoe that is more like a trainer and takes account of comfort and fashion. Most top bowlers work with the manufacturers to find something that balances the two. The ideal boot is light and resilient but still supportive, especially around the ankle. All bowlers are different. Marshall, who was so light on his feet, bowled in something like slippers—albeit with spikes in the sole—if the ground was dry but reverted to the tried and tested form of boot if the ground was soft or damp. Garner needed a work-man's footwear whatever the conditions.

The best and most classical action of the modern era was Lillee's: sideways on, eyes looking at the target from the left side of the left arm, right wrist perfectly behind the seam of the ball, head steady, front leg braced, left arm pulling the upper body into a complete flow-through. After starting out in Perth as a tearaway, Lillee applied the science of body and mind to the art of bowling fast, and wrote a fine book about it. He returned from serious back surgery to become a more complete bowler and year upon year added pieces to his jigsaw. By the time he packed it in as the world's leading wicket-taker, he had created the perfect template for others to study.

LILLEE AND THE MIRACLE MATCH

For all Lillee's magnificent Test-match performances, nothing was quite so dramatic as the Gillette Cup (one-day) semifinal he won for Western Australia against Queensland at the WACA in 1976. In what has been dubbed 'The Miracle Match'—the title of an excellent 2014 book by Ian Brayshaw, who played in the game for the home team—Lillee refused to bow in the face of near-certain defeat. Western Australia had been put in to bat by Greg Chappell and bowled out for 77. Rod Marsh rallied his players: 'There's a big crowd here. Let's not let them down. Let's make 'em fight for it.' Lillee's message was a little more raw: 'Fight for it be buggered. We're going to beat these bastards.'

Which is exactly what they did. Inside two hours, Lillee accepted the man-of-the-match award for figures of 4 for 21 from 7.3 eight-ball overs. He bowled Viv Richards for nought, had Chappell caught at the wicket by Marsh for 2 and knocked over David Ogilvie and Denis Schuller to complete the rout. When Viv Richards, who played all of that season for Queensland, was once asked if he remembered the Gillette Cup game at the WACA, he replied, 'Man, barely a day goes by without me remembering it.'

Lillee was a primal force. His long mane of dark hair, bristling moustache and flapping gold chain combined with an unbuttoned shirt and general snarl to give the impression of a pirate on the high seas. He ran in from such a distance, and with such menace, that the following eye became mesmerised. Upon reaching the crease at fever pitch, he released the ball with an authority and intent given to few others. He was, of course, blessed with myriad skills. By the end of his career, he could deliver everything from his original and beautiful outswingers to seamers and cutters with masterful changes of pace and angle. He overwhelmed the meek and confronted the strong, challenging them to match him blow for blow.

At his best, Lillee was the most dynamic and charismatic bowler of the age. If that Gillette Cup performance on the fast and bouncy Perth pitch stopped most of Australia in its tracks, his 11 wickets on a low pitch in the Melbourne Centenary Test of 1977—each one of them captured with innate cunning and unimaginable reserves of stamina—caught the attention of the world. The photograph of the winning moment when he traps Alan Knott leg before wicket and turns in his appeal to raise an arm to the sky is one of cricket's most enduring images. No other bowler could have made so much of the unresponsive surface. It was during this wonderful cricket match that John Arlott, commentating on radio, said, 'The seagulls on the top of the stands are as vultures recruited by Lillee.'

The Miracle Match is an excellent read, providing a more than useful social biography of the time and revealing profiles of the great players of the day. Just four months after the match, the cricket world was rocked by the formation of WSC. In the book, Kim Hughes, who batted at four for Western Australia in the game, says, 'Talking about the money we got that day—and it was the same for all of us, from the captain down—we later found out that the bloke on the gate, a lovely old fellow, got more than we each did for playing! And it was a huge game, televised Australia-wide and featuring such world stars as Richards, Chappell, Thomson, Lillee and Marsh, with a big crowd in attendance. Unbelievable entertainment and all we got for the part we played was 18 bucks. A ten, a five, a two and a one—all notes in those days!'

Lillee, who was winning a lot of matches and signing a lot of autographs for eighteen bucks a day, and was sick of the rip-off, had already spoken to his manager, Austin Robertson, about some breakaway matches for big money. Needing muscle and money, they approached Kerry Packer, who told them to hang tight for just a few months because he had an idea of his own they might like. No kidding. Packer has long been considered the villain who stole the old game and replaced it with the new. The reality is that it would probably have happened anyway. The players were ripe.

PROC AND SNOWBALL

If Lillee's method was testament to the orthodox, Procter was a vivid example of the unorthodox. Describing his action is difficult. My guess is that he sprinted to the wicket at a pace hitherto unseen, at least by any bowler in control of the delivery of the ball. Where Lillee had menace, Procter had venom; where Lillee had side-on outswing, Procter had chest-on inswing. Upon reaching the crease, he all but threw himself at the batsman, giving the impression of releasing the ball from the wrong foot. This was an illusion but all the more confusing and alarming for it. His arms worked like helicopter blades and the ball truly flew at the batsmen as if propelled by machine. It would skid and swing, and when he rolled his fingers across the seam it would bite and cut. He frequently operated from around the wicket, swerving amazing in-duckers back towards the stumps as panicked batsmen searched in vain for the line of the ball. He recorded four first-class hat-tricks and more in other forms of the game.

Umpires were sometimes as unnerved as batsmen. Tommy Spencer did not dare judge Nigel Cowley lbw from the last ball of Procter's wonder-over at Southampton because it would have meant 5 wickets in six balls—instead of a mere 4 in five—3 of them trapped in front. At Cheltenham against Yorkshire, Richard Lumb, Bill Athey and John Hampshire were all given out lbw by Kenny Palmer, who said after the sixth ball: 'Over, and thank fuck for that.' Boycott was the non-striker and says they were all stone dead. He likes to add that Sir Len Hutton said ruefully, 'The good player were at t'other end.'

Along with these two, my own favourite was John Snow, who was different again. Goodness knows what made him tick but only rarely did it seem to be bowling. Sometimes it was as if he was playing cricket under protest—the title of his book is *Rebel Without a Cause*—and they used to say he was a bit of loner. I'd say his mind had other interests that didn't necessarily marry with a game of cricket and on the days when the two collided, it looked like he didn't give a damn. Anyway, he was frequently alone in an England shirt: wasn't it always just Snow? Or was it always Snow and everyone else? Snow and Higgs, Snow and Brown, Snow and Jones, Snow and Ward or Willis, Snow and Lever, Knight, Price, Old, Hendrick—a whole raft of them. Lucky old Fred Trueman, I say, to have had Brian Statham. And lucky old Statham to have had Frank Tyson.

I was umbilically attached to the screen when this vicar's son from the parish of Pershore Vale bowled for England and I said many a prayer in his favour. I can still see that little stutter at the top of his shortish run and then the break into a rhythm that was without apparent strain and certainly without self-importance. He was more front-on than Lillee, much more side-on than Procter. He was less swing bowler than lethal seam and bounce bowler. His right shoulder, arm and wrist operated in perfect harmony with the left side of his body to give a whiplash effect that snared the very best. He won the Ashes that I had listened to by wireless in 1970–71, with help from Geoffrey I should add, who was at his very best. Ray Illingworth loved 'Snowball' and wrapped him in cotton wool until the Test matches, at which point he unleashed him on Bill Lawry's Australians. Indeed, so great was the 'Snowball' effect that by the end of the tour the opposition had become Ian Chappell's Australians.

The short ball that hit Terry Jenner in the head caused a right old barney. Illingworth defended his man and tactic in a rousing set-to with umpire Lou Rowan. The crowd grabbed hold of the vicar's son on the edge of the boundary, before bombarding him with bottles, cans and partially eaten pies. Fearing for the safety of his players, Illingworth then led his team from the field of play without permission from the umpires, returning after seven minutes when the ground was cleared and the crowd settled. Later, when recalling the emotive nature of the tour, Basil D'Oliveira said to Snow that the ultimate thing in life was to play for England. Snow pointed out that 'the ultimate thing in life was death'.

I toured with him once to the Middle East, in the days before Sharjah and Dubai routinely attracted cricketers, and instead of watching the bat while fielding I found myself entranced by his run-up and action. At 40, he still had whatever 'it' is, and those few days spent on the field of play with him are among the most treasured of my time in the game. I bump into him occasionally and am still in awe. A single observation from John Snow is worth a thousand words from many a pretender. Two hundred and two Test-match wickets at 26.66 don't tell the story. At least, not all of it. Ask the batsmen. Ian Chappell puts Snowball alongside Andy Roberts as the best fast bowler he faced.

THE WEST INDIANS

No reflection on fast bowling during the past 50 years can be complete without an appreciation of the West Indians. These men made the heart beat faster and the hairs rise on the back of the neck. They gave rise to opinion, both positive and not so positive, and changed the modern game. It is rare now to see an attack outside the subcontinent made up of fewer than four fast bowlers. But none of these attacks, with the arguable exception of England's in the glorious summer of 2005, can be broken down into such an impressive array of component parts. Sure, they bowled hostile and fast. But they bowled with brains and beauty, too.

Collectively, West Indian fast bowlers have spread fear. Individually, they spread the gospel of the game with warmth and knowledge. At Hampshire matches, umpire Ken Palmer used to say 'Give me Maco, captain. I like to hear him coming, boy. I like the pitter-patter of them tiny feet and then whoosh, he's gone. I love him, boy, get him down my end and the game will move forward nice and quick.' So I did.

Marshall learnt from the teachers before him. First among these was Roberts. 'I am a warrior,' said Andy. 'I have a job to do and when I go on the field I have no friends. If a batsman gets injured, it is very difficult for me to go and look at him because if he gets up again the very next ball may be another bouncer. No, the sympathy is in here,' he said, tapping his chest. 'You may not see it but it is here.' Roberts wishes he was remembered for his outswinger but knows that the two-speed bouncers for which he is famous made the legend. He was a careful planner with a photographic memory and made fools of batsmen who took the first, easy-paced bouncer for granted. Immensely strong shoulders allowed him to maintain a short-pitched barrage longer than most. Clive Lloyd recalls a particularly vicious assault on him during a Shell Shield match in Guyana. The next morning, a bruised and weary Lloyd asked his mate what it was about.

'For hooking me for six in Dominica,' said Andy.

'Christ,' replied Lloyd, 'that was five years ago.'

Michael Holding talks about the Roberts brain, the way he studied batsmen and measured their strengths and weaknesses. He recalls a Test in India that Andy missed through illness: 'He sent out a message for me to bowl around the wicket to Syed Kirmani and pitch it up at leg-stump. I had unconditional faith in him so I did just that and next over Kirmani lost his leg stump.'

I played one game for Hampshire with Roberts at Basingstoke in 1978 and caught my first catch off him at first slip, low by my left boot. Jim Foat was the batsman. Roberts rushed over to me and then told the captain to pick me for every game. Imagine it: caught Nicholas, bowled Roberts. There are a few more caught Nicholas, bowled Marshalls, I'm relieved to say.

Holding just bowled bloody fast. He was a beautiful athlete, born of running, jumping and hurdling—a consequence of which was the accurate placement of his front foot so that he was never confronted, or restricted, by no balls. An intelligent man, he soon became an intelligent bowler. 'As far as I am concerned bowling is about action and reaction,' he has said. 'What do I need to do now to combat that action by the batsman? That's what I'm thinking about when I walk back to my mark. It is a continuous process. Remember what has gone before and apply it.' With time he developed wider skills, nipping the ball off the seam and offering occasional reminders of his extreme pace to keep the enemy honest.

Of all the Holding stories, the one about the over to Boycott in Barbados in March 1981 is the best. Our favourite Yorkshireman, the gentleman from Fitzwilliam whose Mum could bat better in her pinny, prepared for this moment by batting indoors on a polished wooden floor to replicate the sheen and speed of a Barbados pitch. It took six balls for Holding to prove it a worthless exercise. The first gloved him, the second beat him, the third zipped into his thigh, the fourth hammered the splice, the fifth homed in on his throat until a padded thumb intervened, and the sixth knocked his off dolly most of the way back to Jeffrey Dujon. Bridgetown exploded. Boycott claims it was an unplayable over. Gooch was at the other end—the best place to play fast bowling, said Len Hutton—and doesn't argue the point. Legend suggests it is the best over by a fast bowler in the modern age of the game. Holding won't hear of it and says he bowled a better one to the Chappell brothers in a WSC match, when he got rid of both. Boycott went away and studied the grainy footage, shot from high above wide mid-on, before coming back stronger.

As if Holding wasn't enough, at a team meeting before the First Test of that tour, Boycott asked Botham how to score off Joel Garner. 'You don't,' was the reply. 'No one does.'

'Really? Christ,' replied Geoffrey, 'I'll go to bed then.'

Garner's great gift was length. From his 6 feet 10 inches plus the distance of his long arm extended to the perpendicular, Garner could make a ball of good length feel like a bouncer. It got 'big' as cricketers like to say and hit the bat so hard it jarred the bottom hand, taking a heavy toll of the right-forefinger knuckle and the base of the right thumb. Then, having forced the enemy back, came the deadly yorker. Nobody before or since has bowled a yorker like the Big Bird, nobody: hard to pick and harder to play, this was the ace in his potent pack. When Garner and Marshall were in tandem at the Kensington Oval in Bridgetown, another game was being played. Add Wayne Daniel and Sylvester Clarke into the Barbados mix and you will find that even Viv Richards left empty-handed. Fast bowlers are gold.

MALCOLM MARSHALL

Go to the Kensington Oval and you will find the ground has been generally overhauled in the name of modernism. The pitch is markedly slower than the days when only Perth matched its carry. The two ends by the sightscreens have been named after Malcolm Marshall and Joel Garner. They were without compare as bowlers, especially on this field. Joel remains the most wonderful man; Malcolm has moved on. He did so too young. He was my best friend in cricket and I miss him most days. I shall never forget Robin Smith calling me with the dreadful news. I was on a train in Europe and shed tears for the remainder of the journey. Maco was loyal, Maco was honest, Maco was strong, Maco was talented, Maco was sensitive and Maco was fun. Now Maco was dead.

I well recall our last conversation. He was shored up in Southampton, sick and weak, before returning to Barbados. I should have driven down to see him but for some reason did not. How I regret that. We talked about the usual stuff—cricket, family, another damp English summer fading from memory, the Bajan sun and, of course, his cancer of the colon. At the end of the call he said, 'Goodbye, Markie,' and I sensed he meant goodbye, not au revoir. His voice was thin and he didn't linger. He just said, 'Goodbye, Markie,' and fourteen unforgettable years of friendship and crusades were over.

Connie, his wife, asked me to do the eulogy. The Sir Garfield Sobers Sports Hall in Barbados was turned into a place of worship for the day and welcomed 2000 friends. The service was broadcast live all over the Caribbean. There was prayer and thanksgiving and music and song. The coffin sat in front of us, Maco peaceful at last inside. Desmond Haynes and Gordon Greenidge bathed him in his final weeks and said I would not want to have seen the bag of bones he had become. For that reason I did not attend the public file past the open coffin the previous day.

I followed Viv to the lectern. He had retired early from his own reading, unable to cope, a mighty figure beaten down by grief. Before leaving my seat, I took a swig of brandy in the hope of settling my heavy and pounding heart. I walked past the coffin, removed my sunglasses and took the speech from my inside jacket pocket. I placed it on the lectern and looked out.

I saw only sadness. First I saw Joel and Desmond, broken men. Then I locked eyes with Andy Roberts and Curtly Ambrose, bleeding men. I noticed Tony Cozier and Prof Edwards, devastated men. I saw Connie and Mali, Maco's son, hearts broken. I saw shuffling in seats and heard coughing. I sensed the trauma. I saw many white handkerchiefs brought to faces, though they might as well have been waving surrender.

I started. I did my best. I finished. I was proud of that. Goodbye, Maco.

Wes Hall followed. Wes the preacher man, not Wes the cricketer. This is how he began. 'Malcolm Denzil Marshall is the greatest fast bowler who ever lived. I know this because I am Wesley Hall, and the one thing Wesley Hall truly knows about is faaaast bowling!'

A few fast bowlers might be thought of as the best ever. In the modern age of the game, Marshall and Lillee are the two who tend to receive most votes. Others mentioned in this breath are Dale Steyn, Wasim Akram, Glenn McGrath, Curtly Ambrose and Richard Hadlee. Fred Trueman would win support, not least his own, as would Alan Davidson and Ray Lindwall, two Australians whose records brook no argument and about whom friend and foe speak in fabled tongue. Going back into the mist of time it is S.F. Barnes who, though not fast, has the figures to beat all figures.

Hall was quite entitled, especially at this moment, to make a decision on behalf of everyone. I think the best thing I can do in illustration of Hall's opinion is tell a story in the present tense exactly as I have recalled it many times before. It is a true story, with only the tiniest hints of poetic licence.

Bournemouth, June 1985
The top two teams in the County Championship are at each other's throats. Having the best of the match, we set Middlesex 265 to win in the fourth innings and quickly reduce them to 38 for 3. Clive Radley has arrived in the middle. He nudges a couple and nurdles a couple more. He is urging his inexperienced partner, Keith Tomlins, to fight on. From the fifth ball of an over, Tomlins finds a single that means Radley must face Marshall for the first time in the innings. We have an attacking field set—four slips, gully and square cover on the off side; forward short leg, leg gully and long leg on the on side. You have to earn Radley's wicket; he gives you nothing. He is heavily protected by the usual gear plus a couple of thigh pads, chest guard and armguard.

Maco is at the end of his run. He has taken 5 wickets in the first innings and just trapped Roland Butcher lbw in the second. Right at that moment he is indisputably the best bowler in the world. Just as relevant, he has injured more batsmen than any of his contemporaries. His pace is electrifying and the way the ball skids when pitched short is life-threatening. He is the talk of the county game. Day in, day out; week in, week out, he swings the ball both ways and is a master of length on pitches that do not necessarily suit him. This is one.

There is invariably tension when he is brought on to bowl. You can't be sure what will happen but you think something will. It might be skilful, it might be violent, more often than not it is game-changing. Everybody watches—that is, *everybody*.

He turns at the end of his run and begins an aggressive sprint, legs working hard, arms operating as pistons, eyes narrowed. At the halfway mark he has found the perfect rhythm and now, 10 yards or so from the crease, appears to be relaxed and at around about full pace. The bars have emptied; the gatemen peer through gaps in the old splintered bleachers. Even the dressing-room attendant takes a breather and diverts his attention from the tea-break to the middle.

Suddenly, inexplicably, Maco stops.

We all stop, and look to him.

'Cappy, cappy,' he shouts to me at first slip. 'I want Cardy across from leg gully, man, I want he across. Cardy, Cardy, you move, man, Cardy . . .' He is screaming these instructions.

We are all aghast.

'Cappy, cappy.'

And I run 50 yards to meet him.

'I want Cardy across, skip, I want he away from leg gully, to a close position on the off side.' He says all this in the thickest of Bajan accents. I am first among interpreters. Thankfully, I get it. 'Fine, you put 'em where you want 'em.' And back I go to first slip.

Cardigan Connor, an Anguillan and second among interpreters, is at leg gully. 'Come across, Cardy,' shouts Maco, 'to the off side, close, near Radley. Closer man, tight, come tight, squarer, tighter, stop, stop, there, Cardy, you got it, there.'

Radley looks confused, certainly flustered. One can only imagine the palms of his hands and the sweat on his brow.

Connor is now at silly point on the off side, 2 yards from the bat. Paul Terry asks if I think Cardy is safe. It's a good question. Certainly, a short ball outside off stump and a square-cut in response spell danger.

I shout: 'Are you sure, Maco? Is he okay there?'

'He's fine. Trust me, Cappy, he fine. Cardy, you're fine.'

Maco, a name that suddenly appears sinisterly apt, returns to his mark.

We all return to where we were a minute or so ago.

He turns again and begins the sprint. This movement and the action that follows are a piece of sporting precision, like the mechanical detail in an expensive watch where the moving parts come together as one and create something fluent, accurate and beautiful . . . Arms working, legs pumping . . .

He is at full tilt now, the gold pendant around his neck swinging hypnotically in the early summer sun. He reaches the crease, body perfectly aligned, eyes level, head steady, fingertips loose down each side of the seam of the ball, thumb tucked underneath it. He lets fly. The ball is fast and rips back into Radley from a tad back of a length. It traps him in no-man's-land—prodding, poking, jumping. Trapped. The ball zips from the bat's inside edge onto the thigh pad and pops up to Connor at silly point.

Radley, caught Connor, bowled Marshall, as planned. Another one bites the dust: another one comes and another one goes, another one bites the dust. Maco goes on a victory dance. Demented, we chase him. Connor is beside himself.

Radley has gone. Phillipe-Henri Edmonds is on his way out. Tim Tremlett arrives from long leg to join the party. 'We're playing cricket on earth and he's buggering about in the universe,' says Tim as we all kiss and cuddle. 'Why do we need Tim at long leg?' I wonder. The ricochet off the helmet, I suppose.

'How many wickets is that for the season, Maco?' asks Greenidge.

'Forrrty-nine . . .' And Maco turns to the pavilion, nods at Edmonds who is now halfway to the middle, and says, 'Look, here comes 50!'

It is the end of the over; we have six balls to wait for more. In the interim, Tomlins and Edmonds take 8 from the over bowled by Raj Maru. Then Edmonds is on strike to Marshall for the first time.

'What now?' I ask hopefully.

'I get he out.'

'Excellent, when?'

'Now.'

'Oh, good. How?'

'Lbw.'

'Good, good. You best set the field then.' Off I go back to slip.

'Rat [Maru, at short leg], come straight, Rat. Perfect, Ratty. Cardy, come back, man, come to me, straighter, straighter, right a bit, there, there, stop there. Okay. Don't move, Cardy, you'll be fine, my brother.'

Edmonds asks if we can get on with the fucking game. Marshall tells him to mind his own business. We used to say that Philip didn't need an armguard because he had seven gold Rolexes up his sleeve. Connor is now at silly mid-off, so a long half-volley and he'll wear a well-hit drive. Maco is in top gear; let it be.

He moves back to his mark, hindquarters swaying much as Sobers' once did when the young Marshall was starry-eyed with the game. He wipes his forehead with one of his two sweatbanded wrists and turns to face us. Then he dips his upper body ever so slightly forward, moves onto his toes and begins that deadly scudding approach. His head is perfectly still, his eyes cold-bloodedly narrow. Thirty metres, twenty, fifteen—the speed and balance are captivating—ten, five, he reaches the crease and sets up for the outswinger. But no, the ball curves in late and fast, striking at its target like a snake. The muscles twitch in Edmonds' tall and strong body but the time is too short for further reaction and the damage is done. The ball crashes into his pads.

'How was zaaaaat?' implores the leaping Marshall. 'How was heeeeee,' we scream, in unison. Near certain of a kill, the crowd bay aggressively. It is a feeding frenzy.

'That is OUT,' says the umpire, raising his finger in this atmosphere of bedlam, a finger so unrelenting that might it as well have been Caesar's decisive thumb in the Colosseum.

Edmonds, stone-dead lbw Marshall, as planned.

———

And people ask how I captained Malcolm Marshall.

So well did he know the opponent and his own abilities that he frequently predicted a dismissal. He learnt his craft from the men before him, perfected it in county cricket, polished it for Barbados and hammered home the advantage at Test-match level. He listened to Roberts and Holding and talked for hours over rum or brandy with Garner. He admired Imran and watched Lillee with a craftsman's interest. He never wasted cricket talk; rather, he channelled it. Either he benefited or someone benefited from him. He held nothing back, on the field or off it.

He laughed generously with the Essex spinners Ray East and David Acfield, who offered to carry his bags from the car park to the dressing room such was their fear of him. Then, when the umpire called play, on came the game face. By eventide, he was available to laugh with them again. Cricket was serious business and not to be taken lightly. But the game was a game and the players of both sides were better for sharing common ground.

Initially, he bowled whippy outswing at a lively pace but not express. West Indies spotted his special gifts before we did, frankly. Charlie Knott, the chairman of cricket at Hampshire, gets the credit for hiring this special talent before it was on the radar.

Malcolm was in nappies when his policeman father died in a motorcycle accident. Much of his upbringing was then spent with his grandmother, who had him immaculately turned out for school, and his grandfather, Oscar, who bowled to an enthusiastic young batsman in the backyard and on the beach. Maco always preferred to bat and would get furious at himself for brainless strokes. In the school playground, you only got to bat if you knocked over the kid in possession of the crease, so he started to bowl, fast.

Like other legends of the speed ball—Harold Larwood, Lindwall, Roy Gilchrist—he was only a little chap, small-boned and slim, but, as C.L.R. James wrote of George John some 80 years ago: 'All power is in proportion . . . pace and body action, he hits many a poor batsman on the inside of the knee to collapse them like a felled ox.' That brave man of Derbyshire, Alan 'Bud' Hill would relate to those words, for Bud once resisted Maco over the best part of a day to find later that the pain he suffered from mid-innings to its close was a shattered kneecap.

Malcolm was attracted to Hampshire by the scores of his namesake Roy Marshall, whom he followed in the Barbados paper *The Nation*. When he read the name Andy Roberts on the Hampshire scorecard, the deal was pretty much sealed as far as Malcolm was concerned. On his debut for Hampshire, in late April 1979, it snowed but he still managed 7 wickets when not wrapped around the radiator.

His greatest asset was an unconditional commitment to any of the teams for which he played. Hampshire became a second home and he felt he often bowled best for the county because of the overs under his belt. Early in each season he would insist on long spells, often refusing a break until he had found rhythm and consistency. This was also the way he developed strength and stamina because, under no circumstance, would he run or train in the gym. His only rule was 400 sit-ups a day—200 in the morning and 200 by night.

Maco was fiercely loyal, hated seeing talent wasted and refused to suffer fools or shoddy manners. He had an ego but it was neither inflated, nor manifested in the way of self-regard. His achievements were the subject of pride not boasts. He intimidated simply by presence and performance. Sure, he was a fearsome bowler but he was a funny, friendly and kindly man. We truly loved him and it was not a love that went unrequited.

Of course, Malcolm Marshall was not perfect. There were bad days and silly days, but not many. He was too smart to make the same mistake twice. Occasionally there was controversy, along with a purist's view that he was a sadistic cricketer who used intimidatory tactics for the sake of it. He, and I—who captained him in more games than any other—completely refute this. He exposed weaknesses with ruthless efficiency but he played within the laws. Umpires were empowered to intervene if they felt he was pushing the limits and those who did were almost apologetic, so much did they respect him.

When he viciously bounced the ill-equipped Pat Pocock in the Oval Test of 1984, his explanation was simple. 'Yes, he is batting at number eleven, but he is blocking every straight ball with the middle of his bat and taking up valuable time in the match. What am I to do, keep watching him block me? Or bounce him a few times and see if he then blocks me so easily? I love cricket, but I am born a fast bowler. My job is to take wickets so that my team can win games. I will do the best for myself and my team every time I go to work.'

He was fortunate to have grown up with the increasingly professional age of the game and specifically the period in which Clive Lloyd led West Indies. He admired Lloyd's ability to manage a collection of strong characters and learnt from him, taking common sense as his first point of reference. Malcolm missed Clive when he left, which is not to say that he thought Viv Richards an inferior captain, just that we all miss the father figure who first brings us into the world.

He loved Viv's passion and responded to the beat of his drum. Viv got lucky too, because by the mid-1980s Maco was the complete fast bowler. The inswinger he had worked on behind closed doors was up and running. It was a lethal weapon in the nets—the most claustrophobic place for us guinea pigs—snaking back at the inner thigh to send waves of electricity from that softest flesh to the brain and back again. These sharp intakes of pain were thrillingly bittersweet, for every one that brought misery to a Hampshire player in practice would bring greater misery to an opponent on the battlefield.

In fact, he seemed to have more fun after mastering the inswinger than at any time in his career. It was as if Pandora's box had opened before his eyes and its evil secrets were to be shown to the world. Given he bowled outswing with an open-chested action anyway, the inswinger was already disguised. The pleasure he, and we, derived from Maco's kingdom of days is with us still now. The only shame is that we could not convert one man's skill and sense of duty into a County Championship winner's medal.

As I write, I think of many examples of his genius. Here are two short stories. One of mind, the other of matter. Or are they both of both?

He didn't want to play at Leicester in 1986, complained of a heavy cold. We were contenders for the championship, so I had to talk him round. If we batted first, fine, he could rest up for the day. If we were bowling first, we agreed he would not bowl that day, just field for a while and be substituted. There was method in this apparent madness: if the others bowled rubbish, I figured he would get the bit between his teeth and ask for the ball. Worst case, he should be okay to bowl in the second innings when, with a bit of luck, we would be pushing for victory. Anyway, Leicestershire won the toss and batted. He wasn't happy but said he'd get bored fielding so he might as well bloody well bowl for a while. The sum of which was a surprising fifteen overs of tidy medium pace without a wicket. Leicester got plenty and declared. We did much the same and left them about 40 minutes on the second evening. Maco was in the most terrible strop, coughing and spluttering, and didn't want to come out on the field. I told him he had to, simple as that. We got to the middle and he said, 'I bowl, skip, off five paces.' Okay, I hadn't expected that. The second ball flew from a fraction short of a length and brushed Laurie Potter's glove: a wicket immediately, perfect. Surprised by such bounce, our man-flu victim lightened up a bit. Peter Willey had made a hundred in the first innings but not so this time. Maco hit him on the pads with an inswinger in front of all three. Jonathan Agnew came in as nightwatchman. No contest.

Now, here's the rub. James Whitaker took guard. Immediately, Maco hit him on the left wrist, just beneath the armguard. It looked painful but Whitaker waved us away and negotiated the rest of the over, just. The first two balls of Maco's next over flew from a length and were somehow beaten down by this hurting batsman. Our boy was off just five paces but we were miles back in the slips. I well remember Jimmy looking back to me as if to say, 'Blimey, I'll have whatever he's had!' The next ball reared from shortish and squared him up, arms and hands reacting in self-defence like a boxer guarding his throat and head. The ball hit him flush on the right forearm. The sound told us all we needed to know and, as Jimmy buckled at the knees, we rushed to his side. The physio came out but there was nothing to be done. He was taken from the field and on to hospital.

Next morning he appeared at the ground with both arms in plaster. He said: 'After they X-rayed the right arm and told me it was bust, I said they'd better have a look at the left wrist while I was there. So they did, and here I am, fucked twice.'

Next day, the flu really set in and it was all for nothing. From 16 for 3 overnight, Leicester saved the game comfortably enough. Whitaker's bones healed well and a burst of late season form saw him picked for the England tour of Australia. He got a test match, replacing the injured Ian Botham at Adelaide. One is better than none. Bravo, Jimmy. Who'd have thought it? All plastered up with nowhere to go one minute and three lions on his chest the next. 'C'est la vie,' say the old folks. It goes to show you never can tell.

In a Benson & Hedges Cup group match at Southampton against Essex in 1992, we didn't get many—170-odd. I said, 'Guys, it's a flat pitch. If we're to win this against their batting line-up, we have to win it now. The first ten overs decide the game; get on it and stay on it.' And Maco just said, 'Don't worry, skip,' like he knew something. He tore in, rhythm perfect from the first epically fast and bouncy outswinger that was his trademark. By the end of that over, he had done Graham Gooch lbw with a beauty that held its line and immediately matched it with an inswinger to John Stephenson. For nineteen balls of magnificent cricket, Mark Waugh defended as best he knew how until Maco slipped him the old three-card trick—two outswingers that Waugh left alone and the inswinger that Waugh expected to go by before watching in horror as it veered into his pads like a guided missile. Essex were 5 for 3. Banish those three from proceedings in five overs and it's a long way back into the game for the rest of them. We won it comfortably and went on the win the cup. It was the first and only time in his county career that Malcolm lifted a trophy at Lord's. When West Indies lost to India in 1983, he wasn't playing; when Hampshire beat Derbyshire in 1988 and Surrey in 1991 he was on tour with West Indies. He desperately wanted that Lord's trophy and was thrilled beyond measure. The photograph of us together with the cup is my favourite.

Sharing summer days with this fabulous man was a good enough reason to play the game in the first place. He was my mate and my unflinching supporter. At his happiest, throwing his head back with that infectious laugh, he was an inspiration to us all. I miss him to this day and shall do so always.

WASIM AKRAM AND OTHERS

I rate Marshall number one but I'm not blind. My guess is that he was the most effective fast bowler in all conditions. Certainly, he gets Viv Richards' vote, as much for the wickets he took on the subcontinent—71 at 23 each—as for any of his other skills. Lillee only visited the subcontinent once as a player and took just 4 wickets. That sways it for Viv. The challenger to Marshall in the man-for-all-seasons bracket must be Wasim Akram, who could make a cricket ball talk while it travelled 20 yards in the air. A dead pitch was irrelevant to Was, who transcended most of the surfaces on which he played.

A surprisingly tall and immensely strong man, he sort of shuffled to the wicket, gathering himself alongside the umpire before taking a short delivery stride and releasing the ball with the fastest arm I've ever seen. He swung the new ball and boomeranged the old, amid flurries of bouncers and yorkers that made him impossible to predict. He used his wrist to remarkable effect, altering its position and the angle of the seam within it, and changed his pace almost every ball.

Legend has it that Sarfraz Nawaz taught Imran Khan the art of reverse swing and that Imran passed it on to Wasim and to Waqar Younis. For what it is worth, Waqar passed it on to me and Cardigan Connor one morning in the nets at Southampton, though you will not be surprised to hear that we made rather less of it than he did. Roberts says he always reversed the ball but that, back then, they didn't call it reverse swing. He says that on days when he couldn't make the thing move in the air, he simply turned it around in his grip and if it went, all well and good, if not, he switched it back. There is no doubt that reverse swing is most effective when bowled fast.

The basic method is to rough up one side of the ball while keeping it dry. The other side can be clean and shiny or damp and heavy. This creates resistance and moves the ball in the opposite direction to normal swing. Thus, to bowl reverse outswing to a right-handed batsman, you position the rough side on the right, which is the opposite of where you would position it if you were looking for orthodox swing. Essentially, the ball creates a slipstream in the air, which becomes a low pressure area or a boundary layer. If this is the same on both sides of the ball, the effect will balance out and there will be no swing. The bowler's job is to make it uneven.

There are natural ways that the ball may become rough, such as use on dry and abrasive surfaces or consistent landing in the bowler's footmarks and other rough areas on or around the pitch and square. Unnatural—and illegal—ways to roughen the ball are to use fingernails to scratch it, or outside agents such as bottle tops or sharp-edged implements. In my view, there is a debate to be had on the continued importance of reverse swing in the game and the methods by which it can be achieved.

Wasim won the 1992 World Cup Final with a breathtaking display of fast reverse swing: the deliveries to Allan Lamb and Chris Lewis are among the most memorable in history. Waqar won many a match with reverse swing because the ball travelled in a straight line so far down the pitch, and so fast, that by the time the swing began to change its direction, the batsman was long committed to the original line. I would say that Waqar reverse-swinging the ball at top pace was the closest to unplayable there has been. His Test match strike rate of 43.4 supports this.

It is a fantastic skill to bowl at full speed and swing the ball. Lindwall could do it, Trueman and Procter too. Lindwall had a low, slinging arm that made his bouncers skid and his outswinger really curve. He had a fine brain for bowling that gave him the edge over most of his opponents. He could read them and then outwit them. Not for nothing did they call him 'Killer'.

Davidson was happy cutting his pace to ensure swing and reckons it was a rare day when the ball refused to respond. Benaud rated Davidson alongside Akram, which gives us some idea of his ability to move the ball both ways and of his physical strength. To this day, Davo's shoulders appear to have been cut from oak, and Benaud used to say that Davo could whizz it past anyone's nose when a hurry-up was in order. He took 186 wickets at 20.53—no fast bowler who has played in 30 Test matches or more has claimed them cheaper than that.

Years back, Malcolm and I were in the bar at the Callers-Pegasus Cricket Festival. Trueman came in, saw him and scurried over. 'Not many as good as us around, Malcolm lad,' he said, before suggesting Maco should get more side-on for the outswinger. No flies on Fred. John Hampshire told me Fred could bowl bloody quick, even Marshall-pace from time to time. Boycott confirms exactly that, highlighting Trueman's smooth action, classical technique and 'gorgeous' outswinger. Of course, he was a tremendous character. Richard Hutton once interrupted one of his tales to ask if he ever bowled a plain old straight ball. 'Aye,' replied Fred, 'it were a full bunger and knocked out Garry Sobers' middle stump.'

Procter swung the ball but only in to the right-handed batsmen. He was another who used the bouncer to devastating effect, forcing even the very best players back into the crease and then pinning them in front of the stumps. His variety was a natural leg cutter, and he was able to run his fingers down and across the seam, creating various drag effects that later became better known when television took us in close to bowlers like Wasim, who mastered such arts. These powerfully built men had immense stamina and were as likely to impose themselves towards the end of a day's play, when the batting side had flicked the button to cruise control, as first up in the morning.

This chapter is dedicated to the thrill of fast bowling but the art of swing is, in itself, a fascination. Few bowlers have truly mastered it. Alan Knott insists Ian Botham is the best swing bowler he saw. All of India celebrates Kapil Dev, one of the game's very best and most attractive cricketers. Modern Australia would sell the Mitchell Johnson–Ryan Harris combination that swung the ball at some 'serious licks'—as West Indians like to say. Alastair Cook understandably throws James Anderson's hat into the ring. Botham rejoices in the sorcerer's skills displayed day in and day out by the boy from Burnley, who grew to be the man with more Test wickets than any Englishman.

Anderson is much admired by Sir Richard Hadlee, who knows a bit about this stuff. Hadlee's performance at Brisbane in 1985 led to one of the game's great fairytales, as New Zealand finally beat the great rival from across the Tasman on their home turf. He took 9 for 52 in the first innings and 6 more in the second. Superb hundreds from Martin Crowe and John Reid, as well as brilliant close catching, completed a near-flawless performance, which was written into the folklore of New Zealand cricket. Hadlee would almost certainly have taken all 10 in that first innings had he not caught Geoff Lawson—Australia's number ten—off Vaughan Brown, running away to his right at mid-on. A quirk is that the match was Brown's debut and that this wicket was the only one he took in his Test career. Lawson thought Hadlee 'unplayable' and rates his match performance among the best two or three he has seen from any fast bowler.

Walter Hadlee's third cricketing son was a disciple of Dennis Lillee and a keen student of the game in general. He moved from cocky tearaway in the early 1970s to become a clinical assassin in the 1980s. He did so without compromising much pace, learning instead to conserve energy and play with minds. We saw a lot of him in county cricket. Trent Bridge became his second home, and the personal targets he set for himself each summer were a story in themselves, so frequently were they achieved. Alongside the mighty Clive Rice, Hadlee turned Nottinghamshire into a crack unit and championship winners.

Sir Richard is a tall man and from a shortish and controlled approach he reached the crease ramrod straight and beautifully balanced. The ball was released with the wrist set exactly behind the seam, from which point on it appeared to track its target. With an uncanny knack for length, he wasted few deliveries and nagged at weaknesses like a bitter spouse. If you made contact in defence the ball felt heavy, hard and unforgiving; if you didn't it would nip and bite as if it didn't much care for you.

On a pitch that offered movement and bounce, Hadlee may have been the most effective of them all. Only McGrath and Ambrose could match him for accuracy. Ambrose was a little quicker and bouncier still but didn't move the ball around quite so much. McGrath was a more relentless examiner of human weakness, cruel in his ways. All three of these extraordinary bowlers were able to set up the enemy and then strike with a near-certain and dreaded conclusion. I have talked to fine batsmen who knew the sting was on but admit they were powerless to resist.

I have the three of them, and Roberts, just a tad behind Lillee, Marshall and Akram. Hadlee and McGrath were happiest in the waiting game, the one in which metronomic accuracy brought a detailed plan to fruition. Ambrose was the most explosive and on the days when the knees were up and the eyes trained in on their prey, I swear he bowled 10 miles per hour faster to take a heavy toll from irregularities in the pitch or vulnerability in the opponent. I think of two spells specifically: 7 for 1 (7 for 25 ultimately) against the Australians in Perth and 6 for 24 against England in Trinidad.

AND FINALLY . . .

Who said this?

'There are a lot of tips about how to get good at fast bowling: hip drive, use of the left arm, flow of the run-up, good speed, strength at the crease, control, head still, energy going down. But you have to have that something else. Something that someone like Usain Bolt has over anybody.'

He is spot on so far.

'Your whole body has to work in sync to get the ball down to the other side at maximum pace, so I need to make sure all my energy is behind the ball. That means my wrist needs to be behind the ball. An easy way to tell is, am I landing it on the seam or am I missing the seam?'

Bingo.

'The pitch doesn't matter at all. I prefer bowling on low, slow wickets like in India, as opposed to bowling at the WACA, where there is big pace and bounce. I know my economy rate will be low; I have the possibility of the ball reversing; it will squat; I can bowl those fast cutters; I can bowl straighter lines. Maybe at the WACA you have to bowl slightly outside off stump. The difference between a good fast bowler and a brilliant fast bowler is the wickets column.'

I would have bet on Marshall saying this had I not read it elsewhere. It is a fascinating interview with Dale Steyn—who is the best fast bowler still playing and one of the few genuinely great ones ever—by Nagraj Gollapudi on Cricinfo. There is much of Marshall in Steyn: the pace through the air, the late movement, the lovely off-stump line, the wicked bouncer. His record compares; his strike rate alone is close to incomparable.

Another question to Steyn. 'What's the difference between good and great?'

'Only when you retire.'

'Why?'

'While you are playing, one day you can be great and the next you can be absolute shit. Fast bowling is a battle. I have run in and bowled a heap of poo and the guy has hit it straight to cover. At other times I have bowled the spell of my life and I just can't find the edge.'

And that, of course, is the game in a nutshell.

Yes, fast bowlers are gold.

CHAPTER 9

When spin meets glove

'WELL BOWLED, DELL'; 'THANKS, MATEY'

In 1984, Hampshire played Kent at Canterbury. The match was badly affected by weather and not much more than half of the last day remained when the captains got together in the hope of agreeing upon a formula for a conclusion. Kent had been 179 for 4 on the first day when the rain came. Over the ensuing 36 hours or so it crept under the covers and now the pitch was wet, which made the equation difficult. Nick Pocock came back to our dressing room chirpy as a morning's lark. He had persuaded Chris Tavaré to declare the Kent first innings and forfeit the second. In turn, he would forfeit Hampshire's first innings and agree to chase the 179 already on the board in the 59 overs that remained. 'Easy,' Pocock said to us, unaware that the poker-faced Kent captain had needed no persuading.

David Turner asked Nick if he had ever faced Derek Underwood on a wet pitch. 'No,' he replied, 'but the plan is simple: we block Deadly and get them off Alderman and Ellison at the other end.' Trevor Jesty asked if he knew why he was called Deadly, to which Nick answered that he did, and then

Trevor asked if he had ever tried blocking this Deadly on a turning pitch. 'Er, no,' he answered, 'but it can't be so difficult that we don't make 180 off the others. I mean, come on, lads!'

Underwood was in the blocks for the fifth over. Our score was 13 for no wicket. He bowled a maiden in which Paul Terry played every ball safely in the middle of the bat. 'See,' said Nick in the dressing room, 'a piece of piss.' The next over bowled by Terry Alderman was a maiden too. At the end of the next over, bowled by Underwood, the score was 13 for 3.

Chris Smith played forward to the first ball, which ripped some of the wet surface out by its roots and caught the shoulder of his bat on the way through to Alderman at first slip. I took guard next and replaced the divot. The close field was five strong: two slips, gully, silly point and forward short leg. I figured the best thing was to play back. The ball went past my chest and was taken by Alan Knott at his shoulder height. He rode the alarming bounce of this ball as if he had done it all his life, which he had. No gloves sounded softer and none looked safer than Knotty's. I now had first-hand experience of this genius, a couple of feet behind me. Awesome. 'Well bowled, Dell,' said the great stumper. 'Thanks, matey,' said the great bowler, the two of them in perfect harmony. Knott and Underwood, Underwood and Knott: sure as cheese and wine; funny as Morecambe and Wise; prolific as Lennon and McCartney.

The third ball of the over hit the splice of my bat, heavy and hard. The thing about Underwood was the speed of the ball—almost medium pace and spinning like a top, which gave it the impression of something deadly—thus Deadly. That, and the relentless accuracy. People said he cut the ball but he didn't really, he spun it at a cutter's pace. The fourth ball of this second over was really evil. Spitting with intent, it attacked the thumb of my right glove, tearing it away from the handle of the bat before it carried on an inevitable path to the poker-faced captain at second slip. He threw it up like a child flicks a Smartie to its lips.

I just made it back to the dressing room to look out from the balcony and see Jesty inch forward to another one of these absurd deliveries only to find his gloves in the way of a ball that seemed programmed to travel from hand to pitch and on to slip. It was a kind of magic: an evil, irresistible magic. The first over to Paul had been a sighter, with the seam up. First take aim. Then fire. His second killed off the match.

Jesty returned to the dressing room and said, 'I mean, "Come on, lads, it can't be so difficult"? Yeah, right, fuck me!' At exactly this moment Nick was taking guard and proceeded to reverse-sweep his way to 17, until Deadly rumbled him with the famous quicker ball, an inswinger that zeroed in on its target as if propelled by machine. Nick's 17 was the top score by plenty. We made 56: a miracle. Underwood had 7 for 21; Richard Ellison 3 for 9. You had to laugh. What an experience. I remembered Barry Richards, the best batsman in the world at the time, saying that Underwood bowled them out for next to nothing on a bone-dry and dusting pitch at Gillingham. He said Deadly got 7 for 18 and then he added, 'God knows how we got the 18.' That day, Hampshire was bowled out for 58, with Richards, unlike us.

Underwood was a freak, perhaps the best slow bowler on a bad pitch who ever lived. It was almost comical to see this high-class sportsman—whose ten-to-two feet suggested a complete absence of athleticism—bamboozle everyone. He was a brave cricketer, as witnessed when he acted as nightwatchman in the days before the helmet and was frequently photographed in mid-air avoiding another 90-mile-per-hour missile: Deadly never said a bad word to, or about, anyone but, boy, did they bomb him. Revenge, I suppose, for previous embarrassments.

Knotty says he was the best England bowler he kept to. They had started together playing schools cricket, Underwood's dad driving them around the county. The affection and appreciation was mutual. Deadly reckoned Knotty could read his mind and loved his mate's input. For all the innate skill and the repeated action, there was an insecurity about Underwood that surprised even Knott.

There is an apocryphal story about Brian 'Tonker' Taylor, the Essex keeper, baffled by the young Underwood when they played together for T.N. Pearce's XI at Scarborough. The first ball of Underwood's first over spun past the bat and kept going past Tonker's gloves. The next ball did exactly the same. The third ball was the quick one, which missed leg stump by a fraction. Tonker, by now well confused and still floundering around off stump, waved goodbye to the third consecutive four byes.

'Deadly,' exclaimed Tonker in east London tones, 'they tell me you're a world-beater. You see these gloves of mine? . . . You fuckin' hit 'em.' Underwood saw the funny side of Tonker's limited skills but later confessed that he had wished Knotty had been around to tidy up for him on a day of first impressions.

Kent has been fortunate with stumpers. Hubble, Ames, Levett, Evans, Knott, Downton, Jones, to name a few. William 'Hopper' Levett was a tremendous character, who mainly stood in for Les Ames when he was away with England. Hopper was in the pub one night, hard on the hops he farmed, when the landlord whispered that a wireless report indicated Ames was sick and that Hopper might be called up the next day. Hopper had heard such stories turn to dust before and decided to drink on. Come the morning, come the call up. Worse for wear, Hopper moved not a muscle when the first ball of the day was left alone by the batsman, and then left alone by Hopper too, as it shot past his right shoulder. The slips looked on in shock as the match began with four byes. Next ball, the batsman played and missed and, again, Hopper remained motionless in his crouching position as the ball whistled between him and first slip for four more. The third ball was down the leg side and the batsman played the most delicate of leg glances. The ball flew towards fine leg only to be intercepted by the flying wicket-keeper who, with body horizontal and left arm at full stretch, pulled off a blinder of a catch. Hopper came up with the ball to find himself surrounded by astonished teammates. 'Not bad for the first ball of the morning, eh lads,' he said. It is a hackneyed tale but stands the test of time. Most cricket stories do.

Knotty barely had a drink in his life, save a small celebratory glass of white wine. His idiosyncrasies were the stuff of legend, as was his adherence to health, wellbeing and practice. On tours, he tended to room with Boycott—two early-to-bedders together—but even Boycott was startled by Knott's dawn routine. To us outsiders, Knott was just the nicest man and most generously spirited opponent.

Above everything, though, were the hints of genius. Boycott says that in Australia in 1970–71 they didn't see him drop a single ball until the first morning of the Seventh Test, and that the moment was greeted with amazement by all and sundry, not least the Australians. To this day, Jeff Thomson talks about Knott's guts against the fastest bowling and about the innovative and infuriating shots he played—notably the uppercut—in 1974–75. As the others were being mown down by Lillee and Thomson, Knott and Greig did all they could to stitch the wounds. Knotty 'drove us nuts', says Thommo. He drove us nuts too. At Bournemouth, we watched in awe as he went down on one knee to sweep Marshall for six. Neither before nor since had we seen such madness make for such brilliance. Marshall smiled and applauded. Everyone loved Knotty.

Dark, neat, lithe, fast-eyed and fleet-footed, he was as chirpy as Godfrey Evans before him but not so extroverted. He had a buoyancy that lifted the team through challenging passages of play and an air of optimism that made even the impossible seem likely. His glove work was economical, his footwork accurate. He taught himself the art of diving safely, so that the ball stayed in the glove, and on occasions his acrobatics were heart-stopping in their brilliance. But it was standing up to the wicket to Underwood that he shone above all others. He took a magnificent catch that day at Canterbury, poaching the rearing and kicking ball with improbable serenity. For a split second, it seemed as if the thing had melted away.

'BOWLED, SHAANE'

'He's done it,' said Benaud on the Beeb, and with that Shane Warne's career was launched into the stratosphere. People had suggested he would be good, though I don't suppose anyone thought he would be quite so damn good as he turned out. Right at the beginning, Martin Crowe said Warne was different because 'He turns it across you, from outside leg to off, rather than from middle and off which is more typical of a leg spinner.' Crowe was a fan. We all were. The show captivated us.

The truest way to judge the impact made by a sportsman is to watch the tactical response of the opposition. So concerned was Sachin Tendulkar that he disappeared for a full week of his life before the visit by the Australians in 1998. He was where no one could find him, preparing for Warne: a battle thrillingly won by the Indian. Warne has always said that Tendulkar in India in 1998 was the one batsman for whom the Australian team had no answer, other than to resort to an off-stump line, a decent length and hope. He might have mentioned the white handkerchief he waved in front of Kevin Pietersen during the first innings at Adelaide in 2006–07. Mind you, he worked that one out. In the second innings, Warne bowled Pietersen round his legs, which started the rot. A few hours later, the Australians had bullied their way to one of the great Test-match wins of all time.

Back to 1993. England were rooted from the minute Warne bowled that Gatting ball. 'He's done it' might just as well have been 'He's done them'. No one ball has created a legend in the way that did. It must be up there with Eric Hollies bowling Bradman for a second ball duck in his last Test innings at the Oval in 1948 as the single most replayed moment in cricket history.

Having said that, Warne bowled a bunch of other deliveries that toyed with the minds of opposing dressing rooms. The flipper to Alec Stewart in Brisbane was no less excruciating for Stewart than the Gatting ball was for Gatt. A group of England players sat on a television platform above the sightscreen at the old Gabba after the Stewart ball and tried to work it out. They kept a close eye on the bloke who delivered it too. I know, because I sat with them. Everything Warne did was mesmerising, which was part of the trick. The ego, the smarts, the self-awareness and self-confidence, the imposition and the theatre were all a part of the package. It was not that each ball was so hard to pick, more that the ball you picked was wrapped up in magic. 'It's not getting it there that counts,' he likes to say, 'any muppet can get it there. It's how it gets there and then what happens when it arrives.' Exactly.

There is much that surprises about Warne but first up is his unconditional love of cricket. To Warne, the chase of bat and ball is more than a game. It is a science—and it is art, theatre and war. In turn, Warne is soldier, scientist, artist, actor and entertainer. Cricket is his serious responsibility and a journey that will take him through his life. You can hear the passion for it in his commentary.

In 2003, he was found to have taken a diuretic, a banned substance. The punishment was a year's ban from the game, which did not go to waste. He found an indoor cricket school happy to open its doors for an hour each morning between six and seven o'clock, at which point the cleaners arrived and he had to disappear. Usually he went alone and bowled at a handkerchief but I was staying a week with him in Melbourne and he suggested I come and bat. I had never played against him and never would, so this was an opportunity not to be missed. He began bowling seam up, not bad either. Then he rolled a few leggies of little consequence except for their high bounce, which was the norm on the concrete base of most indoor playing areas. Then he set me challenges—block an over, slog an over, six to win, 12 to win, etc. Then he said: 'Right, you ready for the real thing?' I was ready all right and shall not forget it.

The leg break hissed, some more than others: there was the big spinner and the little spinner, the side spinner and the over spinner. The topspinner fizzed and then bounced alarmingly, hitting the splice of the bat or my gloves. The googly, or wrong 'un, also bounced more than the norm but didn't turn as much. After a couple I could read it okay. The slider was the one I most remember, a telling delivery that threatened to be something it wasn't: a leg break that skidded straight on but did so very quickly, like it had been bowled on glass. He told me that most of the other stuff—zooters and such—were no more than bluff and mind games. I was enthralled. We went back and did it all again the next day. The ball reacted off the surface in a way I had not previously experienced. It was like unravelling a mystery, knowing that a single moment of indecision could cost your life.

I played spin pretty well and made hundreds against Anil Kumble (twice) and Abdul Qadir. Way back, in 1981, I faced Bishan Bedi in a couple of exhibition matches in Dubai. I have no idea why but I was in Keith Fletcher's England XI against a combined India–Pakistan team, which included most of the greats: Imran, Kapil, Viswanath, Bedi, and so on. Bedi's orthodox left-arm spin was an act of pure beauty and so captivated this young batsman that he stood transfixed by the ball, falling hopelessly for its arc and flight. As the spinning orb closed in, it became a temptress, hovering just beyond the young batsman's reach. 'Wait, wait for it to come to you, it will come but wait, have patience,' said Bedi, amused by my groping response. Bedi had it, as the old pros like to say, on a string.

Back in the counties, I battled against John Emburey and Phil Edmonds, as fine a pair of tricksters as you will meet. There was Deadly, of course, and the underrated, pipe-puffing Norman Gifford. I wish I had seen Erapalli Prasanna in the flesh, for Ian Chappell has him top of the finger-spinning league; Graeme Pollock reserved that title for Fred Titmus. Many a South African throws Denys Hobson's hat into the wrist-spinning ring. Pakistan was right to shout from the rooftops about Qadir, in the way India hailed the mighty Kumble. But none of these were Warne. Warne was a force of nature.

Shane Keith Warne took 708 Test-match wickets with leg-spin, the hardest skill in the game. Had he played in the age of the decision review system, he would have taken a hundred more. Warne was the result of an Australian dynasty that began with Arthur Mailey and Clarrie Grimmett. It took in Bill O'Reilly and Richie Benaud, before a few 'nearlies'—Terry Jenner, Kerry O'Keeffe, Jim Higgs, Bob Holland and Trevor Hohns—became the fellows he decided to walk by on his way to the summit. He studied them all, embracing the best of each. It has made him impossible to emulate, for he became the collective noun of leg spin and its consummate master.

On the way back from the indoor school, I asked who taught him the practicalities of this stuff. He said Jenner was a fine coach and great mate. Jenner was his go-to, his checklist. Jenner told him to 'spin up' and drive his right hip. He also reminded him, with some frequency, that leg spinners need a lot of love. Warne said that Benaud passed on to him the advice he had received from O'Reilly—'Go away and rehearse six consecutive perfectly pitched spinning leg breaks. It'll take you three years.' I asked Richie about this and he purred before adding about Warne: 'He did it in two, which began to tell us how good he was.' Perfect, I'd say.

It takes two to tango, and the sight of Ian Healy whipping off those bails with such relish became a standard for the game. Healy's career was the result of a lot of hard yakka; he is a man who leaves little to chance. If Knott is not the best wicket-keeper I have seen, Healy is. I can see him now, low in his crouch, athletic, energised: 'Watch the ball, move, stay down.'

His description of keeping to Warne is riveting. 'There's Warne's slow walk in, the build-up of energy through the crease, and the release. The flipper would have been detected two strides earlier and this is not it. This is the leg-spinner, last seen leaving the hand, blocked by the batsman now. How much will it turn? Think he just rolled it, rather than ripped it, but it's heading for the big hole outside leg-stump.

'Stay down and move late, I keep telling my legs. This could do anything off the pitch and, by then, it will be behind the batsman. But must ignore him and he will only further distract me as I try to isolate the ball. It should slide down leg, but will it? That's the dilemma, and I must wait and watch before deciding to move low and strong. Gloves low and relaxed enough to give with the ball, and in it goes cleanly. Pat yourself on the back, take a deep breath and settle in again. The first ball of the spell is done, 30 overs to go.'

The 1993 series in England is almost always remembered for the Gatting ball but Healy's stumping of Graham Thorpe at Edgbaston, from a high bouncing ball that really spun, was a majestic example of eye, hand and instinct rewarding years of work. Healy says that Rod Marsh gave him the basics, simple little gems that he has passed on to all who have asked, and the rest of it is down to interpretation. His style was to show the gloves to the ball and then exaggerate the 'give' so that it became habit.

Healy's opening line 'There's Warne's slow walk in,' is worth further examination. The walk in is the start of a marker, a statement that tells the batsman this is all about me, not you. There is the pause at the start of his approach, the little stutter of his feet, the walk itself, the slight acceleration, the leap and then the explosion at the crease, followed by the drive of the body and the powerful follow-through. After this comes the great exhortation, the ooh and the aah, the look and the stare, then the comment, the goading, the adjustment to the field and the aside to a nearby fielder, before it all begins again.

Often he would summon Healy or Mark Taylor, or they would call for him, and the two would meet mid-pitch to talk about the weather or the women in tight T-shirts a tad wide of mid-on. The poor batsmen assumed this to be some master plan, a weakness spotted and the necessary science applied, but it was just part of the show. After one such interlude, Shivnarine Chanderpaul lost his stumps to the last ball of the morning session on the fifth day of a Test match West Indies might just have won. With 71 off 68 balls, the little Guyanese had given the run chase a thrilling impetus, until Warne reminded everyone who was boss. It was some ball, more remarkable than the one to Gatting. But that is the thing, a single moment in the mystery cost Chanderpaul and the West Indians their life in the match.

'Bowled, Shaane.' 'Thanks, maate.' Two masters, mainly unbeatable.

'WELL DONE, *MACHANG!*'

Even from a distance there was no mistaking the most distinctive bowling action in cricket. Such a singular mystic: so many friends, a few enemies. 'Will the pitch spin? Is it hard, will it bounce?' he daily wondered, as if the array of off breaks, leg breaks and straight-onners required nature's assistance. Say what you like, Murali Muralitharan claimed 800 Test wickets, which makes him the most prolific bowler of all time and one of the greatest cricketers to have graced the fields of gold.

I did a show with Murali on Channel 4, a sort of innocent or guilty job, in which he volunteered to bowl in a rigid brace, cast with steel bars and resin. In other words, he subjected himself to a televised inquisition during which he delivered every one of his magical, mystery balls and gave us a tour of his action and body. He had a wrist like rubber, that moved with a remarkable super-rotation; an elbow that was double-jointed and could hyperextend; and a shoulder that revolved on a horizontal plane.

He bowled his off spinner and topspinner pretty much as normal, the brace seemingly irrelevant. He bowled the doosra effectively, if slower than he might in a match and possibly with fewer revs on the ball. It was difficult to be sure whether this was because of a lack of adrenaline; because the weight of the brace restricted the speed of the shoulder rotation; or, simply, because the brace did not allow his arm to straighten. When we were done, I put the brace on my own arm. It was impossible to bend or flex the arm in that brace. Before the inquisition, his critics said it was impossible to bowl a doosra without straightening the arm. Wrong. Difficult but not impossible. The vitriol thrown at Muralitharan has been unkind and uneducated. The fact that he has reacted without bitterness tells us much about the man.

Behind him has been an army of support. First among them Arjuna Ranatunga, the one they called Napoleon—a tough fellow with an incisive take on cricket, a love of food and the appetite for a fight. Ranatunga gave no quarter over Muralitharan, indeed he raged against the machine against his man. Then there was every other Sri Lankan on the planet, and Tony Greig too. More recently, Mahela Jayawardena and Kumar Sangakkara have led the resistance. Kumar should know. He stood and watched from pole position. He could read the devil in the delivery and make sense of it. Kumar is much feted for his batting and much under-feted for his work with Murali. Slight of hand and swift of foot, he was the glove for Murali's fingers. Bloody hard graft, keeping to a magician.

Not that you would have known it. Sangakarra just got on with his job in a typically determined and restrained manner. It takes courage to keep wickets and a mighty commitment to maintain Test-match standards with both bat and gloves. A sweet nature belied his ruthlessness, for he was no angel behind the stumps, applying sharp wit and withering language to vulnerable opponents. He was professional, well trained and practised: a man who trusted rehearsal before instinct. The antithesis of M.S. Dhoni, say, for whom instinct is all. In the end, wicketkeeping held back his batting. Ambitious for records, he stood aside as keeper and duly became more prolific on the scoreboard. For a while, Murali missed the sage advice that came from behind the wickets but they soon rediscovered one another. Between them is nothing but admiration, for the roads travelled and the landmarks passed.

At breakfast in Birmingham one morning, I chatted with Sangakkara and we wondered whether any cricketer had contributed so much to the success of his team as Murali. Bradman maybe, but bat and ball cannot compare. The nearest is Hadlee, whose Kiwis won 22 Tests with him and lost 28.

Without him they have won 61 and lost 137. Now, here is a deal-closer. With Murali, Sri Lanka have won 54 and lost 41. Without him they have won 21 and lost 51. In those 54 Test-match victories, the man with the rubber wrist took 438 wickets at 16.18 apiece, striking at a wicket every 42.7 balls bowled. As a point of reference, Warne took 510 wickets at 22.47 in the 92 Tests Australian won with him on board, striking at 51.2.

Murali averaged 6 wickets per Test—the only bowler of the 66 who have taken 200 or more Test wickets to take 6 or more wickets per match. The naked figures are the naked truth, whether you like it or not. Make your complaint to the MCC or ICC if you think there is a cross against his name. Between them they have altered the law to increase the degree of allowance and, we might say, interpretation. It is these institutions that allowed Murali to keep on playing. As Michael Atherton said: 'More power to *their* elbow.'

The Sinhalese for 'mate' is *machang*. This phrase was a constant in the Muralitharan–Sangakkara relationship: 'Well done, Murali; well done, *machang*.'

'WAIT, IT WILL COME, HAVE PATIENCE'

The best spin bowlers provide the ultimate test of skill and nerve. It is cat and mouse they play, a game of hunter and hunted. The batsman requires stealth and composure because the spinners who know their craft make the ball float and swerve and dip. The Gatting ball turned a long way from outside leg stump across to off stump, but first it swung from off to leg and then it dipped, which gave Gatting the impression it wasn't there at all.

In general, decisive footwork and the softest hands separate the expert from the journeyman. The best way to pick a leg spinner is from the hand but, if that fails, watching it off the pitch will have to do. Ideally, the length of the ball should also be determined from the hand—'See it early, play it late,' said the old coaches. Garry Sobers, who played only back to fast bowling, went mainly forward to spin bowling—until, that is, the moment when he picked the length as short and sprang back into his crease to cut, drive and pull. The key is to get the head set forward to the bowler and to the line of the ball and from there let the body position itself naturally.

The bat, not the pads, should lead the way and be angled to ensure the ball drops down to the pitch when defending. The pads should be a second line of defence only. Sobers hates pad-play—'You've got a bat, use it,' he says. By so doing, you hope to eliminate the bat-and-pad catch close to the wicket.

It is important for batsmen to use their feet to come down the pitch but not necessarily to hit boundaries. By getting to the pitch of the ball, it is easier to defend and work singles to keep the strike rotating and the scoreboard moving. There is an art to this, especially as meeting the ball as it pitches opens up both sides of the wicket and upsets field settings. These battles are absorbing and take time. Warne is very good at predicting when one side or the other will crack.

In the masterclasses we have done on television in England, Australia and South Africa, Warne talks about maintaining mental pressure on a batsman. There are many ways to do this: dry up runs, then offer scoring opportunities that have risk attached; leave areas of the field vacant, especially those that require hitting against the spin; have fielders saving singles rather than protecting boundaries; question intent; encourage batsmen to take you on; remind them of previous successes or failures; fly a kite—in other words, bowl a wide ball that spins a mile but that he cannot reach, only watch; bowl into the rough made by the previous bowler's footmarks; applaud him when he least expects it; tease him; stare at him for no reason; stare at him for good reason; and so on and so forth. Warne played games that few others thought about and won many a moment with them.

The best example of this came on the last day of the Test match in Adelaide in 2006–07, when any chance of either side winning appeared to have gone. Both teams had made more than 500 in their first innings. England were 59 for 1 in their second, 97 ahead and only a day left. We chatted on the fourth evening and Warne told me, quite certainly, that Australia would win because the Poms would look to play defensively for the draw and he would do the rest. Apparently, he said this to Ricky Ponting and then led the team talk the next morning.

He hated losing (though it must be noted that he does so graciously and that he speaks well of most of his opponents) and even when he had none for plenty, the belief that a wicket could be taken governed the whole match. It was as if there was only Warne—no crowd, no media, no urn—only Warne and the match to win. Such a menace. 'I might get slogged,' he says, 'or I might knock 'em over but I'm not going to die wondering.'

Sure enough England froze. He knocked over Andrew Strauss, albeit controversially; unravelled Pietersen; found a Jaffa for Ashley Giles and a wrong 'un for Matthew Hoggard. The chaos he caused created chaos in general. On a flat pitch, England threw themselves off the cliff. Lemmings, or just the legacy Warne began to create at Old Trafford in 1993?

At the time, I had not seen anything better than the way Pietersen played Warne in the first innings of that Adelaide Test—the white-handkerchief moment. Pietersen then matched or bettered it against the Indian spinners in Mumbai six years later, when he made 186 from 233 balls and, along with Alastair Cook, hauled England back into the series. Brian Lara conquered Muralitharan in Sri Lanka in 2001–02, making 688 runs in three Tests at 114. Barry Richards, who was commentating, judged those runs as the finest against spin he had witnessed.

(Surprisingly, given the rich palette from which to choose, Richards picks two relatively unheralded innings against spin as among the finest he played. First, 69 against Bedi in a tight Hampshire win on a dustbowl at Northampton; and second, 71 not out, in a match Hampshire lost, when he carried his bat against Titmus and Edmonds on an equally difficult pitch at Southampton—testament, perhaps, to the thrill of outfoxing the foxes.)

All of which leads me to recall the best batting against spin I saw on the field of play. My second County Championship match was against Gloucester at Basingstoke in 1978. I marvelled at the contrasting methods of Zaheer Abbas and Mike Procter, one a master of touch and placement, the other a powerful striker of drives and pulls.

John Southern, our tall left-arm tweaker, said Zaheer was impossible to bowl to because of the speed with which he picked length. Fully forward and fully back, the Pakistani made anything a fraction off length look foolish, while anything off line just looked easy. He said Procter intimidated simply with his presence. One straight-driven six was lost in a field. After that, John dared not overpitch and so Procter stepped back, opened his stance, and pulled him flat into the scorers' hut for six more. History records that John took just a single wicket in the match and that our off-break bowler, Nigel Cowley, was not called upon at all. Gloucestershire's left-arm spinner, John Childs, took 12 for 58. In contrast to the sparkling play we saw from Gloucester's adopted sons, we homegrown folk were rooted to the spot, terrified of a mistake. A bit like our bowlers.

All of which leads me to a favourite story about spin bowling. Procter was a wonderful all-round cricketer but his off spinners are not as well known as the other, more imposing aspects of his game. In the 1970s, he played a few seasons for Rhodesia in the Currie Cup—good bucks, I think—and the pitch in Bulawayo turned square. Transvaal were visiting for a Currie Cup clash of note and, concerned by a lack of options among local slow bowlers, selected a young Welshman, David Lewis, who ran a garbage-disposal business and had played a couple of games for Glamorgan in his youth.

Lewis was a tremendous character and a most popular figure in the Johannesburg cricket community. Though he was taking wickets with his leg breaks for the Wanderers Club in the strong first division of club cricket, doubts lingered about his ability to convert these relaxed weekend performances to the hard-nosed Currie Cup. The doubts proved justified as Lewis struggled to land the ball on the cut strip in Bulawayo and Lee Irvine, keeping for Transvaal, threw himself left and right to limit the damage. Ali Bacher removed Lewis from the attack after seven overs, 0 for 32 in the first innings and five overs, 0 for 16 in the second. When Lewis returned home he told his delightful wife that he wasn't sure Bacher was quite the captain he was cracked up to be. 'Kept taking me off just as I was getting going,' he said.

Anyway, at the denouement of the match, Transvaal were clinging on for the draw. Procter, operating in tandem with the huge left-arm spinner Richie Kaschula, was ripping his off spinners out of the dry and dusty pitch. Lewis was to be last man in and was no sort of a batsman. Johnny Waite, arguably South Africa's finest wicketkeeper-batsman—though Irvine may argue the point—was the Transvaal manager and quickly spotted the potential for disaster. He took Lewis to a tennis court behind the pavilion and asked him what his tactic would be against Procter. 'Lap him, manager, I'll lap him. I'll put a big stride down the pitch and sweep every ball,' answered the garbage-disposal man. 'No, you bloody won't,' said Waite, 'You'll block him as if your life depended on it!' Whereupon he began to coach Lewis in the art of defending against off spin.

'Get forward and kick it,' said Waite, 'or, when it's a touch fuller, lead only with your bat and block it. Under no circumstance go with bat and pad together.' Waite demonstrated and then threw balls for Lewis to put the plan into practice.

They heard the crowd roar at the fall of the eighth wicket and returned to the pavilion with fifteen minutes left in the match. Waite was panicking. It was another to Procter, who now had 7, this one caught at bat-pad. 'Ach, no, not like that boys. Come on, Lewey *boetjie*, try it again,' he said, and Lewis kept at it in front of the dressing-room mirror. 'You've got to take the close catchers out of the game,' he urged himself. 'Kick it, block it, anything, but you must survive somehow. Get forward, man.' At that moment the ninth wicket fell. Lewis was in a corner of the dressing room still rehearsing defensive prods when Irvine said: 'Lewey, you're in.'

There were now six minutes remaining on the clock and three balls left in the over. Glamorgan's Lewis dragged his heels from the dressing room and set out to save Transvaal's bacon. 'Lead with your bat, David,' he muttered to himself, 'or kick it away with your leg. Whatever you do, get forward. Bat or leg, block it or kick it but get forward, get forward David boyo, save the day.' Head down, nervous and way out of his depth, Lewis reached the crease and looked up to ask the umpire for a guard. Before the words 'middle and leg' could come from his lips, there was horror. Complete horror.

Procter was 60 yards away. The wicketkeeper and slips could barely contain themselves. They had taken up position 25 yards back. There were five slips, a gully, leg gully, short leg and silly point.

'Hello, here's trouble,' said Lewis to the short-leg fielder.

To himself he said, 'Shit, I might die here.'

Procter turned at the end of his mark to unleash hell. Barely a muscle in the little Welshman's body moved. The ball whistled past the brow of his eye before flying into the gloves of the towering Howie Gardiner behind the stumps. Procter growled. The second ball was one of those wicked inswinging yorkers that had blown away more world-class batsmen than David Lewis cared to contemplate at that moment. He leapt for his life, or his toes, and the ball, which was shooting just a fraction past leg stump, caught the back of his boot and ricocheted to the gap at square leg. The non-striker, Danny Becker, screamed at Lewis to run the single. Lewis, unable to ascertain his position or mind, found his native instinct take over as he careered to the other end in a flurry of arms, legs and fear. The once rosy Lewis complexion had turned white. Time stood still, everyone suspended in disbelief.

The Rhodesians snapped out of it in the nick of time. The clock was running down. The mighty Proc was not to be denied. He shouted at the stumper and fielders to close in. He walked back two paces and with a gently flighted off break captured the final wicket of the match. Becker, caught Kevan Barbour, bowled Procter 13. There was Castle lager and cane and Coke through the night. Procter, one of the three most devastating fast bowlers in the world at the time, had taken a career-best 9 for 71 with spin. You ain't seen nothing like the mighty Proc.

Lewis, meanwhile, remained unbeaten. And alive.

PART 3

Talking and writing about the game

In the Channel 4 studio with Richie Benaud,
our conscience and our guiding light.

CHAPTER 10

Media days

Simon Barnes once wrote that John Arlott considered cricket not a matter of life and death but 'just a matter of life'. What a contented life it can be, well expressed in Arlott's simple lines about watching a game at Worcester in the late 1930s:

Dozing in deck-chair's gentle curve,
Through half-closed eyes I watched the cricket,
Knowing the sporting press would say
'Perks bowled well on a perfect wicket.'

The writers and the poets came to the game because they recognised its bloody-mindedness every bit as much as its beauty; Arlott knew that best of anyone. It is a game of emotions and contradictions: the strong and the weak; the calm and the headstrong; the faithful and the cynical; the foolish and the wise. It is a mixture of ritual and an opportunity for art, theatre and entertainment. Nothing is more graceful than one aspect of cricket and more infuriating than another. This in itself is stimulating. Cricket consumes and spits out, which is why so many cricketers have hurried their own passing.

Thanks to the internet, it has never been easier to be a cricket writer. Anyone can write and many do. The range is stupefying, stretching across many a divide—from academics to comedians and musicians, for instance. Recently, I was sent a piece by Felix White, the guitarist in the Indie band, the Maccabees. He steps out with Florence, she of the Machine. It was good stuff, misty-eyed about his Nasser Hussain, Graham Thorpe and Mark Ramprakash of long ago.

But we must be careful. The age of the internet and of social media has led to an unparalleled output of judgement. Every slip of word or pen is magnified. On one hand, this is a good thing because it improves attention to detail, but on the other it is less good, because it leads to more cautious journalism.

Sir Neville Cardus, begetter of *The Guardian*'s sporting faith, once said to the novice Frank Keating, 'You'll enjoy sports writing, as long as you get on the front foot at every opportunity.' Cardus headed up what Paul Stevens called 'the holy trinity', with John Arlott and E.W. 'Jim' Swanton. 'All cricket writers have been influenced by Cardus, whether they like it or not,' concluded Alan Gibson in his 1975 eulogy. 'They tried to copy him or to avoid copying him.' Cardus kept his readers 'hovering between tears and laughter', added Gibson.

Cardus's obituary of Douglas Jardine in *The Guardian* is compulsory reading. '[Jardine] was a tall hard-boned personality, having none of the unction often associated in his period with cricket. His was realpolitik. He determined in the early 1930s to wrestle back the "ashes" from Australia, and to put Bradman in a reasonable, if still high, place. All the howls and winds of the world would not deter him . . . He had, off the field, a canny wit and gifts for fellowship. On the field, even a Harlequin cap did not lighten or brighten a pervading air of relentless purpose. Against Australia he played cricket to win. He was perhaps the first to lead the reaction against Edwardian gesture and romance and the humbug of a "may the best side win".' It is interesting that the 'ashes' are in quotation marks and spelt with a lower case 'a'. This suggests that the legend of the Ashes, as we know it today, was yet to take form.

I knew Arlott pretty well and stayed with him on Alderney. Each morning post-breakfast he emerged from the cellar with a basket of wine, six bottles carefully chosen for weather, mood and menu. His library of crammed bookshelves rose from base to pinnacle like a beehive. My eye spent hour upon hour wandering this labyrinth, my hand brushing many a spine. John wrote much as he spoke, with words that flowed like a rich and deep river. He captured simplicity and made it poetic.

Swanton was very different, both at work and play. He was ferocious about detail—'less of the ugly word "on", young Nicholas, more of the "leg"-side,' he once wrote on a card to me—and, about values—'clean flannels, Christopher, clean flannels', he would frequently say to Chris Cowdrey, who was throwing himself around the field in T20 fashion back in the 1970s. Jim was wedded to the game, undoubtedly ambitious and hugely opinionated. At a lunch, word reached him that I had proposed the theory that a blend of the two Richards would surely make for the next best batsman after Bradman. He made his way past tables of diners to tap me on the shoulder and say, 'I hear you think the Richards are almost as good as Bradman. I saw Hammond and believe me, Hammond has them both in a corner.' In the course of the address at Jim's funeral at St Stephen's Church in Sandwich in 2000, Archbishop Runcie said: 'Let's face it, Jim was not a man plagued by self-doubt.'

For all this magisterial assurance, Jim was kind to newcomers, encouraging their appreciation of the game within the unimpeachable parameters he had set himself. He was good company, if frightening on the golf course, and gave one a perspective that began with watching W.G. Grace from his pram and ran to the end of the 20th century.

It is easy to forget how much of the game has gone before. The well-documented heyday of the Hambledon Club in Hampshire occurred a century before Fred 'The Demon' Spofforth bowled out England at the Oval in 1877. The laws of the game were first recorded in 1744 but there is enough evidence to suggest that forms of cricket were played in medieval times—a shepherd with his stick, stone and wicket gate. Cricket has baffled those not brought up with it and bored some who have. But it has charmed those who know it and now enthralls hundreds of millions of people, who watch, listen and read with ever-increasing hunger and an ever-evolving opinion.

ADELAIDE OVAL, 1994–95, 7.45 pm

The day's play and its ensuing responsibilities were almost over, the press box was emptying. My sheet of paper was blank, bar some scribbles. I was meeting John Woodcock and John Thicknesse, two gargantuan figures of the press box, for dinner at the Adelaide Club in half an hour. Woodcock walked behind me, looked over my shoulder and said, 'If you can't think of a good first paragraph, dear boy, tell them what happened.'

I packed up ten minutes later and was at the club bang on time, having not written a word. Writing came later, well oiled, at around midnight. It is a wretched thing about filing from Australia that the desk in London is open all night. Woodcock said it was easier to find something to say after a drink or two. The next morning I said that what might apply to him certainly did not apply to me. The piece I wrote was nonsense. (Not again, I hear you cry!)

Another single phrase, or sentence, that resonated came from Sir Michael Parkinson, who told me that Alistair Cooke—the Cooke of *Letters from America*, not the Cook of

10,000 runs for England—once handed in an essay at university that he believed to be a masterpiece. 'Murder your darlings,' advised Sir Arthur Quiller-Couch his estimable if rather eccentric tutor. If only I had. My flowery prose, and particularly its exaggerated alliteration, was in homage to Frank Keating, whose words had captured my heart. But none of us is Frank, not close. More of that in a while. First, here is the unusual tale of how my media career came about.

A NEW YORK MINUTE

My sixteen years with the London *Daily Telegraph* began by fluke. In the autumn of 1991, I was invited to play two exhibition games for England against the West Indies in Toronto and New York. Twelve of us were paid £4000 each for the US trip and, though the TCCB didn't much approve, these were the days before central contracts, so we were free agents and the four grand was handy.

I missed out in Toronto but stood in for Michael Atherton at the disused ball park on Randall's Island in New York. I opened with Graham Gooch on a bouncy matting surface, which was hardly ideal given I had spent more than a decade in the dressing room at Hampshire telling Malcolm Marshall that I'd hook him into oblivion if we ever played against each other (I had assumed we wouldn't). You will not be surprised to hear that he gave me the chance for two out of the first three balls in the match. The first whizzed past the grille of my helmet. The second I left alone, a tad outside off stump. The third was the same length as the first and, instead of swaying out of the way, I took it on. Silly boy. The mis-hit spiralled into the clear blue sky with Maco screaming 'mine', while clearing other eager West Indian fielders out of the way to take the catch himself and joyfully usher me from the field of play.

The pitch was bloody difficult. Robin Smith, Alec Stewart and David Gower made a few as I recall, but our sum total was no more than 160 in 50 overs. The West Indies won pretty comfortably, Desmond Haynes crashing it about the place. Haynes, incidentally, was one of only five of us who had made anything of baseball a couple of days earlier. After the first game at a swish stadium in Toronto, we all had a hit against a couple of local pitchers. Dessie was good, as was Viv Richards. Robin did fine too. They were the only ones to whom I'd have offered a contract. Gordon Greenidge and Allan Lamb might have been asked back for a second look. The rest of us were rubbish.

We were going to have another go in New York but it didn't work out that way. The crowd at Randall's Island was about 15,000, mainly expat West Indians and Wall Street boys out of London, who loved the match. Don't let Shane Warne or Sachin Tendulkar tell you they are the pioneers of international cricket in the US. I still have the colourful poster at home, the only piece of cricket memorabilia I possess. I saved it because the match was played on my birthday and, given it is the one England team sheet on which I have been included, it will stay a while yet!

Anyway, both teams were awarded a man-of-the-match prize by the sponsors: Haynes for West Indies, Smith for England. We had agreed to split any cash but were told the award was a gift, not money, so Lamb suggested we draw straws. After common agreement and with much laughter we drew in batting order. A short straw for Gooch, pause, a long straw for Nicholas. Game over. Blimey. I opened the envelope and pulled out a letter from British Airways saying I had won a round-the-world ticket in business class. Lucky bastard. Smith's jaw dropped: bad decision, that draw. The guys suggested I use it that coming winter and join them at the World Cup in

Nicholas and Steve Waugh—Southampton 1989. Looks like I've got the upper hand . . .

Yup! A hundred against the Aussies. What a feeling.

England A at Victoria Falls, where I picked up cerebral malaria. During this tour Mike Atherton and Graeme Thorpe proved they had all the necessary qualities for Test match cricket.

The Judge—brave, strong and defiant. He remains a popular and much-loved figure.

Against England at the St John's Recreation Ground in Antigua in April 2004, Brian Lara reclaimed his world record score ten years after first passing Garry Sobers' unbeaten 365, which, incidentally, was made in Jamaica in 1958. Matthew Hayden had borrowed the record from Lara with a blistering 380 against Zimbabwe in Perth in 2003. But Lara was not to be denied and, with England once more the whipping boys, he went on to 400 this time. His unbridled joy is captured here.

Shane Warne. Few cricketers, if any, have made such an impact on the game. What a photograph—such power and presence.

Wasim Akram winning the 1992 World Cup for Pakistan. His ferociously competitive instinct matched his remarkable skills. The two balls with which he knocked over Allan Lamb and Chris Lewis (the latter shown here) are the stuff of legend.

Ian Healy stumping Michael Atherton at Headingley in 1993. 'Stay down and move late, I kept telling myself,' said Healy about standing up to the stumps for the spinners.

Andrew Flintoff consoles Brett Lee at Edgbaston in 2005. A wonderful moment at the end of a wonderful match.

The great Gilchrist, Straussed and Flintoffed at Trent Bridge, 2005. Interest around the UK was at fever pitch and this catch was replayed so often it became a part of everyone's lives.

Michael Vaughan with the urn in the dressing room at the Oval—he says he was thinking, 'Thank god for that!'

The toss in Brisbane at the start of the 2006–07 Ashes. Australia batted, Steve Harmison bowled the wide of all wides and Ricky Ponting set out his marker with a big, big hundred. There was a cruel beauty in the 5–0 revenge.

The King claims his 700th Test wicket at the MCG on Boxing Day, where else! This was another moment of magic to Andrew Strauss, who has been on the wrong end of a few. The photograph says it all.

Muttiah Muralitharan, Kumar Sangakkara and their national flag. Sri Lanka is a small island with a huge heart. These two mighty cricketers are in the pantheon of the game—one has 800 Test match wickets, the other 12,400 runs.

Something was funny—the day the Sydney Cricket Ground goes pink, 5 January 2010.

Our own Abbey Road. *From left*: George, Paul, Ringo and John—a rather more Fab Four than Tub, Binga, Heals and Nicko.

Michael Atherton and Mark Taylor: two highly regarded custodians of the game.

'Out of my way, Nicko, there's a demo to do here,' says Michael Slater. We have plenty of laughs preparing to go on air each day.

With Geoffrey Boycott, both of us grumbling about another Vaughan tweet.

Constantia Uitsig in Cape Town. Jeff Thomson bowled here and Graeme Pollock batted. It was a special place, made more special by the landlords of the day, David and Marlene McCay.

The feisty and brilliant Virat Kohli, worth the admission money alone. Kohli is the most recent in the line of truly exceptional Indian batsmen—from Gavaskar, through Tendulkar to Kohli—whose batting evolved around the demands of the era in which they played.

Joe Root while making 256 against Pakistan at Old Trafford in July 2016. This superbly well-crafted innings makes me think he, too, will one day be included among the elite.

Dale Steyn runs in . . . menace in motion.

A.B. de Villiers—genius in pink. A.B. leads a group of brilliant modern batsmen, each of whom is redefining movement, range and risk.

Two good men embrace: Mitchell Johnson and Ryan Harris, the architects of England's fall from grace in the summer of 2013–14. Respected judges suggested they were as potent as Thomson and Lillee almost 40 years earlier.

Michael Clarke and Brendon McCullum walking out for the toss at the World Cup Final in 2015. Their words—at the service for Phillip Hughes and at the Cowdrey Lecture, respectively—gave cricket much to consider and to embrace.

The game goes back to work in Adelaide after the tragic loss of Phillip Hughes two weeks earlier. The 63 seconds of applause was heard around the world.

Martin Crowe at the MCG on the day of the World Cup final in late March 2015. It was the last time we saw him. The name lives on through his brother Jeff, who is now an international match referee. The Crowe family have given much of themselves to cricket; the game has been lucky to have them.

Since 2005, Chance to Shine has brought cricket to 3.5 million children who otherwise would not have played the game. 'It's not what kids can do for cricket but what cricket can do for kids,' is the ethos around which we have raised millions of pounds to fund the programs that are taking cricket back into schools and communities. Few aspects of my life in the game have been more fulfilling.

When the last word of this book was written and the send key pressed, Leila and Kirsten breathed a sigh of relief and we took off to the sunshine in Greece, August 2016.

Australia in February–March 1992. (They knew I wouldn't be selected in the team!) No one was happier than Smith. 'Leader,' he said, 'you can bowl at me in the nets.' Right.

Wind forward three months. Chris Moody, golfer and friend, telephoned over Christmas. He said he was off to the sunshine in the new year to play four tournaments and asked what I was up to. I told him about New York. 'Well, here's a plan,' he said. 'Leave a month or so earlier and come and caddy for me in Thailand, Australia and New Zealand.' And a plan it was.

The day before we left in mid-January, Christopher Martin-Jenkins called to ask about my trip. He said the sports editor of the *Daily Telegraph* was interested in taking a piece a week from life on the road with the European Tour and from inside the England dressing room. I swallowed hard and jumped at it. The sports editor, David Welch, then called to confirm the details and offer me £100 per column. I swallowed harder: space in a national broadsheet and money too.

In Thailand, at the Johnnie Walker Classic, Chris made the cut on the mark. It was a nerve-shredding experience. Golfers don't make a cheque unless they make the cut. With courage and skill, he birdied two of the last three holes to do so. This is a hard-nosed business, a mile away from the general perception of a pro golfer's life. So impressive was the way in which Chris held himself together under this severe pressure that I rushed back to the hotel room and wrote about it. I then called London and dictated to the copytakers. The next day, David Welch called to say how much he enjoyed the piece and that he would now like two a week and would pay £100 for each of them. That was January 1992. I was still writing on sport for the *Telegraph* sixteen years later. Then, on a cruel evening in March 2008, a new sports editor rang from his crackling car phone to say it was over. 'We're moving the paper in a different direction,' he said. 'More news, less comment.' I was furious and I miss it. Occasionally I think I can hardly grumble: I might have drawn a short straw on Randall's Island.

Welch was an inspirational leader. He knew and loved sport, if occasionally applying a cynical eye to the idealism of some of his writers. The *Telegraph* was the first paper to go to a separate sports pull-out, and to justify it he hired some of his favourite writers and looked after them well. When he stood down, his number two, Keith Perry, continued on the same path. Only when Perry was moved upstairs did the direction of the sports paper change.

There was many a slip, even more panics and occasionally utter embarrassment. Once, after a subeditor told me he had cut a whole paragraph, I shouted down the line: 'Cut it, bloody cut it? It's poetry.' That had them howling at the Christmas lunch! For most of the time that the *Telegraph* was my master, I wrote by hand and filed by telephone to the copytakers at the desk in London. Sri Lankan names caused great confusion, as did phone lines from India. Reverse charges were accepted but not all exchanges could provide the option. In Jamshedpur, I was convinced the copy would not make its intended desti-nation and in Ahmedabad it did not. Only with the advent of the new millennium did we learn how to send our thoughts by the early incarnations of electronic mail. I was useless with the technology, however, and still am.

My favourite filing memory comes from Adelaide on England's 2002–03 tour of Australia. I wrote at the close of play, in between sending links for Channel 4's highlights package of the day. I pressed send, into the *Telegraph*'s embry-onic 'direct input system' and set off for the bar. Then dinner. Then the bar again. A moment or two before the clock struck midnight, I returned to my room and found a message from the sub on the desk in London asking when they might expect my piece. Initially calm, I pressed send again, and called the office. Nothing. I immediately recalled a story of the cricket correspondent of the moment so frustrated by this system that he threw his laptop into the hotel swimming-pool. I squirmed and, though mine was old and faulty, I chose to keep it dry. It was 1 pm in the UK, a little too early for the skeleton crew of copytakers to have arrived and, anyway, there were few of them left by the dawn of the 21st century. It was a line of work made almost redundant by the power of the internet. Midnight in Adelaide, lunchtime in London and no subeditor likely to bail me out by taking 1000 words of dictation, so what to do?

Bravely, I emailed my piece to Tony Greig, who was staying in the same hotel, and then telephoned his room. Greig is early to bed and to rise. He was in the deepest shiraz-infused slumber and took a while to register my stupidity. However, one tiny thing lay in my favour. A week or two earlier, I had written an enthusiastic tribute to him and, especially, to his Herculean efforts against Lillee and Thomson in 1974–75. He had liked that and puffed out his chest. Trembling, I explained my dilemma. He was neither best pleased nor much interested, but he sensed my distress. He asked what the hell he could do about it and I said, 'File it for me from your laptop,' which was a rather more recent and reliable piece of kit than mine. He agreed. Phew.

Up the lift I went, down the corridor of the fifth floor and knocked on 517. I shall never forget what I saw. At 6 feet and 7 inches, the former captain of England and now the most prominent voice and face on global cricket television, was standing half-asleep in his striped pyjamas. I resisted the photograph. He asked me in. The room was freezing cold, a condition I was later to find applied to any commentary box he could so influence and to the inside of his car and home. Greigy loved aircon; ice-cold aircon loved Greigy. The engines of his sparkling new computer roared into life. I shivered. He saw my email. We typed in the *Telegraph* sports desk direct-input address and he pressed 'send'. Eureka! Then he said, 'Now fuck off.' Fair call.

THE FOURTH ESTATE

The cricket writing in Australia has always been superb. Arguably, Peter Roebuck became the most irresistible read in the land. Even Greig wanted to know his take. Certainly, no other cricket writer has managed to invade the players' space and mind with such authority. Martin Crowe once said that Roebuck's insight was eerie and off-putting, which I suppose is a compliment. The finest essayist is Gideon Haigh, who takes the game into a parallel universe. His intellectual approach is often misunderstood, for it challenges the prosaic and one-dimensional thinking of which many players, administrators and television folk are guilty. The game would do well to hear him more clearly. Greg Baum is another who hits the mark more often than not. His consistency and slick use of language and phrasing are a treat. Mike Coward provided a neat combination of history and romanticism. Today, Malcolm Knox and Peter Lalor lead the way for other aspiring correspondents.

Their founding fathers were Jack Fingleton, Ray Robinson and Bill O'Reilly. Fingleton retired from playing on the eve of the Second World War and soon found himself at the right hand of powerful politicians in Canberra. He was to forge close relationships with several prime ministers and begin a career that combined his role as political correspondent for the ABC's Radio Australia with cricket journalism. A disciple of Cardus, he wrote a number of stylish and influential books, some of which were at first condemned for their persistent attacks on Bradman. The one that really got Bradman's goat was *Cricket in Crisis*, long considered the best first-hand account of the Bodyline controversy. In it he criticised Bradman's unorthodox approach of backing away to leg against Harold Larwood. This was one of only a very few occasions when Bradman was moved to reply in a book of his own, *Farewell to Cricket*, where he questioned Fingleton's own ability and therefore his authority on the subject.

The root of this mutual dislike was religion. In the 1930s, Australia was largely divided along sectarian lines. Those of Irish Catholic descent—Fingleton, O'Reilly, Stan McCabe, Leo O'Brien and Chuck Fleetwood-Smith—were in one corner of the dressing room, while the Protestants, led by Bradman, were in the other. Bradman and the ACB accused Fingleton of leading a group who were undermining his captaincy. This left a sour taste and their relationship never recovered. Legend has it that Fingleton and O'Reilly laughed hysterically when Bradman was bowled by Eric Hollies for a duck in his final Test innings at the Oval.

O'Reilly, by all accounts, was an extraordinary man with a biting wit. He wrote in the same aggressive manner as he bowled leg spin. He was an Australian cricketer of the old school, his talent nurtured in the bush and hardened by the realities of life. His fiery Catholicism got him into various levels of trouble but the more they disciplined him, the more he attacked them. I sat next to him in the press box once, for about half an hour, while he chatted with Roebuck. He was 80 years old, wore a collar and tie, and asked where I was from. He seemed to know more about London than I did.

He first encountered Bradman at Bowral. Bradman was a diminutive teenage figure then, whose pads came almost to his waist, but he made 234 not out nonetheless. There was no friendship between them but there was immense respect. O'Reilly described the little master as the supreme genius of cricket. Bradman said O'Reilly was the best bowler he ever saw or played against.

Ray Robinson was thought of as the man who changed the face of Australian cricket writing. His attention to detail was Swantonesque, and his descriptions of mannerisms and performances so accurate as to be almost real, though never romanticised. He enjoyed the complete trust of the players, something that no journalist today can claim. According to Bradman, 'Ray lived as he wrote, honestly, modestly, sincerely and always respected a confidence.'

His book *On Top Down Under* is considered among the finest about the game, capturing as it does the essence of all the Australian cricket captains. Namely: 'Bradman made the purple patches of others look like washed-out lilac'; 'Bob Simpson had a mind no easier to change than a £100 note'; 'Richie Benaud had the faculty of making snap decisions that did not snap back'. The latest edition has been updated to include the captains until the end of Mark Taylor's reign and, suitably, that work was completed by Gideon Haigh. Perhaps Gideon will keep going.

Robinson made a single hiccup in an otherwise long and exemplary career, and it brings me back to the issue of slip-ups. In his book *The Wildest Tests* he described a dozen Test matches that had been disrupted by crowd violence. In it, he misquoted a proverb when writing about a riot-filled Eden Gardens in Kolkata: 'If a Bengali and a Cobra confront one on the road, one should kill the more dangerous first—the Bengali.' In the original proverb, a different community, not the Bengalis, is described as more dangerous; this comment, coming as it did from a respected author, put noses out of joint. It was an honest mistake, but were such a thing to be written today, we can only begin to imagine the outrage on the many social media platforms available now.

I was recently guilty of a damaging error myself. Writing a preview of the World T20 tournament for Cricinfo, I spoke of India as unbackable favourites and, specifically, M.S. Dhoni as a Caesar figure, in line for a triumph granted by the Board of Control for Cricket in India (BCCI). Towards the end of the piece I felt obliged to mention the other teams too, suggesting that England could upset the odds and, maybe, Australia too. I suggested that South Africa would fall at a knockout hurdle and lazily gave the rest a sentence each. Collectively: Sri Lanka, Pakistan and Bangladesh were short of class, I wrote, but useful in the conditions; 'West Indies are short of brains but have IPL [Indian Premier League] experience in their ranks,' I continued, 'and New Zealand are worth a look, strong and savvy.'

Having seen the West Indies capitulate in Australia the previous summer and, worse, noticed how the senior players failed to support Jason Holder's courageous efforts, I wrote them off with an inconsiderate stroke of a pen. I had not even researched the West Indian team to see who remained from the 2012 champions or to digest the fact that Darren Sammy was still captain in the T20 format. I have long been a Sammy fan.

Sammy saw the piece and latched onto my three words 'short of brains'. He fed them to his players and to the press conferences in the lead-up to the semifinal and final. He fuelled the fire that was already blazing in West Indies cricket: board versus players; players association versus some of the players; Mark Nicholas versus players; whole world versus us. I could hardly blame him.

On the Saturday evening before the final, I wrote another piece for Cricinfo, apologising to Sammy and his team. I was not happy with the finished version, so left it overnight. When in doubt, do nowt. I had also tried to get Sammy's private email address but failed. On the Sunday, the situation changed. Ian Bishop replied to my email with Sammy's address. West Indies beat England in a thriller to win the tournament.

At the post-match interview he let rip, sparing no one and certainly not me. My words, he said, were a strong motivation for his team.

This is an excerpt from the piece I filed to Cricinfo.

The first thing is to loudly applaud West Indies cricket on a golden day. The women were magnificent. The men more than matched them. The finish was a miracle: a thing of devastating power, of a certain beauty, and of destiny.

The second thing is to say that the West Indies cricketers who beat England in Kolkata today and triumphantly lifted the T20 World Cup play smart cricket that is both entertaining and hard to resist. There were scatty, improbable turning points that swung the match this way and that—so many of them that it was hard to keep track. In the end, the very fact that West Indies pulled it off was the most epic thing about it.

The third is to offer an unreserved apology to Darren Sammy, a man I hold in the highest regard, to his team and to the coaches around them for the throwaway phrase I used in a recent column on these pages. I would have made the same apology whatever the results of the day but I do so now in the knowledge that the people of the Caribbean will be celebrating long into the night and well into tomorrow. The spirit of the romantics will be with them and from thousands of miles away the rest of us can almost taste the rum, feel its punch and dream of the day when we return to the lapping shores of those incomparable islands.

I also wrote a personal letter of apology to Sammy via email. He will have received it about three hours after Carlos Brathwaite's winning hit in Kolkata. India is five hours ahead of London. When I awoke the next morning he had replied:

Thank you so much for this email. I must admit I was truly disappointed to see that a man who I truly respect and admire could write such about our team. But I'm also a believer that everything in life happens for a reason and this was one of the driving forces that drew us closer as a unit. Once again thank you for the apology. It is greatly appreciated. I will pass on your message to my teammates. Hope all is well on your side. God bless you and your family.

The following day, he wrote again to say that his team also accepted the apology and that most of them had read the piece on Cricinfo. 'We have all moved on,' he said. Right there is proof that cricket is a beautiful game.

The players make it so, while the writers and commentators paint the pictures and spread the gospel. The go-to conscience of the game during my time in cricket has been John Woodcock. He began as a BBC cameraman on Freddie Brown's tour to Australia in 1950–51 and graduated quickly enough to have become cricket correspondent for *The Times* by 1954, a position he held until 1988. Eloquent, always sprightly and driven by history's long counsel, the Sage of Longparish saw that the game belongs to the players, and that their responsibility is to pass it on to the spectators and to the next generation. *The Times* is lucky to have Michael Atherton continuing John's line of entertaining prose, intuitive analysis and reason. Mike Selvey has done much the same for *The Guardian*.

There is no doubt that a previous life playing cricket matters to many readers who have played it themselves. There are superb writers who can turn a phrase but not unravel a technique, or give a sense of how an innings, or over, is crafted. But it takes a variety of styles and approaches, not to say backgrounds and accents, to bring cricket off the page. No one ever wrote in a more beguiling fashion than C.L.R. James, for example, and his book *Beyond a Boundary* is widely considered to be the finest written about the game. The book's key question is inspired by a line in Rudyard Kipling's poem 'English Flag': 'What do they know of England who only England know?' James, an Afro-Trinidadian, asks in his preface: 'What do they know of cricket who only cricket know?' To answer the question, he puts the game into both historical and social context, discussing the strong influence it had on his life and explaining how it helped his understanding of class and race.

The book I most dip into is *The Highlights: Frank Keating*, edited by Matthew Engel. In the introduction, Engel writes that Frank's 'imagery was breathtaking and vocabulary audacious: he was indeed the "onliest Frank"'. He offers three reasons for the love affair between Frank and his readers. One is the writing: 'As Winston Churchill said of Harrow, his education was interrupted only by his schooling. And like Neville Cardus 50 years before, he marched into *The Guardian*, always a paper full of posh university men, and, with barely an O-level to his name, wrote them under the table. He didn't seem to know how things weren't meant to be done.'

Second was his charm:

> He made lasting friendships . . . often improbable ones: the convivial Frank hit it off with the stoical and abstemious Graham Gooch as he did with his more regular bar-companion, Ian Botham. It is true (and the great Cardus had a similar habit) that the quotes he extracted were inclined to sound a bit, well, Keatingesque. But I never heard anyone actually complain. He never misrepresented anyone's thoughts; he just made them more eloquent.
>
> As Mike Atherton pointed out in a characteristically perceptive piece in *The Times*, this would be impossible nowadays. In the major sports, press and performers are

rigidly segregated; there is minimal contact, controlled by public relations officers. The drivel that results, Mike might have added, is not just bland and boring, but—though accurately transcribed—inherently falser than Frank's cavalier interpretations.

The third 'and most important' is that his charm came across to the readers: 'They sensed that Frank was as starry-eyed and uncynical about sport as they were and shared their own delight in the personalities and their character. He was their representative at court side, touchline and boundary's edge. In all of that, he was the onliest.'

I have the happiest memory of driving from London to Herefordshire to speak at Frank's request at the annual end-of-season dinner of his local cricket club. We had the most marvellous evening, for there has been no one in cricket with whom I would rather spend a night of beery banter and festive feast.

BSKYB

It was on my first tour to Australia as a journalist for the London *Daily Telegraph*, in 1994–95, that I badgered Sky's producer of cricket to give me a run on air. John Gayleard, a red-bearded and red-blooded Australian, was no pushover—far from it. But he could feel my enthusiasm. Throughout my life I had copied and mimicked Benaud, Lewis and Laker; Arlott, Johnston and Trueman. I thought I had a story to tell. The game had not come so easily to me as to, say, David Gower or Mark Waugh, but I was certain I could explain how they, and their like, had got there and what they were now doing out in the middle.

The First Test was at the Gabba and finished with England, and me, well beaten by Australians. I stayed on in Brisbane with the former Wallaby captain and sports journalist Andrew

Slack, playing golf, talking cricket and rugby, and saving on hotel rooms. Early on the first morning of the Second Test in Adelaide, Gayleard called Slack's home and asked for me. One of his commentary team was ill, he said. If I got my backside to Adelaide in a hurry, he would pay me £200 to work on the day's play. Slacky drove me to the airport in some haste. I walked into the Adelaide Oval around midday. Nervously, I settled beside Bob Willis and began the audition for a career.

At the close of play, Gayleard asked me to do the next day too. Then in Melbourne, he told me I had three days' work. In Sydney, three became five. In Perth I was straight-up offered the whole match. It was there that he took me to the director's truck and made me watch the moment when Graham Thorpe went to a splendid hundred. He played the tape back and asked what I thought of my own commentary. I cringed and said that I wished I wasn't talking over Thorpe's celebration. 'Exactly,' he replied and then played it back with the commentary taken off. Since that day, I have tried to announce and applaud a cricketer's landmark as it happens, often ecstatically, and then let the pictures of the players and the crowd do the rest.

A few weeks later, he called from London in the middle of the Australian night. I was in Melbourne covering the Australian Masters golf for the *Telegraph*, and in the deepest, most satisfied sleep having interviewed Tom Watson that afternoon. John offered me a job with Sky. That woke me up. I was contracted to Hampshire for a final year, so could not accept it. That shut him up. I said I could start in October. We agreed to talk again. The very next day, Sky's head of sport, Vic Wakeling, called. He said October was fine but that he wanted me on hand to do stuff on camera whenever available during the summer. Vic and I then met up in a Hampshire pub in May, when he said that, in time, he wanted me to present the cricket.

Sky had made the most brilliant start to their coverage of cricket in the Caribbean in 1990. England played well, the pictures were magnificent, the production carefully thought through, and the commentary team of Greig, Boycott, Tony Lewis, Michael Holding and Tony Cozier absolutely top-class. Writing in *The Times*, Sir Tim Rice said: 'I have seen the future of televised sport and it is a dish.' From a conservative, this was some endorsement.

Frankly, viewers liked Caribbean sunshine in their living rooms at home. It was a winter treat to set alongside the thrills of the live Premier League football games. The audacity and size of that first premiership deal had shaken the accepted stream of television consciousness to its core. Now the gloves were off. Sky made money and spent money. Cricket was valuable because it filled hours of airtime, attracted advertisers and audiences, and provided compulsive summer viewing when the footballers were on sunbeds. Sky was a big player, and the terrestrial networks were caught off guard.

I signed up full time in the autumn of 1995, immediately after retiring from professional cricket eighteen years after first walking with a kitbag into the county ground, Southampton— a kid with a dream. I was sad to say goodbye and experienced a short period of withdrawal and depression in the immediate weeks that followed. Day upon day I asked myself, 'Why have you given away a life you've loved?' before breaking down and retreating into solitude. There were three good reasons: I was 36, slow in the field and my arm had gone; I had resigned the captaincy after the best part of twelve summers, and it was time to move out of the next man's way; my head told me it was time to go and do something else. Ian Chappell has always echoed the thoughts of Keith Miller: 'I wanted to retire when people were asking why did you, not why don't you.' It was tight, but I hope I made the deadline.

Wakeling and Gayleard gave me every opportunity. I hosted the 1996 Benson & Hedges Cup Final from the top of the pavilion at Lord's. There is nothing so terrifying as going on air live to camera for the first time. You wonder not how the words will come out, but *whether* the words will come out. Willis, Botham and Paul Allott were good mates and highly professional colleagues. Lamb, Mike Procter, Derek Pringle and others who auditioned over the winters and summers of 1996–97 were pretty much as nervous as I was. I have watched some of the early stuff back and won't be watching it again. Gayleard was good at clearing a path, but not interested in allowing us editorial input. He had come to Sky from Channel Nine in Australia, where everyone did as they were told by the boss. He was a hard bastard and we had our rows but he grounded me in the business, and I thank him for that. When we worked together again later, specifically at the 2007 World Cup in the Caribbean, we had some fun.

Wakeling wanted a more identifiable platform for one-day cricket. He asked Bob and me to come up with a structure and take it to Lord MacLaurin, who was new in the chair at the ECB. At this time, the BBC had all the rights to international cricket in the UK, while Sky had the rights to all England matches abroad. Wakeling badly wanted one-day cricket in the UK, and more if possible. We came up with a soap-opera-themed format for domestic one-day cricket, a minimum of five England one-day internationals at home and at least one Test match, all live on Sky. MacLaurin liked it and liked even more the idea of a free commercial market for the game. International cricket was on the list of government-protected sporting events, so he took the plan to Chris Smith, then Secretary of State for Culture, Media and Sport. With barely more than a nod of the head, Smith agreed to the general principle. In the summer of 1998, cricket was moved from list A to list B and, from that moment on, the television rights game changed completely.

Smith said: 'My decision to accept recommendations on cricket allows the sport more freedom to negotiate a fair price for flagship events. This is something for which the ECB and county clubs have specifically asked. I expect to see this freedom used responsibly, with continued access for all viewers to a substantial proportion of live Test coverage and any new income derived for cricket to be devoted to improvements in the facilities needed to play the game and to raise standards. If these expectations—especially the test of achieving substantial live coverage on free-to-air television—are not fulfilled, then I may of course need to review the listed criteria again.'

This felt important at the time but not seismic. How wrong we were. It was seismic, all right. It was the single biggest game-changer to televised cricket there has been in the UK. The people at Sky were delighted. When the ECB put the rights out to tender, Sky came in hard. So, surprisingly, did Channel 4. The BBC was underprepared.

On Friday, 16 October 1998, I came off the golf course in Troon, Scotland, to be told that Channel 4 had won the rights to televise live all but one of the home Test matches, along with the NatWest Trophy. Sky Sports had a live Test, the one-day internationals and other county, women's and junior cricket. It was scarcely believable. The split deal was worth an unprecedented £103 million. The BBC was left with radio coverage only. Both Channel 4 and Sky had highlights of the matches they did not have live. Channel 4 added another £13 million worth of marketing and promotional commitment to the pot.

The next night I finished playing golf, showered back at the hotel in Troon and made my way down for dinner with the other seven guys on the tour. We began talking about Channel 4's likely approach. A general concern was that it might try to be too funky. The chief executive, Michael Jackson, was quoted in the papers saying his channel would 'revolutionise the coverage of the game', seeking to 'reflect a younger, multi-cultural audience'. Cricket was a 'thrilling and exciting game', he said, and Channel 4 was keen to attract new fans. He made it clear that the network's bid had been accepted because 'our and the ECB's interests coincide, not because of the size of our cheque book'. One of the guys read this out to the rest of us from the morning's newspaper but was interrupted by the receptionist, who said there was a call for me at the front desk.

The voice at the other end was that of Bill Sinrich, who ran Trans World International (TWI), the television production arm of International Management Group (IMG). I had worked for him on productions in India and the West Indies. He asked if I had heard the news and added that he had brokered the deal. 'Good job,' I said. Then he dropped a bomb. Channel 4 wanted me to lead their coverage. Lead? Yes—host, commentate and drive editorial. My heart skipped a beat or two. He added that the most exciting chapter in the televising of British sport was about to open and that we would be in it together. I said, 'Calm down, Bill.' But he was right. He paused before saying goodbye and then said, 'You need to quickly realise that most people have a seminal moment in their life. This is yours. Channel 4 have a blank chequebook—for the production and for you. Believe me, this is your moment. See you Tuesday at 9 am.'

It was hard to keep schtum over dinner.

On the following Tuesday, Channel 4 offered me the job. In the room were Jackson; David Brooke, head of strategy and marketing; Karen Brown, deputy head of programming; and Andrew Brann, finance director. It was a lively meeting, in which pride and enthusiasm drove their ambition. They shared everything, talking as if I was 'in'. Brooke had masterminded the coup and pushed for me to be at the forefront of the production.

Brown was onside. The other two went with it. They all asked what the network should do first. I said, 'Sign Richie Benaud.'

We discussed the styling. There had been a quote from within the network about taking cricket away from the domain of 'crusty, grey-haired old fogeys'. They endorsed that, making a wise exception for Benaud, who was, as they pointed out, anything but crusty. They didn't want blazers, though, or company motifs. Jackson left the room before the rest of us and, as he closed the door, he turned back to say, 'Wear what you think is right. Just one thing though: no ties.'

We went to air live the following summer, at Lord's—the Second Test between England against New Zealand—in ties but not blazers and no motifs. After the first day, reviews were generally kind. The best of them came from Ian Wooldridge in the *Daily Mail*, who said that any worries about the nature or standard of the coverage could be set aside. 'I feared the worst,' said the influential Wooldridge. 'I have rarely been more profoundly wrong.' Then he said, 'If you had chained a child to Channel 4 midmorning Thursday, he would have learned more about the heritage, technique and mystique of the game in two hours than I learned in two years at school.' He was generous to 'bouffant-hair-styled' me and reflected on the authority brought by Benaud. Everyone did. In the *Telegraph*, Giles Smith wrote: 'Frankly, you could assemble a documentary series entitled *Penetrative Sex around the World* and just so long as each programme opened with Benaud saying "Morning, everyone", no one would be the least bit upset.'

It had taken me less than a week to agree on a deal. I went to tell Viv Wakeling of my decision. He was upset, as was I in a way. Sky had given me the break and I had imagined a long career there. Jeremy Thompson, the face of news and current affairs, called to say he thought I was making a mistake and that the future was satellite TV, about which he was undoubtedly correct. But it wasn't a mistake; Channel 4 was where the flame burned brightest for me. I rang Bob Willis, who sounded disappointed but, typically, wished me well; Botham, who said I had got it wrong and that he would miss me, which was so bloody sweet and un-Beefy-like; and Paul Allott, who was pleased for me and saw the move as irresistible. Much water has flowed under the bridge but the four of us are still close friends to this day. I didn't have the courage to contact John Gayleard. I knew what he thought and it wasn't good.

At this point, Wakeling had a problem: no presenter for the England tour to Australia. He was signing David Gower to replace me but David was otherwise committed that winter. He asked me to do it. I said, 'Of course, though what about Gayleard?' 'Your problem not mine,' he said. 'You'll handle him.' Hardly, but we got through.

Meanwhile, the team at Channel 4 were on a charge. Benaud was secured within a month, amid general delight, as was head of sport Mark Sharman, who had been Wakeling's number two at Sky. Just before Christmas, Mark shook the world of sports television production with a decision that virtually nobody saw coming. Instead of awarding the production rights to TWI and Sinrich, he went left-field and gave them to Sunset+Vine, which was led by Jeff Foulser and Gary Franses. Sinrich was devastated. An intense man, he died in 2007 while being treated for depression. He was just 50. His part in that defining series of events will be relevant for evermore.

THE CHANNEL 4 YEARS

Most English cricket lovers have a view on Channel 4's coverage. These are mainly kind, sometimes so enthusiastic as to have made the memory of it almost a cult. Others are vanilla and occasionally there has been negative criticism. For example, the advertising breaks upset viewers who were used to uninterrupted coverage on the BBC, and complaints were made when we left live play to go the soap *Hollyoaks* or *The Simpsons* at 6 pm on weekdays, or to the racing on Saturday afternoons. People fondly remember the commentary team of 2005—Benaud, Greig, Atherton, Michael Slater, Boycott, Nicholas and Simon Hughes, the analyst in the truck—but the early years were not blessed with such quality and depth. I came in for some stick—hyperbole and exclamations being the main grumble—but no one appeared to doubt the passion, enthusiasm or energy that I, and we, gave the seven years during which Channel 4 held the rights.

Most of us had been brought up watching the game in black and white. The coverage was straightforward, conservative you might say, with a single camera at one end and barely a raised voice from a commentator. There were next to no 'add-ons' and certainly nothing that was deliberately in place to 'enhance' the viewing experience. If you liked cricket, you watched. If you didn't, you didn't. I loved it, so I watched every ball I could. Black and white or not, the heroes of the hour made for compulsive viewing. But I don't recall ever thinking that the television coverage made the game either beautiful or exciting. Colour television came to our home in the early 1970s, but the BBC kept the rhythms of the cricket broadcast pretty much the same as they had always been. As the former England all-rounder and then BBC *Test Match Special* summariser, Trevor Bailey, pointed out on the day Channel 4 was awarded the rights: 'Cricket is not a thrilling and exciting game all the time. It's essentially a situation game and it's the situation which creates the excitement, not the television.' True and not true.

Our aim was to bring the game to life for the viewer. We were modernists but realists too, eager to respect the game's history and translate its archive. We took the housekeeping out into the sunshine and, when the rain came to challenge us, we turned the studio into a theatre. We recruited the players to tell their story and the administrators to explain theirs. We invited sportsmen and -women from other fields, musicians, actors, writers and even politicians to share their joy in the game. We ran clinics and masterclasses, demystifying the inner game and busting jargon. We took cricket to the towns and villages of middle England and even to Northern Ireland. We ran competitions and offered guided tours of our private space. We even beat Tim Henman, playing on court number 1 on the middle Saturday of Wimbledon, in the ratings. Duncan Fletcher, the England coach, said we changed the perception of the game at a time when the British public and the national cricket team most desperately needed it. He added that the team's performances improved concurrently with Channel 4's overall sense of optimism. We tried to be both inspirational and aspirational and, mostly, we succeeded.

Superb camera men gave us lovely, soft pictures, and the audio team created the ambient sound techniques used so successfully by Channel Nine in Australia to bring the 'sound' of cricket to the fan at home. Lou Bega's *Mambo No. 5*, which made it to Number 1 in the pop charts, worked brilliantly as the title music. The titles themselves and the graphics had the right blend of artistic appeal and practicality. Some of the innovations worked and some did not, so we kept plugging away. We ran a live highlights show every evening that was a nightmare to get on air and not to everyone's taste. We used the Saturday-morning *Cricket Roadshow* to have a bit of laugh and demystify cricket's introspection. Sybil Ruscoe proved that women had a place in covering a game too often associated with men. Live bands played in lunchbreaks and the channel threw money at community projects and big-screen cricket events in parks and town centres. We advertised, marketed and promoted. It was a love affair with cricket and we stopped at nothing to make the lover special and everyone else appreciate her.

Gary Franses, the producer, Hughes and I put hours into Hawkeye at the Roke Manor Research Centre outside Romsey in Hampshire, where they more usually developed technology for the military's guided missiles—weapons that could consistently hit their target a mile away. We figured they could manage 22 yards' worth of lbw. By the time Hawkeye was ready to go to air, hundreds of balls had been bowled in the nets at Lord's. The result of each one was recorded and matched against Hawkeye's data. It was perfect, every time.

Meanwhile, the resourceful Hughes was developing another important part of the Channel 4 coverage—an appliance and brand he was quickly to make his own, the Analyst. Initially, he shared the role with Dermot Reeve, but lateral thinking and a unique ability to bring something to air on television without the slightest hint of ego gave him a seat that has been much copied since but never bettered. If anything, an endearing self-deprecation came through and enhanced his message. From a tiny corner of a dark broadcasting truck came many an Analyst's moment of magic.

Of all the gizmos aired on Channel 4, the least convincing was the Snickometer (having said that, Snicko has improved out of all recognition since 1999 and is now a valuable part of both the viewing experience and the umpires' decision-making process). But people loved it, mainly because Benaud loved it, and what Richie says . . .

Benaud was hired by Channel 4 when he was 68 years old. He stayed until we went off air, by which time he was 75. He spent most of these seven wonderful years behaving as a colt and encouraging us to push the boundaries. Only very occasionally did he miss a beat or, indeed, suggest that we had. He has been cricket's greatest salesman and its finest television communicator. 'Never forget,' he would say, 'that you are a guest in people's homes, so don't irritate them.'

I would put Ian Smith, the former New Zealand wicket-keeper; Bill Lawry, the proud Victorian who captained Australia after Benaud and Bob Simpson; Ian Chappell, who followed Lawry as Australian captain; and Tony Cozier, the informed and understated Barbadian, in the premiership with Richie. Right up there with them are two figures, both larger than life, whose colourful lives have been the subject of many an interpretation.

You are either for Geoffrey Boycott or against him. He does only black and white, no grey: his fans, or otherwise, offer the same in return. I am conclusively for him. We got him into a seat on Channel 4's coverage eventually but it took some persuading and, strangely, it was adversity that helped sway opinion. Boycott's recovery from severe throat cancer was a thing of monumental character, like his batting. The difference, though, was that when at the wicket he felt he had to prove himself to the world. In the battle with cancer, he was proving something to himself while, at the same time, fighting for the love he has for his wife, Rachael, and daughter, Emma. This mellowed him.

During a tea-break in the 2003 Lord's Test, I interviewed him live, the first time he had spoken on television about his illness and the journey to recovery. It was tender and real, showing a man who had travelled the long road home. Even the naysayers were struck by his warmth and the gentle hints of self-deprecating humour. By the start of the next summer, he was one of the Channel 4 number. He did not disappoint. We work alongside each other to this day, in the Channel 5 box with Michael Vaughan and Simon Hughes, and spend most of our days laughing.

Greig had hoped to work for Channel 4 since he heard the rights had left the BBC back in the autumn of 1998. Initially, the key executives in the corridors of power at Channel 4 wanted a younger look, from a broader base of the game's multinational society. If they couldn't find that in Britain, they were happy to look elsewhere, but not to Greig. Greigy had been brilliant for Sky in the early days of satellite TV, cranking up the model (a remarkable contradiction for one so wedded to Kerry Packer's free-to-air Channel Nine) and sprinkling stardust on even the dreariest day of Test-match cricket. He was convinced he could do the same for Channel 4 but the channel was not for turning.

Not until 2005, that is, when Franses, a long-time admirer of Greig, convinced Karen Brown that his association with both England and Australia, and the insight that brought, would be the icing on the cake of our commentary team. Franses was proved dead right. Greigy was tremendous value, throwing himself at that summer and proclaiming, with typical abandon, that it was the best production of cricket he had ever worked on.

Maybe, maybe not. Greig had been a central figure in the development of the Channel Nine cricket story, one that set a new standard for sport in general. The man from whom Greigy had learnt pretty much everything was David Hill, the original executive producer of WSC and a part of Packer's inner sanctum. Hill founded Nine's *Wide World of Sports* in Australia, went with Rupert Murdoch and Sam Chisholm to BSkyB in the UK and on to Fox in the US. He was the first great innovator in global sports broadcasting and a master of narrative. ('Sport as drama and sport as soap opera—that's what people want to watch on television,' Hill said when he teamed up with Chisholm at Sky.) Murdoch described him as 'a dynamic and imaginative leader who changed the experience of nearly all major sports on three continents'. If I had a television wish left, it would be to work with Hill.

It was watching Channel 4's coverage of the 2005 Ashes (the first Ashes series in the UK that the Nine Network had not bought since Packer began foraging in the global sports-rights market) beamed live into Australian homes on the SBS Network, that Kerry Packer realised his own coverage needed a spring clean. He told Sam Chisholm, whom he had dragged out of retirement for a brief second period as CEO of Nine, that Channel 4 was 'doing it better than us' and then told him to sort it out.

There is no doubt that in 2005 we were at the top of our game. The coverage of that summer won us our third BAFTA, and the channel generously asked me to receive it on behalf of the team. I did so on the day my daughter, Leila, was born— Sunday, 7 May 2006—so 'quite a day', as Richie used to say when the cricket had sparkled.

I had met Kirsten, Leila's mother, four years earlier. Her marvellous looks, wise counsel and splendid humour had utterly captured my heart. Now we had something even more spectacular than a BAFTA to share. On the stage, with the glitterati of British television scattered across the dining tables on the ballroom floor of the Grosvenor House Hotel, I said: 'I'd like to be able to tell you that this is the most wonderful thing that has happened today, but I can't, because at half past two this afternoon my daughter was born!' Whereupon, enthusiastic applause and a cheer or two broke out. The BAFTA sits proudly at home, a bookmark to the unpredictable story of life. Leila tells people about the day it was awarded and Kirsten smiles.

The first BAFTA had come in 2000, as much perhaps for the novelty and imagination in our work as anything else. Franses was the glue that held together a talented group of career television folk. Nobody has taught me more about the values of the business and the detail that makes every moment of live television seem so splendidly undetailed. For me, and I would guess for him, too, the Channel 4 years were both the pinnacle and the happiest of a working life. I had not thought that anything could match playing the game but I was wrong. Showing it off on television matched it absolutely, maybe even pipped it at the post.

In the middle of December 2004, our world came tumbling down. I was in a hotel room in Adelaide after a day on air for Channel Nine when the telephone rang. Channel 4's director of sport, David Kerr, told me that all the rights for live coverage of English cricket had gone to Sky. I stood, rooted to the spot, digesting the news I feared most. There had been two clues.

The first came in the Caribbean nine months earlier, when I was working for TalkSport radio and the London *Daily Telegraph* on the England tour. Mark Sibley, then commercial director of the ECB, was genuinely concerned about Channel 4's ability to withstand the financial pressure of the existing cricket deal, never mind another, more expensive one. In fact, he could not see the channel bidding a remotely competitive number, and he was proved right. As we talked, he looked across to the other side of the bar, where key figures in Sky's rights acquisition team were buying drinks for their commentators, who had just finished broadcasting the day's play live into English homes. They were in the Caribbean as guests of the ECB, said Sibley, and they had a lot of money to play with.

The second came a few months later at the drinks reception before the Cowdrey Lecture at Lord's. I was sharing a drink and a laugh with David Brook, who had by now left Channel 4, when the non-executive chairman of the ECB's marketing committee, Giles Clarke, pushed his way into our conversation to say that he didn't know what we found so amusing because within a year or so we were unlikely to be televising cricket. It was an odd moment. Or, as Brook called it later, a chilling moment.

A great deal has been said and written on this subject. My belief has always been that cricket needs visibility on free-to-air television. The breadth and quality of Sky's coverage is superb, but fewer people are watching cricket than ever before. Test cricket, in particular, is special in that the action unfolds over four or five days. It relies on viewers dipping in and out of the coverage in order to keep in touch with the story. Once you lose touch with the narrative, you lose the plot. Notwithstanding the rapid rollout of digital platforms, free-to-air channels have the ability to capture the casual viewer as well as the committed fan and, therefore, still have a place as broadcasters of national events. At the end of the summer of 2005, kids were out with bat and ball wherever you turned. It felt as if the game had become, like football, a part of the community. Eleven years on from Channel 4 cricket's last day on air, there is barely a pick-up match to be found.

The ECB had long done a deal with Sky: Channel 4 had no chance. The channel dithered and then missed the chance to make a formal, higher bid in the second round of the tender process because on that December morning in 2004, the ECB chairman telephoned the director of programming at Channel 4 to say that he was on his way to London to announce that the rights had been awarded to Sky. It is true that Channel 4 could not have come close to matching Sky's huge offer—in effect, Sky doubled the existing joint agreement—but not necessarily true that the network had fallen out of love with cricket. The hope was to change the balance of the arrangement that had been in place for the previous seven years but Sky and the ECB had already moved on, together. Under pressure, Channel 4 could have offered a little more but Sky wanted the lot and money talked.

In defence of the ECB, Sky has truly committed to cricket, both as wallpaper and drama. No *Simpsons*, no

Hollyoaks, no news, weather forecasts or racing, just ball by ball—guaranteed. 'It is a myth that football made Sky,' said David Elstein, later Sky's head of programming. 'Football *embedded* Sky. The major increases in subscriptions came when the multichannel package was launched . . . The others came with cricket. Cricket is when Surrey [by this he meant the Home Counties and indeed most of provincial England] discovered Sky.' The England team has been the clearest beneficiary of Sky's monopoly. The money used to fund central contracts for the players, and all that goes with them, has led to greater professionalism in the best sense of the word. Elite coaching and training have improved, and investment into the level below international cricket is bearing fruit. Now the ECB must pay greater attention to participation, in both clubs and schools.

In Australia, there is legislation to keep home Test matches on free-to-air television. Cricket Australia is happy with that, for it underpins the sport's popularity. At the very moment I heard the Channel 4 news in my Adelaide hotel room, Cricket Australia released a statement: 'We continue to support legislation because it ensures a maximum audience for the game, particularly in the vast, remote areas of Australia. Our view is that the promotion of the game is best served by as much access to it as possible. Our preference is for the 2005 Ashes series to be on free-to-air TV.' Though, of course, that specific preference did not materialise.

This milk is long spilt. The fact is that the move to downgrade cricket to sport's B list left it open to raids from all avenues of a rapidly changing pay-TV business. British Telecom are now a force in the sports-rights market, along with other service providers. The BBC remains mute on the subject of televised cricket but continues to commit wholly to the game on radio and the internet.

Test Match Special may have changed but its ethos remains as driven by that subtle balance between information, picture-painting and entertainment as it did when John Arlott, Brian Johnston, Christopher Martin-Jenkins, Fred Trueman and Trevor Bailey were the voices of reason, colour and laughter. The modern masters of the medium are Jonathan Agnew, who learnt from these fine men, and Jim Maxwell in Australia, who has long commanded the ear of cricket lovers around the world. Another favourite is Harsha Bogle, the Indian of many talents, whose wings have spread to television. Such skills are given to very few, which is why the language and tone provided by McGilvray and Arlott all those years was so important to the game and its audience.

Channel 5 was awarded highlights rights and asked me on board. We make a good program that goes out every evening at 7 pm for an hour looking to tell the story of the day through cleverly edited pictures and our appreciation of them. We are proud of the show and delighted by the viewing figures that frequently touch upon a million and, on days of high drama against Australia, have been double that. But they barely scratch the surface. On the final day of the Ashes in 2005, Channel 4 had the official figure of nine million people umbilically attached to a screen somewhere in Britain. Had the network been able to record numbers in offices and public places, that figure might have doubled.

That golden summer of 2005 changed the lives of many people, not least the English players. It was to change my life, too. I had never done anything more stimulating or fulfilling. I understand that we did not win the heart of every cricket lover, but we won the respect of the vast majority. I miss it to this day.

CHAPTER 11

Australia again,
and a call from Kerry

Kerry Francis Bullmore Packer died at 10.40 pm on Monday, 26 December 2005. He achieved more in his 68 years than most other men dare to dream of. With him went a piece of the Australia the world knows best—a deal done hard, on a handshake.

With days to live, he had delivered what was then the biggest deal in Australian sporting history, as Channel Nine and Foxtel came together to secure the television rights for the Australian Football League. They paid AU$780 million. He died peacefully three days later at his Bellevue Hill mansion in Sydney's Eastern Suburbs. His system—his kidneys to be precise—finally gave in.

I remember his passing vividly. Nine had covered the first day's play of the 2005 Boxing Day Test without a hitch. At seven o'clock the next morning, my phone rang. It was Steve Crawley, head of sport. He said Kerry had died and that I would pick up on camera straight after the 9 am news bulletin, announce his death for those who did not already know and then host a show about him that would lead into our preview of the day ahead. That woke me up. I started to think about what I might say before falling back on John Woodcock's advice from eleven years earlier: 'If you can't think of a good first paragraph, tell them what happened.'

I was oddly emotional about a man I barely knew. We had met once, less than a year before.

A CALL FROM KERRY

There was once a red phone in the Channel Nine commentary box. It was a direct landline to the producer from the man who owned the network. When it rang, everyone froze. Well, nearly everyone. Richie Benaud simply raised an eyebrow. The stories of this phone are the stuff of a legend that relates sackings, schedule changes, commentary roster intervention, commercial instruction and run-of-the-mill bollockings in equal measure.

My journey with Channel Nine began early in the Australian summer of 2003–04. I was in Sydney, doing very little for a week after watching England win the Rugby World Cup. I went to see Alan Jones, the popular—if sometimes controversial—radio broadcaster and celebrated speech writer for various prime ministers. Jones gets around. He has also coached in both rugby codes, worked in musical theatre and backed aspiring musicians, artists, and sportsmen and -women. Above all, perhaps, he owns and loves racehorses. Few people have covered such ground.

Famously, he coached the 1984 Wallabies on their unbeaten tour of the UK and struck up a close friendship with the captain, Andrew Slack. Slack introduced us way back—February 1987—when I was travelling across this vast continent and staying wherever there was a bed and a beer. I had heard of the way Jones inspired many young people with his unique take on motivation and performance. Clearly, he had a brilliant mind and an ability to persuade young talent into justifying itself. I was treading water in county cricket and running out of time to play for England. Slacky thought I should meet Jones. His wife smiled and said: 'Interesting idea. He's different. Good luck.' A date was set.

A week later I pressed the buzzer of Jones's urban-cool Newtown apartment. He would not let me up until I had satisfactorily answered the entry-level question: 'How much do you want it, champion? How much do you want to play for England?' 'Er . . . a lot, I guess,' I feebly answered. He pressed the buzzer and up I went.

He came to the door with a kind smile and a glass of champagne. A piece from Wagner's Ring Cycle was pumping through the sound system. He was different all right—thoroughly engaging, with a theory for everything and an answer to most things. I loved his enthusiasm and genuine interest in my career and future. I left after midnight, empowered.

Intermittently, we stayed in touch. Some fifteen years later I was in his office for coffee. We talked mainly about Jonny Wilkinson and English rugby until he switched tack and said that Slack had told him I was looking to spend more time in Australia. True, I said, but only if there was work in the media somewhere. He suggested I call David Gyngell, the new Nine CEO, about a gig with the channel. I said no chance, either of me calling or of him being interested. Tony Greig had been down the same road on my behalf a year or so earlier but Gyngell had boned the idea almost before Greig had fired off the email. Both Jones and Greig indicated that Benaud was at the end of his hosting days and Nine were unsure about his replacement. Thus, Jones persisted and I resisted. Then he picked up the phone. 'Put me through to David Gyngell,' he said to his PA. 'Christ, man, what are you doing?' I protested.

'G'day, Gyng . . . Now look, champion, I've got Mark Nicholas in my office, the host of Channel 4's coverage of cricket in the UK. Yes, mate, Mark Nicholas. He's your man to take over from Richie. No, mate, he's in my office now . . . Yes, mate. He's here for a day or two yet. Well, he'd better be . . . Yes, good . . . I'll tell him. Bye, mate.'

Down went the phone.

Jones told me to give it fifteen minutes and then to call Gyngell's PA immediately, which I did. She was charming and we agreed to a meeting at 10 am the next day at Channel Nine.

Gyngell was surprisingly enthusiastic about me becoming part of the network. He wondered if I was thinking of moving to Australia full time. I repeated what I had said to Jones—it was a case of the work available. He was eager for me to stay and commentate on the First Test between Australia and India at the Gabba, which caught me completely off guard. He called the producer, Graeme Koos, and told him to set it up. I could sense Koos making a fuss, wondering how the heck he would justify this to his commentary team and the viewers. Gyngell told him to pull his head in, give me a proper go and let him deal with the spin-offs. Then Gyngell said he would pay me a thousand bucks a day.

I shall never forget the look on the faces of the other commentators when I turned up at the Stamford Plaza Hotel in Brisbane. There was a room set aside for wardrobe fitting and I was told to head there for a blazer and tie. Mark Taylor and Ian Healy greeted me warmly and then asked what brought me to Brisbane. Greig came in full of the joys of late spring and dropped his jaw. Bill Lawry laughed. Benaud and Chappell barely blinked an eye. My guess is that Gyngell rang Benaud for endorsement. Thus Richie was expecting to see me and had told Chappell en route. Simon O'Donnell, who was hosting the coverage alongside Richie, must have been as surprised as Taylor and Healy but hid it well.

It rained most of the first day, so there was a lot of awkward hanging around. When I finally picked up the microphone, I did so on the back of an understated throw from Greigy, who said, 'It's 1 for 42 here at the Gabba, and to pick up commentary are Richie Benaud and Mark Nicholas.' And I could hear Australia say, 'Who?!'

Michael Slater tells a nice story about sitting in the seat next to Richie for the first time. He was working for Channel 4 at the Lord's Test against the West Indies in 2000. The first thing every commentator does when he arrives at the ground is look at the commentary roster. In those days, a slot alongside Benaud was the highest seat in the business. Slater sat nervously for seven or eight minutes, unsure of how to go about following the great man's minimalism. Then Brian Lara under-edged a ball from Darren Gough that shot past leg stump and, instinctively, Slats grabbed the mic to say, 'Ooh . . . that's just snuck under Lara's bat.' Pause, long pause. 'There is a word "snuck" in the English language, isn't there, Richie?' asked Slats. Longer pause. 'I can think of one or two 'ucks, Michael,' said Benaud, 'but "snuh" isn't one of them.'

It was one thing to sit down next to Richie but quite another to do so for the Nine Network. Nervousness hardly begins to describe it. The palms of the hands go clammy, the mouth dries up and simple disciplines such as listening to the director via your earpiece go out of the window. Channel Nine's cricket coverage had held me captive since WSC had caught us all off guard. It set a standard that inspired a new way of thinking about televising sport. The four full-time commentators—Benaud and Chappell, Greig and Lawry—could form and divide opinion, educate in the ways of the greats and entertain in a fashion that encouraged imitation and parody. The comedian Billy Birmingham had made the four of them cult figures with his Twelfth Man albums. The hair, the hats, the clothes and the voices were public property. The game was the soundtrack of summer and these four men were its face, feel and sound.

Thus, I was beyond nervous. Thankfully, I knew a bit about the Indian team and offered some offbeat stuff that went down okay. As the match progressed, I calmed down. Over the five days, the team were generous to me and we got through. I said goodbye and travelled north to the Sunshine Coast for a look around. A couple of days passed and I was in the process of booking flights back to the UK when Gyngell called. He wanted me to stay for the Adelaide Test, starting the following week. 'Kerry is flying in for that weekend, to listen to you!' Thanks, Gyng.

I had a golden moment in Adelaide, suggesting that Anil Kumble should switch to bowl over the wicket to Adam Gilchrist, who was swatting his round-the-wicket offerings into the stands. I said he could knock him over from around the wicket and if so, the boost to the Indians might well inspire them to go on and win the game. Well, Kumble switched to around the wicket and bowled Gilchrist next ball. It was a magnificent Test match, won against the odds by a buoyant India. Within 24 hours Gyngell called asking me to stay on again: 'This time for Melbourne and Boxing Day,' he said.

I flew to Melbourne for Christmas and played golf with Shane Warne at the Capital—a private club owned by Lloyd Williams, who had built Crown, the magnificent hotel in which the commentators stayed. Lloyd played with us and during the round Warnie gently suggested to him that Packer should think seriously about me coming to work for Channel Nine. They were great mates and, apparently, Lloyd did just that to surprising effect. Thanks, Warnie.

On Boxing Day morning I walked nervously into the commentary box. Three times I had shaken hands and said goodbye to these guys and now it was g'day again. After Christmas salutations all round, Lawry looked up from his lead commentator's seat and said: 'Merry Christmas, Mark. You're not having my job, however hard you try!' The Brisbane Test had been a breeze, not that I knew it at the time. Melbourne was trickier—the more often I turned up, the more I trod on eggshells. By the Fifth Test in Sydney, I felt in everybody's way.

I was staying with Michael Slater at his perfectly positioned Bondi apartment. He had been unwell and was fighting back. We had long breakfasts, hung around in the sunshine, were in and out of the surf and linked up most evenings with Jo, the girl who was to become his wife and who did more than anyone to get him back on track. Most of all he wanted the chance to commentate on Channel Nine, having made an excellent impression with Channel 4. We spent hours talking about the future, imagining a day when the two of us, along with Taylor and Healy, might inherit the mantle of 'the tight four', as Greigy liked to call the group who had been at it since Packer won the rights.

At the end of the summer, Gyngell offered me a contract for the following season. The network would try me in front of camera, he said. Slats seemed pleased, pointing out that at least we knew there was a way through the door.

Thus, back to Australia I came for the 2004–05 season. Koos put me in front of the camera for two minutes each lunchtime to ad lib a summary of the morning's cricket. It was a screen test. Then I started presenting segments, such as tea. This was especially awkward for O'Donnell but he barely raised an eyebrow. Hats off to him, for never once did he indicate that he felt compromised. What he felt deep down is entirely another matter.

The second match in the VB one-day series was in Hobart on a cold and damp mid-January day. While calling a quiet passage of play, I sympathised with the spectators, who were wrapped up, and the Pakistani fielders, whose bodies refused to do as they were told in the conditions.

As the players were leaving the field for the break between innings, Koos's mobile phone rang. He looked around the commentary box and mouthed, 'It's Kerry . . .' The red telephone was long gone; the boss had not called in a while.

'G'day, Mr Packer . . . Sure . . . let me look . . . No I think he's gone to lunch . . . Ah no, he's here, hang on.'

And he mouthed again: 'Mark, it's Kerry, for you.' Even Richie looked up with interest.

My heart thumped, wanting to burst from my chest. Beads of sweat gathered above my brow. My legs went to jelly. I searched for saliva but found none.

'Hello.'

'Son, it's Kerry Packer.' His voice was throaty, like gravel, and low. 'Son, stop bagging the fucking game.'

'Pardon, Mr Packer? I'm sorry, I missed that.' It was a bad line. I moved across the room.

'I said stop bagging the fucking game, son. Celebrate the game, talk it up.'

'But Mr Packer, people tell me I'm too busy talking the game up and that I should toughen . . . '

He raised his voice. 'I'm not people, son, I'm the boss. You listen to me.'

By now, I'm bent sideways at the far end of the commentary box, dying of humiliation and desperately in search of a better signal.

'I'm trying, Mr Packer. It's not a great line. I think it's better here. I think I'll hear you better now.' I wished I could not have done.

'Son, stop telling us how fucking cold it is in Hobart and how the fielders' are wringing their hands and how people are wrapped in anoraks and having a shit time. The only people having a shit time are those of us at home who have to sit here fucking listening to you.'

Kapow!!!

And he wasn't finished.

'And son, we're a commercial network. We sell the game. It's not over till it's over. I don't care how far in front the Aussies are, it's never over. Our business is numbers, son, eyeballs.'

'Yes, Mr Packer.'

He was on a roll now.

'And another thing, when you're next in Sydney, come and see me. Ring my secretary and make an appointment.'

'Yes, Mr Packer, when should I . . .'

'Are you fucking deaf, son? I said come and see me when you are next in Sydney. And son, bring those two other young blokes, Taylor and Healy, with you.'

'I will, Mr Packer.' I promise I will.

'Goodbye, son.'

And down went the phone.

The world stood still. Contorted and beaten, I stayed rooted to the spot in shock. The room was quiet. Most of the guys were at lunch. Koos had stayed behind and came to . . . well . . . console me, I suppose. He tapped my shoulder and prised the phone from my fingers. Max Kruger, the scorer and statistician for longer than most could remember, asked if I was all right. Yes, I was fine. Koos said the call sounded pretty hardcore. I said it was. He asked how I felt about going back on camera after the break and I admitted I wouldn't be comfortable. He suggested giving it a miss and that he would come straight up with the commentators who could fill the couple of minutes' overlap until play began. Then he told me to go for a walk and get some air.

I wandered aimlessly towards the beach, which is right behind our commentary position. Having taken off my shoes and socks, I walked along the sand, all hopes and aspirations lost in translation. Packer's perception of me was so far from my own that I weighed them up against each other and came down in favour of his. Confidence shot, I reckoned I'd be on a plane back to the UK within a week.

I did one half-hour commentary stint in the run chase but didn't trust myself to say much more than the occasional 'Good shot'. Benaud gave me a few conciliatory looks. Greigy jumped all over it saying that Kerry got everybody once, even Lawry. 'He puts a marker on most people who represent the network,' said Greig. 'Take his call as a compliment.'

Bill told the story of Kerry calling him on the red phone during the first year of WSC and telling him to 'Stop copying Benaud and start fucking talking.' He added that he hadn't stopped talking since. 'After all,' he says, 'Kerry was paying the wages, not Richie.'

Lawry is a wonderful man; tough, of course, but kind of heart. He was a plumber by trade and delights in telling the rest of us that we have never done a day's work in our lives. He and Greig struck up an unlikely friendship. They had dinner together most evenings, Greig with his huge glass of shiraz and Bill on something soft. Their on-air chemistry was a mystery but it worked so well, and was so funny, that some television folk swore they must have had a scriptwriter.

Taylor and Healy were pretty cool. They said they were looking forward to the visit, though they wouldn't have betted on quite how soon it would come.

At almost the very minute I landed back in my Hobart hotel room, the phone rang. It was Gary Fenton, then Nine's head of sport and an ally.

'You okay, my boy?'

'Yeah, I'm fine now, Gary. Thanks for calling. Look mate, you tried, Gyng tried, we tried. Some things are not meant to be. I really appreciate your support these past two . . .'

'Hang on, it's not that bad!'

'Really?'

'Oh, it'll be fine. Kerry just wants to get his claws into you blokes. I've rung to say you're booked on the eight o'clock flight to Sydney in the morning with Tubby and Heals. The boss wants you at his office in Park Street at midday. I'll meet you in Starbucks across the road first. See you then, mate.'

As I was digesting this news, the phone rang again. This time David Gyngell.

'I hear the old man gotcha.'

'You could say that, Gyng.'

'Must have been a good one, mate, even by his standards, because James [Packer] was sitting with him watching the cricket and heard him going hard at you. James just rang to tell me, reckoned you copped it and could do with a call.'

'Well, that's good of him. And of you, Gyng, thanks.'

'Anyway, call him back and tell him he's talking shit.'

'I'm sorry . . . ?!'

'Call him back and tell him he's talking shit. Seriously, it's the only way with Kerry, and he'll respect you for it in the end. He wouldn't have you on the network if he didn't think you were up to it, so call him and stand your ground.'

'Are you fucking mad?'

'No, mate, I mean it.'

'No way, Gyng.'

'Your call. Anyway, glad you're okay. Make sure you give as good as you get tomorrow. If it's any consolation, I get one of these a month. I've learnt to give it back to him. It's the only way. You're doing a good job, mate, hang on in there. Catch up soon.'

And he was gone.

I mean, honestly, call him back and tell him he's talking shit? Mind you, Gyng was Packer's godson; I guess that helps.

PARK STREET, SYDNEY

Taylor and I drove to the airport and met Healy in the Qantas lounge. A night's sleep had bestowed courage upon us.

'I've got Fujitsu, the board of Cricket Australia and numerous other things to get on with. I'm not taking any shit from Kerry. If he doesn't want me, fine, I'll be off to do something else,' said Taylor over a strong cup of coffee.

'Yep,' followed Healy, 'I've got the car-wash business, the travel company interests, the board of the Cricketers' Association. I'm right.'

'Yeah, me too,' I added. 'I've got Channel 4, the *Daily Telegraph*, and work in South Africa and India. I'm outta here too and good riddance.'

Fenton was waiting for us in the Starbucks opposite Packer's office in Park Street. He had the old commentary manual with him, sepia-toned and frayed at the edges, the one David Hill had put together at the start of WSC in 1977. 'Kerry wants you to read this before you go up.'

'He's kidding isn't he? This thing is so outdated, Richie has forgotten it.'

Fenton told us to keep calm. He needn't have bothered; our early morning fizz was going flat. By the time we crossed the road, entered the lobby and pressed the button for the lift, silence and the shuffling of feet had taken over. Then Tubby said: 'You got Channel 4 remember, Nicko, and you the car wash, Heals.' 'Yeah, right,' we said, and giggled like schoolkids outside the headmaster's office.

Packer kept us waiting for half an hour—did so with most people, apparently. Intermittently, we talked in hushed tones but apprehension had taken hold. We wondered what was about to happen to the rest of our lives. Then the secretary invited us in.

He was standing at the door of his office, a most impressive man. It was the first and only time I met him. Though diminished by age and illness, he was tall and still strong enough to intimidate. He looked over his glasses at each of us, shook our hands one by one in a solemn sort of way, and ushered us to seats on the other side of his fine desk. He sat down and lit a cigarette. His suit jacket hung by the door. He wore a white shirt, tie and braces. The time was 12.30 pm.

I had to pinch myself. This was the man who, pretty much single-handedly, dragged cricket out of its past and into its future. Writing after his death, one eminent correspondent suggested that Packer mirrored Oscar Wilde's definition of the cynic: 'A man who knows the price of everything and the value of nothing.' He knew the price all right, but the thing about Packer was that he knew the value too. Cricketers have been thanking him ever since. And those who haven't, should.

Without warning, he launched into a spellbinding attack on our commentary. He talked quietly but firmly and with a sense of threat. His words were less advice than instruction and the long and short of them was: stop telling us something is interesting, the viewer can decide whether it's interesting; don't use that word 'clever'—it's a game of cricket, that's all; stop asking questions of other commentators and excluding the viewer; stop telling us about shit weather; cut out the in-jokes—we're not interested in your tennis and golf games or your fish and chips; keep women, kids and blokes who don't play the game in the loop by keeping it simple and explaining it for dummies; call the fucking game, not the peripherals; tell us about the game but don't analyse everything—it's not science, it's a game, and all that analysis is boring; call the game; know the players, know the figures, know the conditions and take us inside the game. Don't lecture. Call the bloody game.

There was a good half an hour in those messages and then he asked if we had read Hill's commentary manual. We murmured that we hadn't. He said to do so. Whereupon, he turned on Healy. 'The other night you called the game against the Kiwis over when they needed 13 an over and they got up. It's never over, son. Listen, you blokes, we're a commercial network. We survive with good ratings and good revenue. Never, ever call a game over until it's over, son. You called the game against the Kiwis over.'

'No I didn't, Kerry.'

Oh my god, did he just say that? And Kerry? Did he call him Kerry?

'You fucking did, son.'

'No I didn't, Kerry.'

'Son, I'm not an idiot. You called it over when they needed 13 an over.'

'I didn't, Kerry. I was rostered off the game. I wasn't even there.'

'You fucking were, son."

It was a robust exchange. I gave the points to Healy. He was right, he wasn't there, which would have been funny at any other time than this. It was me who called the game over.

By now, Packer had his feet up on the desk. He chain-smoked and studied Taylor and Healy closely. He barely acknowledged me, preferring to use the time to work forensically through two men who were to drive the machinery behind Australian cricket for a while to come. Maybe he thought he had covered me on the phone.

He finished with Healy and switched to Taylor, focusing on his position within Cricket Australia. He wanted to know everything. Tubby let some general stuff loose and kept the big issues of the day to his chest. When Kerry challenged him, he replied that it was Kerry himself who approved Taylor joining the board and that he couldn't now betray it. He asked how Taylor saw the future of cricket television rights and, rather than skim across something he knew relatively little about, Mark returned the serve. For the first time, Kerry half-smiled. He figured they were going to be 'fucking expensive' next time round but that Cricket Australia shouldn't take him for granted. He wanted that one taken back to the boardroom. 'You can tell them, son.' And Kerry was right, of course.

Then he reverted to Healy and to the Cricketers' Association, of which Healy was chairman at the time. He didn't want to see another battle between the players and their employers like the one in the late 1990s. Were the current players happy, he asked, and if so, why were they always on the take? Healy knew his arguments and put them across with typical conviction. They sparred with each other. Kerry listened, as he had to Taylor. Then he said that the players shouldn't take anything for granted either, and certainly shouldn't get greedy. Healy agreed and said he would let them know. It was riveting stuff.

It began to occur to me that Packer was taking us under his wing. Perhaps he knew how ill he was and saw the chance for a last throw of the dice with three young fellas who were to carry the torch he had first lit when we were wide-eyed teenagers. The longer we sat there, the greater the privilege became. While writing this book, I called Tubby to see if his memory of the day matched mine. It pretty much did, and he added: 'The main message that I felt he wanted to get over was that "he" was always watching, that the three of us were the new custodians of the commentary box, and that the game needs continuous monitoring with as much positive noise as we can give it.'

The message came over loud and clear, after which Packer opened up the conversation. The future of limited-overs cricket was a particular concern. Were we serious about this 20-over stuff, because it was no good to him—could hardly fit the ads into the breaks and, anyway, it was all done in three hours, so what sort of a commercial-television model was that, he asked. Then bonus points in one-day matches, then fielding restrictions. After that, bats, helmets and over rates in Tests. Then no balls and Bradman's take on the back-foot law. From there came back-foot play.

He stood up, which we assumed was the signal for us to go. It was three o'clock. As we pulled ourselves from the chairs, he told us to sit down. Tea and coffee arrived. He picked up an old bat and said it was the one Sobers used in Melbourne in 1971–72. He encouraged us to feel how light it was and then showed us how Sobers defended on the back foot from a front-on position, like Ian Chappell, he said. 'There's too much bullshit about playing side-on,' he added. Then he showed us another bat, Bradman's. He imitated the Don's pick-up and asked who else did it like that. I offered Viv Richards and Geoff Boycott. He nodded. We were all talking freely now.

He asked if we followed golf. Indeed we did. He smiled. From the same corner as the bats came Jack Nicklaus's persimmon-headed driver. He waggled it and talked about the change in golf-club technology. He said that Nicklaus hit it onto the par-five 18th at the Australian Golf Club with that driver and a six iron. Still riveting. Frankly, pretty much everything he said was gold, even when it was nonsense and there wasn't much of that. He loved talking sport and touched on rugby league and tennis, too. After the initial broadside, it was as if he had asked some mates around for tea and biscuits.

At four o'clock, he ran out of steam. 'Take care of the game,' he said, 'because it won't take care of itself.' It was with a warm handshake that he bade us farewell. That was it, the only time I met Kerry Packer. Unforgettable.

EPILOGUE

At the time of WSC, the establishment attitude to Packer, and to the players he recruited, was excruciatingly arrogant. In England, most administrators, journalists and former players reacted to him with mere disdain. But in Australia there was vitriol. The secretary of the ACB, Alan Barnes, said of the players reputed to have signed for WSC, 'They are not professionals, they were invited to play, and if they don't like it there are 500,000 other cricketers in Australia who would love to take their place.'

A few months after our meeting at Park Street, the board of Cricket Australia, as it had become known, marked its centenary by naming the two most influential figures in its history. The first, Sir Donald Bradman, was no great surprise. The second was a show stopper: Kerry Packer. Bob Merriman, then chairman, said, 'Kerry still has a deep passion for cricket. He still wants laws changed to make it more entertaining. His ideas are proactive and sensible.'

Less than eight months later Kerry was dead.

———

I took careful note of John Woodcock's simple advice when opening our broadcast—or 'telecast', as Greigy loved to say. 'Good morning, everybody, welcome to the Melbourne Cricket Ground. We begin today with the sad news that Kerry Packer has died.' Benaud, Lawry, Greig and Chappell were alongside me and for an hour, as we showed vision of the many people and events Kerry had touched in his cricketing life, they talked about the man, his impact and his legacy. The recollections and anecdotes were at once moving and revealing, funny and inspiring. Almost immediately after play began that day, both Ros, Kerry's wife, and James, his son, sent us messages of thanks for the way the cricket program to which he had given birth had honoured his passing.

On the day of the state memorial at the Sydney Opera House, two huge flags fluttered at half-mast high upon the Harbour Bridge. The Queen Elizabeth II, a magnificent ship, lay at anchor—a coincidence, maybe, but also a fitting tribute to a man treated so badly in the UK almost 30 years earlier.

Packer changed and improved cricket. He emancipated the players for their benefit and for his. To some it was a scandal, to the rest of us it was a brave new world. In his tribute, Benaud—dressed in the cream blazer Packer had suggested he wear in front of camera so as to be 'different from the others'—told the full story of cricket's reformation laconically and brilliantly. Benaud, of course, had understood from day one the brave new world Packer would be able to create.

He followed the Australian Prime Minster, John Howard, and preceded an understated but beautifully delivered reading of Rudyard Kipling's 'If' by Russell Crowe. The finest eulogy came from James, who captured the essence of the man who had steered his life. A single sentence summed it up: 'There was no more binding contract in my father's world than when he shook your hand.'

My experience was just a fragment of Packer's output, and yet all the characteristics were there—belligerence and the bully; clarity and the mentor; loyalty and the boss; warmth and the friend. I went into the meeting at Park Street frightened and came out of it enlightened.

He knew his own mortality better than most. After he took up polo at the age of 50, he had a heart attack and there is some dispute about the length of time he was clinically dead. Some say eight minutes, others twelve. Anyway, he came back to announce categorically: 'I've had a look and there's nothing fucking there.' This was not disputed at the memorial service where there were no prayers or hymns but instead 'C'mon, Aussie, C'mon' and 'Waltzing Matilda'.

Afterwards, on the steps of the Opera House, Shane Warne lit a cigarette and said, 'Bloody marvellous service.' For a bloody remarkable man—who may, or may not, still be watching over us.

TURNING BACK TIME

Back in April 2005, a strange thing happened at Channel Nine. Lynton Taylor returned as a senior consultant. His brief was to oversee sport, news and entertainment as well as mentor Nine's executive team. Taylor had been at Packer's right hand during the WSC years and was now back, at Packer's behest once more, to ease the load on David Gyngell. The appointment had exactly the opposite effect. Gyngell was already exasperated by the ongoing interference of what he called multilayered management systems, and the introduction of Taylor was the final straw. On Monday, 9 May, he resigned as CEO, expressing his frustration to Packer when he went to Park Street to explain his decision. He was 38 years old and walked out on the job he had coveted all his life. Kerry was his proxy godfather, James his best mate. He must have had good reason. (Gyngell was to return to the network a couple of years later, help save the business from bankruptcy and forge a remarkable new deal for cricket.)

I heard the details of his resignation a month or so later in London, when Gary Fenton rang to tell me I had been sacked. Gyngell's silence had been a concern but I hadn't seen it as quite this terminal. Fenton was genuinely sorry. I was pissed off. I had put a lot into trying to make this work, both emotionally and practically. I had turned down opportunities in England and India, eager to make the Australian adventure fit, and was now left with a mighty hole to fill. Not that I was remotely surprised, having always figured that a call would come one day. The timing of it was odd, that's all.

Completely out of the blue, a month later, Fenton called again. He hedged a bit, as was his way, before casually asking if I was free in early October to 'host' Nine's coverage of the Supertest and one-day matches between Australia and the ICC World XI. He emphasised the word 'host'. Weird. Sacked one day, promoted the next. I accepted and decided to take more of the initiative.

While covering the matches, I insisted on a few ideas of my own. These included moving out of the studio and opening the program alongside the pitch, in the sunshine, before hosting the toss live. Rob Sheerlock, Nine's director, who had made such a big impression on Channel 4's coverage, was delighted to shake things up and said as much to a couple of senior Nine executives standing at the back of the production truck when we went to air.

There was just the one Test, in Sydney, and then three one-day games at the Docklands Stadium in Melbourne. The series fell flat. No one said a word to me about why I was there or whether there was a future for me with the network. I was booked on a flight home to the UK a couple of days later. Then another strange thing happened. I was walking into a restaurant in Sydney for lunch when the phone rang. It was Sam Chisholm, who introduced himself as the man who used to run Nine and BSkyB and was now back at Nine in Gyng's job. I had to smile. I had never met him but if you worked in the business and didn't know who Sam Chisholm was, you were already out to lunch.

In effect, he said I had been fired by mistake and that he was now in the hot seat and he wanted to correct the mistake. Chisholm had run Nine in the glory days before leaving for BSkyB in London, where he dreamed up the Premier League. If he was back at Nine, some people would be running for cover. I said he had better be quick, because I was flying home the following evening. He invited me to his office at ten the next morning.

James Erskine is the best manager/agent/deal-maker in Australia. At Mark McCormack's request, in the late 1970s he set up IMG's Australian arm, with Michael Parkinson as his key client and sales point. In the mid-1990s, when Mark McCormack refused Erskine's request for equity in IMG, he left to set up Sport and Entertainment Limited—in effect, his own version of the same sort of thing. Michael is still on his books; Shane Warne too. James steered the Australian Cricketers' Association through the uncomfortable waters of its first collective bargaining agreement with the ACB—the issue Packer referred to while we were in his office. He knew the field, the players, their masters and their paymasters like no one else. He was also a close mate of mine. I called him for help with Chisholm. He said to call him back and tell him there would two of us the next morning. Chisholm laughed and said he was much looking forward to it.

For more than half an hour, the pair of them talked about the old days—Bert Newton, Paul Hogan and Kerry, of course. Sam told a very funny story about going to the Ascot race meeting in the UK with Kerry and Bruce Gyngell, David's father. Apparently, Kerry kept an old Mercedes at the Dorchester Hotel but fancied something smarter for the trip down the M4 so wandered over to Berkeley Square to see what he could find in Jack Barclay, the world's oldest and largest Bentley dealership. He liked the look of the dark-blue one in the window, asked the young lad at reception if it had a full tank of petrol and, when assured that it had, wrote out a cheque. The next day, Sam and Bruce arrived at the appointed hour and the three of them set off in this beautiful car, Kerry reading the paper and the other two chatting away. By Knightsbridge, an agitated Kerry told his driver to turn around and head back to Jack Barclay. Kerry climbed out, had a look in the window and then went back to reception. It was the same lad at the desk.

Is the white one for sale, asked Kerry, and has it got a full tank of petrol? Yes, and yes, came the replies. Whereupon he wrote out another cheque. Then he walked out to the street, poked his head in the window and said to Sam and Bruce: 'You blokes drive yourselves to Ascot. I want to read the newspaper in peace.'

Sam asked me what I wanted to do at Nine. I said, 'You called me, you tell me why I'm here.' He said Kerry liked the Channel 4 coverage of the Ashes and wanted Nine's cricket to have the same feel. The board concurred, he added. He said Kerry wanted me to front it and commentate on it. When I left the room 45 minutes later, I had a four-year contract with Channel Nine.

GOING TO AIR

Each day, on each outside broadcast production, is pretty much the same. A couple of hours before play, the producer holds a meeting with the crew. Sometimes I go to that, sometimes not. It depends on cameras and whether any hosting positions are complicated. Channel Nine have some exceptional camera men and we all know each other well enough to read what the other is thinking. This is hugely valuable on live TV, where we frequently wing it. All of us have input but the director makes the final decision. Sheerlock can think on the go like few others and therefore our morning preview shows have a nice loose feel to them.

I have never worked to a script on cricket, or with autocue or teleprompting. I prefer to note down bullet points and then ad lib. Structured television is fine in a studio, often necessary in fact, but the great outdoors is for exploring.

There is a run sheet that details the various segments of the show and their timings. We have usually discussed this the night before with the producer. Mark Taylor is always good for an idea, as is Warne. In fact, all the guys have thoughts about the day just finished or an overall picture of what might be interesting for the viewer the next day. Everyone has their strengths. Ian Healy is brilliant at summing up the previous day's play in any prescribed time frame. Michael Slater has the rare ability to take you inside the mind of a top player with his animated batting demonstrations. Any of Warne's masterclasses are a must-see and, in general, his alternative thinking makes for terrific television. Both Warne and Taylor are expert at crystallising match situations and explaining where they might lead. Healy thinks laterally about all aspects of cricket and Slater does drama like no other. I like listening to Ian Chappell talk about technique and, in particular, the need to simplify it. In England, coaches always seemed to overcomplicate the game. In Australia, they mainly keep it simple. Or the best of them do.

The commentary box is far more relaxed than visitors expect. Everyone has their own space and taps away on laptops, one eye on the play, the other on lunch. We have half-hour commentary shifts that are mapped out on a daily roster by the producer. These used to be 40 minutes long but David Hill noticed that if the game was not 'blazing hot', the commentators drifted off, especially later in the day and if the spinners were on. So he shortened the time on air which, in turn, meant there were more slots to fill. Bill loved that.

Steve Crawley, head of sport after Gary Fenton until he moved to Fox early in 2016, expanded the idea to three commentators per shift partly because the network had employed so many of us and partly because he wanted more conversation applied with a greater sense of urgency. I think this works but it's only at its best if each of the three commentators understands their various roles. Historically, every shift had a lead commentator and an 'expert' summariser. Now there are two summarisers and they need to watch each other like hawks, avoiding repetition or exaggeration. To a degree this format was introduced by Gary Franses on Channel 4 cricket, which launched the 'Analyst'; then Sky appointed the 'Third Man'. Other networks have caught the bug, notably Star Sports in India and SuperSport in South Africa. At Nine, the third person is another commentator rather than an expert with a specific brief. As I say, it's fine if the discipline is good but I worry that it is used to show off more 'names' and 'voices' rather than to enhance the experience for the viewer.

Getting a day of Test-match cricket to air is a challenging task. There are 26 cameras, eight video desks, audio, lighting, racks, editors making numerous play-ons and play-offs, as well as music pieces to open and close segments and for highlights packages. There are two production assistants, two vision mixers, three people on graphics, many miles of cable and stage hands to move it and the rest of the equipment around, three large production trucks and three smaller ones. There are teams for Hawkeye, Snicko and Hot Spot, engineers, technicians and an entirely separate production unit for the lunch show with Slats. Add in nine commentators, a scorer and statistician, the director, the executive producer and the head of sport, and you have about 90 of us to be transported, housed, fed and watered. This is a job done uncommonly well by Nine's head of sports production, Ron Castorina. The man is a marvel. In fact, with a load like that it's nothing short of 'marvellous' that we get on air some days.

In mid-February 2015, our coverage received an almighty roasting in *The Guardian* from a young journalist, Geoff Lemon. His angle was that we had diverged from the subject, which was the cricket itself. Instead, we had gone in-house and blokey. He had a point. As a group, we have never openly discussed Lemon's piece—a wise move, I think, as doing so might have led to personality clashes. But we all saw it and during the summer that followed made significant moves to bring the whole thing back down to earth. Only others can judge whether we managed to do so. Now we have a new head of sport and a new executive producer of the cricket coverage. They will have their own interpretations of how we best move forward.

We have missed the patrician air provided by Benaud. When you heard it from him—and remember, the modern commentator is both caller and promoter—it was believable. Many a 'beeyoutifull topspinner', for example, was simply the one that didn't spin; many a promo for *The Farmer Needs a Wife* was explained tongue-in-cheek, which gave it perspective within the coverage of a tight session in Test-match cricket. Officially or not, Richie was our captain and our conscience. From the very beginning, Lawry called him the 'captain of the commentary team', something that Billy Birmingham—aka the Twelfth Man—picked up on with enjoyable mock motivational speeches to the rest of the team. Actually, Richie gave nothing of the sort. Instead, he gently encouraged while only occasionally offering little pearls of wisdom that could not be ignored.

Of all his sayings on the art of commentary, the one that stands out to me is 'engage brain before mouth'. This would save us all a lot of embarrassment. The idea that you 'don't speak unless you can add to the picture' is all well and good but most cricketers who have played at the top level can find something within the game, if they know where to look, that might not occur to the majority of viewers. Richie preferred minimalism; it's as simple as that. In others, he liked enthusiasm, and in Lawry he found the perfect antidote to his own self-styled economy. He adored Bill, or Phanto as he called him, and they bounced off one another with a timing and presence given to few comedy double acts.

In a way, he rode above the game, keeping his opinions to himself and, whatever the provocation, carrying on regardless. Goodness knows how often he must have despaired of all that went on around him—the two things that really made his blood boil were throwing and match-fixing—but somehow this never invaded his television space, a space he reserved, almost wholly, for affection and appreciation of the game that was his life. In general, things were 'quite brilliant out there' or just 'marvellous', and they left the viewer basking in his friendship and knowledge.

Why don't more commentators follow Richie's lead? Mainly because emulating him is impossible. The dry wit and comedic timing were a gift; his depth of understanding was the product of more than 70 years up close and personal with the game. Silence was among his most effective weapons and not many producers out there want silence anymore. During the World Cup, I got an email from the executive producer of Star Sports that urged me to talk more. The Indian audiences want a constant flow of stories and information, he said. Evidence, I suppose, that the televised cricket of the moment is geared to the values, standards and expectations of a young, social-media-crazed audience who have no time in their lives for silences. Only Benaud could transcend that.

CALLING AUSTRALIA HOME

There is a small corner of North Bondi where the point stretches out to sea and the waves lash at huge rocks that have withstood their attentions for hundreds, maybe millions, of years. It is called Ben Buckler and it is there that I have lived from late October through to March in the years since Alan Jones first called David Gyngell on my behalf. Sydney is a wonderful city with an incomparable lifestyle. As the American writer Gore Vidal once observed, 'Sydney is the city that San Francisco thinks it is.'

Not a day goes by without a comment on the cricket, whether it be over a morning splash in the surf, a jog to Bronte and back, or a cup of some of the best coffee in the world at any one of the numerous cafes that help to make this a little piece of paradise. In Australia, cricket is life. It remains the one national sport and on any summer Saturday afternoon the virtuous circle of Australian cricket is on view. School, park, grade, district and state cricket underpin the national teams. At the Easts Club on Bondi Road—formerly Waverley Cricket Club where, at one time or another, Tony Greig, Geoffrey Boycott and Malcolm Marshall all trod the boards—training and practice sessions on Tuesdays and Thursdays are oversubscribed with youngsters and yeomen alike. All summer long, the back pages of the newspapers are full of cricket talk, whether success or scandal. On beaches, the scores are shared via social media and live play is streamed via smartphones. In bars, teams are discussed and players anointed or otherwise. Cricket matters.

More than a decade ago now, two pimpled teenagers— drainpipe jeans and tats—poked their heads out of McDonald's on Bondi's Campbell Parade, smirked at me and said, 'You're no Richie Benaud,' with which I wholeheartedly agreed. Super sledge, that. What most interested me was that they watched cricket so closely. The new Richie thing dogged me for a while but it was balanced by friendly encounters and general support. Nowadays, I feel as much a part of the scene as any surfer strolling back home from the beach and engaged in conversation about the day. A surfer's currency is the waves; mine is bat and ball.

The subjects I am asked about most are Richie Benaud and Shane Warne, the best Australian players, the future of Test cricket and the impact of T20. During the time I have held the Nine microphone to my lips, an array of wonderful cricketers has lit up the game before moving gracefully into retirement. It has been my privilege to talk about their performances and to interview them so often they must surely have thought, 'Not Nicko again!'

I have already said a great deal about Shane Warne. It is enough that he was named one of *Wisden*'s five cricketers of the 20th century and continued to play at a high level in Test-match cricket until January 2007. After retiring at the Sydney Cricket Ground, he went off to captain the Rajasthan Royals and win the first IPL. Typical. I cannot think of a cricketer who has so dominated front and back pages, which is testament to his celebrity and his addiction to risk. Even Ian Botham's colourful journey pales alongside Warne's 25-year journey. Of the attributes I have not previously discussed, it is his respect for the game that most stands out. The other day I asked Michael Vaughan about batting against him and he said, 'Warnie gave me a lot of respect, never abused me once, just "Good shot" if I played one, and he always came up to me after the match and said, "Well played, mate," if I'd made a few.' Sure, there have been boorish moments, of which Warne is now embarrassed, but these should not be confused with the cricketer who understood his place in the history of cricket and, more specifically, his conviction that no one, not even he, is greater than the game. In Chapter 9, I said he had become the collective noun of leg spin. It now occurs to me that may not be a good thing for no other leg spinner has a chance.

Warne would be a certain selection in most people's greatest Australian team, probably in their all-time World XI, too. Only Bill O'Reilly comes close among Australian spinners and Muttiah Muralitharan from elsewhere. Other Australians of Warne's era who qualify for such consideration are Glenn McGrath, Adam Gilchrist, Ricky Ponting and Matthew Hayden.

BENAUD'S GREATEST TEAM
Back in 2004, I was involved in a fascinating project with Richie Benaud, in which he chose his best team for a DVD, *Richie Benaud's Greatest XI*. We made it with my brother, Ben,

who had his own production company. Benaud researched in great detail. He was at pains to point out that his final choices reflected the team he would most want to represent 'him' and was not necessarily meant to be the greatest cricket team ever. This was a sensible parameter, because it allowed entirely subjective thinking and invited no argument. In each position, Benaud selected three options, 'in the same way I have always chosen teams, with the final eleven on the left-hand side of the page and two back-up players to the right, so that in effect I was looking at 33 players with three reasonably well-balanced sides able to take the field'.

Benaud chose Adam Gilchrist to keep wicket and bat at number seven after Garry Sobers. I still have the notes he wrote at the time: 'In 50 years of playing and watching, I have never seen anyone strike a ball more cleanly than Gilchrist and no one has reached keeping dismissals and batting targets faster in the history of the game so far as keepers are concerned.' I interviewed Gilchrist in Adelaide, immediately after he decided to retire, and was struck by his self-deprecation. He had a good, if not flawless, approach to the spirit of the game and was eager to be generous to colleagues and opponents. I would call him an athletic and effective wicketkeeper rather than a natural, and just about the most dangerous middle-order counter-attacking batsman the game has seen. Benaud's other options among stumpers were Rod Marsh and Ian Healy—further proof of how well Australia has been served, especially as there was a place in his heart, if not his list, for Wally Grout.

Glenn McGrath missed out on selection by a hair's-breadth. Dennis Lillee won the slot at number ten, ahead of Ray Lindwall and McGrath. Benaud said, 'Glenn McGrath is one of the great pace bowlers the cricket world has seen. Not blisteringly fast, he is beautifully accurate and with a host of variations that make him so dangerous to batsmen.' He might well have gone on to talk about McGrath's ability to prey on weaknesses, both in mind and technique, and an unerring ability to home in on the opposition's key players or captain. Like Curtly Ambrose, he took devastating advantage of conditions or surfaces that suited him and, in general, brought more stress to the beating heart of an opposing cricket team than anyone except perhaps his cohort, Warne. What a pair they made.

Benaud's team and his options read thus:

Jack Hobbs	Len Hutton	Victor Trumper
Sunil Gavaskar	Arthur Morris	Gordon Greenidge
Don Bradman	Wally Hammond	George Headley
Viv Richards	Greg Chappell	Graeme Pollock
Sachin Tendulkar	Frank Worrell	Brian Lara
Garry Sobers	Keith Miller	Ian Botham
Adam Gilchrist	Rod Marsh	Ian Healy
Imran Khan	Richard Hadlee	Kapil Dev
Shane Warne	Bill O'Reilly	Abdul Qadir
Dennis Lillee	Ray Lindwall	Glenn McGrath
S.F. Barnes	Fred Trueman	Harold Larwood

When the idea was first put to me I decided that as this was to be my team, it would be one I would like to watch and be with during whatever mythical matches it might play, that the players would be first of all brilliant cricketers and quite probably characters as well, and that they would be good mixers with the opposition.

I have met all of the final eleven and when I narrowed it down to 33 from scores of players, I had met all but one. One of the many aspects of my selection that I would pay a great deal of attention was those who stood out as having had a beneficial effect on the game, those who stood out as champions and who are remembered as being outstanding in their era. Also, if they had an influence on cricket itself.

It would be superfluous to have a coach with a team of this quality and character, but I do have two men I would appoint to other positions—Keith Miller as twelfth man and Frank Worrell as manager. Miller, as player and captain, could fill any position in the team; Worrell was the best I ever saw at man-management. As the first black cricketer to be 'allowed' to captain West Indies away from the Caribbean, he was one of the reasons why the face of cricket in Australia and perhaps in other parts of the world was changed forever because of that Tied Test series.

The selections tell you much about the man. The clues are everywhere. Over the days that we took to record the film, we talked about his life in and around the game. The greatest things in which he was involved were the Tied Test, WSC and Old Trafford 1961 when he bowled out England to win the match—'without which I wouldn't be sitting here talking to you now!' The greatest things from afar were Australia beating England in the First Test in 1877, the Warne ball to Gatting, the first one-day international in 1971 at the MCG and the 2005 Ashes series—'the most exciting battle I have watched,' he said.

The worst things were the match-fixing and bribery scandals that have haunted the game. They left him with an empty feeling, he said, and a particular sadness about Hansie Cronje. He was interesting on sledging, which, he pointed out, has always been around in some fashion or another. It astonished him that the players found time for it, given his own need to concentrate entirely on the job at hand. He liked the spirit of cricket initiative started by Colin Cowdrey and Ted Dexter, and said it should be no hardship to embrace the spirit of the game at the same time as trying to win it. 'Subtly, MCC have posed the question of whether it really is *impossible* to win a cricket match without sledging your opponents,' he said. And he hoped not.

He was hugely positive about the playing standards. 'The cricket in the past two or three years has been the best I have seen in a period of playing and watching that covered more than 500 Tests and 57 years.' I can't help but wonder if he would say the same now.

He felt that cricket in Australia was in good shape thanks to forward-thinking administrators. I had an update from him on this in 2013, when he applauded Cricket Australia for having former players such as Mark Taylor, Allan Border and Wally Edwards on the board. He spoke well of the CEO, James Sutherland, and of Tim May's work on behalf of players. He had briefly considered administration himself but was put off by the folk who ran the game in the 1960s and 1970s. And anyway, he said, his media work around the world made it all but impossible.

He loved his time with Channel 4 cricket. 'When BBC lost the rights I didn't expect any more television work in the UK because the first press release for Channel 4 said, "We won't be employing any grey-haired old fogies in our commentary box." So in my own press release the following Sunday I wrote, "I'm sure David Gower and Tony Lewis can look after themselves, but I can't imagine who else they might be talking about!"' The seven years with Channel 4 were among the most exciting and innovative of his life, he said, with the flair of young people to hand every day. Gary Franses and Rob Sheerlock—who had come from Nine—were the best producer and director, respectively, with whom he had worked. More generally, he was hugely proud of the way Channel Nine and then Channel 4 had broadcast the game. 'The most important thing for me and for the viewer is enjoyment. I've had it every day from the minute I have arrived at the ground until the minute I leave. I hope the viewers have too. One thing I can tell them is the extraordinary amount of work from many people behind the scenes that goes into making it happen.' At the time of our last detailed chat, he was delighted that Channel Nine had secured the cricket rights once more, 'making sure viewers are able to watch, at no cost on free-to-air, the best cricket matches involving Australia'.

And to conclude: of all the things that he had enjoyed with his mates in the game, nothing could quite match the shiraz grape.

CHAPTER 12

2005 and all that

The title of this book is meant as an appreciation of cricket not a summary. I see the game as beautiful, which is not to say that things can, and do, detract from its appeal. These might be anything from one-off extremes such as match-fixing or throwing to ongoing concerns such as the imbalance between bat and ball or the tardiness of over rates. Some issues are not immediately obvious but become a worry over time. Among these has been the increasing gulf between the best teams and the worst. By 2005, England had become so feeble against Australia that the Ashes lost something of its magic. Test cricket needs competitive Ashes cricket because it is the market leader: the worst possible outcome for both the sport and television is the likelihood of only one winner.

Much as Kerry Packer liked to see the Poms beaten, he saw increasingly little commercial value in the series as they were and, therefore, chose not to bid for the rights to the Ashes of 2005 in England. Hindsight proved this a mistake but the evidence upon which he made his judgement was simple and persuasive. The Australians were not only the best team in the world but one of the great teams of all time. The chances of a meaningful audience sitting up through the night to watch them hammer England again were slim. (Good crowd numbers and even better television ratings for the two 5–0 thrashings that have been handed out on Australian turf since 2005 suggest the locals like the taste of English blood, but to expect them to arrive bleary-eyed at work through the winter months, in the cause of what was, back then, considered a one-horse race, was too much.) Therefore, the public network SBS, with its multi-cultural remit, took Channel 4's pictures and commentary and made itself very popular among the surprising number of Australians who did, in the end, sit up through the night. They had good reason. They were watching one of the most fantastic series of cricket matches ever played.

There is a theory that fewer people in Australia have the deep love of cricket so apparent in England, where the many amateur varietals of the game still thrive. In Australia, people enjoy the outdoor life for its own sake, and look to play sport competitively. They hope Australia does well but, arguably, less for the aesthetics perhaps than for the result. They expect famous deeds, of course, but not from tall poppies. Australians like their sports folk to remain the neighbour they once knew. I don't agree with the theory. I am certain Australians love cricket every bit as much as the English and, in particular, continue to love Test cricket, which has played such a huge part in the country's development.

———

After sixteen barren Ashes years, during which time there was no Botham or Gower to paper over the cracks in English cricket, Michael Vaughan swapped team sheets with Ricky Ponting at Lord's in mid-July 2005 boasting a few blokes with a bit of ticker and plenty of talent. Throughout the six weeks or so that followed, Vaughan barely slept. The cricketers of

England and Australia knocked seven bells out of each other and, this time, it was the English who were left standing. Most people agree that it was the greatest series of them all. Certainly, the Ashes was back on the map. Andrew Flintoff and Kevin Pietersen, among others, became household names—talk show, game show, *Hello* and *Grazia*—because of their part in the hard-fought victory. It was the summer when all of England—and most of Australia, it should be said—saw cricket as the beautiful game.

FIRST TEST, LORD'S

Channel 4 started its coverage of the most eagerly awaited Test match in my memory with a pre-recorded sequence that opened from the small lobby outside the England dressing room. One underrated aspect of any cricket television broadcast is the work done by the camera men. In this instance, Bob Blocker harnessed a Steadicam across his shoulders and around his upper body so that he could film players and pundits on the move. The plan was for me to replicate England's walk from the dressing room to the middle, a walk that is very different at Lord's because the players have to negotiate their way through the members on their way to the pitch. For this, Bob had to be led backwards down two flights of stairs, through the Long Room and out onto the field. The members needed policing and didn't like it much, so it needed to be a first take.

I stood underneath the sign that said 'Home Dressing Room' and began with something like: 'In just a short while from now, Michael Vaughan will lead his team from this dressing room, down these stairs, past portraits of Sir Donald Bradman, Douglas Jardine, Keith Miller and Sir Len Hutton along their way to the middle. The great history of the Ashes was forged by these men and by so many more who have best illustrated the cricket rivalry between England and Australia that began in 1877, just down the road from here at the Oval, where the Ashes urn will be pres . . .' And as we were about to enter the Long Room, we had a technical fault and had to start again.

Members shuffled, some anxious to see more of television's fussy detail, others looking to hurry to their protected seat. Take two: 'In just a short while from now . . .' And this time we nailed it, down the stairs and then winding a path through the packed and feverish Long Room, out through the double doors, down the concrete steps, through the little white gates and onto the great green baize. By the time I said my last word, my heart was pounding fast enough to burst from my chest. For some inexplicable reason, a pre-recorded piece to camera is more nerve-racking than anything live. I guess with live you just do it; with a pre-record you can keep doing it again and again, and nobody wants to do that. It was the first time the MCC had allowed such access, and the pictures of a pavilion hitherto unseen by 99 per cent of the population were well received.

(Colin Cowdrey told a nice story about Bradman walking to the wicket at Lord's for the first time in 1930. Up to that point, England had not seen the best of him and so treated his arrival with little of the deference that was to follow. Bill Woodfull and Bill Ponsford batted serenely through the morning session and into the middle of the afternoon, when they were interrupted by King George V, who was not prepared to wait until the official tea-break to meet the teams. After the line-up, play resumed and immediately Ponsford was well taken by Wally Hammond at slip. Thus, at first drop, out came Bradman for the first time at Thomas Lord's magnificent ground. As the young Australian danced down the steps of the pavilion, the steward doffed his topper, opened the small white gates and, with pride but no prejudice, said, 'Good luck, Mr Bradman.' At the close of play three hours later, Bradman was 155 not out. The crowd rose to him. He took off his cap, raised his bat to acknowledge the applause and was about to climb the steps when the same steward again doffed his topper and said: 'Well played, Mr Bradman!' To which Bradman winked and replied: 'Useful net for the morning.' He went on to 254 and often referred to it as his best innings.)

From there I went to the pitch for the toss. Ricky Ponting won it and chose to bat. The atmosphere fizzed with electricity and the captains were nervous: Ponting betrayed by the speed at which he talked (even faster than normal); Vaughan by the angling of his head slightly away from the camera lens and by the raising and twitching of his left eyebrow. (My ten-year-old daughter blames such responses on 'nervocitement' and explains this further by saying that they only happen to her when she is essentially happy to be doing the activity that is making her so apprehensive. She could go far.) Vaughan was certainly looking forward to the day; you could see that in his eyes. He went off to rev up his four-man pace attack and with him went an enormous roar from the already full house, which was most unlike Lord's.

For 25 minutes out in the middle, our pundits got stuck in: Tony Greig bullish about England; Geoffrey Boycott reckoning McGrath and Warne would sway it—'bowlers win matches and they are the best'; Michael Slater excited for Matthew Hayden and Justin Langer walking out to bat where he made his first Test hundred before famously kissing the badge on his helmet; Michael Atherton sanguine about all things, keen for Flintoff to seize the moment but realistic about the bank of Australian talent. We all talked about Pietersen's first Test and the fact that Warne had pushed for his inclusion. Pietersen had left Nottinghamshire to team up with 'the King' at Hampshire. Naturally, he had made an impression, though the day I went to Southampton to watch him bat he scored just ten subdued runs. Having said that, he looked the business—set-up, body shape in defence and attack, the straightest of bats and sharp footwork—and I was moved to agree with Warne. Boycott was in favour too. At a couple of minutes to eleven o'clock, I threw to Richie Benaud in the commentary box, who said, 'Morning, everyone.' Two simple words that locked it in. Benaud, the starter's gun, had given the go-ahead and they were off.

After which, it went like this. Steve Harmison hit Langer on the elbow and Ponting on the grille of his helmet, a truly significant blow that brought a bloodthirsty audience to life. The thin red trickle down the cheek of the Australian captain was captured by a thousand lenses and transported to every corner of the cricketing firmament. Australia, it appeared, could be hurt too. (The first sign of this had come a few weeks earlier at the T20 match at the Rose Bowl, outside Southampton, when the animated crowd inspired England to an overwhelming 100-run victory. Australia was noticeably shaken by the confrontational nature of England's play and the passion of the support.)

In response to Harmison and the out-of-character Lord's crowd, Australia's feisty batsmen played their strokes but wickets fell at timely moments for the home team. By the time Vaughan recalled his strike bowler—a man hewn from the mining communities of England's north-east—to pick off the tail with 4 for 7 in 14 balls, the gauntlet had been thrown down.

There is always an Aussie happy to pick it up, it is what they do. In next to no time, Glenn McGrath removed Marcus Trescothick and Andrew Strauss to catches behind the wicket; then he castled Vaughan, Ian Bell and Flintoff. This was renaissance seam bowling and confirmed McGrath's pre-eminence in the art form.

Meanwhile, just a mile or two away, there was an explosion at Shepherd's Bush tube station. Then one at the Oval tube, then Warren Street tube. While cricketers did sporting battle, terrorists did war. In the media centre, eyes that would not usually leave the cricket were suddenly attached to the news. The juxtaposition of events was surreal. Twenty minutes into the afternoon session, another small explosion took place on a bus on the Hackney Road. Extraordinarily and thankfully, they all malfunctioned: the detonator caps fired but the bombs did not go off. Come rush hour, people travelled home with only mild disruption. The fear though was that 7/7—the dreadful attacks of two weeks earlier that cost 52 lives and left 700 people injured—had not been a one off, after all. The front pages were full of the potential of the horror, the back pages full of McGrath and company. One of that company, Jason Gillespie, said he would fly home if there was another attack. The ECB and the police came together to tighten security at all the Test grounds. Even amid the fantasy of Lord's, there was no avoiding the reality of a disturbed world.

The match was won and lost by Kevin Pietersen catches—well, sort of. He dropped three sitters, the most important of which was in the second innings at cover off a Michael Clarke punch that deserved to have cost him his wicket. Clarke went on to bat as if the gods liked him. Overall, I think we can say they do. Turning back time a day or so, Pietersen might have finessed a first-innings lead for England had Damien Martyn not taken a superb catch running back to the grandstand. The South African born batsman had just smeared Warne over mid wicket for six and fell for the trap of trying again. It had been a sparkling debut innings, remembered for that first slog-swept maximum that echoed like a gunshot and for the towering strike over mid-off and into the pavilion off McGrath because it was so damn figjam—'Fuck I'm good, just ask me'—and, of course, because it didn't happen to McGrath very often. Everyone could see a star had been born; the English among us just wished he would catch a bit better.

Anyway, Pietersen's sidebars are only a part of the story. The hard fact was that England were bowled out cheaply twice: in the second innings, the final five wickets collapsed in just 46 balls. All this felt like *Groundhog Day*, and there was nothing beautiful about it at all. Packer, it seemed, had got it spot on.

Back to the bombs. I couldn't help thinking about 1981 and the way 'Botham's Ashes' joined forces with the wedding of Prince Charles and Lady Diana Spencer to lift the nation out of its depression. For cricket to have similar impact again, England had to play as it had done under Michael Vaughan for the previous eighteen months, which was bloody well. From this wreckage at Lord's came confirmation that Pietersen was a find, and both Harmison and Flintoff were frightening attack dogs. They say that if you have to, you can write the story of the Second World War on the back of fag packet. Applying this theory to England's hopes after the First Test of 2005, you would say: 'Score more runs and catch your catches.'

(Postscript: Queen Elizabeth II met the teams as prearranged at the tea-break on the first day. As we watched the line-up, an Australian leant into my ear to say: 'You know, Keith Miller briefly stepped out with her sister.' I said I did. 'Well,' he continued anyway, 'in 1953, Lindsay Hassett reminded the lads to arrive at the ground the next day with best bib and tucker because they were heading for a reception at the palace straight after play. Miller said: "Aw shit, not for the third night in a row!"')

In the London *Daily Telegraph*, we had more space than a fag packet. Boycott said, 'The result has dashed a lot of hopes. Now the players have to stop talking a good game and perform. It doesn't do any good to be making catty comments about the opposition and going out and losing to them like that.'

I wrote an out-of-body piece: 'The First Test should never have been played at Lord's, it should have been at Edgbaston on a flat pitch, where nationalistic fervour scores runs, takes wickets and might help to hold on to that wretched ball when it flies through the air. The administrators blew this, along with most other things they have a crack at. Not your fault, lads, their fault.'

During Ashes series, Australians often ask me who I support. The trouble is you can take a fellow out of England but you can't take England out of the fellow. Some deal with it and others slag me off. I'm either a traitor, licking the nuts of all Australians (an English view), or I'm a Pommy who should piss off back home (an Australian view). The truth is, I love cricket and try to celebrate its players. It is really no more complicated than that. Except during the Ashes.

Since I am writing about the England that Vaughan captained while sitting alongside him in the commentary box, I asked him for a short summary of his feelings after the First Test.

'Honestly, I thought we were doomed. Done for. I couldn't tell the lads that, so I thought I'd better act up. I said it was blip, nothing more, and added that Edgbaston would reveal our strengths. Deep down, I didn't believe it, I just thought the baggage of all the previous defeats would be too much for us to carry forward. Shows how wrong you can be!'

(The morning after Lord's, I received an email from Simon Denehy, a close mate who worked in the financial markets in the city. The email was titled 'Dreams do come true' and talked about the omens that were pointing to an Ashes win. Up to mid-July 2005, it said, the Dow had run pretty much in parallel to the way it had run back in 1981. In 1981, Prince Charles had married; *Coronation Street*'s Ken and Deirdre got married; there was a new doctor on *Doctor Who*; Liverpool won seventeen league games but only finished fifth; Norwich and Crystal Palace were relegated; and Liverpool won the European Cup. Up to the point of the start of the Lord's Test in 2005, Prince Charles had remarried; *Corrie*'s Ken and Deirdre the same; there was another new doctor on *Doctor Who*; Liverpool won seventeen Premier League games and finished only fifth; Norwich and Palace were relegated; and, wait for it, Liverpool had just won the Champions League final in one of history's greatest football comebacks. So Simon certainly wasn't writing off England.)

SECOND TEST, EDGBASTON

First up, McGrath goes over on his ankle and is ruled out of the match. The pitch is the colour of Bondi sand. The weather is okay (it's Birmingham, so okay is good). Australia have hungry batsmen, at least three of whom are among the greatest to wear the fabled green cap, and England are on the bones of their arse. Up goes the coin, down it comes in Ponting's favour and he says to Vaughan, 'We'll have a bowl, mate.' Of course you will, Ricky. After interviewing them both, I throw to the break with the news that Australia have won the toss and will bat first. Christ, you'd have thought I had dropped the 'C' bomb. It all went off. First the producer, then the director in my ear: 'Mark, Australia will *bowl* first. Please confirm that to the viewers straight after the break. Please acknowledge you understand this. Australia are bowling.' Indeed.

'Welcome back to Edgbaston where the news is that Ricky Ponting has won the toss and the Australians will bat first.' Next, apparently, the head of sport rang. Not happy. After which, Gary Franses, a producer who likes a dotted i, was again in my ear. 'No, they bloody well are not, they're batting for Christ's sake, have you got that? The Aussies are batting, I mean bowling, the Aussies are bowling.' Even Gary lost it. Before I fully digested this crisis, Greig and Atherton, who were out on the pitch alongside me, muscled in to say Australia were bowling.

This was an incomprehensible decision by Ponting, so unexpected that I had pre-programmed his response the split second the coin landed in his favour, and was unable to remove the copy from my thick head. Frankly, I was a mess and let Greig and Atherton carry most of that preview segment. Eventually, I threw to the next break with the right information. Duh.

Mike Denness inserted Australia at Edgbaston in 1975 and lost by an innings and plenty. This, on the back of a hammering in Australia a few months earlier. He was sent a letter addressed to 'Mike Denness, cricketer.' It read: 'If this reaches you, the Post Office think more of you than I do.' People really care about this stuff. It's the Ashes, the bloody Ashes.

Notwithstanding my own inability to comprehend Ponting's decision, I quickly learnt that a number of those in the away dressing room felt much the same. Given England made 400-plus in the day, rollicking along as if footloose and Ashes free, you could understand why. Here, at last, was a chink in the armour that had been unbreached since 1987. I mean, Australians bat first when the coin lands in their favour. They just do. I have studied the replay of this toss. Vaughan has a hint of a smile while listening to Ponting.

For the next couple of days, the teams played high-octane cricket, most of the highlights of which came from Andrew Flintoff. He made powerful, blacksmith-like runs in both innings, including a couple of sixes that sent this commentator into a frenzied state. Flintoff had taken Geraint Jones under his wing, defended his honour and his glove work, and then catalysed a hitherto unseen aggression in his batsmanship. (At one stage in the series, Flintoff was asked about a dropped catch off his bowling by Jones. He replied by saying something like, 'A lot of people are questioning Geraint's wicketkeeping but none of them are in our dressing room.')

Flintoff bowled very fast in this match and, with Simon Jones, found some deadly reverse swing. One over in the second innings set England on their course—six deliveries of such ferocity and impact that even the crowd smelt blood. Probably, it was this over—and the final result of the match, of course—that moved the country to pay closer attention. In the over, this mountain of a man from Preston removed Langer with the second ball and Ponting with his last. In between, he beat Ponting as if he were a county triallist groping for a contract. The air of resignation on the face of the Australian captain as he walked from Edgbaston's pasture told us of the progress England had made.

Other eye- and ear-catching happenings from the first three days of the match are easily recalled: the opening onslaught by Trescothick and Strauss; Flintoff's strange shoulder injury that did anything but hamper his batting; Warne's outrageous spinner that went past Strauss on the outside of his pads to hit leg stump, his 100th Test wicket in England; another Warne delivery, this time to Bell; Ashley Giles snaring Adam Gilchrist; Harmison's memorable slower ball to Michael Clarke in the final over of Saturday's play; the noise, the sheer volume of noise. The Eric Hollies Stand might have been the Kop.

To the nub of the thing, and the photograph. With just two wickets to take, the ground authority announced that if the match finished quickly, ticket holders would be welcome to have picnics on the outfield. (Best not to say anything until the fat lady has done her bit, is the moral there.) Mind you, a persuasive majority of the people who arrived at Edgbaston for the start of play on Sunday morning did expect England to wrap it up within, say, 45 minutes—if not quite the fifteen mentioned over the PA. Warne and Brett Lee were not among them. Applying the 'blondes have more fun' principle, they set about the 107 runs left to make. Lee took a pounding while Warne gave one. England began with an attacking field that left vast spaces for Warne to chip and carve. But the thing about Warne down the order is that he can bat like he is up the order, so he drove, pulled and cut too. Lee saw as much of the physio as of Warne, so often was he mashed on the hand and body by England's West Indian-style attack.

In no time, the football crowd of Saturday became a snooker crowd on Sunday and the general unease was not lost on Michael Vaughan's increasingly exasperated men. A hearty slice of luck went their way, however, when Warne trod on his wicket while trying to flip Flintoff through mid wicket—9 down now and 62 still needed. In came Michael Kasprowicz. No worries: not for Kasper and Binger anyway. They nicked and nudged and occasionally threw a punch at English hearts and minds—40 runs came in no time, or so it seemed. With 15 needed, Simon Jones dropped an awkward chance at third man—'at that moment I thought it had gone,' says Vaughan—and with 4 needed Lee creamed a square drive directly at the sweeper posted on the cover boundary. A single then, not *the* four. Phew.

In the commentary box and adjoining studio, the tension led to demented behaviour. A technician who hadn't smoked in years drew deeply on a Marlboro Light. Another left the studio and paced along the back balcony, refusing to watch. I got up and down, went for a wander, giggled childishly, felt my hands and armpits turning sweaty, asked daft questions and answered them myself with the idea that what we were seeing could not be true. Surely our eyes were deceiving us. Benaud barely missed a beat, his vital signs remaining steady and clear. Thankfully, it was Benaud who had the microphone in his hand at the moment of truth.

The greatest skill of a sports television director is to choose the pictures that best tell the story. This sounds obvious but it is not straightforward. That summer, Channel 4 had 26 cameras, all with a different brief. Of these, up to twenty offered an angle on the immediate action. Thus, Rob Sheerlock had to make a snap choice from twenty options, along with aligning his choice to an instinctive feel for the likely route taken by the commentator. Sheerlock is without peer in this regard. He reads a commentator's mind.

On strike now and with 3 needed, Kasprowicz hesitated over whether to play or duck a short delivery from Harmison. His hands flailed at the ball, deliberately or otherwise, and it brushed one of them on its leg-side journey through to Geraint Jones. Jones fell to his left and intercepted the dying missile inches from the closely mown grass. His gloves wrapped around that ball to hold it tight as he rolled over and then sprang from the turf in the sudden knowledge that he had won England the Second Test by 2 runs.

Benaud followed Sheerlock precisely. He saw that Jones had held on.

'Jones!'

Then Sheerlock switched shots to the umpire, Billy Bowden, who slowly raised his crooked finger.

'Bowden!'

Pause.

Then to Kasprowicz.

'Kasprowicz the man to go and Harmison has done it.'

Sheerlock changes shot to Lee.

'Despair on the face of the batsman.'

And then Sheerlock goes to Vaughan and England.

'And joy on the faces of every English player on the field.'

And that was all he said, at the end of one of the greatest cricket matches of all time. It sounds easy but it isn't. The temptation is to explode with rhetoric but Benaud knew less was more. Such were the pictures that words were superfluous. Mind you, he sure sounded excited.

At this point, most of England's cricketers became demented. Flintoff, however, had taken note of Lee on his haunches, head bowed and stricken by defeat. One warrior stooped to console another, offering a hand in tender support. Many a camera was firing away but not all upon the chivalry between Flintoff and Lee. One that did allowed its owner, Tom Shaw, to flog the picture far and wide. It is the image by which we best remember the series. In the *Telegraph*, Boycott said, 'Of all the wonderful things to come out of this match, the nicest was that as soon as England won, Flintoff went straight over to Lee to congratulate him on his efforts. Flintoff had been trying to knock his block off all morning, remember. This was a great piece of sportsmanship.'

Martin Johnson wrote, 'There is no more vibrant form of the game than Test cricket . . . the survival kit for a spectator used to be a sandwich tin and coffee flask, now it is incontinence pants and blood pressure pills.' Matthew Hayden said, 'For a long time now the cricket world has been waiting to see us in a dog fight. Well, we have that fight on our hands now and we won't shy away from it.' Marcus Trescothick: 'I have never felt physically sick at the end of a cricket match before. We came in expecting to have such a great day but when Australia needed only a handful of runs I was thinking: "Oh my god, how are we going to get over this?"'

As for Vaughan: 'I knew then. I could see it in the players' eyes. The belief flooded the dressing room, especially Fred. I thought, "If we bat first in the next two games, we've got a great chance." I did a complete 360 from Lord's. I suddenly just knew.'

In the commentary box, Gary Franses sent a text to Jeff Foulser, chairman of Sunset and Vine, the company producing the coverage for Channel 4. It said, 'There's a DVD in this— The Greatest Test.' The ECB agreed. We had week to get it on the market—editing, voicing, packaging, distribution, all in a week. By the time we got to Old Trafford, *The Greatest Test* was in the shops and selling out—55,000 had gone by the end of the series. Then, in September, we made a ten-hour box set of the whole series. It sold more than any sports DVD ever in the UK—about 670,000 copies. Gary also made *Hidden Ashes*, a gem that runs for an hour and shows the sights and sounds of the summer that did not make it to air on the live coverage at the time. Who would have thought it? Three cricket DVDs out of one series. Edgbaston made it all possible.

Edgbaston was the best cricket match I have ever seen.

THIRD TEST, OLD TRAFFORD

It took ages to get into the ground. The traffic queues snaked the streets of Stretford and Trafford Park. In the end Michael Slater and I got out, dumped the car for twenty quid in someone's front yard and walked—or ran, actually. We rehearsed late and suddenly the toss was upon us. Vaughan won it, batted on a beaut of a rock-hard Peter Marron pitch and made 166 himself. Surprisingly, McGrath was back, seemingly immune to the detached ligaments in his right ankle. The second ball of his tenth over bounced more than Vaughan expected, which might have been a bit of luck because Gilchrist could only finger-tip the thinnest of edges over the bar. The third ball ripped through the England captain's extravagant drive and uprooted his off stump. Had Steve Bucknor not spotted McGrath's overstep, history might be different. Vaughan's fling with Lady Luck seemed to lift his batting spirit. The regal air returned, the Vaughan of Australia 2002–03, peeling off exemplary cover drives and the swivel pull that has driven bowlers to distraction. He stroked Jason Gillespie out of the series and by the second evening was hugging his great mate Giles, whose 3 wickets then helped reduce Australia to 214 for 7, 31 short of avoiding the follow-on. But, please, who enforces the follow-on anymore. Get modern, Mark.

From that unpromising position Warne made 90, many of them in a fruity partnership of 86 with Gillespie, a bowler who once made a double-hundred in a Test match. (Oh, cricket, what a box of tricks you are.) Warne doesn't do Test hundreds; he ensures he is caught on the leg-side boundary if anywhere near. He had been missed twice by Jones G on the wet Saturday, during which only fourteen overs were possible. But what overs they were! The cricket lurched around, unpredictable as a drunk, and Jones found himself on the wrong end of the spectator's derision. Warne simply observed that he was out of his depth. It was in the aftermath of this match that Flintoff was moved to defend England's wicket-keeper.

What else in this match for the insatiable Warne? Test wicket number six hundred, that's what else. Trescothick was the victim, Gilchrist the man who caught it from the back of the West Countryman's bat. Warne acknowledged the crowd by holding the ball aloft and kissing his wristband, a gift from a pretty girl—his daughter, Brooke. The band signified strength and reminded us that whatever else kept popping up in Warne's colourful life—and throughout the summer, the break-up with his wife was tabloid news—he only had to cross the white line to remind everyone of a ferociously competitive spirit and those sublime cricketing gifts.

Strauss made a hundred with a sticky plaster on his ear, having been smacked on the side of the helmet by Lee in the first innings. Ian Bell and Geraint Jones hit a succession of shots that suggested they were growing into this Ashes stuff, before Vaughan declared, leaving the old enemy 108 overs to make 423. The two gum-chewing left-handers, whose series had not gone well, negotiated the new ball safely enough. They were to fight another day, the last day.

On the third evening of the game, I went round to the Australian dressing room to get a shirt signed for Chance to Shine, as agreed with Warne. The attendant called for him and out he came in undies, dragging on a Marlboro Light. He was immensely proud of the 600th wicket and of Brooke's present to him. Reluctantly, he said no to the shirt because, apparently, the guys had heard some of my commentary and thought I was barracking for the Poms. You can't win. But he signed it, and the following winter the others happily agreed to sign a bat. Their reaction was a curt reminder of the bubble in which a team lives through a demanding period of televised sport. The scrutiny wears down even the most temperate. We all needed to take a breath. At this point, England, and Warne, were holding up best.

By 9 am on the fourth morning the ground was full—20,000 more people were stuck outside, me among them. Lancashire had decided to sell tickets for a tenner each and reckoned that might attract 15,000 people. Forty thousand came, many of whom camped out for the night. At 7.30 am the streets were alive with cricket fans, all heading one way. When the gates were shut, desperate men were shoving £10 notes through the bars, begging for a seat. Like Flintoff, who had driven from home, we skipped down a one-way street to avoid the logjam. This time I completely missed the rehearsal and went pretty much straight on air with the preview show. I vowed to get up earlier at Trent Bridge. Those already inside the ground were beyond excited.

It was a day for the ages. The scoreboard read Australia 371 for 9 when it was done: match drawn. But, as so often with cricket, that score hardly told the story of a bewitching series of events. Lee finished exhausted on the ground for the second consecutive Test, this time hammering the turf in joy after surviving the final 24 balls with Glenn McGrath for company. The ninth man out was Ponting, who played one of his, or anyone's, best innings. That he made 156 was worthy enough, but that in so doing he continued to provide an uncommon sense of threat to an otherwise rampant England made his demise all the more painful. Caught at the wicket down the leg side, he walked from the field imagining that the match was to be lost and surely felt he did not deserve that. Rarely can a man have felt lonelier in this 'team' game. Solitude is no state for an Australian team sportsman. Australians are in it for one another and for the identity of their land. This is borne out by the team song, 'Under the Southern Cross I Stand', and the rewritten last line— 'Australia, you fucking beauty'. Ponting is the definitive article of this inherent 'Aussieness'. He is a defender of the faith, blindly on occasions, but the brilliance of his batting and fielding and the sheer force of will he has brought to the Australian cricket team are among the game's most convincing achievements.

As things turned out, Ponting got the draw he deserved. Balls whistled past heads, bats, gloves and bails as Flintoff and Harmison strained every sinew but simply could not take the final trick. Upon the umpires calling time, the Australian balcony leapt about with a manic zeal. Out in the middle, Vaughan gathered his men and said, 'Look at that balcony, lads, and watch the mighty Australia celebrating a draw with us. We've got 'em now.'

Martin Johnson wrote, 'It was like the Colosseum inside Old Trafford, with the crowd roaring for lbw every time the ball hit the pad and the umpires getting booed—like the old Roman emperors—if they gave the thumbs-down.' Derek Pringle wrote, 'In setting up the endgame, Strauss battled a cut ear and indifferent form to make 106. As he swished his bat and removed his helmet at reaching the milestone, the field dressing on his left ear recalled Van Gogh's harrowing self-portraits, though Strauss did have a smile on his face.' Simon Hughes said, 'Australian cricketers are like cockroaches. You can damage their legs, cuff them on the head and poison their knees, but you can't crush them. Their spirit is unbreakable. Left for dead overnight, they have regenerated and are back hunting their prey.'

I remember all of us being utterly exhausted.

FOURTH TEST, TRENT BRIDGE

By now, the whole of Britain was across the cricket. Channel 4 was averaging an unprecedented five million viewers a day. At Warner Music off Kensington High Street, Nick Stewart, head of one of the record divisions, called me to say that every single television in the building was tuned in to Channel 4. He wondered if we might explain things a little more deliberately, because the audience had morphed from long-term devotees of the game to newbies in drainpipe pants who needed lbw deciphered. A family of friends who, previously, had not been enamoured of cricket, came with me to Trent Bridge and stayed for the entire match. We scalped a couple of last-minute tickets for them and they rabbit on about it to this day.

If the abiding image of the series was Flintoff consoling Lee at Edgbaston, Patrick Eagar's wonderful photograph of the horizontal Strauss catching Gilchrist in the slips during the Australian first innings at Trent Bridge runs a close second. The vignettes between Flintoff and Adam Gilchrist had been required viewing long before Strauss gave us the old razzle-dazzle. At least, they had been if you were English. The key, as Vaughan points out, is that Flintoff *wanted* to bowl at Gilchrist. More than that, he wanted Gilchrist to know that he wanted to bowl at Gilchrist and he wanted the Australian dressing room to know too. He might have been the only bowler of the day with such a desire, given the physical and mental damage inflicted on so many by the man Benaud called 'the cleanest striker of a cricket ball I have seen'. This time, the ball moved a little away from the Australian off the pitch and found the thickish outside edge of a bat we had once thought only had a middle. It flew to the left of Strauss at second slip, just above waist height, and Strauss flew with it. From our perfect view in the commentary box, Strauss, horizontal and at full stretch, appeared frozen in time. As I write I can see it, and feel it.

Commentating, the usually understated Atherton repeated, 'What a catch!' Until it dawned on everyone that it had really happened. Fred lifted Straussy high off the deck, as if it were a line-out. The great Gilchrist, Straussed and Flintoffed.

Harmison's height and bounce, Simon Jones's pace and late swing, Hoggard's control and consistent outswing made for a handful. But a fully fit Fred, so immensely strong and bullish, was the game-breaker. Fred hit the pitch hard, the bat hard and the gloves hard. He bowled a nasty throat ball and a searing yorker. Above all, he made the ball swing, especially the older ball, which he reversed late and dramatically from around the wicket at Gilchrist. You could argue that the series needed some Gilly gunfire to make it whole, but that would be to deny cricket its right to defy the odds.

Surprising things happened at Trent Bridge. It is a most wonderfully atmospheric cricket ground. Ponting had Vaughan caught at the wicket, for example. I repeat, Ponting was the bowler and Vaughan was caught at the wicket: some death! Flintoff batted in orthodox fashion and inspired the best from Geraint Jones, who batted a bit like Ponting. Then the England new ball kept hitting Australian pads and the umpires kept raising their finger: Damien Martyn and Ponting were both lbw victims, having edged the ball onto their pad. Such deaths! In the second innings, Ponting was run out by a substitute fielder of whom no one had heard. They have now. It was Gary Pratt, of course. What a death. Surprising things happen at Trent Bridge, and spiteful things too. Ponting was not in the least bit pleased. His view was that England had played loose with substitutes all series and, marching up the pavilion steps in high dudgeon, he gave England coach Duncan Fletcher a mouthful. Fletcher retained a splendidly impassive mask. Pratt was on for Simon Jones, whose injury was genuine, so much so that Jones didn't play again in the series. Martin Johnson wrote something like, 'Whatever the rights and wrongs of the Ponting run-out, there were two Pratts involved.'

The oddest thing was the follow-on, such a quaint and distant notion. Kolkata 2001 had put the heebie-jeebies up all captains whose team led by more than 200 on the first innings. It is easily forgotten that V.V.S. Laxman played one of history's four or five greatest innings to set up the Kolkata great escape story. The statistics in favour of the follow-on are compelling: between the first Test match in 1877 and the end of the 20th century, captains went for it on 225 out of 261 opportunities, from which 168 matches were won and only two lost. Since 2000, captains have taken the option on 84 of the 136 possible occasions and Kolkata was the only embarrassment, albeit a nasty one. Mind you, there are good reasons against it nowadays—the prevalence of back-to-back Tests and the lack of the long-lamented Sunday rest day, among them. In Vaughan's case, the only reason against enforcing was Warne and the danger of allowing him to bowl last on a dry and tired pitch.

But Vaughan is not much spooked by history. Neither had he allowed his men to play the series in fear of Warne— though, by heaven and hell, Warne was trying to convince them otherwise. For the first time in almost exactly twenty years, an England captain took the follow-on plunge. An hour later, Simon Jones limped off. Two and half hours later, the Aussies were 129 for 1. Vaughan says he was pretty spooked then. Finally, after 78 overs of Australian batting in the match, Ashley Giles was thrown the ball. From this point on, the left-arm spinner played a telling part in the narrative.

(I must quickly tell a Giles story. A local Midland potter was a Giles fan and made a limited edition of celebratory mugs in honour of his testimonial year, each imprinted with the words 'Ashley Giles: The King of Spin'. Except that when they came back from the factory there was a misprint. An 'a' had crept into the word 'spin' so Giles was now anointed the King of Spain, a moniker that stuck.)

Immediately, the King of Spain coaxed a mistake out of Justin 'Alfie' Langer, who prodded to short leg—a wicket that disturbed the rhythm of the Australian rearguard action. Then Martyn called Ponting for the Pratt single. At the close, Australia were still 37 behind with the top four back in the hutch.

The fourth day was as good as anything at Edgbaston three weeks earlier, or at Headingley or Edgbaston in 1981. It tested our patience and challenged our emotions. It simply could not be trusted. Both teams fought as if they knew the wounds of defeat would not heal in time for the Oval. People who had paid chunky sums of money for tickets were caught looking away or wandering round the cricket for a breather. Everyone, everywhere was on edge.

Some cope with this better than others. Warne copes with it better than anyone. Indeed, you might argue that he breathes the oxygen of 'edge'. After Clarke and Simon Katich had added exactly 100 together, Warne hit Giles into the crowd a couple of times while making a fuck-you 45. Lee, who had landed a blow or two that needed fetching from the street in the first innings, merely hit roofs and stanchions this time around. England were left with 129 to win.

The omens of Headingley 1981 were suddenly upon us. That famous day, Australia had required 130 but crumbled to defeat by 18. At Edgbaston two weeks later, the same Australians had required 151 and, withered by Ian Botham's spell of 5 wickets for 1 run in 28 balls, lost by 29. Usually the English crow about Headingley 1981; now nobody dared to enter conversation about it. The facts were that Australia had enforced the follow-on, reduced England to 135 for 7 and then been royally beefed to all parts of Headingley—an innings that drew the phrase 'into the confectionery stall and out again' from Benaud, in one of his more elaborate moments of commentary. Yet, even after Botham's stupendous assault—you name it, he hit it—there were just the 130 for Kim Hughes's team to make. John Dyson set off at a canter and the Australians reached 56 for 1. Famously, Mike Brearley switched Bob Willis to bowl down the hill and, well, we know the rest. Now, at Trent Bridge 24 years later, England made 32 against the new ball in five overs. Which was when Ponting called upon Warne. Or maybe Warne called upon Ponting.

He began with a flat leg break into the rough outside off stump. Trescothick played forward, bat and pad together, and was caught by Ponting close on the off-side. Simple as that. His seventh ball was a higher leg-break that Vaughan edged to slip. Strauss fell to a leggie that ripped out of the rough and carried from the inside edge of his bat to leg slip. Then Bell flipped a Lee bouncer into the greedy hands of Kasprowicz at long leg: 32 for no wicket had become 57 for 4.

I have seen four bowlers who could manhandle the opposition in this way. It comes from the power of personality. Lillee, Procter and Botham are the others. Warne preys upon insecurity, or uncertainty, like no other. Then he strikes, with a poison for which there is no antidote.

However, even the King cannot bowl from both ends. Surprisingly, given there were so few runs with which to play, Ponting turned to Shaun Tait at the Radcliffe Road end of the ground. Pietersen and Flintoff saw the moment and licked their lips. Boundaries flowed. Sensing the shift, Ponting recalled Lee, who charged in to knock them both over. The fear set in again, like a Stephen King novel. Geraint Jones fell next, Warne's venom working its way through the veins of the England dressing room. Lee besieged umpire Steve Bucknor to answer his call as another rocket ball pounded into Matthew Hoggard's pads but the Yorkshireman survived the Jamaican and then calmly drove twice through extra cover, first for two and then for four. His wife said she had never seen him drive a ball for four. He had picked a good time to impress her. As Warne searched for flight and spin, Giles eased a half-volley for a couple. On the dressing-room balcony, the tension manifested itself in contorted faces and daft, desperate expressions.

Each negotiated delivery received roars of approval, each run scored brought a cacophony. With two needed, unsung Ashley reached out and worked two balls from Warne to leg: the first hit Katich at short leg, the second headed out to the mid-wicket boundary. At the sight of this, everybody English went mental. The winning runs had been made and the seemingly impossible—to at last beat an outstanding Australian team and reclaim the Ashes—was now very possible.

Above all things at the end of this marvellous match, I remember the way the players of both teams embraced one another. Hard-bitten rivalry became mutual respect at the instant of a push to mid wicket by a tall left-arm spinner. The sun shone upon many a smiling face, whether capped in blue or green. Vaughan led England's players down the pavilion steps to greet the two unbeaten batsmen and eleven vanquished Australians. He and Ponting warmly shook hands and shared a joke. Nottingham's outpouring of joy spread across the land: godspeed to London and the Oval.

After numerous interviews and a fascinating soliloquy from Boycott about how hard it is to get over the line against Australian cricketers, we came off air in state of euphoria. Even the crew had taken to pacing the corridors of the media facility with the rest of us when things got nervy, and throwing hats in the air at the moment England won.

Kirsten was with me for the match and we drove back to London after the C4 highlights show, which I voiced live over edited pictures. It was a hard enough gig after a dull day, but after a day such as this it became the most gruelling half-hour of interpretation and storytelling imaginable. She drove the twenty minutes to the motorway with me crashed out in the passenger seat before I woke abruptly and took over. I swung onto the M1 heading south, hit the accelerator pedal and was settling into *The Rising* by Bruce Springsteen when the phone rang. This is an almighty name drop, but I shall tell the tale anyway.

The caller was Mick Jagger, with Charlie Watts, in a hotel room somewhere in the US. They had watched most of the match on Jagger's laptop, courtesy of a Slingbox and were beside themselves with excitement. Charlie wanted detail: how lucky was it Flintoff got Clarke on the stroke of lunch and wasn't it luckier still that the umpire gave Katich out? Jagger wanted sensation: the Gary Pratt moment, for example, and what it must have felt like batting against Warne. He said that when Jones was caught having a mow at Warne, Charlie went and hid in the bathroom. Jagger has always liked cricket, and is rightly credited with bringing Sir Paul Getty to the game. He says that in the 1970s, Getty lived in Chelsea so he would go round to cheer him up. In the summer, they watched the cricket on the telly and the Rolling Stone began to teach the multimillionaire about the game with which he was to fall in love. I first met Jagger at Getty's beautiful private ground in Oxfordshire, then stepped out for a while with his PA. We have remained friends since and he comes to the cricket occasionally, sometimes hanging out in the commentary box to the amusement of Boycott, who takes the mickey out of his clothes, shoes or long hair. The two Stones were on the phone for an hour, finally saying goodbye as we passed Luton Airport. The Ashes of 2005 had hooked everybody.

In the London *Daily Telegraph*, Michael Parkinson said, 'Eight million tuned into the last knockings of the Trent Bridge

Test. That's as maybe. But how many were looking? This Test series has an epic grandeur capable of making all other big sporting events seem puny by comparison . . . This is now a formidable England team with a tough, intelligent captain and an appetite for a scrap. They are united with a team spirit and common purpose . . .'

Matthew Hayden wrote, 'In years to come people will scroll through the history books to learn about the remarkable series that took place between England and Australia in 2005. Should we get up at the Oval, it's something I'll read about day in, day out. If not, I'm afraid the books will gather dust on the shelf.'

Michael Vaughan again: 'To be honest, after Trent Bridge I was more nervous than I had been all summer. Finishing the job is hard, especially against that lot. I wasn't sleeping much, and every possible angle and outcome went through my head. I kind of began to pray we would pull it off. We had come a long way; I couldn't stand the thought of letting it go.'

FIFTH TEST, THE OVAL

Of all the Tests, this is the one I remember least well. A case, I suspect, of so much happening that it became a blur. Notwithstanding the interruptions for bad weather that gave the whole occasion another dimension, it was an immense game of cricket: a match with the power to define careers. Australia had to win to retain the Ashes, England to draw in order to claim them back. For all England's dominance over the three middle tests, the score was 2–1 in the home team's favour. That was all.

On the Test match merry-go-round, players and commentators, administrators and ground staff gather around the pitch each morning to chew the cud. On 8 September 2005— very late in the summer for Test cricket—there was a collective apprehension in the air. The match referee brought the coin with him and Vaughan, who is by his own admission 'a useless tosser', was relieved to see another feeble flick land in his favour. I remember thinking how I wanted England to make it through the match as much for him as for anyone or anything else. He had led his team with calm authority during long weeks of high tension and heightened passion. He thought quickly on his feet, using his bowling attack with the same shrewdness that had characterised Brearley's captaincy 24 years earlier. There was something of Raymond Illingworth's steel in him too. For sure, he is up there among the very best England captains.

Bat, bat and bat again was his mantra against Australia, and Strauss and Flintoff rewarded him absolutely. Strauss plays down the quality of his own batting, especially against Warne, but he held firm as the great spinner took the first 4 wickets of a Test match for the first time in his life. Having been 81 for no wicket, England found themselves 131 for 4. Strauss needed help and found it from Flintoff, who played an innings more in keeping with his classy Trent Bridge hundred than the boisterous affairs at Edgbaston. The pair put on 143. England made 373. Surely now . . .

We should have known better. Alfie and Haydos found their mojo with well-crafted hundreds. Hayden had not been himself since Simon Jones picked up the ball in his follow-through and winged it back at the startled batsman in the one-day international at Edgbaston, a match England won with almost as demonic a performance as the one in the T20 game at the Rose Bowl. Worse, from Hayden's point of view, was a rogue story that accused him of refusing to sign autographs for kids. No doubt about it, the Team England machine had worked the press to its advantage. But now Hayden drove and pulled with his more usual gusto, while Langer nudged, jabbed and cut with typical vigour. Australia was not going away. Conspiratorially, the rain trimmed Saturday's play to not much more than three hours. These belonged to the Australians until the ground staff raced the covers to the middle with an almost indecent relish.

English supporters sang and danced while Australians stripped to the waist and made as if the sun was burning their torsos—slip, slop, slap. On Sunday, the Australian batting reverted to series type. Clarke and Gilchrist were trapped in front by Hoggard, who dealt with Lee and McGrath as well. A fired-up Flintoff took care of all but one of the rest. The last 5 wickets fell for 11 runs as gung-ho batting tactics rebounded. Mind you, this gave England a tricky period in bad light and Warne duly snared Strauss before the umpires came to the rescue of Trescothick and Vaughan. The players left the field at 3.40 pm and, for the two and half hours until play was officially called off, the English sections of the crowd had another knees-up. It is rare to see such celebration upon an umpires' offer of bad light.

Thus, after seven tumultuous weeks—and seven memorable years—we arrived at the witching hour. On 12 September 2005, the Ashes went back to England and Channel 4 said goodbye to cricket. It was also the day that Richie Benaud made his last broadcast in the UK. He had been at it since 1963 and was much loved. With the rights moving away from free-to-air television, he had decided to call time and to enjoy the south of France for longer periods than his work had previously allowed. I do not mind admitting these three events stirred emotion in a way that is hard to describe. Joy and sadness fought one another for our attention; this was the day of pride and a fall in more ways than one.

PRESENTING THE ASHES

First up, we had to bring the climax of the series to air. The television running order—or run sheet in Australia—was assembled by the producer, Gary Franses. My respect for him is unconditional. He consults, appoints and cajoles. He put out fires and regulated ego. Once, I did something daft and he had the courage and sense to tell me. Another time, he was part of a decision with which I wildly disagreed but had to live. Otherwise, for seven summers and many a spring day shooting the breeze of the challenges to come, we got along famously. We are very different, which is probably the secret.

Each morning, four stapled A4 sheets were distributed to every key member of a vast crew. Some of them, each at the helm of a smaller but important entity, would have been a part of the meeting from which the running order was created. Up to a point, it was a collaborative and democratic process. Until Gary put his foot down.

The first page listed the requirements of the day and the various on- and off-air times. The second page was self-explanatory—the commentary roster; the ego thing. Six commentators for 24 shifts means four per person per day, which is exactly as Gary wrote it most of the time.

Page 3 was the 30-minute lead-in to the day's play. The timings were important, because Channel 4 is commercial and therefore ruled by advertising. We had to hit breaks because the slots were pre-paid. I frequently kicked colleagues in the shin, which meant, 'Pleeese shut up, we gotta go.' At Channel Nine we now have an hour-long lead-in show, which can take some filling. During that half-hour period on Channel 4 in the summer of 2005, we seemed tight for time every morning. Essentially, the brief was to summarise the story of the day before and set up the potential of the day ahead. To do this, you need good vision and graphics, a player interview or two, and commentators with something to say or demonstrate. Each has a skill of his own and Gary was masterful at having the right person in the right place at the right time. Believe me, that is rare.

This is how I saw those various skills. Tony Greig loved to educate the viewer with examples both practical and theoretical. His passion for the game was undimmed by age or exposure, and no one researched cricket's current affairs like Greigy. In addition, he loved to stir things up, supporting the underdog and rattling the favourites. Michael Slater brought the same energy and enthusiasm to the commentary box that characterised his enterprising and often brilliant batting. If the job needs one thing above all else, it is enthusiasm. Michael Atherton appraises even the most controversial aspects of play, or the players, with a calm intelligence. He was the perfect foil to Geoffrey Boycott's more pointed approach. Boycott does his own view, straight, like no other. If his job is to be an expert on cricket, he is damn good at his job. Of course, he polarises opinion but isn't that the point? Benaud was the start-up man and the finisher, and most things in between. His role in the success of the coverage cannot be overstated.

My job is to get the best from the talent, leading it to the subject at hand and asking questions that the viewer at home might ask themselves. On commercial television, I have to weave in and out of breaks, so be able to plan a question with a view to the length of time the answer may, or may not, take. Ideally, you go soft to start and then work towards the more serious issue. But if time is short you cannot delay. Sometimes the producer or director will have a specific angle or an alternative point. Equally, there may be a problem with a camera or some vision and then the presenter has to turn on a dime. This means the commentators must turn with him, something Atherton does particularly well.

Michael Parkinson once said to me that you need an ego to do the job but no ego in the job. I see myself as the middleman between the product, which in this case is the game, and the audience. My aim is to get the product across simply, intelligently (I hope) and with enthusiasm. And to hit the clock when need be. Michael has been a tremendous supporter and, along with my wonderful stepfather, Brian Widlake—whose fine television and radio career ended at about the time Hampshire were winning a few trophies—has provided me with informed and generous advice.

The fourth page was the 40-minute lunchtime show. On the first day of the last Test, for example, we were talking to Richie, skimming across his life in the game before getting through some housekeeping in the second segment. Page 4a was my notes. As I've said, I'm not a believer in scripting live television. I think it takes away from both intuition and instinct. I have bullet points and look to interact with guests, rather than drive the thinking. Occasionally, guests dry up and then I earn my money.

Generally, there would be a run sheet for tea as well but by the end of a series like this, we winged it. The narrative of the summer of 2005 was a run sheet in itself.

AFTER 16 YEARS, THE URN RETURNS TO ENGLAND

England had to negotiate a 98-over day without too much going wrong, simple as that. There was excitement in the air—or 'nervocitement' actually—because nobody was completely at ease with the position in which their team had finished the afternoon before. The rude awakening from the previous day's bad-light party hangover was the realisation that Warne and McGrath had long perfected the humiliation of English batsmen. The glass-half-empty brigade suddenly saw the potential for more of the same. As for the Australian faithful, not much since Lord's had suggested their team were in the right parish to pull off a miracle. The Oval was full to bursting as spectators peered through the morning mist. We made a decent half-hour's telly, 'Jerusalem' boomed with grandeur, and out came Ricky Ponting's Australians.

McGrath had missed the Trent Bridge Test with an elbow problem but now he was back doing what he does best. Vaughan and Bell had their off-stump indecision clinically exploited by the man they call the Pigeon, and Warne accounted for Trescothick and Flintoff at the other end. The pitch was offering wicked amounts of spin and the King was all over it. It occurred to us that this was the last time we would see the pair of them together in England—McGrath and Warne, that is— and that cricket might never have seen such a partnership of fast and slow, so fierce in its collective intent. It is not enough to simply call them great bowlers. They are very great sportsmen, who transcended their game and rewrote its history.

There was a saving grace for England in the form of a South African. Since Greig first made the journey from the Eastern Cape to the south coast of Sussex, many a Southern African had followed him. Liveliest among them was Allan Lamb; most powerful was Robin Smith; most demure, Graeme Hick. I dare say none of these gifted three could have played the innings now put before us by Kevin Pietersen, a brazen lad from Pietermaritzburg. My, how long it seemed since that off-driven six off McGrath at Lord's. But it was a mere 50 days, and K.P.'s bravado was intact. He had made a poor fist of defending his wicket before lunch so, over a ham roll, he asked Vaughan how best to go about the business of saving the match and securing the Ashes. Vaughan said, 'Your game is to take 'em on, to attack, so go do just that. An hour from you and we've won the Ashes', which summarised his general approach to the series. Attack when possible but stay in Australian faces if not.

Obediently, Pietersen took 'em on all right. Warne had dropped him at slip, a straightforward chance in front of his face, and was immediately made to pay with a couple of those slog-sweeps that take no prisoner. Lee bounced him at great pace and watched in amazement as the ball disappeared into the ether. Only once did Pietersen get the shot wrong, and Tait very nearly pulled off a catch on the long-leg boundary that would have impressed even Strauss. One pull stroke, from a 93-mile-per-hour ball that was barely short at all, came back past the stumps from which Lee had delivered it. Benaud said he thought it was coming through the television screen. Nobody could quite believe what they were seeing. If Ponting played the finest defensive innings of the series, and Flintoff and Geraint Jones had combined at Trent Bridge for the most thrilling dovetail, Pietersen now stole their show. This was an everything innings and doing just as Vaughan said it would.

Nonetheless, Geraint Jones and Paul Collingwood—who had been brought into the side to replace Simon Jones and so fortify the batting in a match that needed runs from England— were rolled over as tea approached. The score was 199 for 7; 205 ahead but not quite in possession of the urn. Giles made his way to the middle, punched Pietersen's glove with his own and never looked like losing his wicket until a tired and exasperated Warne breached his defences just before the close. By then the King of Spain had made 59 and the match was saved. He would probably say it was his best innings and it may more than have doubled the value of those mugs.

To finish the story, we must first finish the Pietersen story. I once suggested that his batting was blessed by genius in the way, perhaps, of Viv Richards. He shrugged off the compliment, saying no one was Viv. But I wasn't saying he was Viv, I was saying he was different—the way Viv was different. By it, I meant that he could do things others could not. There is something crazy about Pietersen, something so alternative and unpredictable that the rules change and, with them, the possibilities change too. In the period after lunch, he barely defended a ball but when he did, it was an exaggerated block or kick after kick at Warne's deliveries aimed into the rough. Then suddenly he would mow one of the same deliveries down the ground for six. Before the series, Warne had urged the England selectors to pick Pietersen because 'he can hurt us', but even Warne might not have known how badly. This South African man in his English coat and with hair of many colours made 158, the exact score another South African man, with a face of colour, had made when batting for England on the same ground against the same opponent 37 years earlier. Basil D'Oliveira's 158 was to change the world; Pietersen's merely changed the order of things.

Richie Benaud was in situ for his final half-hour of commentary. We had all wondered how he would say goodbye and reckoned it would be short and sweet. Not so short as John Arlott who, famously, did not actually say goodbye but simply handed over—'and now it will be Trevor Bailey and Christopher Martin-Jenkins'. Gary pushed Richie a little and established that he did have something in mind, something typically well prepared. As Pietersen drove to mid-off, this much-loved former Australian captain said, 'There's been all sorts of music here today: "Land of Hope and Glory"; the national anthem; before play, "Jerusalem". I carry a lot of music around with me, and a favourite is Andrea Bocelli and Sarah Brightman singing that duet, that wonderful duet "Time to Say Goodbye" . . .'

Pause. Pietersen plays forward to defend.

'And that's what it is, so far as I'm concerned, time to say goodbye . . . Thank you for having me. It's been absolutely marvellous for 42 years. I've loved every moment of it and it's been a privilege to go into everyone's living rooms throughout that time. What's even better, it's been a great deal of fun.'

Pause. Pietersen loses his off stump to McGrath.

There was no change of tempo or key.

'But not so for the batsman, McGrath has picked him up! Late in the day, he's got a beauty through Kevin Pietersen;

308 for 8 now and Pietersen will get a standing ovation . . .
He's getting one from Shane Warne now [Warne goes to shake
Pietersen's hand before the noise of the crowd takes over].
A roar to end all roars.'

A few lines later, he threw to the next commentators and
that was that. Goodbye, K.P., goodbye, R.B. There was barely
a dry eye in the commentary box and not many more in those
living rooms. It occurred to me while writing that we shall
never know how he would have signed off had he not been
interrupted by McGrath bowling Pietersen. Anyway, Benaud's
day was not yet quite done.

The very end of the Test match was a bizarre anticlimax,
as if the gods had run out of steam. After Warne finished off
England, Australia briefly batted but then accepted the offer
of bad light. More cheers. Eventually umpires Rudi Koertzen
and Bowden pulled the stumps from the ground and the hugest
cheer rang out around south London.

By now, I was on the other side of the ground waiting to
interview the players. The noise of the crowd was so loud
that it was impossible to hear via my earpiece what else Gary
had in mind. I grabbed a couple of the players before their
first lap of honour and then noticed a change in the crowd's
attention. Heads turned to the big screen at the Vauxhall End
of the ground and the wall of sound changed from feverish
nationalism to loud and resonant applause. As one spectator
stood, so did another, until everyone at the Oval was standing
and applauding. And then I saw why. Richie was crossing the
outfield alongside Tony Greig. Gary had sent him over to be
with me for the last word. I shall never forget the extraordinary warmth of this moment, when 21,000 people spoke as
one for the whole of the country. It was a level of respect and
admiration accorded very few. Greigy says that Richie shed a
tear. Richie never denied it.

The Oval has seen many a telling and often glorious day. This was of the best, to rank with 1953 at a guess, when Denis Compton hit the winning runs against Lindsay Hassett's team. While medals were handed out to the umpires and players, the atmosphere was spirited and festive. Then Vaughan received the Ashes urn, or its replica, and I remember thinking, 'Wow, I bet that feels good.' The euphoria of the crowd was remarkable, a sure sign that cricket had a part to play in the lives of British people. Certainly, the feel-good factor was every bit as powerful as it had been in 1981. Twenty-five years on, a pair of tickets for a day's play at the Oval had sold on eBay for £1115 and a penthouse with a view of the ground was let for the week at twenty grand. The quality of the contest and its narrative drama had captivated a new audience and these fans, along with the established lovers of the game, had something communal to celebrate.

We interviewed all the team either before or after the laps of honour. It really was quite a do. Then we—the Channel 4 team this time—said goodbye after seven years' commitment to something we loved so deeply that letting go took a very long time. Years, in fact.

As I packed my things, I vividly remember thinking how wonderful the spirit had been between the teams. I think this must have been because the Australians were generous in defeat. There were no misgivings, not openly anyway, not even any sullen faces as Vaughan held aloft the prize. In fact, there were smiles and, later apparently, happy hours spent in the England dressing room with beer and champagne to loosen the tongues of warriors who understood the fates of the game they played.

The next day there was a bash in Trafalgar Square, which I had the great privilege of hosting with David Gower. On the most beautiful morning, tens of thousands turned out to pay tribute to Vaughan's team, who emerged from the open-top bus understandably the worse for wear after a night, and morning, on the tiles. Some choice of venue, England expects and all that. Afterwards, Kirsten and I walked most of the way home, the wonder of it all washing over us.

ASHES REFLECTIONS

The general view is that this was the greatest Ashes series of all. Ricky Ponting called it 'the best he played in', which, given he made only one substantial score himself, is a good marker; Michael Clarke, looking back now but a pup at the time, agrees. Benaud thought it pipped 1981. I hardly need say where the England players rated it. There were monumental performances from Andrew Flintoff and Shane Warne; surprising frailties in both predictable and unpredictable characters; and nerve-shredding tension in three of the five matches.

Australia was slow to react to England's swing bowling, aggressive batting and desire to win. Vaughan led the side with uncommon purpose and belief. Whatever he did between Lord's and Edgbaston was genius. Whatever the Australians did in that time, which was not much, suggests they made the assumption that England were already shot.

The fortunes of the two wicketkeepers bears particular scrutiny. Both dropped catches, Jones more than Gilchrist, but then Jones caught two beauties that respectively decided, and threatened to decide, outcomes. The one to win the match at Edgbaston is not celebrated as perhaps it should be. The rebound off Strauss to get rid of Warne at Old Trafford was an instinctive thing born of a lifetime playing sport. Jones used the same instinct to flourish with the bat, accelerating England's innings at times when the Australian bowlers had the door open, only to see Jones, mainly with Flintoff, slam it shut in their face. Conversely, Gilchrist was an increasingly discombobulated figure. The most spectacular cricketer of the age was unable to counter Flintoff's hardball pace and late swing delivered from around the wicket. The longer the series went on, the more obvious the confusion became: stick or twist? Too late.

In most other Ashes series, Warne's 40 wickets at 19 and 249 runs at 27 would have secured victory. Voted one of *Wisden*'s five cricketers of the 20th century, he emerged through the first years of the 21st century with his game modified by the march of time and the results of injury. But the mind, surely Warne's most defining weapon, remained as alert and strong as it had ever been. Hour upon hour, day after day he lifted Australian spirits and redeemed hopes. His performances were Herculean but the army alongside him lacked edge and imagination.

Flintoff provided infectious enthusiasm and joy. He bowled long spells at the limit of his capabilities, batted with increasing assurance and fathered a four-pronged pace attack that had a nice blend of speed, bounce, swing and seam. For fifteen years England had called for the new Botham. For the time being at least, the search could be called off.

Botham himself watched in admiration from the Sky commentary box, where highlights of each day's play appeared every night. He was pleased that Headingley 1981 would no longer be the go-to filler on the big screen during rain delays. Back then, His Beefiness displayed many of the qualities on show from Flintoff and Warne—notably strength of body and mind, and a force of will that carried the day. For all the attention paid to the Headingley miracle, Botham's magic was every bit as relevant in the next two Test matches of that series. At Edgbaston, where they say lightning struck twice, Botham came back to bowl with the Australians 105 for 5 in pursuit of 151. Brearley told him to 'Keep it tight for Emburey', who had just dismissed Graham Yallop and Allan Border. Forty minutes later the match was over. Botham conceded just a single run while taking the last 5 wickets in dramatic fashion. When he bowled Alderman, he sprinted down the pitch, grabbed a stump and holding it aloft ran from the field as if possessed. That picture became almost as iconic as the one taken of Flintoff and Lee by Tom Shaw 25 years later. In the Fifth Test at Old Trafford, Botham played his finest innings, memorably hooking Dennis Lillee off his eyebrows much as Pietersen had flayed Lee at the Oval. Another stroke off Lillee went back past the bowler at head height with such speed that had Lillee not followed through so fully, the ball might have ripped his head off. The best of Botham carried the whole nation. No single figure has had such an impact on English cricket. Grace, Hobbs, Hammond, Jardine, Larwood, Hutton, Trueman, Compton, Boycott, Gower, Flintoff, Vaughan—none of them quite matched Botham's ability to turn a game on its head and thrill the crowd while doing so. Grudgingly, most Australians came to rather admire him.

Do Ashes series truly define English and Australian cricketers? Not always, but often enough to make them the pinnacle of ambition. Botham influenced more matches than most others and, doubtless, would like those happy memories recorded on his gravestone. Vaughan's men of 2005 would say the same. The very nature of this chapter concentrates on England's remarkable victory, but over the 128 years of Ashes cricket, it is Australia that holds the upper hand having won 130 Tests to England's 106. The series are locked at 32 each, which augurs well for the future.

'England's win is sure to do a lot of good for Australian cricket. Here in England I have been gladdened by the absorbing interest in the game, especially amongst schoolboys. That is, unfortunately, not the case in Australia, where interest has waned alarmingly. Well played, England. You deserved it, and the Australians will not begrudge you the thrill of it, but I hope that you do not hold on for too long. Australia did, and has cause to regret it.' These words were written by Bill O'Reilly after England won at the Oval in 1953, under Len Hutton. The point of them being that the cricketing health of both countries is imperative in sustaining the legend and inspiring the next generation.

Australia's response to 2005 was a thing of cruel beauty. On home turf in 2006–07 Ponting's mighty team tore apart Flintoff's England, winning all five Tests in commanding fashion. At Adelaide, Warne played the lead role in turning an unpromising final day into a story so good they made a movie about it. *Amazing Adelaide* was produced and distributed almost as quickly as *The Greatest Test* had been eighteen months earlier. At the end of the series both Warne and McGrath retired from the game, taking their last bow at the Sydney Cricket Ground with a jaw-dropping 1271 wickets between them (Warne 708, McGrath 563). In 104 Test matches they played together, the total is a record 1001 wickets. No other duo has sung so prolifically from the same song sheet. Ponting was soon to discover how challenging life would become without them.

The winning captains since that day have been Andrew Strauss twice, Alastair Cook twice, and Michael Clarke, whose team of 2013–14 sought and achieved the same level of vengeance that Ponting had enjoyed in 2006–07. It is surely true that Ashes cricket defines the captains. 'Jardine's Bodyline tour', 'Bradman's Invincibles', 'Illingworth's Ashes', 'Chappell's Australians', 'Gatting's side of 1986–87', 'Border's all-conquering team of 1989' are the collective terms by which these teams and their place in cricket history are remembered.

Strauss won in Australia in 2010–11, a rare feat among English captains. Since the Second World War, only Hutton in 1954–55, with Frank Tyson at his fastest; Illingworth in 1970–71, with Boycott and Snow at their best; Brearley in 1978–79, against those Australians not recruited by Packer for WSC; and Gatting in 1986–87, with Botham, have pulled that particular rabbit from the hat. Peter May took a marvellous group of players by boat to Australia in 1958–59—arguably the most gifted team to leave British shores—and was thumped 4–0 by Benaud's exciting young side. Australian captains have had more to crow about on English soil. Bradman, Benaud, Simpson, Ian Chappell, Border twice, Mark Taylor and Steve Waugh have all enjoyed the English summer and the prize at the end of it.

Today, the captains are put through the ringer by a voracious media. Newspapers feed from their every utterance; news channels fill hours of rolling time with press conferences pre- and post-match, often latching onto nothing more than passing observations. Immediately after the toss at every international match played in England, the captains complete three separate interviews, for Sky, TMS and Channel 5. They do the same when it is over. These obligations are honoured with patience and mainly good humour.

The most open have been Vaughan, who delighted in the opportunities given to him by the new wave of social interaction, and Clarke, who wore his heart on his sleeve in a way that many Australians could not bring themselves to trust. This was a pity, for Clarke's heart is good and kind, and his head the equal of any cricketing man. It was a wonderful moment when he lifted the World Cup, coming as it did so soon after the loss of his great buddy, Phillip Hughes. Through that desperate period for Australian cricket, Clarke kept alight the candle of hope.

Ponting gave little at the beginning of his tenure. So high were his own standards that he was sometime puce with anger at a poor performance by the team. But as the power of that team diminished, he adapted the angle and delivery of his message. By the end he had learnt to be media savvy, so much so that his move into broadcasting already has shape. I should also add that Ponting was among the very greatest cricketers, especially able at turning the screw. His innings had a certainty about them, an impression given as much to the opposition as to the viewer.

Strauss was very smart with the media, using press conferences to discuss the narrative of the team and post-match flash interviews to clearly explain the moment. He was careful not to let the Pietersen affair cloud his general optimism for the progress he and the players made together, but it wore him down in the end. He is an excellent choice to lead English cricket forward in his ECB role as director of England cricket, already proving the merit of tough and decisive moves that have cleared the way for a hitherto unseen freedom of thinking in England's play.

Cook is a stubborn so-and-so and naturally wary. Part of this comes from his own reticence in front of the camera or behind a microphone; the rest from his feeling that those in glasshouses (press boxes and commentary boxes) should be more careful with the stones they throw. He believes that modern cricket is the equal of, or has improved upon, any other era in the game's history—an argument over which he cannot be swayed.

Cook gives an immense amount of his time to good causes, arriving with that devastating smile and an impressive aura. More often than not he stays longer than required, happily paying attention to those less lucky than cricketers. During variously challenging periods in the job, he has been at his wits' end. But he is no quitter and the England team has regenerated under his calm authority.

Remarkably, he has made more runs than any England batsmen. When he passed the 10,000 mark at Chester-le-Street, he proudly raised his bat in the knowledge that he is one of only twelve men in the game's history to have celebrated such an achievement. Rather charmingly, he was delighted by this and chose not to hide it from the camera. We are in an age of vanilla relations between player and press but he confessed to immense self-satisfaction, for once rejoicing in his own achievement rather than attributing it to the greater whole of the team.

To me, the Ashes were always the dream. My father told me about Miller, Harvey and Benaud on one side; Compton, Trueman and Dexter on the other. My destiny was not to play a part but to talk and write about the players who do and the matches that cast a spell over two distant countries united by their past and by the games they play. It is tremendous fun. The Ashes is all it's cracked up to be and everything that Test-match cricket should be. The 2005 series confirmed this to a great many people and, all too briefly, brought the game back to the streets, parks and playgrounds of England. We had pined for a competitive Ashes series and we got one. Even Australians gave thanks for that.

CHAPTER 13

A crystal ball

Spring in England, 2016 . . .
A funny thing happened in London today: the sun came out and there was no need for layers of clothing to enjoy it. I thought of the county cricketers peeling off jumpers and swapping hand-warmers for suncream in their pockets. Well, maybe not. This is Britain, not Bangalore.

Spring is the most glorious time, bringing as it does the rebirth of cricket and blossom. In attics, men look out old boots, leather dried and cracking, soles with September's grass still sticking. Once, it was the time to pour linseed oil over a bat's face, but now they barely knock 'em in before smiting sixes and missing straight 'uns. Groundsmen tend emerald-green turf, still theirs for now but soon the possession of white-clad warriors who prod and poke, land, pitch, run, fall and scuff.

Cricket pavilions have their doors opened to that scent of stale kit and clothing, and of damp wood. Shafts of sunlight evoke memories of previous deeds that led to a walled garden of photographs and a club dinner of jokes about first-ballers and no balls and free hits and the young lad who made neither head nor tail of his pitcher of ale. Upon old hooks are old shirts and in lockers lie the odd sock and a pair of batting gloves that number two lent to number ten, who forgot to return them. Spiders emerge with stealth, aware that summer brings warmth but no peace.

What of practice? Nets abound, so many on astroturf now. Boys play away in shirt sleeves and their fathers in woollen jumpers that betray their history. Joints scream and muscles twitch but eagerness wins out. The wonder is that winter has been survived. (Written with apology to Neville Cardus.)

———

In Bengaluru right now, and all over India, there is a very different cricket from the nostalgia invading British senses at the start of a new season. British rule has long gone—hooray!—and the 9th IPL has the nation in thrall. Back in February 2008, the first IPL player auction offered untold riches to cricketers from far and wide. Each franchise was permitted to spend millions of dollars on attracting players with high levels of skill, power and appeal. Almost overnight, the game moved away from a long-established set of institutionalised parameters to a free market. Sony Pictures Television bought the rights for close to a mind-boggling billion dollars, and it wasn't long before the rest of the world was dipping its toes in these sparkling waters. Nearly a decade on, the IPL has survived all manner of distraction and accusation to remain at the forefront of commercial cricket.

While county cricketers wheel away in front of next to no one, crowds flock to matches between teams about whom most of us know nothing. In some cases, we haven't even heard of them. Who does Brendon McCullum play for? Gujarat Lions, of course. And Kevin Pietersen? The Rising Pune Supergiants, naturally. After all, M.S. Dhoni is a Supergiant these days (I've always seen Dhoni as a giant), lest you had lost of track of the Chennai Super Kings' suspension from the tournament during investigation into their practices. The players swap teams faster than my mates and I once swapped Dinky Toys. What does this tell us? It tells us about market forces, that's what.

The IPL cricket is louder, larger, more insistent and more addictive than anything before. Players have attitude; it is the 'new' thrusting India. They are promoted to stardom long before they have achieved anything of real significance. Some of them may ask what is 'significance'? American gridiron football has a player who does nothing more than come on to the field to try to kick a goal, after which he leaves. Is this act significant? You bet your life it is. So when a kid from the backroom of Dhoni's newly acquired empire comes on to take the catch that wins the day—a kid called Deepak Chahar, say, or Ankush Bains—don't be surprised or begrudge him. The kids serve their apprenticeship at the coalface these days, not in a void beneath the bowels of the capped players dressing room. And when they do so, millions of people depend upon them.

You have to love it. Switching between channels is a surreal experience: two utterly contrasting designs, methods, styles, wardrobes and support of exactly the same game. Sort of. Sky shows Nottinghamshire and Yorkshire at Trent Bridge, where the otherwise flamboyant Alex Hales is admired for the disciplined way he survives 52 balls to reach double figures and goes on to accumulate a total of 34 runs in 115 balls spread over 145 minutes. There are only 120 scheduled balls in one whole innings of the game on the other channel. Goodness knows what Cardus would make of that.

Press the remote and Sky also shows the Gujarat Lions against the Delhi Daredevils in Rajkot where Rishabh Pant plays 'normal cricket' (his own words) to score 69 runs in twelve balls fewer than Hales's double-figures milestone. It's either crackers or it's cracking entertainment. I'll barrack for the latter, though I suppose it's a bit of both.

Face it, cricket is coping remarkably well with its time lapse—one form of the game is played in the past, the other in the future. Both have relevance for the follower and commitment from the participants. One looks after traditional technique and values, the other revolutionises both. One can define a man, the other can make him rich: the lucky few have definition and money.

How *did* Lalit Modi, the businessman who founded the IPL, do it? Kevin Pietersen, for one, has called Modi a genius. He was talking, of course, about the introduction, deliberately or otherwise, of the freelance cricketer within the franchise model. Chris Gayle, when first approached, was so aghast at the amount of money that he could barely compute: 'I'm like, how much?!' And who is to say he is not worth it any more than any elite player who is hugely highly paid in any other sport.

Most likely, Modi set out to create an electric, modern tournament, something so bright and sassy that the new generation could identify and interact as it does with popular culture in general—music, fashion, celebrity. From it came unimagined spin-offs, as the law of unintended consequences provided opportunities so extreme that county cricketers are now excused their contracts in England to honour their contracts in India. Modi's timing was as good as Kerry Packer's nearly 50 years ago.

Back then, the secretary of the ACB responded to Packer's heist with extraordinary arrogance. Wisely, this time around Cricket Australia handed out 'no objection' certificates as if they were confetti. Cricket has moved fast, every bit as fast as it did when Packer first made the 'Lights, camera, action' call at the Sydney Cricket Ground. Once Packer got what he wanted and what cricket so badly needed, he moved aside and the game settled down to find its rhythm for modern times.

Which is exactly what must happen now. Cricket needs a global common ground; it needs sympathy, rhythm and union. Modi's call of 'Lights, cameras, *auction*' has shown the way forward. Cricket's leaders must respond while the game is still trending. There is a place for all people and for all formats, but not for self-interested governance.

International cricket is run by the ICC, whose board is made up of people with vested interests in their own country's health and progress. Recently, India, Australia and England broke away to form a cabal that compromised those left behind. The big three bullied their way into a takeover of all immediate ICC tournaments and, more generally, wrested away hostile control of the governance, finances and future of the world game. Some might say good riddance to the pusillanimous ICC as we knew it. Others would argue that the game cannot be truly represented without a reconstituted ICC, whose main board should consist of independent cricket people and followers who are prepared to take responsibility for a long-term view.

To survive the move into a commercial marketplace and at the same time remain artistic, cricket needs a clear vision. I say this with some confidence, because classical music has survived the invasion of popular culture; books have survived the assault of social media; and true art has survived its pretenders. The age in which we live is fast-moving, but it is not one-dimensional.

Test cricket needs to adapt, in the way that concerts and galleries have adapted. It has to reflect the space and time available. T20 cricket has lifted cricket's morale and introduced new audiences to the game. It has found sensible commercial models and applied them to a successful experience for the viewer. There is a view that it is modern, gauche and contradictory but so were Jackson Pollock, George Orwell, David Bowie and the Sex Pistols, and they all became a part of our lives.

The T20 behemoth can lead cricket into its next era. More than anything else, T20 and the structure of international cricket in general needs clarity. What do we have at present and what do we want of it in the future? The IPL, for example, is now too long—not for its own sake but for its place in our hearts, minds and a sensible global schedule—and yet it still has the power to make us peep behind the curtain. Then, when the final stages come, we settle down to watch, however long it has taken us to get there. The Big Bash League competes daily with Test cricket, an unnecessary collision when Australia has the space to separate it and allow them both to breathe. England desperately wants an equivalent. The Caribbean Premier League needs further profile and investment. It is the route forward for West Indian cricket, leading a revival in the game that is inherently loved and followed by proud people.

Broadly speaking, most cricket lovers have no problem with a divisional structure for Test cricket, as recently mooted by the ICC. Frankly, they would run with anything that brings narrative to an important and historical game that is being overrun by T20. Promotion and relegation provides general interest and new teams might rise to the challenge of justifying themselves at the high table. As much, though, as aspiration would be rewarded, the danger is that the more vulnerable countries will be compromised beyond their control. There are three or four teams in the second division of the County Championship in England that seem destined to stay there. Were these teams New Zealand, Sri Lanka or West Indies—all of which have found life hard at Test-match level at some stage during the past five years—would they, or the game at large, find themselves unable to sustain their participation? The standards between the two divisions have grown wider in county cricket, and they would surely do so in Test-match cricket as well. One argument says that is a good thing, a natural cull of sorts that allows the elite few to concentrate on one another. The other argument says that there is only a limited number of teams. Given we are trying to broaden the base of the game not narrow it—while at the same time maintain high standards— we should not ask too much of those with limited resources, in case they become a victim of the cull.

I much prefer a World Test Championship, played within a four-year cycle of international cricket's major competitions. This allows for the retention of the Champions Trophy—which, incidentally, was abandoned to make way for a Test-match championship, then reinstated as a cash cow—but not for more than one major T20 event in the cycle. After the tremendous success of the recent World T20, the ICC's chief executive, David Richardson, said he was not in favour of increasing the number of World T20s for fear of killing the golden goose. Now we hear there are to be two every four years. Thus, I worry for the goose.

T20 is the zeitgeist. It has financial muscle, global audience appeal and television commitment. Franchised domestic tour-naments are beginning to take a shape, though non-negotiable windows in the calendar would improve that shape further. Freedom of movement for the players is better understood as an essential part of the game's future blueprint. T20 can help the game grow, but it must not become a monster, devouring all in its path. The ICC should set the parameters for T20 in every corner of the world and adapt Test cricket and one-day cricket to sit alongside it.

If one-day cricket is to have sufficient profile, it needs a less-is-more policy, and quickly, before the public's patience wears out. We know the World Cup works. We think bilat-eral series are still attractive, though ticket sales are no longer quite so convincing. One-day series should be restricted to a maximum of three games, making the tickets hard to come by and the memory sweeter and clearer. All bilateral one-day cricket should be World Cup cricket, as proposed by Australia a couple of years back, with the points making up a league table that decides entry and seeding for the World Cup as we know it. The Champions Trophy is a useful tool for 50-over cricket, reiterating the essential bridge it provides between the shortest and longest forms of the game, and reminding us of its ability to parade a full complement of cricket's skill sets within the time frame.

A World Test Championship need not be complicated. Every four years the top four teams during the course of that period would meet up for a festival of Test-match cricket played over a month or so in the country that leads the table at the point of its conclusion. At this event, they would all play each other once and then the top two contest a multimillion-dollar final. If matches were drawn, the team highest in the original table would go through. The same tie-breaker would apply to the final, thus providing an added incentive during the 'league' stages.

In the way that Test cricket needs a story to tell, it is really no different from the IPL. Time is required for a crescendo before focus switches to the climax. Over four years there is space for the ten full member nations to play each other home and away over a minimum of four matches and a maximum of ten. The ten-match scenario is there to allow for the Ashes, the series that has done more than any other to keep Test match cricket alive and mainly well. This makes for a minimum of 36 matches per country or, in the case of England and Australia 42, over four years—fewer than the big boys play at present (India have 13 home Tests in the 2016–17 season alone). Ideally, bilateral tours would consist of three Test matches, three one-day games and three T20s, but in reality that may be too much cricket to fit in the timeframe. There will be a price for England and Australia to pay, both in terms of player fatigue and fiduciary responsibility. Money made from extra Ashes matches must surely go into the pot for the staging of the month that we might come to know as the 'ICC Test Championship Festival of Cricket'—and assume a sponsor's name in there somewhere too.

At the end of this four-year period, the team that finishes last in the Full Member League table would lose its Test-match status and the team that wins the Associate Test Championship—staged concurrently with the World Championship to include finals during the same period and in the same country—would gain Test-match status.

Above all, the ICC and all the member nations must be empowered to market this with the same enthusiasm as they market T20, because unless the game sells its vision passionately and extensively, we cannot hope to persuade outsiders that we have something relevant and attractive on offer. Then we need to sell the tickets at a sensible price, offering packages for families, kids and schools. Finally, a proportion of these new matches needs to be seen on free-to-air television, in a simultaneous broadcast with a satellite network if need be.

Somehow, Test cricket needs to be given back to the people. To mix proverbs, the horse will have to be dragged to the water because in most parts of the world it has long bolted. The key is not to give up but to believe in its potential ourselves and improve the model. A suspicion lingers that key administrators have lost faith in the five-day game, preferring the ease with which they bankroll their problems through T20.

The costs of a World Test Championship will be high, but the Champions Trophy pot and a share of the proceeds from the franchised T20 tournaments that are dependent on the players provided by the full member governing bodies, is the only way forward. Everybody must buy in to this bigger picture, or the moment will pass us by—and that is *everybody*: the world of cricket in union.

FORWARD TO THE FUTURE

Now, let's take the game deep into the 21st century. Test cricket has survived, but only within an elite circle of players and continents. There is now a collective called the Superpower Series, which is played once a year over short dedicated periods by Europe, Africa, the Asian subcontinent and Australasia. It reflects the slick round-robin model shown us by Kerry Packer during cricket's first great revolution and, backed by multinationals, it is richer and more glamorous than even the IPL. The players who reach the final earn film-star status and companies battle for the rights to use their image and sell their brand.

The matches are scheduled over four days with a minimum of 100 overs bowled on each of those days. No innings may last longer than 120 overs. There are two breaks of half an hour but no official drinks breaks during play. A second new ball is available whenever the bowling team wants it. No more than five fielders are allowed outside the 30-yard ring at any stage of any modern-day cricket match. The Superpower Series is allocated by rotation and the home continent gives up the right to choice of innings. Only in matches between the three guest continents does the toss of a coin take place.

The dissolution of the Test-playing countries as we knew them was both controversial and painful but has proven to be a master-stroke in rejuvenating the purest form of cricket. At the same time, there was a strong lobby to get rid of the draw, which the new age fans see as anachronistic. Their view is that the team that scores the most runs over four days wins the match and their determination forced a global referendum on the subject. The vote was open to all cricketers in the world who had played a first-class match, everyone who had umpired in one and anyone who had sat on their national board of control, for however long. Surprisingly, the hawks who wanted to oust the draw got a right thumping. The overriding view was that the drama and tension brought about by saving a game was often as thrilling as the excitement of winning one. In addition, it was pointed out that the draw offered an escape clause for the team that was on the wrong end of the pitch or conditions, or simply played poorly for a session, and provided the opportunity for a display of the character that makes Test cricket unique.

The quality of pitches comes under the expanded brief of the International Cricket Board (ICB) match director, who works closely with each venue and the groundspeople in the build-up to the Superpower Series. Their responsibility is to the spectator every bit as much as the players. The match director also controls all contentious issues that have been taken out of the hands of the umpires—such as ground, weather and light, boundaries and the use of substitutes, as well as the many day-to-day decisions that are driven by the need for objectivity and common sense. Outside of playing the game, the job of match director has become the most sought-after in cricket and is highly paid. Appointments come directly from the main board of the ICB, which is made up of independent directors, none of whom has a role within their own country's governing body. As required, this main board has a subdivision that includes each of the four international match directors and one former cricketer from each of the countries represented in that year's Superpower Series.

The pink ball is an unqualified success. People fondly remember the time in Adelaide, back in 2015—goodness, how long ago that seems—when it was first seen in a Test match and how, rather generously to the manufacturers, the curator left more grass on the pitch to ensure the ball lasted the required duration. Not now. Cricket balls are of excellent quality and have benefited from technology that has ensured a strong, proud and lasting seam.

People still tell jaw-dropping stories of the days when bats were like railway sleepers but limitations on their weight and depth have also contributed to a more even balance between bat and ball. (There was an entertaining moment at the air-meet global sport's history convention in Chicago recently when the lecturer, Roger Federer, unveiled an air-tight display chamber in which was housed a driver used by Ben Hogan, the tennis racquet used by Lew Hoad when he won the Australian and French Opens and Wimbledon in 1956, and a bat used by Dennis Compton. The students in the audience laughed, at first refusing to believe they were the real thing, and even the black-and-white movies shown of each of those great sportsmen in action failed to convince. As most of them insisted, sport has moved on for the better; the old days were all very well, they said, but, you know, please. Federer smiled: 18 grand slams, the last of them at 38 and the kids just didn't get it.) Anyway, I digress. The point is that it's not all one-way traffic for batsmen these days.

Almost 50 per cent of Superpower matches are played into the evening. The players grumble about venues such as Durban and Brisbane, where the high levels of humidity lead to awkward sessions for batsmen but as Jacques Kallis and Mark Boucher have said, batting in Durban was always damn difficult when the clouds hung around. (Into their mid-sixties now, Kallis and Boucher still play eighteen holes a day at Els Park on the outskirts of Cape Town.)

The only country in which the pink ball is not necessary is England. Experiments to play day–night Test cricket fell foul of the weather and, frankly, England's vainglorious efforts to play Test matches at night were part of the reason the cricket community decided to rethink the whole damn product. What has worked well is the change to playing hours in the height of summer. Once every four years, when the Superpower Series comes to town, the matches are scheduled to start at 12.30 pm and finish at 7.30 pm. At last, those who rule have recognised that the best part of many an English summer is the early evening.

Thankfully, the DRS is out of the hands of the players. Each of the three umpires, who rotate the roles out in the middle and on the sideline, have personalised touch-screen tablets, which offer everything that the television coverage provides. Immediate replays are on hand to help their decision-making which, incidentally, no longer includes the calling of no balls. The sensors first put into the return crease and popping crease back in 2026 have worked a treat. Umpires and players have a terrific relationship, mainly because so many of the variables have been eliminated.

In the Superpower Final last month, Europe finished the seven-hour day an over short of bowling the required 100 and was fined 17 runs, the amount of the most expensive over of the day. They lost the final to Asia by 16 runs, so we were denied a tie and a shootout for the winners' medals, which are struck from gold. The captain of Europe, the straight-talking veteran Archie Vaughan—son of the man who led England to the Ashes in 2005—said he had no sympathy with his players. 'Any side that can't bowl 100 overs in the day deserves everything they have coming,' he said to millions of people worldwide at the post-match media frenzy. At this, news reporters tracked down the former Chairman of the Asian Cricket Union, Mahendra Singh Dhoni, for comment. Late middle-age, and the long commitment he made to the military after retiring from cricket, has caught up with the great man and he prefers the quiet life. He was delighted by Asia's win, even in the circumstances, he said, but really couldn't talk about over-rates given the amount of time he had been out of the game—almost 25 years!

The 50-over game is now the 30-over game and is played by fifteen countries. There is no limitation on bowlers, any of whom can be substituted for high-quality fielders but may not return to the field once they have left it, unless the reason is injury. Because all 30-over cricket is played under the banner of the World Cup Cricket League, there are bonus points for taking 7 wickets in an innings. In this form of the game only three fielders are allowed outside the ring in the first ten overs, four in the next ten and then five in the final ten. Playing 30 overs per side has become the ultimate cricket, a perfect period during which to display myriad skills and satisfy all audiences, whose members range from those who fell for the game at the turn of the last century to those who now regard 'air-hop' as the simplest way to commute every morning. Tickets for the World Cup, which is held every two years, are at a premium given the ease and speed of global travel.

Fans have tired of twenty-over cricket. The desire for something faster, shorter and brighter has forced the hand of administrators, who are searching for the new utopia. As in the football codes, 90 minutes is considered long enough to hold the attention of a new audience. The idea of ten-over cricket is causing a bit of a stir: 30 consecutive balls from one end and then 30 from the other. The 7-wicket bonus point initiative in the 30-over game has helped even out the contest between bat and ball. Inspired by this, the ICB's elite captains' committee met by satellite and agreed to trial eleven-a-side ten-over matches in which only seven players can bat. When the sixth wicket falls, the seventh batsman continues with the last man out as his runner.

There was an alternative put forward by the MCC—the old club recently admitted children, by the way—from an idea first given it by Ted Dexter in 1998, which suggested that if the team batting first lost 5 wickets or fewer, the team batting second would only be permitted to send seven batsmen to the crease. If the team batting first lost 6 wickets, the team batting second could only use eight batsmen, and so on. Though the captains liked it in principle, they agreed the practicalities could confuse the crowd, so went for option one, first mooted by Martin Crowe in 2014.

Four bowlers must be used in the new Max10 competition, but each of them can bowl for any number of overs the captain sees fit. Only three fielders are allowed outside the ring for the first three overs and then five for the remainder of the innings. No one, of course, is allowed to enter the double-hit red zone. So far it has gone well, even in America, where the feeling is that baseball has not adapted sufficiently to appease impatient kids. Cricket has caught on in cities with a strong immigrant culture and a desire to make their own choices. The hard-skin fluorescent ball trials have gone well, says the Chairman of the ICB, Misbah-ul-Haq, and the new ball is certain to be used in the exhibition matches scheduled for Hawaii. In general, the visiting Max10 franchises from overseas are a fresh, exciting attraction and there is now a push to take the next Superpower Series to the States.

Generally, the live cricket experience gets a big tick on ASM—advanced social media. Essentially, television is so good that venues are doing all they can to match it. The chip that comes with the entrance pass offers the spectator myriad options for demands such as travel, catch-up video, access to player interviews and insight into performance—such as the speed of the ball, the amount of swing or spin, and the time a fielder has to react to a catch. The new domes provide fantastic interactive facilities that link to the chip, while sellout crowds also enjoy the chance to win holidays and cars in the competitions run on their personal in-seat consoles. The keypads allow them to order food, beverages and merchandise that arrive in seconds—but not alcohol, which is limited to private areas. The retractable roof provides the best of both natural and artificial light and weather. Finally, hats off to the designer of the new hydro-turf pitch, which can now be adjusted to play harder and faster if the much-needed new shorter version of the game demands it.

Seems like Max10 is here to stay.

BACK TO THE FUTURE

Some of the above is far-fetched. Some of it is for real. I think Test cricket can be played over four days with a minimum of 100 overs per day. I fear that drawn games will, one day, become an anachronism but we should not forget that many a first-class, four-day match finishes undecided amid great tension. Therefore, the international game is not necessarily writing itself a suicide note by shortening its most precious format.

I think match referees should have greater responsibility and profile, and that they should closely monitor the quality of pitches, in hand with neutral experts who travel the world before Test-match series. Every pitch and venue has its own flavour; the key is to retain that flavour but not exaggerate it for the unfair benefit of the home team.

I believe in a future for the pink ball in any essentially dry climate. Adelaide was far too fantastic not to be repeated there and elsewhere. The pictures perfectly told the story. Test cricket was very special over those three days and the pitch did not need much of a trim for the contest to be perfectly balanced. The players remain wary of something they know very little about. Packer would tell them to get on with it. Time is short; Test cricket needs an energy the players are oddly unwilling to provide.

I have long thought that the ideal short form of the game is 30 overs per side, and that a restriction on bowlers diminishes the spectacle for the crowd. I doubt that T20 cricket will remain unchanged, even in my lifetime. Brilliant as it may be now—exactly what the game has needed—it is the lowest common denominator of the moment. People tend to move on from lowest common denominators.

SUMMER IN ENGLAND, 2016 . . .

In late June, I was at Oak Tree Primary School in Mansfield, outside Nottingham, with Chance to Shine. We opened a new non-turf pitch for a school with good facilities in an area that otherwise finds day-to-day life difficult. The children were terrific value and appeared happy enough to listen to my enthusiasm for the game and to meet James Taylor, the Nottinghamshire and England batsman, who has suffered heart problems so severe that they forced him out of the game. You would never have known it from his bright and positive demeanour. The sun shone, the kids laughed and the winner of the bowl-out on James's team won a replica Ashes urn. He called it his best day ever. All was well with the world, relatively at least.

In the middle of the summer of 2003 my bat-making pal, Duncan Fearnley, asked me to a fundraising meeting for the Cricket Foundation, the game's charitable arm in the UK. After listening to the variously worthy ideas that circulated the table—lunches and dinners, golf days and the like to raise small tranches of money to support cricket development—I suggested that there was a bigger and more relevant picture out there: cricket in schools, or the lack of it. I had long been appalled at research that told us 88 per cent of schools in Britain did not play any meaningful form of the game. Equally, I had tired of the elitist tag attached to cricket, a game born of mining communities every bit as much as country houses. My instinct was for the foundation to change direction and focus all its attention on regenerating interest and participation in the game where it mattered most, in schools. To my surprise, the folk around the table agreed that we should investigate the idea further.

A week or so later, at Worcestershire's county cricket ground, Duncan talked to Mervyn King, who had just become governor of the Bank of England. Mervyn had similar thoughts and agreed that the three of us should meet in London. We got on well, sharing a similar passion for the game and a sadness about its lack of reach. Over the next two months, we met more often and began to hatch a plan. I thought we would need £10 million to make an impact in schools. King said £50 million. Ossie Wheatley, the former Glamorgan cricketer and then chairman of the Cricket Foundation, clearly understood the practical issues we faced at the grassroots of the game and began to think through the logistics of a pilot program. At first seeking autonomy from established institutions, we resolved to fund and organise our own programs. Mervyn brilliantly sold our vision to Charles Clarke, then the Secretary of State for Education, and Ossie had the government's Sports Lottery people onside. I went to the private sector and persuaded Sir Tim Rice to give us a million quid, god bless him. The government matched every penny and pretty much does so to this day.

We employed Wasim Khan, the former Warwickshire and Sussex batsman, to run the pilots in 72 schools across urban, inner-city and rural environments. Mervyn came up with a simple and effective campaign slogan that lives with us to this day: 'It is not what kids can do for cricket but what cricket can do for kids.' Thus, we told people that we were not driven as much by unearthing Test cricketers as by simply giving children an opportunity to experience the game that had meant so much in our lives. Our gospel was that team sports matter and that cricket matters most: our aim was to enrich the lives of girls and boys across every ethnic divide in our communities. We launched Chance to Shine in May 2005. It was to be a memorable summer in many ways.

Wasim came on board full time, first as operations director and then CEO, to deliver our vision. Recently, Luke Swanson came from Pearson (the book and education company) to continue Wasim's work. The ECB is firmly with us. Eleven years on, we can proudly say that £52 million of funding has allowed three million children at 11,000 schools to play cricket who would not otherwise have done so. More than one and half million of them are girls. Clare Connor, the former England captain and now boss of women's cricket at the ECB, insists that Chance to Shine has done more than anything to normalise the idea that cricket is for everyone.

I vividly remember the day we launched our Street program, designed to focus on special needs within inner-city communities. We were on a council housing estate on the outskirts of Greater Manchester, and the kids were playing on a large hard-court surface we had built for them. Our coaches were working with the local police, who had taken to umpiring and coaching the kids themselves. I spoke to the sergeant in charge of the area. He said that Chance to Shine had taught the local police force every bit as much about the children as the children had learnt about them. He said people on the estate had begun to trust the police and the more they played cricket together, the more they found that even the most challenging kids became friendly and supportive.

Our programs are inclusive, engaging and played in the spirit of the game. Last year alone, 346,000 children benefited from them. At the end of 2015, the UK government published a new strategy for sport that set the agenda for Sport England, our largest funder. The three themes are: the power of sport to deliver vital social outcomes, including individual and community development; the value of engaging people who are typically less likely to engage in physical activity; and the overwhelming importance of giving young people the opportunity to play sport in general. And these are exactly the things we do.

Here are two examples:

As a child, Soyfur Rahman struggled at school, really struggled. He had travelled from Bangladesh to Bethnal Green in East London and didn't speak a word of English. Luckily, cricket was there to help him. His school, Hague Primary, was one of the first to receive support and coaching from Chance to Shine. The innovative head teacher even created a rooftop playground for the children to enjoy cricket at every opportunity. Soyfur was a good bowler and he quickly impressed his new classmates. Respect turned to friendship, and with that came a stronger self-belief. Soyfur's English improved and his love of cricket grew so much that he joined the local cricket club in Victoria Park. Today, ten years on, Soyfur has become a full-time employee with Middlesex Cricket and is coaching with Chance to Shine back at Hague Primary. Soyfur's cricketing journey has come full circle.

Eleven-year-old Jordan, from Nottingham, had changed primary schools ten times and was expelled from the last two. Both her parents were in prison and several foster placements had been tried without success. Jordan had frequent episodes of violent and verbally abusive behaviour but then, through a Chance to Shine coaching scheme, she discovered a talent for sport. Jordan was in the school team for a cricket festival where she impressed, and regularly attended after-school cricket sessions at the local cricket club. Her outbursts lessened considerably, her school attendance increased dramatically and she showed a talent in maths, art and other areas of sport.

Cricket breaks down barriers. It creates social skills that bring people together and it helps form friendships that last a lifetime. Chance to Shine really is a dream that came true. Now the dream is to reach a million more, and another million after that. And one day to see a cricketer receive his, or her, first international cap and hear them say, 'Chance to Shine changed my life.'

EPILOGUE

A beautiful game

Cricket is the most artistic of all games and, to me, the most beautiful—hence the title of this book. Cricket is difficult, frustrating and unfair, but the bounty of its rewards is plentiful. Players have a singular power to make or break the game, as does the behaviour of the weather. Matches are sometimes dull, and the amount of time taken in becoming so is a constant source of amazement to those who are not wedded to their charms. It is a game of vignettes, which give it layers, but these layers are not apparent to everyone. The expressions of the participants give it human drama but this, too, is subject to understanding.

Cricket is celebrated in verse and song and on canvas. It can be as brutal as it is balletic, as true as it can be false. Those who play it must take risks and, in so doing, know they may be betrayed. As I have discussed in an earlier chapter, it is surely why the writers came to the game, to wallow in these contradictions.

I find it aesthetically satisfying because it is a game of straight lines but one that still has a place for awkward angles and rugged edges. The perfect example of this among modern batsmen is Virat Kohli, who has made hundreds in all three forms of the game that both acknowledge and defy the textbooks. During the 2016 IPL, he played innings after innings that were worth the admission money alone. In the Test series between England and Sri Lanka that finished in June 2016, James Anderson bowled beautifully but with an idiosyncratic dip of his head as he released the ball. This certainly defied the textbooks but has not stopped him becoming England's leading wicket-taker. These two cricketers happen to please my eye, both geometrically and artistically, which may be one and the same. They are confrontational characters, who express themselves in a direct manner because they are trying to master a devil of a game. They need the wisdom of Solomon and patience of Job, along with athleticism, skill and a keen eye for a ball. We can hardly blame them for an off day.

My time playing cricket coincided with a golden age. The 25 years between 1970 and 1995 featured an array of cricketing genius—of Sobers and Procter; Botham, Kapil, Imran and Hadlee; two Richards; Chappell, Pollock, Miandad, Tendulkar and Lara; Lillee, Thomson, Holding and Marshall; Wasim and Waqar; Knott and Healy; Warne and Muralitharan. It is reassuring to see some more of it about today.

Can genius be applied to sport? Of course it can, as easily as to anything else. Genius is mystical and beyond convention. Genius does not imply a player is the best, just that they have taken their sport to a previously uninhabited place. This is why genius in W.G. Grace's day is every bit as relevant as in A.B. de Villiers' day. Both have clearly taken their game out of its existing parameters. They are not comparable because the parameters are not comparable, but they set the bar of the moment and, if unable to improve upon it themselves, watch on as others surely do so. In Grace's case it was a long time before anyone caught up, and I have already argued that we are still waiting for Bradman's chaser. It could be that we wait forever for the man who reinvents the skills paraded by Warne and Muralitharan.

I have wondered about the spirit of the game, surely its greatest strength. There has been a lot of anger out there of late and an increasing amount of greed. The good guys are as good as they ever were but the less good have a loud voice, some of them in important positions of power. I like India at the head of the game but with that position comes a pastoral responsibility that cannot be ignored. Australia and England must encourage India to look after the game of cricket at large, not just the Indian interpretation of it.

Everybody should read, or listen to, Brendon McCullum's compelling 2016 MCC Spirit of Cricket Lecture. McCullum's adventurous brand of cricket won many admirers and there was genuine sadness when he retired from the game early in 2016. The lecture, given in the name of the widely respected Colin Cowdrey, was something else again. In it, he says that 'cricket was meant to be a game, not a life or death struggle', and he explains the root of an ethos that is at the heart of cricket's enduring appeal:

> I want to talk of the other really significant happening that affected my approach to the game. The events leading to it took place at the Sydney Cricket Ground on 25 November 2014. On that day, Phil Hughes suffered injuries that were to prove fatal . . . Phil was a good man . . . The outpourings of grief that followed the tragedy were testimony to how much he was loved . . .
>
> The way that Phil's death affected what happened [to our Test series against Pakistan] didn't go unnoticed by those who witnessed it. Cricinfo saw it this way: 'The Kiwis were badly affected by the incident and didn't even celebrate any of their achievements. A remarkable thing to note here is that

they barely applauded a wicket. Consider this: just the two bouncers bowled today and no close-in fielders in front of the wicket! Takes some doing and still they won the game in four days to level the series 1–1 . . . full marks and hats off to the Kiwis for the spirit they have shown throughout the series. Certainly an example set for all the other sides to follow and act upon. Long live their attitude.'

The realisation of how we achieved the result through the manner of our play came sometime later. The team had drawn strength from one another and from [the highly regarded sports psychologist] Gilbert Enoka's [theory of] 'no consequences' [that] brought a 'joy of life' in a cricketing sense that was richly ironic but, nevertheless, liberating. The big thing I took away from this Test is the way Phil's death affected our mind-set and the way we played in the rest of the match. It was so strange, and yet it felt so right, that after Phil's death we didn't really care anymore about the result. Because nothing we could or couldn't do on the field really mattered in comparison to what had happened to Phil. Our perspective changed completely for the rest of my time playing Test cricket for New Zealand, and we were a much better side as a result.

Many observers have said that we were playing the way it should be played; as gentlemen who respected the history of the game. People undoubtedly warmed to the fact that we no longer sledged the opposition.

We worked out what would work for us, based on the traits of being Kiwis. To try to be humble and hardworking and to enjoy what we were doing. It is vital that you understand that we were never trying to be 'nice guys'. We were just trying to be authentic in how we acted, played the game and carried ourselves. For us, sledging in an abusive manner just didn't fit with who we believed we had to be. It wasn't authentic to being a New Zealander.

This is not the time to go through a microscopic examination of 'what is sledging' and to seek to define it. Everyone has a view of how the game should be played and everyone is entitled to their view—Jeff Thomson probably shouldn't have called Colin Cowdrey 'fatso' and told him to 'piss off'. But it's a great story and Colin had broad shoulders from all accounts.

The truth is that cricket is unique—you spend a lot of time out there, 'in the middle'. Humorous comments made in the heat of battle are gold. And when Colin Cowdrey's funeral took place at Westminster Abbey (with 2500 people in attendance), it was Thommo who carried the Australian flag. Enough said.

In terms of our New Zealand side, we weren't righteous in our stance and demanding that other teams follow our lead, but for us it was so good to play free of the shackles— to genuinely love the game again, to acknowledge and enjoy the opposition. And for me, when I pulled back the curtains in the morning, wherever we were, I smiled when the sky was blue and felt the same anticipation I did growing up in Dunedin.

And so, in reflecting on my fourteen years of international cricket, I again acknowledge my numerous failings and mistakes throughout my career. But I also celebrate that when I retired from international cricket the New Zealand team, through the contribution of everyone, had rediscovered its soul. It's now a team that our country is proud of. Our followers know that New Zealand won't win every game or be the world's best team, but I think they are able to look at the team as a representation of our culture.

Right there is the spirit of cricket. It is with McCullum's words resounding in my head that I say thank you to a beautiful game.

Love is lost

If I should go before the rest of you,
Break not a flower nor inscribe a stone.
Nor, when I'm gone, speak in a Sunday voice,
But be the usual selves that I have known.
Weep if you must,
Parting is hell.
But life goes on,
So . . . sing as well.

Joyce Grenfell

People come and go, places change. Cricket is a game made up of good souls; the bad ones can be counted on a single hand. It so happens that most of my closest influences and friends have not hung around for as long as I would have liked.

My father Peter, Malcolm Marshall, Colin Ingleby-Mackenzie, Peter Sainsbury, Richie Benaud and Martin Crowe are among the cricketers who most touched my life in the game. Constantia Uitsig in Cape Town was a ground on which I felt cricket's unbridled spirit: when it was sold, a piece of the game went with it.

Given I have already devoted a part of this book to Marshall, the space here is for others. Mainly, these are the pieces I wrote after I heard of their passing, sharpened for the purposes of these reflections. I have written about Constanta Uitsig knowing that the man who created it, David McCay, is fighting a battle with cancer. I have not written about my father. Any cricket story I have to tell is because of him.

MARTIN CROWE, 1963–2016

'Marty goes to rest', first published on Cricinfo, 4 March 2016
Last night I dreamt about Martin Crowe. Fit, able, strong, gifted; bald, smiling, sick; angry, incisive, raw; modern, playful, intuitive. Then the dog barked and I awoke. Outside it was dark. A chill wind rustled the bare branches on the huge plane trees in the nearby park. For some inexplicable reason, I remembered our golf game on Waiheke Island, Christmas Eve 2002: Martin and Jeff together against Audrey, their mother, and me. She said we would win because the boys were bound to compete with one another more feverishly than with us. She was right. Such mighty competitors.

Then I looked at my phone, and the text. No. Oh no. The chill ripped through me.

Jeff said Martin had gone peacefully with Lorraine and Emma by his side: a beautiful wife, a beautiful daughter, the loves of his life. Jeff was thankful that the 'brutal pain' was over. We all must be.

Another text, this one from Michael Clarke expressing dismay and adding that Martin will already be talking technique with Phillip Hughes. Then Ian Botham, Wasim Akram and many more who are not so well known—all with a line of affection and appreciation. Brothers in blood, brothers in arms, brothers in cricket deeply shocked by the loss of one of their own so young, so vibrant, so alert.

I made tea and thought of that extraordinary piece of writing on Cricinfo, 'The Masks We Wear'. In it, Martin spoke sympathetically of Jonathan Trott who, in a depressed state of mind, had returned home early from England's tour of Australia. Martin said he had been in similarly confused territory himself at the start of his career. 'Expectations were high . . . I cried a lot, moods ebbed and flowed, emotions ran hot. Then I found a mask and began to fake it until I made it.'

Oh tortured soul be free. Martin thought less of himself than we thought of him. By a distance. He battled his mind, beat up on his heart and yet, was always a beautiful man.

For me, an intense relationship began at the Parks in Oxford in 1981. I had played for MCC against the University and a kid with a Kiwi accent asked for a lift back to London. We talked cricket all the way home, throwing ideas at one another with youth's abandon. He fancied a short-form game even then: the germ, of course, of Cricket Max. He spent that English summer at Lord's, an overseas recruit to the MCC ground staff, and dreamt of a hundred there. Next time I saw his name, it was on the team sheet against Australia. Christ, the kid is up against Lillee and Thomson! He didn't do much good but was hardly the lone ranger. Just nineteen years of age and hung out to dry.

We met again at Southampton in 1984. He struggled to 50 in a pretty ordinary Somerset side, who played a pretty ordinary county match against a pretty ordinary Hampshire side. We laughed about that since. Within a year, he was making hundreds in Test cricket and Hampshire were gunning for the championship. The game and its players never stand still. In the evening he told me about New Zealand pinot noir and suggested I drop the Graham Gooch impression and go back to an orthodox stance.

He really liked the orthodox. Right up to his passing, he urged the same from Ed Cowan and stuck around long enough to see it working. 'Still head,' he would say, 'weight on the balls of your feet, balanced moves—sideways, forward and back.' We spent hours on these things in the Indoor School at Lord's—tinkering, toying. Wasim Akram thinks him the best batsman he bowled to. Most agree that a close-to-perfect technique and a great hunger for the game set him close to the pantheon but that self-doubt, linked to ever deeper analysis, denied him an unarguable place within it. I argue for his inclusion: few have achieved more and fewer still have given the game more. When the ICC brought him into the Hall of Fame, his joy was unbridled.

Cricket had been a long struggle. Not for lack of talent but for lingering suspicions, mistrusts and uncertainties. There were quarrels with colleagues, teammates and administration, then later with producers and heads of sport. He tired of these and wished for harmony. He was incandescent about the treatment of Ross Taylor, a friend and protégé, when the captaincy was taken from him. He said so publicly and for a while this influenced his judgement of Brendon McCullum. But McCullum always knew that the Crowe heart lay entrenched in the game and, specifically, in New Zealand's interpretation of it. Unsurprisingly, Crowe could not help but come to admire the McCullum way.

Marty's great pleasures came first from his two girls then from close friends, wine, food, golf, art, design, style. He turned up at our place in London before dawn one morning and, restless after the flight from Auckland, rearranged our bookshelves and rehung the pictures. The joint looked a whole lot better by breakfast.

He loved London and thankfully twice fulfilled the Lord's dream: the innings in 1986 was good; 1994 was something else. That gammy knee could not deny a masterpiece presented at the game's greatest theatre. This innings may not have been his best given the terms of engagement but it was, he thought, the purest.

Almost certainly, the 188 at the Gabba (Hadlee's match!) in 1985 was the most hardcore, and hundreds in Guyana in 1985 and Lahore in 1990 the most efficient against all-conquering attacks.

Another must be mentioned, though of a social nature. Paul Getty's XI versus the Australians 1997 at Wormsley, plenty of middle-order batsmen but only one opener. Marty, not having held a bat since retirement a couple of years earlier, played and missed at three out of six in Glenn McGrath's first over. From the third ball of the next, he eased onto the back foot and drove to the extra-cover boundary. He made 115 not out. It was breathtaking, and beautiful of course. By heaven, he was a lovely batsman to watch. We should have won but the rest of us could not climb the same ladder. Generously, Mark Taylor's Australians came into our dressing room to shake his hand and share their beer. Michael Slater said, 'I spend hours in the nets trying to bat like that and you come out after two years and . . .'

A further text has just come through from Jeff. I have asked which of his brother's innings he most rated. Lahore, he says, or the three innings at home in 1987—all against the West Indies—that defined him. Then he adds, 'His 174 against Pakistan in Wellington was mapped out on a piece of paper six months prior as we flew to Fiji!'

Deep analysis was not only applied to his batting. Captaincy, coaching, commentary and committees, innovation, progress, prediction and, finally, writing all benefited from this remarkable mind. In my experience, no one has been able to see into the crystal ball like Martin. Cricket Max was genius of its type, a forerunner of the modern T20 game and of where it might well go ten years down the line. His blueprint for a World Test Championship was a bad miss by the ICC and remains so. His thoughts on the television production of sport and the rhythms of good broadcasting are priceless. Martin did not always say what people wanted to hear, but rarely could they argue successfully against him. Beneath it all was an unflinching passion for the game, a love and knowledge so deep that sabbaticals were required to ease the tension between him and his life's pursuit.

The last time we saw each other, almost a year ago now, we took a gentle walk from Bondi to Bronte in Sydney. We rested on the grass bank above Bronte beach and talked about the past, present and future. He was at peace at last, he said. Though the year of remission in 2013 had proved to be a wicked temptress, he was back in the fight of his life. He resisted further chemotherapy, preferring instead to feel alive and mentally strong for these extended days with Lorraine and Emma. The journey through illness had brought him self-discovery and a hitherto unseen lightness of being. He let go of demons and explored friendships. He loved his brother and could now tell him so, rather than refuse the two-foot putt for par. He had not realised quite how much the death of his father in 2000 had troubled him, but with time to think and pray, he had even come to terms with that loss.

Recent communication has been by text, email and a few phone calls. The mind has been willing but the voice has been weak. There has been something charming about a fearless gladiator so in touch with his own mortality. Suddenly, out of nowhere last month, an email was sent to Jeff and me. Through the haze and drugs of pain relief, it talked cricket again, a final offering to the game. Jeff is convinced it was meant for the world. Jeff knows the beauty of the game like few others and best understood his brother's remarkable mind.

First ball: off the long, eternal run.

People in administration (the good and the ones doing their best but not reading the brief properly) come and go, you know, a cyclical thing. And so Srinivasan has gladly departed and Giles Clarke's time is waning. Interestingly,

Cricket Australia are beautifully on the front foot and, for daring measure, are even dancing down like yesteryear, such is their newfound confidence at the helm. A year on from creating a stinky breakaway, the garden smells rosier again, and it is grand to see a potential shift back to the central truth. The Big Three were rightly targeted by an aggressive media, who saw the poor getting poorer fast and the divvy-up unfair and unsubtle. Bye bye, Srini. This first, fast curving first ball was you.

Second ball: respectful, 4th stump, consolidation of line and length.

Davie Warner has a second child, named Indi, very cool and diplomatic. He also has a damn good respect for the game too. Nothing but goodwill coming from the Warner Family in recent times. As a result, a heap of focus on notching up daddy ton and, take note, he stands in waiting for the most important office in Oz. Yes, sad that Brad Haddin got mad and didn't see the exit sign with a smiley face flashing brightly as he departed. That being so, my sympathies with him around his family hardships through a period where there is no escape. It's a hard act to please all. But that's what almost all individuals have done over the last year, governed by strong leaders who have instructed their teams to forgive and forget. Thus they inspired youngsters and their families to follow this vital advertisement for cricket as we all reeled and mourned Phil Hughes. That ball grew us up real fast.

Third ball: pink this one and swinging late, then seaming and bouncing, all under a darkening sky and a floodlit stadium.

Pink balls need greasy conditions, apparently, to make it last the correct amount of overs. I say leave the pitch alone and decide over a few tests on a mark when a second new pinkie is needed. Patience, and a few more games, then the mark will become clearer—as opposed to juicing up conditions which dramatically alter the landscape. The purpose is defeated if manipulation comes first over mystery. Easily fixed in time. Yet, I believe, the horse has already bolted with Test cricket. By not sticking with the proposed Test championship concept set down for 2017, the chance, the obvious window, the golden egg, has gone. Not that it won't be tried sometime, but the die is cast on Test cricket—it's dumbing down and mediocre standard of participation. It has historic meaning still but has become costly and slow, and has been overtaken by T20. The West Indies have fallen, but they will rise again for sure, dressed in full three-hour action gear.

Fourth ball: leg-spin mode and spinning fast from leg, a side where a boundary sits obsolete with no chance of catches from a top edge off these modern bats—the fans are as busy now looking to claim (and protect family from) those skiers, as busy as any outfielder has been.

Ten years ago, Australia played NZ in the first ever Twenty20 International at Eden Park. Thirty-thousand turned up on a balmy night and saw Ricky Ponting, a true great, irresistibly caress the ball to all and sundry for 98 glorious runs. In the com box we wondered, and worried a touch too, about the effect this would have long term—on everything.

As the leg spin is released, forget our long term musings because that momentous wonder we had way back has just hit home. When I read Stephen Fleming's quote about 80,883 attending the Big Bash derby match at the MCG on Jan 2, between the Stars in green and the Renegades in red, I felt it. Fleming, not one for throwaway attention, made a call that was forthright and honest, yet said clearly to state a moment in time for all to take notice: 'To have more than 80,000 at a domestic match [outside of India] will send absolute shockwaves through the cricketing world.'

Cricket Australia, who for long periods of the game's history has been a leading light, had had a quiet time lately. But not anymore. When you can invite that humungously friendly family support to watch a three-hour game, with supreme facilities, and not just break crowd records but obliterate them, then you get what Fleming is saying. It will only get bigger and better. Meaning something else won't.

Fifth ball: chucked, overstepped, and lethal in its intent.

And so it took a Renegade, Chris Gayle, to take centre stage next, sending another shockwave into the ether via a boundary line interview with a female journalist. The effect of the content delivered by Gayle was undeniable and created a din and a reaction so strong everyone took notice. It reminded us of our greatest wake-up in humanity—the need to see the end of blatant discrimination. Worst of all, it was live on air, rammed down a close-up camera, hitting us at the family home or a community gathering somewhere. Young children were watching, transfixed by the exciting energy that Fleming passionately expressed. This need never happen again around cricket. Instantly, I sided with the Stars above and condemned the Renegades.

Final delivery: normal light is fading, dinner is in the air, families gather. Lights are on to full effect.

Another T20 match is about to begin. Many of them now, all around the globe. All of them in properly bona fide competitions with a massive following throughout, often night upon night in prime-time television, always aiming to deliver a dose of fun and fever, and a winner crowned at the end. And cleverly, everyone has deemed that all is needed to make the ground full is a Family and Friend Pass, at forty or fifty bucks, ensuring folk come together. Just buy a pass and roll on up. By making up numbers to fill the pass, the admin continue to fill the fans seats and all benefit. And, as the younger wannabe man-fan readies himself for another sizzling fast head-high crowd-catch, the family flavour rises to fever pitch.

The future of cricket far into the night is safe and sound, by virtue of the game settling into proper competition, well marketed towards a family environment that ensures— no, guarantees—value for all. Meanwhile, a Test match, searching for connection to a fast-moving modern world, is played somewhere, but without enough context or support, and with dwindling hope for its own future. How can they who rule the game have done this?! Australia must act again if no one else will.

Twenty20—as Fleming said on 2nd January, 2016— created a wave and no one has got off the ride that might well have to sustain the game eternally. With a tweak here and there . . .

Martin Crowe removed his mask and put a creative mind to rest. By being so spiritually aware of what lay beyond the physical world, he became an irresistible conscience for those of us left behind. The game ignores his teachings at its peril.

What shall I most miss? The wisdom, the kindness, the childlike simplicity of the humour, the lack of ego, the rants— yes the rants, and how!—the high standards, the hard but fair marking, the counsel given and taken, the shared love of so many things that stretch heart and mind. Above them all is friendship.

Farewell, great thinker. Farewell, great player. Salute, dear friend.

RICHIE BENAUD, 1930–2015

'The day Richie died', first published on Cricinfo, 10 April 2015
He was father, uncle, brother and friend. He was our conscience

and our guiding light. In an age of much madness, he made sense. He held firm when others doubted and let go when those around him needed to fly. His wise counsel was without compare, his kindness unconditional. There was something elemental about him, like the wind and the rain. And he was summer's sunshine. But now he has gone.

Yes, Richie Benaud has gone. It has to be repeated to feel true. A flame that burned brightly for 84 years has flickered of late and now died. There is a darkness. If you have grown up watching cricket, you have grown up watching Richie Benaud. He was a constant in all our lives. The memories, the sights and sound of him, will live with us forever.

We, that is, the Channel Nine commentary team, last saw him in person at the Sydney Cricket Ground in November. When he arrived on the outfield in front of the Members Pavilion where we had gathered, there was a general shuffling. Unseen and virtually unheard of for a year since the car crash that all but ended his life in television, the news that he was to appear at the Nine Network's launch of the 'Sizzling Summer of Cricket' was greeted with immense excitement.

The crash had damaged a couple of vertebrae, and the suggestion of surgery to the Benaud spine had lingered for most of the previous Australian summer. He made no fuss, of course, but admitted that he was far from ready to bowl 30 overs off the reel on a hot Sydney day. The surgery never happened. Apparently, a natural fusion was already taking place. Instead, the medics found some melanomas. Radiation and chemotherapy are not anyone's game. The treatment had taken its toll. I suggested that it had been a rough year. 'Roughish,' he replied, with the understatement that has been a hallmark of his life.

Anyway, Richie turned up bang on time for the photo shoot and, though our joy in greeting him was uninhibited, we were all sad to see him so diminished. He carried himself with fortitude and typical grace, but he was clearly weak. It seems absurd that he retired from the commentary box in England ten years ago, but it is fact. On that early September day at the Oval in 2005, the producer of Channel 4's cricket coverage, Gary Franses, had sent him across the ground to be alongside me and the others in our commentary team to say goodbye. Channel 4 had lost the rights to cricket in the UK.

The crowd rose to him with as much bonhomie as they had to the England team that, moments earlier, had won the Ashes after a summer of cricket that held the nation spellbound. Moved by their enthusiasm and warmth, Benaud shed a tear.

He has been good to us all: always by our side, a constant source of wisdom and encouragement. No one has sold the game of cricket with greater skill, few played it with greater flair.

When Mark Taylor switched from the playing field to the hallowed Nine Network commentary team, he called the fall of a key Australian wicket 'a tragedy'. Benaud let it rest for a couple of hours before gently tapping Taylor on the shoulder and whispering, 'Mark, the *Titanic* was a tragedy.' Taylor said that Benaud had once used 'tragedy' while commentating himself. (Later during the summer, we heard it on an archive clip. Gold!)

His minimalism was a lifestyle, best illustrated in his television work both in front of the camera and behind the microphone: 'West Indies cruising to victory here, all Carl Hooper has to do is keep his head as Shane Warne switches to bowl round the wicket into the rough outside leg-stump.' At which point, Hooper charges down the pitch and has a mighty heave at Warne. The ball spins and catches the leading edge of Hooper's bat. It is about to drop into Steve Waugh's hands as Benaud says, 'Oh, Carl,' and nothing more.

The Benauds have been private people. He and his English wife, Daphne, live in an apartment in Coogee and watch the surf roll in each morning. After a long lay-off they had started their 40-minute sunrise walks again, not a minute more or less. These had given him relative strength and given her breathing space. They were inseparable. Her loss will be beyond pain. When Richie bought the drinks he would always say, 'Don't thank me, thank Mrs Benaud.' She is a terrific woman who began life in and around the game as PA to Jim Swanton years ago but fell in love with the dashing former captain of Australia.

They lived in summer for 50 years, travelling across the world each April and September to cover the game for myriad networks and newspapers. Benaud's crusades to English shores actually began as a player in 1953, when he came by boat with Lindsay Hassett's touring Australians. They were at sea for five weeks and made their way around the shires for the five months that followed.

At the end of the summer of 2002, we took him to lunch at the Ivy in London. The room was full of the great and the good—Frost and Parkinson, Mrs Beckham, Michael Winner to name a few—but it went silent when he glided in. You should have seen the punters gawp. And the waiters, too. In general, Richie kept himself to himself, which is a powerful weapon. Because of it, public appearances were something of a parade.

His cricket can be summed up easily enough—a fine leg spinner, a dashing batsman, an excellent fieldsman but, above all, a brilliant and intuitive captain. Peter May brought a team of stellar names to Australia in 1958 and was beaten 4–0 by Benaud's young adventurers. It was ever thus. Australia has cricket in its soul and Benaud will always remain a part of that soul.

I miss him already. I'm sure we all do. To have him back among us that day in November brought such pleasure. Bill Lawry was there too, up from Melbourne where he looks after his beloved wife, Joy. Bill was very funny on the stage, telling Richie that the melanomas might be a bane now but, back then, with his hair flowing, shirt unbuttoned almost to the waist and gold chain sparkling in the sunshine, he looked a million dollars. They were quite a pair, Bill with his comedic talents and Richie with his natural dry wit.

The last time I saw him at all was on the telly in a quite brilliant Australia Day advertisement for Australian lamb. Captain Cook is at sea, on *The Endeavour*, one supposes. A mobile phone rings. He reaches into the pocket of his naval frock coat and answers it. The scene switches to Richie, tongs in hand, back home at the barbeque. 'Cookie!' says Richie. 'G'day, Rich,' says Captain Cook. 'Fancy an Australia Day barbie round at my place?' asks one great man of another. Cook looks to his second-in-command and then to some of the midshipmen around him and asks if they fancy it. Of course they do! Richie then calls various other iconic figures in Australia's history, including Ned Kelly no less. They are all in. Have a look on YouTube, it is well worth it. The ad tells us much about Benaud's sense of humour, timing and perspective. And it tells us the extent of the esteem in which he is held by all Australians.

When modern cricket folk talked of aggression and sledging as part of the game, Richie raised his eyebrows and cringed. Such attitudes were not part of his game, nor of the game played by Keith Miller, Garry Sobers, Ted Dexter or the Nawab of Pataudi. If modern cricketers want to do the Benaud legacy justice, they should reward his unwavering faith in their abilities and performance by ceasing such mean-spirited behaviour as of today. The day Richie died.

I just googled the word 'dignity'. It says: 'The state or quality of being worthy of honour or respect.' There you go, that is Richie Benaud in a simple definition. From the first day of a glorious cricket career to his last as a universally admired and loved communicator of the most beautiful game, he was the very best. Our privilege was to have sat at his table.

PETER SAINSBURY, 1934–2014

(I could not attend the thanksgiving service for Peter but wrote a few thoughts that were read out by Shaun Udal.)
Well, Sains, it is time to say goodbye. What a man you have been, what a husband, father, grandfather, cricket player, cricket coach, counsellor and friend. Without hesitation, and with immense admiration, we can say—and I suspect most in the room today would say—that we loved you and will miss you more than you could ever have known.

You brought warmth to our lives. You brought perspective to our thinking. You brought enthusiasm to our chores. You never grumbled, you never spoke ill of other folk. You were kind and generous of spirit. You brought dignity to our souls.

I have pictures of you painted before my eyes. There is one of you batting—cap tilted, strong grip, keen eye, thou shalt not pass and though shall come over to my side! There is one of you fielding—quick little steps, low centre of gravity, safe hands. There is one of you bowling—'Thank you, umpire' as the cap is handed over, easy approach, pure action, nagging and accurate pitch of the ball, fools playing for the turn. There is one of you in the morning—bright and cheery for the day to be done. One of you at lunch, furious after a sloppy morning from those in your care. One of you at the close, gently cajoling, buying beer, listening, learning, passing on to others. And my favourite picture is of that wonderful face, screwed up in deter-mination and concentration, the truest grit I ever saw.

We regret not listening to you more. Your way was not to force but to encourage. You knew more than you knew and offered more than you know. You were our pastoral care and our shining light, come fair wind or foul. You were our friend.

How we loved it when you sneaked away from parties without saying goodnight; how you screamed blue murder at Robin Smith for smacking those practice balls into the flats; how cross you were when we fielded badly; how happy you were when we beat the odds; how you manipulated the fines system to even up the lucky and the not so lucky of the week just gone; how you showed us optimism and joy in the simple things we often miss ourselves; how you dressed smart and played smart. How we loved how your modesty prevailed.

And you were gifted. Very gifted, though you would have none of it. After all, Sains, you did something none of us Hampshire cricketers have done—you won two championships and believe me, without you, the winning might not have been the winning. You were special, unique. You were hard, you were soft, you were fair. You could laugh, you could cry . . . and you did both in the Lord's dressing room on that magnificent day in 1988 when your beloved county finally made it to a Cup Final and went on to win in style. Your joy at that achievement was our joy too.

You were our friend and no finer friend has there been. To Joycie goes our love, our sympathy and our thoughts. And also to Sara and to Paul, who share this dreadful loss with their mum.

Sains, rest well. You gave this life all of yourself. You left nothing out there . . . but golden memories.

COLIN INGLEBY-MACKENZIE (1933–2006)

First published in the Daily Telegraph, London, 3 July 2006
On Thursday last week, the world bade a final farewell to Colin Ingleby-Mackenzie. Seventeen hundred people, maybe more, filled St Paul's Cathedral to appreciate and applaud a life less ordinary. Ingleby-Mackenzie, Hampshire captain in the late 1950s and early 1960s, MCC president in the late 1990s

and bon viveur through a lifetime, died on 9 March of a brain tumour. Poor Colin, there was so much life left in him. He was a remarkable man, whose rare ability to fill a room with laughter and hope characterised his life. Indeed, Colin was the climate of optimism.

He was an amateur in the true and best sense. His light touch and extraordinary enthusiasm made him a force for good without compare. When he first played for Hampshire, it was a dour club still fighting to reassert itself after the Second World War. The captain and secretary at the time, Desmond Eagar, identified him as the man to inspire a mixed bag of cricketers beyond their promise. Eagar got it spot on. 'I decided to abandon the evils of gambling, knuckle down and lead a successful team,' wrote Ingles in his book *Many a Slip*. At least the third bit caught on. In his first team talk he set the tone: 'Let's enjoy the game and above all let's entertain or perish,' he said, and then would frequently begin a three-day county match by urging the boys to win in two and if not, then lose in two, so 'either way we'll have a day off!'

From there, the only way was up for Hampshire cricket, as the players, supporters and all those who came into contact with the club flew in the wind beneath Ingleby's well-spread wings. Hard-bitten pros were suddenly sipping brandy and Bollinger in the company of lords and ladies, knights and nawabs. Strings of gorgeous girls and high-society folk lifted morale in the dressing room. Gatemen and ground staff were treated as equals, and all of them, from each corner of his rich tapestry, were seduced.

There was good reason. Cricket matches had become an adventure, a gambler's alternative to anything that had gone before, as daredevil declarations illustrated his ambition and belief. Bowlers such as Derek Shackleton, Butch White and Peter Sainsbury bought into them and played above themselves. Even opposing captains started to declare with the intent of providing a spectacle, and the Hampshire lads cashed in. As Leo Harrison, his stumper and friend, pointed out: 'He could charm anyone, even the enemy.'

But it was his own men he had changed the most. There was nothing feudal about his leadership, no side to his character, and no meanness in his mistakes. The players fell head over heels for him and his capacity for fun. Even when he lost the plot, when the Ingleby went one way and the Mackenzie another, they were happy to be captained by the hyphen.

Hampshire's first championship was won on 1 September 1961, amid delirious scenes at Bournemouth. From it came the legend of 'Happy Hants'. Given the strength of Surrey and Yorkshire at the time, it was a phenomenal achievement.

After Eton he went into the navy as a submariner, and though he began business life with Slazenger very soon after national service, he received instant immortality at the start of a new career in insurance. Due in to the office at nine in the morning on 1 February 1959, he arrived at midday on 18 March after a holiday in the Caribbean he simply could not leave. This jaunt had been preceded by a tour with E.W. Swanton's XI, which he captained. Concerned about the team's erratic form, Swanton suggested a curfew. 'I'd like everyone in bed by 11, Colin,' Jim said. 'Oh, I don't know that's such a good idea, Jim,' replied Ingleby. 'We start play at 11.30!'

By the mid-1990s he had committed himself to country-house cricket at Sir Paul Getty's private ground, recruiting and managing high-quality teams in festival matches. These occasions allowed us the last views of him with his soulmates, Denis Compton and Keith Miller—all three of them lovers of the turf, the turps and the totty, and all howling with laughter together.

If Ingleby was the right man at exactly the right time to lead Hampshire, it was the same story 40 years later when he was elevated to the presidency of the MCC. The sensitive issue of female membership had bubbled beneath the surface for some time, and Ingleby's charm, diplomacy and steel rode the storm of losing the initial vote on a technicality and returning to the polls, so to speak, six months later to win the day. The world would never be the same again. Neither will it be without Ingleby.

CONSTANTIA UITSIG, 1991–2012

David McCay lay flat on his hospital bed at the Newlands Clinic in Cape Town. Diagnosed with lung cancer that had spread to the spine, he had major surgery to stabilise the spine and prevent paralysis. Recent years have not served him well. The empire he built fell to dust. Painful material losses include a game lodge, a farm in the Karoo, the family home and Constantia Uitsig (*uitsig* is Afrikaans for 'view')—the magnificent wine farm, hotel and collection of three restaurants that attracted devoted fans from far and wide.

His beautiful family has regrouped. His eldest daughter, Kate Louise, was married in Kirstenbosch National Botanic Garden as dawn broke on the 20 February 2016. The party drifted into dusk and beyond. David, somehow, was there. He wore a grey beard and long silver hair: he might have been Richard Harris at the start of *Gladiator* if you took no more than a glance. The wheelchair supported his immense frame comfortably and the cravat that nestled beneath his beard was distinguished. It was his first venture into the sunlight for seven weeks.

At his best in the late 1960s, McCay bowled medium-fast swing and seam at a standard good enough to play games for Western Province. His deep love of bat and ball inspired the final piece of the Uitsig jigsaw: an absolutely beautiful cricket ground that he cared for with his own hands. He ran a team that played casual—and not so casual—club cricket against anyone who wanted a game. Few could resist the effortlessly magnificent setting in the Constantia valley, the humbling presence of Table Mountain and the crystal-blue skies that make summer days in the Cape among the most wonderful experiences on earth.

I met David right there, as he was holding court on his patch. His team hammered the Heartaches, Tim Rice's team, with whom I toured in the late February of 1993. On a 38-degree day, Tim put McCay's lot in to bat—Tim has a theory that his best chance of a draw is batting second, dear Tim—and they gave us a 'klap', as the Afrikaaners in their number might say. The declaration came at 350 and our mob collapsed into the swimming pool, where drinks were served.

Batting at number four in the run chase, I was supposed to make a hundred and give us a shout. I never even took guard. A ten-year-old boy ran me out at the non-striker's end after Tim Graveney's suicide call. I lost the plot right there. By the time I reached the dressing room, no one was safe. Bats, gloves, pads, you name it, bounced around the walls while expletives echoed across the valley. You'd have thought I'd been run out by a rival for a place in the Test team.

I didn't take to McCay, thinking his declaration absurdly late and his ribald laughter at my dismissal more than patronising. It transpired that he didn't think much of me either, carrying on as I did. I was the captain of Hampshire and behaved like a spoilt kid. The boy who ran me out was his son, who came on to field when McCay briefly left to fire up the coals for the hog-roast. McCay thought that very funny.

Anyway, at the barbecue by the pavilion in the evening he came over with a cold beer and said he was sorry not have seen me bat. Not many people have said that. And then he invited me back to play anytime. Indeed, he said, if I was ever in town I should call and we could play golf or have lunch. The upshot of the inauspicious start was that from 1993 to 2008 I never stayed anywhere else in Cape Town. Uitsig became a home away from home, and the McCay family my family. I love them all and sure loved that cricket ground.

The standard of cricket at Uitsig was good. David had plenty of mates who could play and plenty of visitors who tell tales to this day of the ringers he often recruited. During the World Cup in 2003, I spent a lot of time commentating and travelling with Jeff Thomson. David said to invite him. I said, 'You're kidding—he's got buggered knees, a dodgy shoulder and hasn't played in years.' David searched for a less telling weakness. I suggested alcohol and oysters. He said offer him the freedom of the winery and the food of the ocean. So I told Thommo he could sit in the restaurant (which was alongside the ground), eat ten dozen oysters and drink all the wine he could stomach if he appeared on the team sheet and bowled five with the new nut. Bingo.

We sat down for lunch soon after midday. At half past one, David won the toss and chose to bowl. Thommo cleaned up a couple of dozen of Namibia's best oysters, nailed a few Castle lagers, met the other blokes in the team, pulled the cork on a bottle of chenin blanc, and changed into whites at 1.50 before bowling the first ball at two o'clock.

It was something to behold. The fastest bowler in history on this gorgeous little cricket ground, shuffling to the crease with those small steps before contorting his seemingly elastic physique into a sideways-on, catapult action that, for a few unforgettable years in the mid-1970s, delivered the ball at a 100 miles per hour. On this day at Uitsig in 2003, I can vouch that he was fast enough, too. An innocent left-handed opening batsman edged to me at second slip and I caught the damn thing at shoulder height away to my left. Christ, I caught one off Thommo! It is in the memory bank for ever and a day. The batsman might just as well have shouted, 'Catch it!' for he too will not forget the moment he was forged into history as another victim of Jeffrey Robert Thomson. The fellow had the scorecard framed and it hangs in his pub.

Thommo picked up another wicket, bowled a couple of shit balls and said so, loudly, before retiring to the stoop at the restaurant and continuing the business he had started soon after midday. Now that might have been the end of the story had we not made a Horlicks of the run chase. Just as that extraordinarily golden evening light began to wrap its arms around Constantia, Thommo had to pad-up. This was tricky, given his six hours on the stoop. Choice language accompanied the exercise, thought quite not so choice as the echo of 'You fucking ripper' when our number ten edged one past the keeper for the winning runs. This delight, coupled with obvious relief, motivated Thommo to call McCay a 'beaut of a bloke' and suggest that the two of them now really got stuck in.

Memories are made of men like Thommo.

Malcolm Marshall and Desmond Haynes played at Uitsig, Graham Gooch too, as did Mike Procter, Adrian Kuiper, two Kirstens—Peter and Gary—Garth Le Roux, Jacques Kallis and many, many more. But none, not even Thommo, caused quite such a commotion as perhaps the greatest batsman South Africa ever produced. I was involved in this one, too.

Graeme Pollock was hired by talkSPORT radio to work with us on England's tour of South Africa back in 2000. Pollock was the nation's favourite son, more so even than Procter or Barry Richards. He had mystique and legend. Everybody in the land of the Springbok was in awe of Graeme Pollock.

The commentary team remained in Cape Town after a match and Pollock was reluctant to give up the suite in town he had been allocated for a whole week by a splendidly sycophantic hotel manager. McCay's team had a game on the Saturday but I was ruled out because of a flight that afternoon to Kimberley for a one-day international the next day. Then I had a thought. David had long coveted Pollock on his Elysian field. We all had. What if David flew us both in and out of Kimberley on the Sunday of the game. That way I got to play and Pollock got to stay in the hotel with his beloved Jeanie. There was a trade-off though. In return for the flight on David's King Air plane, Pollock would have to turn out for Uitsig too.

This took some persuading. Geeps, as he is widely known, had been long retired, and his knees made Thommo's look like a new pair. But persuade him we did, with the offer of lunch and a few beers.

Anyway, the moment came. I was at the wicket when he came in at number four, the position in which he had batted all his life. He was 56 years old, with a body going on 70, the ravages of a life on and off the field having taken their toll. He took guard, looked around the field and crouched into that most familiar stance—feet set wide apart, bat resting on the ground between them. The first ball was a tad wide and left alone. The next, much the same but cut with jaw-dropping authority to the boundary behind point. He couldn't run, so he blocked or hit boundaries. He scored 50-odd, mainly through point and cover off the front foot. He leant upon that right foot of his as if it were a crutch for his left.

His commanding presence was matched by only the very best—Viv Richards and Garry Sobers first among them. Age cannot wither the outline and the little manifestations of character. Signs of the old magic were still there. Like the leopards of the African bush, the spots on these fellows never seem to change. It is the way they carry themselves—an intimidation of sorts, simply through presence.

It was the most terrible disappointment when he was out. I don't remember how, just that everyone sighed the deepest sigh. It was the last time he batted and we were there to see it. Better still, I was at the other end. He stayed for a few drinks and the South Africans gathered around him, feasting on his every word. Graeme was, after all, voted the country's cricketer of the century and, at a time when South Africa was starved of international sport, his mighty deeds sustained the nation.

The next day David's plane flew us in and out of Kimberley. We felt very important, and one of us was. The cricket in the match between Zimbabwe and England was pretty poor. Deep down the great man must have thought he would eat these fellows for breakfast. Boycott was working with us and said exactly that. He added that he, Boycott, would gobble up anything Graeme left on the plate.

On Monday morning, back at Uitsig, I wandered over to the cricket field. David was watering the square. We hit golf balls from the beautiful turf at the edge of the outfield—starting with wedges, moving through the irons, until we finished by smashing drivers far into the valley. We had lunch and then went nearby for nine holes. These were the hazy, lazy days of summer—an incomparable time.

Sitting alongside him at the clinic, I thought back to Thomson and Pollock and to all the genial club cricketers who had enjoyed David's wonderful hospitality. I pictured the backdrop of the Constantia Valley and the vibrant colours of the fauna, mountains and sky. I remembered the clean sounds of bat and ball, the bellowed appeals, the kind applause and the endless laughter among cricket folk whose simple pleasure was a day in the sun.

And I remembered the last time the sun began to drop over the mountain and how our stories were told in shadows.

Postscript

These pages have become more autobiographical than planned. I hope that has not made them too dull to read. Though they drift in and out of my life in cricket, the main aim has been to concentrate on the people I have admired and the events that have surrounded me. To adapt the first line from Simon Hughes' award-winning book, *A Lot of Hard Yakka*, I may not have been the greatest cricketer going around but I have sure rubbed shoulders with a few who were.

I was crazy about the game as a boy and thought of little else. Naturally, I imagined I would play for England but it didn't turn out that way. Instead, I have written and talked about cricket since the day I stopped playing it professionally in 1995. One of the gifts of such a life is travel, and the places I have seen and the folk I have met have been the greatest joy. One day, perhaps, I shall write about the vibrant colours of India, the vastly changed canvas in South Africa, the friendly smiles in Sri Lanka or the sheer joy of cricket still evident in the Caribbean. For the moment, it is mainly between England and Australia that I have hopped, skipped and occasionally jumped.

I hope the book has been enjoyable and informative. If not, no blame can be laid at the door of the friends I have made at Allen & Unwin and Atlantic Books. Thank you to Patrick Gallagher and Tom Gilliatt in Sydney for the chance to tell these stories and Tom, most particularly, for his straight-shooting support. Also in Sydney, and always at the end of the telephone when needed, has been Angela Handley, whose editorial ability and patience knows no bounds. Nearby are Nicola Young and Aziza Kuypers, whose attention to detail has ensured a readable text. In London, Will Atkinson and Clare Drysdale have been the best of sounding boards and companions. In Southampton, Richard Isaacs has corrected my economy with the facts and looseness with the figures at the turn of many a page. I am indebted to you all.

More generally, over the years I have dipped in and out of other people's thoughts on the game to further inspire my own. My thanks and admiration for the volumes they have written go to John Arlott, Jack Fingleton, Richie Benaud, Frank Keating, Mathew Engel, Mike Brearley, Peter Roebuck, Sambit Bal, Gideon Haigh, Michael Atherton, Ed Smith, Martin Crowe and Mark Greig. Intermittently, I used previous work of mine that appeared in the London *Daily Telegraph* and on Cricinfo, a fine place, so thanks are due there as well.

A life in cricket is a great privilege.

Mark Nicholas
London, August 2016